EDWIN J. BROWN is Chairman Emeritus of the Department of Education at the University of Santa Clara. Previously he was Dean of the University College at St. Louis University and of the Graduate School at Kansas State Teachers College, and taught at Michigan State University and the Universities of Oregon and Colorado.

ARTHUR T. PHELPS is Assistant Professor of Education and Director, Teacher Education Program, at the University of Santa Clara. He received an M.A. in English from Canasius College, where he lectured, and an M.A. and his Ed.D. from Columbia University. Under the sponsorship of the National Science Foundation, Dr. Phelps directed summer programs at the University of Santa Clara for gifted secondary school students interested in science and engineering.

# MANAGING
# THE CLASSROOM

## The Teacher's Part
### in
### School Administration

EDWIN JOHN BROWN
CHAIRMAN, DEPARTMENT OF EDUCATION
UNIVERSITY OF SANTA CLARA

ARTHUR THOMAS PHELPS
DIRECTOR OF TEACHER EDUCATION
UNIVERSITY OF SANTA CLARA

SECOND EDITION

THE RONALD PRESS COMPANY · NEW YORK

Library of Congress Catalog Card Number: 61–7744

PRINTED IN THE UNITED STATES OF AMERICA

# PREFACE

This book, designed as a text for courses in classroom management, acquaints the teacher with the administrative responsibilities of elementary and junior high school classroom work and instructs him in handling routine matters expeditiously. With emphasis upon the development of democratic school citizenship, it treats the classroom as a community, with the teacher as its government and the pupils as its citizens.

The book is organized into four parts. Part I defines the nature of management and the responsibilities of the teacher-administrator, relating these to the school and its program of activities. Part II investigates the actual conduct of the classroom. It instructs the teacher in ways of achieving discipline, in procedures for effective guidance, and in incentives for motivating learning. Part III offers an operating plan to help the teacher with administrative details. Procedures are outlined for testing, marking, reporting, and promoting pupils. Suggestions are given for organizing the curriculum, preparing the daily program, conducting the class, and improving study techniques. Part IV delves into the personal and professional relationships essential to the growth of the teacher. The importance of personality in human relationships, the maintenance of good mental health, proper personal conduct both on and off the job, and means of professional improvement are treated at length.

At the end of each chapter a practical teaching or classroom problem is described and followed with a series of questions. In addition, there are study questions on the chapter materials and selected and annotated references. These supplementary aids may be used for written assignments or for class discussion to test the reader's comprehension of each topic.

A text can go only so far toward making classroom management a part of the student's thinking. Always the student must see management as a means to an end, never as an end in itself. In a way, a teacher's management of a classroom is somewhat comparable to another subject the pupil is living, a subject which might well be called personal responsibility. This is the line of approach this text takes throughout.

EDWIN J. BROWN
ARTHUR T. PHELPS

Santa Clara, California
February, 1961

# CONTENTS

v

## Part IV
### PERSONAL AND PROFESSIONAL GROWTH

PART I

# THE NATURE OF CLASSROOM MANAGEMENT

# 1

# THE SCHOOLS OF TODAY

Life in the United States has changed profoundly in the last hundred years. An upstart nation which gloried in its isolation has become an essential part of a world order. Self-sufficient farmers and frontiersmen have been transformed into interdependent mechanics and professionals. A broadened suffrage includes all citizens, both men and women, regardless of color or creed. A people that once demanded nothing but freedom to expand to the west has spanned a continent and finds its only remaining frontier in outer space. To expect education not to change under such conditions would be to expect the impossible. And so it is, education has changed.

So, too, has the concept of classroom management changed. Once it was sufficient that the teacher should preside at a raised desk before a class restricted by seats bolted firmly to the floor, a monarch in his class—a benevolent monarch perhaps, but still a monarch. Today such a concept is not acceptable. Authority the teacher still possesses—indeed, must possess if the educational process is to be carried on. But his authority is the authority that proceeds from depth of understanding in a field of knowledge, from competence in many aspects of a demanding profession, and from the maturity of judgment and strength of character which should be found in the individual to whom parents entrust a large share of responsibility for the education of their most cherished possession, their children.

## CHANGES IN ATTITUDES TOWARD EDUCATION

Schools are involved in a process of evolution as are other phases of American society. Many changes have taken place in the general attitude toward education, a few of which are noted here:

1. Basic to all education in the schools today is the belief that what is learned should improve the quality of living.

2. Learning is planned to be gradual and continuous. It is not discrete or saltatory.

3. Attention is focused far more upon teaching children to handle ideas than upon forcing them to memorize words.

4. The child is best educated as a unit organism, as a whole. He is treated as an individual with special abilities.

5. It is recognized that learning takes place to a great extent through sense impressions. The child hears, sees, touches, uses the materials with which he works. Audiovisual aids are in general use.

6. Activity, learning by doing, characterizes the child's daily work. Memory work is used only where no other approach to learning will serve.

7. Facts are learned where they will be useful in the child's thinking processes. No longer is there an irrational emphasis upon multitudinous petty facts.

8. Group activities are the rule rather than the exception.

9. The classroom is considered a dynamic unit of American society with emphasis upon the exchange of ideas, many of which originate with the pupils. The old daily lesson-recitation approach is pretty much a thing of the past.

10. The classroom creates a natural social setting; it involves the child in a child's society.

11. Much emphasis is given to the out-of-class learning of children. No longer does education mean only the acquisition of academic knowledge.

12. The mental health of the child is considered to be of significant importance. A child who is unhappy in his school life will usually have difficulty in learning.

Not all of the foregoing changes are accepted by all of the thousands of schools in the United States. Change in the thought processes of a people is always slow, and much of the old, especially those portions which in themselves have some solid utility, is still evident.

Although a clean-cut statement of the basic attitudes, or better perhaps the ideals, of American education is difficult to formulate, the following statements of attitudes toward American education today will probably not incur serious disagreement:

1. As a Christian nation, America insists that the individual personality is sacred. The recognition of a Supreme Being, in all schools, whether public or private, is everywhere acknowledged. The term "godless schools" does not rightfully apply to any American schools. The public schools are non-denominational, but they are not godless.

2. Because of the sacredness of the individual, the potentialities of each child must be given every consideration.

3. The thought is always kept in mind that democracy is essentially a type of behavior. A major part of learning is in the realm of behavior, and a child learns to behave democratically.

4. *Freedom,* so often used as a watchword, is not meant to imply absence of all restraint. It is considered synonymous with *liberty,* meaning a disciplined and responsible freedom.

5. Freedom develops from accepting responsibilities. A child earns freedom; it is never a gift. The child is taught to accept increasingly greater responsibilities.

6. The right of the child to make choices commensurate with his maturity, which in turn parallels his citizenship development, is recognized. This is to say that a ten-year-old child makes ten-year-old choices, makes ten-year-old mistakes in his choices, and exercises the rights and privileges of ten-year-old citizenship.

7. In a general way each child in school is given opportunities to participate in experiences which lead to growth. The experiences are many and the growth is not only intel-

lectual and social, but also physical, emotional, and spiritual.

8. Formal schooling is a significant portion of a child's experience, but it is never considered as being sufficient in itself.

9. In all schools each child should be taught to think for himself. A child who thinks for himself will grow into a man who thinks for himself. This is but saying that the schools are consciously training for democratic living.

10. The development of habits and skills, as well as the acquisition of knowledge and understandings, is a highly significant part of all formal schooling.

## ATTITUDES TOWARD LEARNING

It is evident that the school of today is basically different from the school of yesterday. Because the ideals or attitudes which govern education are quite naturally reflected in the teaching and learning situation, it follows that the teacher must operate from some basic principles of learning which are more or less fixed; they must become a part of his innermost being.

For an understanding of American education, it is necessary to record the contributions of comparatively few men. Among these are: Rousseau with his ideas of growth, of naturalism in learning, of self-activity for the learner, and of recognition of the individual; Pestalozzi with his understanding of children, his doctrine of interest, his development of the sense-training idea, and his method of object teaching; Herbart with his interest in educational philosophy and in techniques, and in the development of a sounder educational psychology; Froebel with his then novel idea of learning to do by doing, his insistence upon play in the education of very young children, and his emphasis upon loving children; and finally, G. Stanley Hall with his enthusiasm for child study and the psychology of the adolescent.

The statements below have been derived from these educators and from others who have contributed down through the years. Hardly broad enough in their implications to be called principles, the statements offer a vantage point for viewing the field of child growth:

1. A child is the most precious thing in the world. All of that child goes to school, not merely the intellectual child. The emotional, the aesthetic, the mental, the spiritual potentialities of the child all are in the teacher's hands.

2. Children learn best by activity, that is, by doing.

3. Education deals with expanding, developing, increasing, and improving the quality of living. It is an unfolding, not an infolding.

4. Since a child learns through his senses, all of the senses (and there are more than five) should be utilized. This implies that he goes more readily from the concrete to the abstract than from the abstract to the concrete.

5. The formal school curriculum is only a part of a child's total learning situation, and the formal curriculum and the child have not inherently a great deal in common. The learning situation includes everything with which a child comes in contact from the time he awakes in the morning until he goes to bed at night. Education is thus a process of adjustment to his total environment, not only to his school environment. From this it is evident that school alone cannot carry the burden of education in this broader sense. The home, the church, television, and the movies all must take on their share of the task.

6. Children differ in abilities. Some children have keen minds but are not gifted physically; some are perfectly coordinated physically but are average or less than average academically; some are gifted in music and art but have a rough time in mathematics; some are mentally keen but are emotionally unstable.

7. Motivation is a key word in all learning. A child learns most easily the thing which interests him.

8. A classroom is a segment of American society. If a child does not fit well into his social group he is an unhappy child, and an unhappy child does not learn well.

9. The teacher is the liaison officer between the child, his home, his church, his friends, his outside activitives in gen-

eral, and his school. A child succeeds not in part of his
activities but in all, because he lives as a whole being, not
as a collection of parts.

10. Learning develops when there are interests and needs to
be satisfied. Satisfaction of interests and needs is realized
by an individual through his own efforts and through the
stimulation of his friends. A child lives in a dynamic
world: this implies action rather than a static condition.

## OBJECTIVES OF AMERICAN EDUCATION

Because education encompasses everything which affects
a person's way of behaving throughout his life, a statement
or definition of objectives is most difficult to formulate.
From a school viewpoint, an educational objective is a standard or goal to be achieved by the pupil when the work in the
school activity or school division is ended. This might be
interpreted as a desired change in a child's behavior as a result of all his school experiences. An immediate objective
for a teacher is in terms of purposes to be realized or accomplished through teaching processes. A teacher's immediate
objective may differ significantly from his ultimate objective,
which is expressed in terms of the final valued results he
seeks to achieve by means of a more continuous education
process.

The Educational Policies Commission, a highly select committee of members of the National Education Association,
in *The Purposes of Education in American Democracy*, sets
down four broad general objectives as follows: self-realization, human relationships, economic efficiency, and civic responsibility.

The first objective, *self-realization*, encompasses everything that deals with the child as a person. This involves a
child's intellectual, moral, physical, spiritual, aesthetic, emotional, and personal development.

The second, *human relationships*, includes everything
which pertains to a child's relationship with others. Through
this general objective, a child comes to know and appreciate

and evaluate all of the services for which he later in life will pay. The great fields of communications, of transportation, of merchandising, all involve human relationships. What a man does in the service of his fellow man—the work of the minister, the teacher, the doctor, the lawyer, the diplomat, the merchant, the dentist, the engineer—all are in terms of human relationships. Through this objective a child comes to realize that if he is to lead, he must serve; that if he is to be loved by his neighbor, he must love that neighbor.

The third, *economic efficiency*, is the broad objective which, if attained, enables the child as a man to pull his weight in the boat. Herein would be the satisfaction of the need for preparing for a trade or a profession. Economic efficiency means just what it says: that the man, through the satisfaction of this objective of education, is able to make an honest, comfortable living for himself and his family.

The fourth objective, *civic responsibility*, implies that through realization to the fullest of his potentialities, through his relationships with his fellow man being thoroughly satisfying, through his ability to be economically efficient, the child, grown to manhood, carries his share of civic responsibilities loyally, efficiently, and democratically. The instrument of the latter academically is in part the great field of the social sciences.

It is evident that whatever is good or bad in any school or school situation has something to do not only with the individual's development but also with values recognized by society. Values are set up by the society in which those values operate. Through education more refined values are given to that society. Education tries to work toward objectives which will make finer values materialize. Education deals with a knowledge of, an appreciation for, and a control of the values that a society believes in. If a society's values are low, education has somehow not done its work well.

In America one of the controlling values, and certainly one of the most significant, is found in the word "democracy." It encompasses in the thinking of Americans the way of life which is most desirable. The objectives emanating from the Educational Policies Commission tend to be synonymous with the ideal America holds of a way of living.

## ROLE OF THE TEACHER

Classroom administration deals largely with the organization and management of a single classroom. The teacher makes the classroom a dynamic part of society, a coordinated, smooth-working, functioning unit. In the classroom, the teacher is an administrator. As a rule the administrator deals largely with the executive function. He does not make or interpret the law. In the teacher, however, one finds vested not only the executive function of government but the law-making or legislative function, and the law-interpreting or judicial function. Of course this is only saying that to a great extent the classroom teacher sets up the regulatory function (that is, makes the law), acts as a judge (that is, interprets his own ruling), and enforces the regulation he has made and interpreted.

**In the Administrative Unit.** In any book dealing with administrative practices, it is well to remember that the basic principles of administration are universal principles. This is saying that these principles fit, with modification, anywhere in the field of administration. If the assumption is true (and there is every reason to believe it is) the administration of a polar expedition to go under the Arctic icecap, of a large stock farm which breeds thoroughbreds, of a great department store, of a city bank, of a church diocese or a conference, of a large city school system, or of a single classroom differs only in scope, extent, working materials, personnel, and application. The basic principles are the same. The teacher is an administrator, and his unit of administration, although it may be comparatively small, is never insignificant. When he makes a mistake someone is hurt. That the classroom, rather than the child or the teacher, is the logical basic unit of administration is only placing the emphasis where it belongs for administrative purposes. For teaching purposes or for supervisory purposes the unit may well be the child or the teacher.

**As a Specialist.** Because of the slow growth of the idea that the classroom is in itself a dynamic unit of society, there has been an attendant slow recognition of the classroom teacher as a highly trained specialist. Not only must he know subject matter—and only the uninformed believe the subject matter of the schools of today is not difficult to master—but he must know child psychology and teaching techniques.

Because in many cases the classroom teacher is in charge of one specific group—a classroom, study hall, or homeroom —with the responsibility sometimes shared but never eliminated, it follows that the teacher has more to do with the all-round development of each child as an individual than does any other person. He is an administrative officer, but not one who works by directives, telephone, or messenger, or from the sanctuary of an inner office. He is on the firing line. When he succeeds, his youthful daily associates grow, not only in terms of the academic function, but equally in terms of the idealistic, the emotional, the physical, the artistic, and the spiritual.

The classroom teacher is the instrument by which attitudes toward life are inculcated in children. He has the job of helping boys and girls, who are soon to be men and women, to realize the ideals suggested. If the goals, the aims and objectives of education are to be realized, it is upon the classroom teacher that the great burden falls. There are no shock troops in front of him. The principal of the school cannot do the job; the city superintendent or the board of education cannot do it. They are too far away. To help accomplish the teaching assignment, a teacher must possess good academic training and an effective personality.

*Professional Training.* Professional training is the first requisite for success in teaching. Teaching is a profession, and a profession is ever an occupation involving relatively long and specialized preparation on the level of higher education. A teacher's background, then, both general (that is, subject matter) and specific (child psychology, methodology, administration) is the basis of his success. A teacher's professional training is in one sense never completed. A teacher can no more rest on what he has than a physician can rest on the training he brings out of medical school. A teacher's in-service training is often the difference between a great teacher and another whose work is marked by mediocrity. In a sense a teacher goes to school all of his life.

Even today, after many years of emphasis from so many sources upon the significance of teacher education, there are those who honestly believe there is little specialized training needed for teaching. It is not unusual for a college professor in an academic field to say or imply to one of his classes that anyone who knows his subject well can teach successfully. At best this is but a partial truth; at its worst it is wholly untrue. One must know subject matter to teach subject matter; on the other hand one may know subject matter and not be able to teach it to children. To illustrate: A good golfer knows golf; however, only a few golf professionals are great or even good golf teachers, and they teach adults; a good football player knows football, but great coaches of football are not overly plentiful and many of them were not even good players; a great scientist knows his science, but may not be able to teach science at all well. It is a matter of transfer of training both within himself and to his students.

There should be no serious conflict between the importance of subject matter and methodology in teaching, but there is. This is probably due to the fact that there are good subject-matter teachers (history, mathematics, science) who have had little or no *formal* teacher-training. Some would argue that they were not trained. It would seem, however, that these people have had much *informal* training. A big-league shortstop has had no formal baseball training, but he is good at a highly developed skill. It is well to remember that he may have had fifteen years of good informal training. Again, he is learning only a skill—and teaching is more than a skill.

The same probably pertains to good subject-matter teachers. They have, through years of contact with teachers, some good, some bad, assimilated the best techniques from these teachers. The poor teaching to which they were subjected made so unfavorable an impression on them that none of it was carried forward. The same would be true of the short-stop. He copied the technique used by the best players he saw, not the worst.

Subject-matter control in the specialized area of teaching tends to increase in importance with the academic advancement of the student. One needs more training in mathematics to teach algebra to ninth-graders than to teach sixth-grade arithmetic. It would seem that methods of presenting subject matter tend to decrease in importance with the academic advancement of the student. Thus, for the Ph.D. candidate, the instructors need mastery of a very important content; the method of study can be neglected to some extent as the advanced student tends to develop his own techniques. This is not saying, however, that there is no need for good techniques at the advanced level. It is only saying that the teacher of children needs better instruction in the techniques of teaching and of learning than does the teacher of the more advanced learner.

*Personality.* If a single item in the teacher's success were to be factored out, an item which in itself must be positive if the teacher is to succeed, the personality factor would be most significant. That is to say, if other factors—mastery of subject matter, good techniques, good physical attributes—are held constant (assuming that all are satisfactory) in two young teachers, but the personality factor is varied significantly—one being exceedingly good, the other very bad—the probability of success is great for the first, the probability of failure is great for the second.

Someone has said that one's personality is the product of his yesterdays. This implies that personality has much to do with behavior patterns. The psychologist would say it is *social stimulus value*. As a part of a teacher's equipment, personality tends to be a composite of all his habits, physical, mental, moral, spiritual—his habits of thinking and doing and being.

With rare exception, the personality of anyone who has gone far enough in formal schooling to be a teacher is generally satisfactory. There are only aspects or phases which need to be improved. This is saying that personality, since to a great extent it reflects habits, can be modified. Always one's social impact tends to be made up of his native endowment plus a composite of his daily living, his reading, his thinking, and his personal habits. A few persons have great natural endowment. They have unusual personality traits (a trait being a characteristic and relatively permanent mode of behavior, an outcome of both heredity and environment) which make adjustment to teaching children easy for them. These are the so-called "natural" teachers. Unfortunately these are comparatively few in number. *Most good teachers make themselves good teachers.* It is possible for one to learn by experience only, but experience is a slow teacher and usually a costly one. Professional training shortens the time needed to achieve experience and does a better job. The teacher's personality, then, as a factor in his teaching equipment, is not an accident; to a great extent the teacher makes his personality what it is. Because of the complexity of the topic, a later chapter is given entirely to this subject.

## DISCUSSION PROBLEM

Below are extracts from statements by educators of the past who have contributed to our educational growth and development. After each man's name is given the year of his birth. With some of the quotations which follow there would be hearty agreement; with others, less agreement. The quotations are from the writings of men whose educational philosophy influenced more or less the period in which they lived. No contemporary educator is quoted. With which ones do you agree?

JOHN AMOS COMENIUS (1592): "Whatever is taught should have a definite use in everyday life. General principles should be taught first, then the details. All things must be taught in proper succession. Never leave a subject until it is thoroughly understood. A perfect knowledge of God, nature, and art should be taught. Things should be taught with reference to the manner in which they came into existence."

JOHN MILTON (1608): "I call a complete and generous education that which fits a man to perform justly, skilfully, and magnanimously all the offices both public and private of peace and war."

JOHN LOCKE (1632): "The business of education is not to make the young perfect in any one of the sciences, but so to open and dispose their minds as may best make them capable of any, when they shall apply themselves to it. . . . It is therefore to give them this freedom that I think they should be made to look into all sorts of knowledge and exercise their understanding in so wide a variety or stock of knowledge."

JEAN JACQUES ROUSSEAU (1712): "Everything is good as it comes from the hands of the Author of Nature; but everything degenerates in the hands of man."

IMMANUEL KANT (1724): "Education is the art of developing man's natural gifts in their due proportion and in relation to their end."

JOHANN HEINRICH PESTALOZZI (1746): "To engage the attention of the child, to exercise his judgment, to raise his heart to noble sentiments: these I think are the chief ends of education."

HORACE MANN (1796): "Education alone can conduct us to that enjoyment which is, at once, best in quality and infinite in quantity."

JOHN HENRY NEWMAN (1801): "Christianity, and nothing short of it, must be made the element and principle of all education."

JOHN RUSKIN (1819): "Education does not mean teaching people what they do not know. It means teaching them to behave as they do not behave. . . . It means . . . training them in the perfect exercise and kingly continence of their bodies and souls. It is a painful, continual, and difficult work to be done by kindness, by watching, by warning, by precept, and by praise, but above all by example."

HERBERT SPENCER (1820): "The purpose of education is to prepare us for complete living. The only way to judge of the value of an educational course is first to classify, in the order of their importance, the leading activities and needs of life, and then measure the course of study by how fully it offers such a preparation."

THOMAS H. HUXLEY (1825): "That man I think has had a liberal education who has been so trained in youth that his body is the ready servant of his will, and does with ease and pleasure all the work that, as a mechanism, it is capable of; whose intellect is a clear, cold, logic engine, with all parts of equal strength and in smooth working order. . . . Whose mind is stored with knowledge of the great and fundamental truths of Nature and the laws of her operations; one who . . . has learned to love all beauty, whether of Nature or of art, to hate all vileness, and to respect others as himself."

JOHN DEWEY (1859): "I believe that the only true education comes through the stimulation of the child's powers by the demands of the social situations in which he finds himself. . . . The child's own instincts and powers furnish the material and give the starting point for all education."

WILLIAM CHANDLER BAGLEY (1874): "From between the opposing forces of soft sentimentalism and hard materialism we can climb to a new plane—the plane of virile, practical, and dynamic idealism. The only kind of freedom that is thinkable today is disciplined freedom. We cannot build our democratic structure on the shifting sands of soft pedagogy. There must be iron in the blood of education and lime in the bone. In the individual, as in the race, true freedom is always a conquest, never a gift.

"For a motto of an educational theory meet for the needs of democracy in an increasingly industrialized civilization, I propose the phrase, 'Through discipline to freedom.'"

CHARLES H. JUDD (1873): "Viewed in the light of the psychology of social institutions, education is seen to be an effort to fit the individual into the general plan of social co-operation. Education seeks to give the individual as much as possible of the organized experiences which generations of minds have put together. Education seeks to drill the individual in the use of these instruments of adaptation which have been perfected by earlier generations. Education aims to make it possible for the individual to master the methods of recording his own contributions to the intellectual wealth of the world."

## QUESTIONS ON THE PROBLEM

1. From the statements recorded above regarding the aims and purposes of education from the time of John Amos Comenius to the present, select the one you like best. Try to be specific in saying why you think it fits your own thinking best.

2. Were the dates of birth of the authors not given, do you believe it would be possible to place these definitions of education in their chronological order solely upon the content of the definition? Can you say why?

3. Rousseau's *Émile*, written about two centuries ago, has probably influenced American educational theory as much as or more than any other book produced. The quotation is from that book. Can you show why this thought as expressed in

the quotation would influence educational theory? Do you agree with the statement? Why?

4. Is there any statement presented from the educators and philosophers of the past which disagrees substantially with the others? Is the disagreement, if there be such, significant? Discuss.

5. Which two statements agree most closely? Add a third which is in practical agreement.

6. Write a one-paragraph exposition of what you consider to be the basic function of formal (school) education in the United States. You may incorporate whatever is usable from your reading. Try to write something that is worth reading in class —limit 250 words.

## STUDY QUESTIONS

1. Try to state specifically the major objectives of classroom administration.

2. From the viewpoint of the tremendous size (and importance) of formal education in the United States, state briefly what you believe will be America's three greatest educational problems in the next twenty years. Be able to discuss each if called upon.

3. Why are the objectives which you listed in the first question more easily attained in the classroom than in any other phase of education?

4. Your text states that the classroom teacher is a specialist. Can one be a specialist and perform duties which are marked by their variation? Doesn't the idea of a "specialist" convey the thought of doing one thing very well? Discuss.

5. Is there danger, under the American ideal of education today, that a child may become a good citizen but be inadequately trained in fundamental skills? Does "iron in the blood of education and lime in the bone" have anything to do with acquiring skills? What would you say is "soft pedagogy"?

6. What is meant by the term "disciplined freedom"?

7. How does "training and conditioning" differ from other phases of learning? Is conditioning not a part of education?

8. What is meant by saying that learning is not "saltatory or discrete"?

9. What is the specific difference between attitudes and principles? Between principles and objectives?

10. Be prepared to discuss in class this statement: "The formal school curriculum is only a part of a child's total learning situation. . . ." (See p. 7, item 5.)

11. Take the item, civic responsibility, from the four objectives set down by the Educational Policies Commission and list under it no less than ten directly or indirectly taught procedures in our schools which are aimed at attaining this objective. To illustrate: (1) A child is taught to respect the property rights of others. (2) Most schools teach a course in Government or the Constitution.

## SELECTED READINGS

BUTLER, FRANK A. *The Improvement of Teaching in Secondary Schools.* Chicago: University of Chicago Press, 1954. Two chapters are especially recommended, Chapters 7 and 9. The first is a clear discussion of social dynamics in the classroom and its application to daily work; the second deals with an overview of teacher planning.

CHAMBERLAIN, LEO M., and KINDRED, LESLIE W. *The Teacher and School Organization.* 3d ed. Englewood Cliffs, N. J.: Prentice-Hall, Inc., 1958. The first chapter, "The Scope of American Education," offers a good summary of the size of America's educational problem at the time this work was published.

GRAMBS, JEAN D., IVERSON, WILLIAM J., and PATTERSON, FRANKLIN K. *Modern Methods in Secondary Education.* New York: Holt, Rinehart & Winston, Inc., 1958. Chapter 1. A good résumé of the place of teaching as a factor in the pupil's like or dislike for high school.

HARRISON, RAYMOND H., and GOWIN, LAWRENCE E. *The Elementary Teacher in Action.* San Francisco: Wadsworth Publishing Co., Inc., 1958. Puts major emphasis upon the teacher as the instrument of learning rather than upon educational theory.

HASKEW, LAURENCE D. *This Is Teaching.* Chicago: Scott, Foresman & Co., 1956. Chapter 3, "These Are the Learners," contains sections dealing with the various ways of studying pupils.

KYTE, GEORGE C. *The Elementary School Teacher at Work.* New York: Holt, Rinehart & Winston, Inc., 1957. Chapter 1, "The Philosophy of the American Elementary School," and Chapter 14, "Organization and Management," deal in a practical way with one phase of the theme of the text you are studying.

LIEBERMAN, MYRON. *Education as a Profession*. Englewood Cliffs, N. J.: Prentice-Hall, Inc., 1956. Chapter 8, "Teachers and Their Characteristics," is closely allied to the theme of this text. Discusses the reasons teachers enter the profession and ways that have been developed to measure fitness for the profession.

MACLEAN, MALCOLM S., and LEE, EDWIN A. *Change and Process in Education*. New York: Holt, Rinehart & Winston, Inc., 1956. Pp. 22, 449ff. Presents a consideration of the work of the teacher in education and discussion of "the wider reaches of preparation for the profession of education."

WILES, KIMBALL. *Teaching for Better Schools*. Englewood Cliffs, N. J.: Prentice-Hall, Inc., 1952. Chapter 6. Is developed around the idea that a group is born; that it emerges when a number of individuals reach some common goals and some common plans.

# 2

# THE TEACHER AS ADMINISTRATOR

"Find out what a child doesn't like and give him plenty of it." That seems to have been the dictum of a century or so ago concerning the three important items in the school program: the child, the teacher, and the process. School, at the lower levels especially, was essentially a discipline in the unpleasant. Parents—and teachers—were inclined to wonder much and worry a little about a boy who said honestly that he liked school. Could he be exactly bright? Possibly there was present some of the thinking of that grim old theologian, Cotton Mather, who with a fine discrimination on the theology of the doctrine of original sin would have argued that children came into the world depraved and that their natural learnings would resultantly be sinful. If they liked anything, it was suspect. School was not a pleasant place as far as children were concerned.

The work of the teacher in those days was strenuous. Ungraded rooms, with the pupils' ages ranging between five and twenty-one, and an enrollment of commonly more than fifty, did not guarantee any teacher a vacation at the beach. The work, though strenuous, was from a methodology viewpoint uncomplicated. The teacher made the assignment in the textbook; the pupil memorized the assignment or at least studied the assignment with a technique based upon memorization; the pupil recited to the teacher. The recitation was found everywhere from the Great Lakes to the Gulf, from the Atlantic to the Great Plains. From a managerial viewpoint the teacher's chief problem was that of pupil control or, as it is more commonly called, discipline. He did not report, grade, program, unify, organize, cooperate, or promote. Critics he did not have unless he did not or could not whip the big boys. If he could not, he did not finish the year—or did not come back for the next year.

Historically the date cannot be placed when the changes in methods of teaching a school and managing a class took place. Class instruction dates back to about 1690 or perhaps a little earlier, when Jean Baptiste de la Salle in France with his Brothers of the Christian Schools taught boys in groups (by ages) as an economy of time factor. In America, the change in classroom management was an evolution that coincided more or less with the development of the city superintendency and the school principalship. Approximately the time was between 1800 and 1850.

The growth of the city school system made necessary the appointment of a city superintendent. The growth of the school building from one classroom to many classrooms led to the appointment of a school principal. With the advent of the city superintendency and the school principalship, a new type of duty developed for the classroom teacher. For the first time he had to make reports; he had to program his classes in relationship to others so that water, toilets, and playgrounds would be available for all; he had to make out report cards for parents; he had to attend teachers' meetings; he was held responsible for annual promotions of students. He became a manager, and school management became a part of the profession. Today this phase of the teacher's work is classed as a normative science, as it is based to a great extent on norms. Today grading, reporting, programming, organizing, unifying, planning, and promoting, all are words in the teacher's everyday working vocabulary.

## PHILOSOPHIES OF SCHOOL MANAGEMENT

The teacher is in a dual position: he teaches and he also interprets and manages. The term "management" tends to be a generic one, as its applications are numerous. A man manages a bottling works; a foreman manages a railroad crew; an administrator manages a hospital; a baseball executive manages a ball club; a farmer manages a wheat farm; a rancher manages a cattle ranch; an explorer manages a polar expedition; a superintendent manages a school system, and a classroom teacher manages a classroom. The same basic principles are present in each situation, for the principles of administration are universal principles; they apply anywhere.

An analysis of management makes it first of all an *economic* organ. It has come about through mass production. To a great extent, as business analysts point out, management is *the* economic organ of an industrial society. Every act, every decision, every deliberation of management has economy as its first dimension. At first glance this would seem to apply only to business management. It should be noted that in a business sense the economy is in money; in non-commercial enterprises (such as formal education) the economy is in time and effort, which in its final analysis is saving manpower, an eventual saving of money. The teacher administers in order to save time and effort for himself and his pupils.

**Effect of Tradition.** Formal traditional learning was transferred to America almost bodily from Europe. As a result, almost from the first there was a conflict between the basic ideals of democracy and a mechanistic schooling which was in its form autocratic. At the time American schools were being established, only a small portion of Europe was democratic in its form of government. It is somewhat surprising that the schools of colonial America were as democratic as they were, considering their autocratic forebears. Because of the European influence (among others), American teachers have found themselves between two powerful forces: the one, a firm belief in democracy as a way of life and a sincere desire to bring as much of it as possible into the classrooms; and the other, the handcuffing, leg-shackling fetters of a European tradition which in itself had a strong tendency to be autocratic and authoritarian. This may explain why teachers have always tended to be more democratic and progressive in their attitudes and pronouncements than they actually are in their practices. Someone has said that teachers are liberals in their pronouncements, but conservatives—almost reactionaries—in their doings. Tradition has always been a limiting thing, whether the tradition be good or bad, useful or worthless.

This does not mean to say that everything that has been borrowed from our European forebears has been bad or worthless. Almost the opposite would be true. The traditional is in itself neither good nor bad. What it means to say is that tradition in itself does not make for freedom and is always opposed to change. Even principles, though sound, are unchanging when set in the mold of tradition. Disraeli is quoted as saying, "Tradition embalms a principle."

In the organization and control of the classroom, the teacher may take one of two routes. In neither does he surrender the authority vested in him by law. Shall he encourage the boys and girls, thoughtfully and democratically, under his guidance to organize their room for daily action; or shall he, as the teacher, kindly and firmly organize it for them? The latter will undoubtedly save him some work. Shall he, using his best training and judgment, set up in detail the plan of the daily activities of the room; or shall he, using that same training and maturity of judgment, encourage and assist the children in *their* room to set up the details of management? Two philosophies of school management, and of living in a democracy, are involved in the simple questions. It need not be pointed out that the second, although it is far more trouble and on the surface seems inefficient, is a direct application of democratic processes to everyday child life; whereas the first, although it may appear to get a job done more efficiently, takes all of the responsibility with its attendant satisfactions away from the children.

**Conflict in Educational Theory.** The teacher in the schools of today is in the in-between position in a conflict of philosophies (if the disagreement can be dignified by that term) or better, perhaps, an argument in which anyone and everyone joins. In this argument as to what shall be emphasized in the schools and as to what the methodology of teaching shall be, philosophers and psychologists are sometimes vocal (they have some right to be); politicians, welfare workers, and ministers express themselves freely; journalists, with little professional educational background, write articles for popular magazines; radio and television personalities contribute their opinions (which are sometimes good); social scientists take a hand in the free-for-all game; and law enforcement officers get into print with their opinions. The National Association of Manufacturers gets out bulletins, and the AFL–CIO takes sides. Somehow out of this babel of voices—the least vociferous of which commonly belong to the most interested people, the parents and teachers, school administrators and boards of education—must emerge a decision which satisfies all. That this cannot succeed goes without saying.

Below are presented some of the conflicts in educational principles which confront the teacher. The differences of viewpoint are not inconsequential, because on them hinges the whole question of where the emphasis shall be placed on what is taught in the schools. What is taught is an interpretation of educational thinking, and the thinking in turn influences the entire political philosophy.

| | | |
|---|---|---|
| Emphasis on the physical and biological sciences and mathematics, as preparation for earning a living. | vs. | Emphasis on the social sciences and humanities as the essence of a democratic society. |
| Authoritarian school management (children need discipline). | vs. | Democratic school management (school is life, not a preparation for life). |
| Firsthand experience (laboratory work). | vs. | Vicarious experience (reading, television, radio, audiovisual education). |

| | | |
|---|---|---|
| Factual learning (one cannot think without facts). | *vs.* | Thought-provoking learning (learning is unfoldment, not infoldment). |
| Teacher instruction (a good teacher lectures). | *vs.* | Free-for-all discussion (learning is an activity). |
| Subject-centered (subjects must be mastered). | *vs.* | Pupil-centered (teach children, not subjects). |
| Extrinsic motivation (incentives are necessary). | *vs.* | Intrinsic (interest) motivation (incentives are artificial). |
| Drill and memory work (practice makes perfect). | *vs.* | Insight teaching; drill reduced to minimum essentials. |
| Conformity to strict rules of behavior (pupils need more discipline). | *vs.* | Spontaneity; self-discipline (a child must be taught to discipline himself). |
| Authoritarian direction. | *vs.* | Much counseling and guidance. |
| Little pupil freedom. | *vs.* | Much pupil freedom. |
| Teacher dominance. | *vs.* | Much responsibility given to child. |
| Emphasis on detailed exactness. | *vs.* | Emphasis on grasp of basic principles. |
| Intensive study of comparatively limited areas. | *vs.* | Extensive study of larger areas and of more areas. |

Each column (or school of thought) presents a definite pattern. The left-hand column would produce something of this type of school: The physical sciences with their concomitant of mathematics dominate the curriculum. Every child gets physical science training of the formalized physics and chemistry type and laboratory taught. Factual learning is stressed at all times and the teacher lectures a great deal. The teacher is subject-conscious at all times, and those who cannot do the work well are allowed to fall by the wayside. The motivation for these pupils is marks, grades, honors, even prizes. Industry tells the schools what it wants from the schools and the schools conform. The teacher in this type of school runs his classes as a patrolman runs his beat—he is in charge and what he says goes. There is much drill and practice work although pupils tend to dislike both. The pupil conforms at all times; rarely is he allowed to express disagreement. The direction is of the "do as I say" type and pupils are allowed little freedom of choice. The teacher dominates every situation at all times. Study tends to be for details, although basic principles are certainly never intentionally neglected. Pupils are not broadly educated, but they are decidedly well-trained. Pupils from this sort of school "know what they are supposed to know" and usually rate high on standardized tests. As a group they satisfy college entrance requirements.

From the right-hand column a school of this type evolves: No more emphasis is put upon physical and biological sciences and mathematics than is given to history, sociology, economics, or English. The humanities are stressed as much or even more than the physical sciences. Home economics, shop work, driver education, and kindred subjects get some time from many students. The child reads much. Learning instead of being firsthand (laboratory), which is comparatively slow and expensive, is through vicarious experiences such as reading, dramatization, committee work, television, radio, and free discussion. Much emphasis is placed upon thought-provoking discussion, and pupils express themselves well. Great freedom both of expression and of activity is permitted. The teacher teaches children first, subject matter second. Motivation tends to be from interest, as the uninteresting is either made interesting for the child or is modified to make it more palatable. Audio-visual aids are used much in study, and school is as a rule a pleasant place for these youngsters. The over-all situation is democratic, and the teacher, though always in command, is often in the background. Spontaneity is the rule and teachers counsel much on each child's personal problems. Children are definitely treated as individuals. The child is taught to take much responsibility and mistakes are taken for granted. Children study extensively and parents are amazed at the breadth of their learning but are sometimes chagrined that the same children, although reading much above their grade levels, are sometimes weak in fundamental operations in arithmetic.

It is a platitude to say that the teacher's attitude toward school management has much to do with the objectives sought. It is never the subject matter which is undemocratic or un-American; it is the manner of handling the school situation. The schools must demonstrate democracy in action, but democracy does not mean failure to live up to one's obligations either as a child or as an adult.

It would seem that a basic purpose of all schooling would be to turn out a person who through experience would be both well trained, where training is indicated, and well educated, where breadth of learning is desirable. A well-educated pupil is, after all, a boy or girl with a broad background of knowledges, insights, and appreciations. He has the educational background necessary to carry successfully the next course of work in his climb up the academic ladder.

## MANAGEMENT AND PUPIL RESPONSIBILITY

One of the broader aspects of management, and without doubt the most significant from the standpoint of citizenship development, is concerned with the growth in responsibleness of the individual child. The child is going to have many responsibilities later; he should be getting some training for them while he is still in school. Individual responsibility tends to grow out of group responsibility; for this reason the teacher should begin by developing a sense of responsibility in the class group as a whole.

**Developing Group Responsibility.** The classroom, with its opportunity for developing this first attribute of American citizenship, is in danger of giving lip service only to the ideal of group responsibility. It is so easy to profess one thing and practice another. Adults are prone to criticize youth for its irresponsibleness, when American life, even the American classroom, has comparatively few responsibilities to give youth and commonly withholds those which are available.

Greater responsibilities can come only to those who have first handled smaller responsibilities well. Responsibility-taking is, like mathematics, in an ascending scale of difficulty. Group responsibilities are the training ground for individual responsibility. Because the beginning teacher frequently has trouble putting his theory into practice, a few suggestions for starting such a program in the classroom are offered.

1. Let the pupils try planning their own assignment for the next day. You work with the class, of course.
2. Allow the pupils to set up the rules and regulations governing the room on such routine matters as leaving the room, using the pencil-sharpener, or makeup work for classes missed. If you find that at first they are going astray, you will, of course, guide their decisions.
3. Make the pupils responsible for good conduct when you are out of the room.
4. Encourage the pupils to set up the regulations by which each can carry his load in room housekeeping.
5. Allow the pupils to make the necessary rules and regulations regarding the care of wraps, books, lunches, and things of this sort.
6. Give pupils the privilege of considering, with your help and guidance, punishments for violations and infractions of rules before offenses happen. (Exercise much care here, as you are the responsible person and the authority rests with you.)
7. Ask for suggestions from pupils as to how room visitors shall be welcomed and made to feel that the pupils are glad they have come.
8. Let the pupils work out methods of distributing tickets for school activities, such as plays and athletic contests.
9. Ask pupils to suggest the best possible way for handling classroom supplies and other materials which are in daily use.
10. Encourage the pupils to make their own regulations governing the use of library books, the dictionary, and other reference material used by their room.

11. If the pupils are allocated any general committee work by the school authorities, see that it is carefully carried out (by the pupils).

12. Encourage the group to function as a class in all group activities at which the whole school is represented.

It must never be assumed that a teacher's work is lessened by setting up the goal of developing responsibilities in pupils. Usually, a teacher finds the work less onerous if he does it himself.

**Developing Individual Leadership.** It does not always follow that, when a group has assumed responsibility well, each individual in the group has assumed equal responsibility. In practice, individuals in the group rarely, if ever, assume equal responsibilities. There will always be leaders and followers within the group. The teacher who takes his classroom management for what it is, an important phase of a child's development, has the problem of making each individual as ready, willing, and efficient as it is possible for that particular individual to be in assuming and executing the responsibilities which are rightfully his. He is going to have many responsibilities later; he should be getting some training for these responsibilities while he is still in school.

Group action must come from individual leadership within the group. The teacher thus starts with the whole and goes to the development of the individual parts. Leadership and responsibility-taking are in some ways synonymous terms but are not necessarily the same thing. Leaders take responsibility, but there are many who will assume responsibility willingly that lack the essentials, other than initiative, required of good leaders. A teacher should expect pupil growth to come from activities such as these:

1. Serving as chairman of any one of the numerous committees through which group action functions best.

2. Carrying out individual assignments made by a committee, the teacher, or any other designated authority.

3. Assuming the responsibilities and duties accompanying the election to any class officership.

4. Assuming the duties of a homeroom official.
5. Accepting the responsibility of knowing and utilizing school rights and privileges.
6. Serving as editor, business manager, or circulation manager of the room publication or as the room's representative for getting news to the general newspaper source for the whole school.
7. Knowing and observing his individual responsibility for the morale of the room. (Avoidance of being a grouch or malcontent illustrates this point.)
8. Acting as traffic-control officer when given the opportunity and serving with "honor and distinction."
9. Acting as an ambassador for his room at public gatherings where each room is to be represented.
10. Being responsible for his own day-to-day behavior to the extent that teacher domination becomes increasingly less.
11. Participating in planning, discussing, and executing all actions which are desirable for a good school citizen.
12. Holding himself responsible, individually, for the school's good name, his class's behavior, his parents' participation in school affairs, and his own everyday acts.
13. Being responsible for his own personal behavior in the hallways and lavatories and on the playground. Consciously he is encouraged to feel that his room and his school's good name is his responsibility when he is at public gatherings or in public places in general.

**Evaluating the Program.** Evaluating the results of efforts to make classroom management function in terms of developing responsibility in pupils is a difficult problem mainly because results are hard to measure. There is no test which can give a teacher an accurate measure. The results seem to be negligible in terms of the effort put forth. Here is where a teacher may be inclined to say, "Oh, what's the use!" He must remember that he is working on a very large edifice and that the day-to-day work of any one individual makes very little showing. If he is to get any satisfaction from his effort, he must notice that in this phase of growth much of the dynamic activity of the group comes from the class itself. The teacher does not do all the thinking, neither does he plan in detail how the work is to be done. The activity does not always follow the course the teacher prefers. Since the group furnishes the thinking and the activity, the thinking may be immature and much of the activity wasteful. The group may carry out the work and make mistakes. The mistakes, if they are not too significant, should be permitted to occur. The group acts as a group, yet each child grows as an individual.

From the standpoint of good learning as well as from that of developing individual responsibility on the part of the learner, the teacher should encourage the pupils to evaluate their own efforts. Anything and everything which has in it a concentration of group effort will follow the four steps of *purposing, planning, executing, and judging.* The teacher is always on the job. He carefully refrains, however, from expressing opinions which may be seconded by those looking for cues. The group decides whether the work of the group and of the individuals in the group was well done. It decides where it succeeded and where it failed to do a good job. As director of the scenario, the teacher never allows any individual to be censured by the group when that individual has tried to do his part well. Children are not only thoughtless in their criticisms, but also severe.

Under this way of working, each child tends to see the whole activity in terms of his part in it. This is what every athletic coach is always trying to achieve. Usually the child does not need to have his failings pointed out, and rarely does he need to be told when and where he fell down on the job. His classmates know and the more outspoken will tell him. No one praises his good work and he is not inclined to overevaluate this himself, as he is conscious of the group censure for one who overapproves his own efforts. A teacher should talk to each child privately if he feels that such action is necessary. A teacher's praise is always in general and for the group; rarely does it single out individuals.

## PRACTICES AND PROCEDURES IN MANAGEMENT

When the teacher has any doubt as to the efficacy of his daily practices in helping to achieve his broader objectives of management, he should weigh the procedure in the balance carefully; if it comes up lacking he should try to discard it. This he may not always be able to do, for many practices of the individual classroom are tied up in the larger domain of school administration. Even when this is not true, traditional practices are usually firmly entrenched.

**Clarifying Aims.** If the dictum that every piece of school machinery should give an educational account of itself is followed, a teacher may find that many of his management practices are suspect. The questions which follow are intended only as a point of departure to aid a teacher in clarifying his general aim in the field of management:

1. Shall penmanship be taught in regular classes each day or shall each student's penmanship be evaluated in terms of his daily written work, and the instruction be more individualized? What is good penmanship? Can any penmanship be called poor if it is produced easily and is clear and readable?
2. Shall spelling be taught in classes, taking the words from a spelling book? Might it be well to scrutinize all written work for spelling errors, check these, and hold each student responsible for learning to spell correctly each word he has misspelled? Does a child increase his vocabulary significantly from learning to spell the words in a spelling book? Will this technique tend to limit the child's vocabulary by causing him to use only words he is sure he can spell correctly?
3. Shall a child be deprived of recess time as a punishment? Upon what theory is such a practice based when it is done? What are the penalties the teacher pays? Are recesses a right or a privilege?
4. Shall pupils be asked to memorize poetry against their will? Shall memorizing poetry ever be used as a punish-

ment? This is a traditional practice which is disappearing. Why should it disappear entirely? Or should it?

5. Shall recesses in elementary school be of fifteen-minute duration? Is there any evidence that this is the best amount of time to use? When would a ten-minute period be indicated? A twenty-minute period?

6. Shall pupils in all the different grades in a large school have a recess period at the same time? What are the advantages of staggering the recess periods? What are the disadvantages of having pupils in different rooms have recess periods at different times? Have modern school buildings given a different aspect to this practice in general?

7. Is "room housekeeping," in the form of having pupils pick up all paper from the floor before being dismissed, a good practice? What are the arguments for it as well as against it in terms of its educational value?

8. For many years schools were operated during the winter months only. Later the time was extended to five, six, seven, eight, then nine months. From an educational viewpoint is the nine-month term the answer? Many schools are now paying teachers for ten months of work. Should our schools all be extended to ten-month terms? What would you say to running schools for eleven months a year, thus finishing elementary school in six years rather than eight? Suppose our schools were under the 6–6 plan. Would this alter the case? European schools do not use an eight-year elementary school. Are they necessarily wrong?

The teacher with well-defined aims in his management, the one who knows with some definiteness what he is trying to develop in his pupils, has laid the groundwork for efficiency. Efficiency, however, is finally measured in terms of results. Results are evaluated in terms of the time expended, the mental and mechanical effort put forth, and the child's development while acquiring the results.

**Justifying Results.** Evaluating classroom procedures in terms of the time and effort expended and the end-results achieved is, of course, much easier to talk about than to put into effect. The daily machinery of roll-taking, of making and giving a test and recording grades, of getting out reports to parents, of making out records and reports for the central office, of using school equipment without undue waste of time and effort—all must be carefully evaluated in terms of the over-all purposes of the school. In theory, at least, each procedure is a means to an end; never is the procedure an end in itself. Paper work of all kinds is suspect if the work is tending to become an end in itself. Tests are worthless if results of tests are not used. Reports must do something; records must serve an educational purpose.

Too often a teacher fails to ask himself what the procedure is accomplishing. As an old farmer said to a young friend who was waxing enthusiastic about purchasing a small combine for harvesting wheat which had been set up by the dealer at the state fair grounds: "Yep, Bob, she does run smooth; and I haven't much doubt that little outfit'll do all that's claimed for it. But there's one thing you're forgettin'. It runs smooth, the belts just hum, there's not a creak or a whine any place in it, but—*there's nothing going through it.*" The test of a machine is what it does under working conditions. The danger in school management is always in mistaking the busy hum of the machinery of classroom procedure for the real accomplishment of educational aims. The turning of the wheels of the machinery must never be mistaken for the actual process of separating the wheat from the straw. No matter how smoothly the school machinery runs, "there's nothin' going through it" when it fails to serve the only persons for whom schools exist, the boys and girls.

Although there is little doubt that all school procedures should serve the educative function or be modified to the point where they do so, there is a question as to whether some of the most common school procedures are really serving the pupils well. A few items of school procedure are offered here for consideration. Not all are in existence in all schools, but all are found in some schools. Is it possible to indicate how the management machinery justifies its existence in each case?

1. Making the flag salute a requirement each day. What is the purpose of saluting the flag? Can patriotism be inspired by a mechanical process? Can you suggest a better way to teach respect and love for the flag? Can you suggest a situation under which a daily flag salute would be indicated as a desirable practice if you believe it is not always good?

2. Testing the entire school system on standardized tests; working up the results and making excellent descriptive-profile charts of results. Results are discussed at teachers' meetings. Suggestions are made that more or less emphasis be given to certain subject fields. No definite program of using the test results in curriculum changes or in any other way is set up.

3. Writing out formal lesson plans for the principal's and supervisor's offices. Plans not utilized except in case of an absence when a substitute teacher takes over.

4. Reading aloud long passages in reading and literature classes when an appreciative audience is lacking. In what type of classes would reading aloud be an end in itself? Is reading aloud a testing process which might well be carried out for each pupil individually?

5. Holding school plays which take much time for practice and ticket promotion and which utilize a comparatively small number of pupils in learning situations.

It is not meant to imply that the procedures suggested above are necessarily bad in themselves. They are merely given as examples for questioning whether certain common procedures really serve the educational purpose for which they are intended.

**Setting Up Routine Procedures.** Routinizing school machinery is never, of course, an end in itself; it is only one of the minor means of accomplishing the purpose for which schools exist. The more important factors of room procedure tend to be matters of judgment and initiative. However, for the efficient operation of the classroom, some phases of management must be routinized at the earliest possible date. Among these, the following are the most conspicuous:

1. The daily schedule. A school's schedule or a room's schedule is the timetable for the day's work. It is followed rigorously. Only exceptional circumstances warrant a change even for a day.
2. Distributing materials. This is always a matter of routine. However you as the teacher distribute materials, follow the same pattern from day to day. Two common methods, both elementary, are in use. (a) Use monitors: These pass out materials (texts, papers, songbooks, etc.) for the one row in which they are seated. (b) Place the materials (for example, if a test is being handed out) in the hands of the first pupil in each row. This allows for an accurate count.
3. The form for writing up experiments and other written work. Be exact in what you want as to form—and stay with it until the form is routinized.
4. Taking the roll for the day. A seating chart which locates each pupil by name in the seat he occupies is the easiest and possibly the most efficient method. In this way you check only vacant seats which are few in number.
5. The formal beginning of the day. Homeroom procedure for a formal opening is considered desirable. The remainder of the homeroom program is not subject to routine.
6. Classroom housekeeping. Pupils (as well as teachers) are inclined to be messy in their housekeeping. The use of wastepaper baskets, pencil sharpeners, chalk and erasers, texts supplied by the school—all are handled to better advantage if the procedure is habitualized.
7. Development of good study habits. The idea of getting busy at once is contagious. Wasting time in getting to work instead of plunging in at once (but in a methodical manner) is a weakness not only of school pupils.
8. Regulations governing, and practice in observing, fire drills. This is a first-day duty. Rehearse until the movement is practically automatic. Habit must function in an emergency as panic tends to destroy the ordinary thinking process.

Later, as the need arises, the teacher takes up such procedures as makeup work for illness in absences of short duration, attendance at general assemblies for the entire school, rules and regulations governing the use of drinking fountains, locker rooms, and toilet facilities, and others of a similar nature.

Some phases of management are never completely habitualized or routinized, and would lose in effectiveness if they were. To illustrate, consider the classroom dictionary. Its placement in the room so that it is easily available to all, the routing of students to and from it, and the regulations as to the number and the duration of times for which it may be used—all these are simple classroom mechanics. However, using the dictionary efficiently after the pupil gets to it evidently requires a higher order of mental output than getting to and from it. Both efforts are skills, the one very simple and uncomplex, the other quite complex. Obviously the going to and from this classroom aid is a matter of routine, and can be regulated. But using the book correctly comes under the head of a mental-methods skill, a skill which is developed at different rates and to different degrees by individual students.

## GROUP TEACHING AND GROUP DYNAMICS

The modern school teaches children in groups, not only because groups are more economical for teaching purposes, but also because children during their waking hours tend to live in groups. The school is a society, a dynamic society at the age level of children. And, although the effect of the group is always present and is always recognized, every good teacher also recognizes clearly the significance of the statement that no two children are alike. Today every school child belongs to a group—and there is always group interaction—yet every child is an individual in that group. The classroom is a dynamic society.

The social and economic pressure of a growing population, with its concomitant of an ever increasing industrialization and the massing of that population in cities, has forced upon formal education a broader function. During this period of America's growth the school took upon itself new aims, new methods, new techniques, and a broader interpretation of its obligations, goals, and objectives. Slow to make changes the schools have always been, because there has always been and even now exists a pronounced lag between what a society in a democracy is experiencing and what the schools in that democracy are emphasizing. Advancements in science, in economic thought, in engineering, in transportation, and in communication all usually exist for years in practice before textbooks and the schools emphasize these things in any way commensurate with their importance in the American way of life. The schools in a democracy are rarely the first to put the old aside, and rarely are they the first by which the new is tried. This, perhaps, is as it should be, since there are many movements which affect American life for a brief period and are then cast aside because they have not stood the test of time.

**The Teacher's Problem.** Today the classroom teacher faces a difficult problem. He must first of all recognize and then evaluate the forces which are acting upon American education. He must know the media through which these forces act. He must keep in mind the larger objectives of education in a democracy. He must be able both to shape and to direct the attitudes of the child as well as to understand the forces which are acting upon the schools. Because he teaches children in groups, it is most difficult to keep the individual child from being submerged in that group. It is usually the most vocal who tend to work their way to the top and thus receive recognition. If the socialization process, which is at the heart of the American school, is to serve its purpose, every classroom teacher as a function of management must consciously seek to keep the class what it should be, a group working together, not a collection of individuals.

In the classroom of the past, what was called group action was rarely that in fact. Usually the idea originated with the teacher, the activity was dominated by the teacher, and the whole effort attained a result desired by the teacher. As in so many other groups, one person or a few persons in the class did all the work. Such action, although it took place in a group situation, could not be considered group action in the true sense. Real group action, in a classroom or any other group, must represent the combined effort of all group members. It goes without saying that the teacher's responsibility is to guide pupils in the process of attaining genuine group action.

The word "dynamics" connotes in itself forcefulness, energy, stimulation, active influence, and in general a functional relationship toward a problem situation. Frequently, group dynamics concerns itself with changing the operation of social forces. Shall a boy, a member of the class, who has no "better" clothes be allowed or encouraged to attend a class "dress-up" party wearing his blue jeans and a denim shirt? This illustrates the type of problem from which excellent group dynamics effort often originates. The class, under the teacher's guidance, looks at a situation which is not only an interesting one for the class, but one which sincerely concerns it.

Here is a typical group dynamics problem which offered itself to all the pupils in an elementary school: the Board of Education ruled that there would be no Christmas vacation, other than Christmas Day, because of the fact that school had been closed in November for two weeks due to a measles epidemic. Pupils, at first, were indignant. Then their indignation went over into reasonable but forceful group action. Through the proper channels they attacked the problem and offered the Board of Education a solution, one which was acceptable to the Board, to parents, and to the children. The effort could properly be called one in group dynamics.

**Steps in Group Dynamics.** As a group effort with the driving power coming from the children, with the basic purpose having to do with change, the usual steps in the process may include (1) a clear statement of what the problem is, (2) selecting some possible ways or means of solving it, (3) considering the steps to be followed in putting the suggested solution into effect, (4) weighing the scheme suggested for getting the task done, (5) carrying out the plan with everyone working, and (6) weighing the final results to determine where the effort was at its best and where it did little. Quite commonly the effort tends to merge the steps and there is necessity for reconsidering the problem after the data are more complete. That is to say, step 5, carrying out the plan, ties up with step 1, a clear statement of the problem, after the pupils find they did not have all the data at first.

Group dynamics has an important place in the classroom. Definitely it is a technique which belongs in the field of classroom management. When applied to the classroom situation, it can be a conscious effort in which pupils help to improve their own learning goals through change, have a part in developing their learning procedures, and work out within the group the best ways of achieving the results set up as being desirable.

## DISCUSSION PROBLEM

### THE DEVELOPMENT OF INDIVIDUAL RESPONSIBILITY
### AS A FUNCTION OF MANAGEMENT

"It is possible, perhaps probable, that I am wrong," said Miss De Vore of the sixth grade in the Lincoln School to the elementary school supervisor, Mr. Black. "I feel that most teachers fail to make their school management really function because they do not see the routine of running a school as a means to an end, rather than an end in itself."

"I'm not sure that I follow your argument," said Mr. Black.

"Well, this is what I mean," Miss De Vore went on to say. "In my own case, I have a feeling that if the schools are citizenship training centers, my biggest job as a teacher is to make every boy and girl have a feeling of individual responsibility for everything that he does—in fact for everything that his room does."

"Oh, I see what you mean. You really believe that your school management isn't just machinery leading to a mastery of school subjects, but that management, in itself, may be just as much a means of accomplishing an important aim as is a history lesson, for instance."

"That's it exactly," said Miss De Vore.

"And this goal or aim, which in a way you're putting in as an extra school subject, you have named 'Individual Responsibility,' is that it?"

"That's exactly what I'm trying to say," said the teacher. "My management ought to make my history classes better, incidentally, but I believe that the 'Individual Responsibility' aim can be developed and satisfied in no better way than through the school management program—in fact, through the school administration program in general."

"I suppose that I've thought about this before," said Mr. Black, "but I don't know that I've had it put to me in exactly this manner. How do you go about getting this Utopian dream realized?"

"You're making fun of me now, and it isn't a Utopian dream. It's a very real thing. I'll tell you some of the things I am doing —and am not doing." Miss De Vore thought for a second, then asked, "Do you remember one day a week or so ago when you visited my room and found me absent when you came in? The boys and girls told me later that you had been in—and that you stayed for only a few minutes. I've been leaving the room frequently lately, while school is in session, just to make the pupils feel that I trust them."

"They respect your confidence, I'm sure," said the supervisor. "When I came in the other day, everyone seemed to be busy. There was a group in the corner working on that products map (that's what it is, isn't it?); another group had their heads together at that table over there."

"I remember now," said Miss De Vore; "they were our Memorial Day assembly-program committee."

"The others seemed to be working on their assignments," concluded the supervisor. "Oh yes, I forgot to mention, Lucille met me at the door and told me that you would be back in a little while and asked me to take off my topcoat. I believe she offered me a magazine to read first. Then thinking she might be failing as a hostess, she decided to sit down and talk to me."

"That's fine," said Miss De Vore, "she had never been told to do that. Tell me everything else you can think of that happened. You see, it's hard to get evidence of a feeling of responsibility from the pupils when I'm here, because all their lives they've been trained to be dependent upon a teacher all the time they're in school."

"Well, let's see, I can't seem to think of anything important. One of the boys shut off a radiator and opened a window at the back of the room. He closed the window later and opened the radiator because so many pretended to be shivering with the cold. Marie—I think that's her name, the one with very black hair and a boyish haircut—collected some papers and put them on your desk."

"I'm glad you've told me these things," said Miss De Vore. "It's some evidence the plan is working."

"The room wasn't as quiet as when you are here," said Mr. Black, "and there were a few who may have been visiting, but there wasn't any real disorder. I'd say there was a lack of restraint rather than disorder." The supervisor grinned.

"You can make fun of my idea, if you want to," said Miss De Vore laughingly, "but I know one thing for sure, this attempt to develop individual responsibility in each child has made me critical of my aims; it has made me stop 'talking down' to children; and it has done away with nearly all my rules. We still have regulations of course. What's more," and her eyes challenged, "I expect my supervisor to help me in realizing my aims if he agrees they are desirable ones."

"He does think they are desirable ones, and he will help all he can. There's one thing evident: you may not always be taking the most direct route, but it is a good road, and I feel quite sure you know where you are going," said Mr. Black as he nodded good-bye and left the room.

Outside the door Mr. Black nodded his head emphatically, and anyone listening might have heard him say, "Boy, I wish I had more teachers who could see the function of management in the classroom for what it should be, a development of responsible young citizens, instead of thinking of management as an end in itself."

## Questions on the Problem

1. Is Miss De Vore's "individual responsibility" aim a good general aim for education? Can you think of a classroom situation where it would be undesirable?

2. Is Miss De Vore right when she says, "All their lives they've been trained to be dependent upon a teacher?" Is there a fine line where dependence leaves off and independence begins? Can you illustrate?

3. Would you judge that Miss De Vore has progressed to a considerable extent in her goal when she takes it upon herself to leave a sixth-grade room unattended even for a short time? Is this a good practice? Why? Why not?

4. In a college class such as you are in today, to what extent do you feel dependent upon an instructor as long as he is in the room? Who is responsible for a feeling of dependence, the pupils or the instructor? Is it our traditional way of managing schools that is responsible for the lack of independence in our pupils?

5. Can you think of aims other than the one of individual responsibility which are desirable goals of management in the everyday classroom? Suggest some others.

6. Can you show how some routine procedure, such as using a pencil sharpener, might be made a matter of individual responsibility?

7. Criticize this statement: The number of *rules* necessary for ordinary school management tends to be in inverse proportion to the amount of individual responsibility felt by each pupil in the room. (Be sure to distinguish between *rules* and *regulation*.)

## STUDY QUESTIONS

1. Is the word "administration" too broad in its connotation for what happens in a single classroom? Can you make a clear distinction between school administration and school management?

2. "One never knows when education takes place." If the statement is, in general, true, is it not possible that a child is being educated to a considerable extent even though he is failing a subject?

3. Has a student who has had three years of the four-year program of a college course, had three-fourths of a college education? More than three-fourths? Less? Other than the diploma, is there any special advantage in finishing a college course? The recognition is given for graduating, not for going to college. Is this sound thinking?

4. Is there a strong probability that a child with a marked feeling of *group responsibility* will fail in a subject? Would you expect the correlation to be high between a strong feeling of

responsibility and academic excellence? Is academic excellence in any way tied up with taking responsibility other than that for doing good classwork?

5. You as a teacher will try to give pupils as much responsibility as is suitable to their development. Will this mean more work for you, or less work? Why?

6. Why does tradition tend to clutter up our aim to make our school management function in developing good classroom citizenship?

7. Can a man be a perfectly good citizen who cannot and does not take responsibility? Do the two elements, of necessity, have anything in common? Discuss.

8. As a teacher in training, you are probably taking a course in teaching methods. Be specific in saying how a methods course differs from a course in management or administration. What elements are common to both?

9. Try to be specific in suggesting those procedures of your high school courses or of college courses which are suspect as far as giving an educational account of themselves is concerned.

## SELECTED READINGS

CAMPBELL, ROALD F., CORBALLY, JOHN E., JR., and RAMSEYER, JOHN A. *Introduction to Educational Administration*. Boston: Allyn & Bacon, Inc., 1958. Chapter 8 is recommended reading. The teacher's role as an influential part of the administrative machinery is pointed out. Indicates how teachers are both decision-makers and policy-makers.

DRUCKER, PETER F. *The Practice of Management*. New York: Harper & Bros., 1954, Chapter 13. This is a text which deals with management and its functions in all phases of business dealings. The basic principles are the same as for school administration.

HASKEW, LAURENCE D. *This Is Teaching*. Chicago: Scott, Foresman & Co., 1956. Chapter 7, "Ends Sought by Teaching," presents some analyses of the goals of teaching, some criteria for choosing these goals, and a portrayal of the school as a segment of a democratic society.

KYTE, GEORGE C. *The Elementary School Teacher at Work*. New York: Holt, Rinehart & Winston, Inc., 1957. Chapter 2, "The Psychology of the Elementary School Child and His Learning," presents clearly how the child's developmental stage influences the teacher's daily work.

MEHL, MARIE A., MILLS, HUBERT M., and DOUGLASS, HARL R. *Teaching in Elementary School.* Rev. ed. New York: The Ronald Press Co., 1958. Chapter 8, "Classroom Social Behavior," is recommended reading. The personal and social adjustment of pupils and the organizational plans which affect this adjustment are emphasized.

MORSE, WILLLIAM C., and WINGO, G. MAX. *Psychology and Teaching.* Chicago: Scott, Foresman & Co., 1955. Chapters 1 and 2. Chapter 1 deals with the work of the teacher in an easy-to-read style. Chapter 2, "What Goes On in Schools?", presents the more or less routine working of the classroom and indicates how, in practice, responsibility is developed in children.

POWER, EDWARD J. *Education for American Democracy.* New York: McGraw-Hill Book Co., Inc., 1958. Pp. 15–30. A semiphilosophical discussion of the meaning of education with quotations from other writers makes this enlightening reading.

# 3

# THE TEACHER AND THE CHILD

The child and the teacher: these are the two factors which are unchanging and which are intimately personal in classroom administration. All other factors are only partially personal elements or are entirely impersonal. Indirectly the superintendent of schools, the principal, the classroom supervisors, and special-subject teachers have some personal relationships with children, but it is the classroom teacher who really knows children intimately. The process of instruction, which represents the interaction between pupil and teacher, and the classroom environment in general are other factors which function through the personal element but are not in themselves personal. The above is intended to say one thing: classroom teachers and their pupils live in an intensely personal relationship, and in no other phase of the educational process does a comparable relationship exist.

## INTERACTION BETWEEN TEACHER AND CHILD

Schools exist for children. If teachers and other school officials can and will remember that the million-dollar plant back of them would have no reason for being were it not for the child trudging up the walk, their personal attitudes toward their work will change.

**Nature of the Child.** Because the child is the reason for the existence of teachers and schools, it follows that to know the child is the teacher's first task.

As is generally recognized, the child is biologically immature. That he spends a greater part of his normal life in reaching maturity than does any other of the higher organisms is in general a positive factor rather than a negative one. He develops slowly because there is so much to develop.

Maturation in the child is never an all-or-nothing proposition. The organism is not immature and then suddenly mature. Maturation comes slowly. From both the physiological and the psychological viewpoints, the structures of the body do not all mature at the same time. Comparatively rapid and comparatively easily measured physical changes take place during certain phases of the maturation process, but the most significant psychological changes seem to develop more gradually and are less easily recognized. All of these factors tend to make the nature of childhood more difficult to understand.

Only comparatively recently have teachers felt concern for children as children. Immaturity was for centuries considered as a physical difference only. Boys were only small men, in much the same manner as a half-grown chicken is, in the housewife's view, a small chicken. The difference was in size only. Because of this slant, everything a child did or said or thought was forced into an adult mold. The objective was to make adults quickly out of children.

As a child matured, he simply added more adult patterns to his behavior. No one recognized that a child's interests were different, that a child's reactions to a given situation were different, that, in brief, a child was not a little adult but was in fact a different sort of person. As a result of this thinking, education consisted of making a child conform to an adult pattern. Knowledge was always in terms of facts, and knowledge was always the basis of education. Education was thus a "pouring-in" process. Enough facts and a child had knowledge; enough knowledge and he had an education.

With Rousseau, and to a lesser degree with John Locke who preceded him, the new concept of education appeared. Its premise was that a child is not a little adult. Rousseau stressed the idea that a child matured in terms of natural laws. Education thus became development of the child, an unfoldment aided and fostered by the teacher, the home, and all the other forces by which he was surrounded.

In America, the development of the kindergarten, the Pestalozzian use of objects and experiences, and the work of Colonel Francis Parker, G. Stanley Hall, and John Dewey focused attention on the child as an individual. Today, all good teachers recognize that the child is a unique *personality:* that all teaching devotes its efforts to a concern for and an appreciation of his growth and development and that a thorough understanding of how he learns is the beginning of all technique both in instruction and in management. A teacher who works with children efficiently understands the interaction between teacher and child and the effect that this has upon the learning process.

**Development of the Child.** The teacher, in his personal relationships, is concerned with the child's entire development. There is no way of developing him in segments or in parts. If teaching and management were concerned only with the development of a knowledge of facts or the development of specific skills, the task would be comparatively easy. As it is, the teacher is concerned with the child's health, safety, play, relationships with other children, character, and moral and spiritual growth—in fact, with everything in his daily life. The development of a child's potentialities or powers is a function of all schooling, whether formal or informal.

The modern teacher recognizes that classroom techniques must not and cannot attempt to provide experiences which affect only a part of an individual. The child's activities involve him as a total organism. When one says that the whole child goes to school, he is saying that the intellectual child is inseparably a part of the physical child. A given experience causes not only a reaction in the part of the organism where the reaction is desired, but frequently also in portions of the organism which no one suspected could be affected. All recognize that the entire organism is affected under the influence of danger, of great joy, or of any other emotional experience. Not all recognize, though, that more ordinary experiences affect the organism in a manner equally definite although not so noticeable. Even under normal conditions no two children are affected alike by the same experience, and evidence is lacking that the same situation will produce the same response in the same child on two different occasions. This is not to say that some of a teacher's experiences with children will not be more involved from the intellectual viewpoint than from the physical, but that in all experiences of the classroom the entire child is involved.

The viewpoint that all of the child is involved in even the most commonplace school happenings has a great deal to do with the daily school program and with the personal factor in that program. Everything a teacher does or plans to do must be evaluated in terms of its effect on the child.

It would seem that when a teacher is teaching reading or arithmetic he is probably doing something significant in the development of character formation. A teacher may be giving his best effort to developing his "individual responsibility" program, and be doing it well, and at the same time be developing attitudes toward life which are more significant than the thing he is emphasizing. This to some extent goes back to the thought that one does not know when education takes place. The instructional program is inevitably tied up with the emotional child, the spiritual child, the intellectual child, and the physical child. The physical may affect the intellectual, and vice versa. A nearsighted (myopic) child may be rated as intellectually slow when he actually is bright enough but cannot see well, and a hard-of-hearing child may be pigeonholed as indolent and inattentive. No one doubts that the question before every teacher at all times should be, What is this total situation or experience doing to the child?

**Importance of the Personal Element.** The personal element in management comes to fruition when the child is considered as an individual. Children do not differ much in size, in the way they dress, in the way they respond to questioning, in their opinions, in the things they enjoy. But they do differ in the more subtle aspects of their nervous and physical makeups and of their emotional lives.

The teacher who fails to accept the child as an individual loses the chance to make the personal factor function. He typically talks down to the child, a patronizing tactic that arouses most children's resentment. He is likely to insist upon adult standards of excellence—to compare the non-comparable—and to fail to see commendable effort and to give that commendation which is so important to the child. He tends to stifle creativity because it does not fit into everyday procedure. Such attitudes on the part of a teacher are not conducive to success in classroom administration.

## THE CHILD AND THE LEARNING SITUATION

For over a half-century child psychologists have been studying how children learn. From these studies several fundamental principles have been derived. It need hardly be said that these principles are stated in the abstract. The teacher's problem is to take the abstract principles and apply them in a practical way to school management as well as to classroom teaching.

Although there are many ways of stating the principles which have been developed, in general the thought is the same in all cases. The principles, as stated below, are not in order of importance.

The principle of *frequency* says that the more often a child does a thing, if other factors are held constant, the greater is the tendency for the same response (doing the thing) to appear under a comparable situation. This is the basis of all drill work in writing, spelling, music, arithmetic, and typing.

*Recency* is the principle of learning which says that, other factors being constant, the response to a given situation which has been used most recently, and used with satisfaction, is the response which the child is most likely to give. It is, of course, fundamental that the words "used with satisfaction" be stressed. Experiments in learning show that recent exercising of the response with disastrous results does not lead to repeating the act. That is, punishment for a recent act inhibits the repetition of the act. From the two principles above, it is clear that a child must practice frequently if he is to learn; he learns more easily if the practice is recent and if it has given him satisfaction.

The principle of *satisfaction* is thus another basis of learning. In non-technical wording, it says that there is the tendency to stop any pattern of behavior when the object causing the effort is no longer there. Satisfaction of the desire, whatever the desire may have been, causes the learner to cease the effort. To illustrate: Lucille won't continue to study an assignment which she thinks she has mastered. Bob won't bring in the wood each evening to earn a promised bicycle after he has been given a bicycle. This principle operates when a car is purchased with a small down payment and a continued payment each month for many months. After the car is driven home, much of the satisfaction is lessened, and the payments each month no longer add much to the satisfaction.

The principle of *punishment*, when applied to learning, tends to have an opposite effect from the principle of satisfaction. It says that, other factors being held constant, any learning response (whether good or bad) which leads to dissatisfaction tends to be eliminated and to be replaced by one which leads to satisfaction. Learning is slowed down or stopped entirely whenever dissatisfaction rather than satisfaction follows the act. This is the basis and reason for punishment. In general, punishment is an inhibiting factor, rather than a teaching factor. It is negative in its results.

*Immediacy* of punishment or satisfaction has to do with learning also. This principle says that the sooner the reward or punishment follows the act, the greater is the tendency to repeat the act in the one case and to avoid the act in the other. It does little for the learning process to punish a child for an act committed a month ago. Neither will rewarding him a month after the act tend to make him repeat the satisfying effort.

Another principle of learning deals with what is spoken of by the psychologists as *symbolic drive*. It is related to reward and punishment. A drive is an internal condition which directs what a person will do in response to an external situation. It is, for practical purposes, a motive. In symbolic drive, the symbol, through previous association with either punishment or reward, substitutes for the actual stimulus. In other words, when Johnny has been punished for getting into the cooky jar, the word "No" from mother (a symbol) inhibits his action in much the same way as a spanking. However, teachers soon learn that too frequent use of the symbol (which in this case is the spoken word) in place of the action (the punishment) fails to secure the desired response. The teacher who threatens and scolds, who tries to make the symbol for the punishment (the words) take the place of the punishment, soon loses control of the classroom.

Children as well as adults have drives and urges. A small number are physiological in nature, in that they are physical tensions which seek for release in activity. Most psychologists break drives and urges down into two classifications, primary and secondary. A primary drive is a direct urge. It tends to be a fundamental, elemental need. Frequently it is physiological in its antecedents. A secondary drive is an urge or strong motivation which has been acquired through experience and education. It comes only indirectly from the needs of the organism. Most urges or drives in children (as far as schoolwork goes) are secondary. Such drives are not fundamental needs of the organism but come about through experience, either personal or vicarious.

Adults rarely realize how much of daily motivation comes from some sort of symbolism, the most common of which is the written or spoken word. Adults have learned to accept the symbol (the word) for the action. The word "Stop" on the highway is a symbol—and a symbol only, but if always obeyed it has the effect of law enforcement. Contrariwise, adults soon pay little attention to the person who talks all the time, or to the highway driving sign which warns every few rods to go slow when there is no evidence of need for the warning. In each case the symbolism is failing in its purpose: to secure attention and to inspire action.

With children, because of the necessity for the symbolism to control urges or drives, the teacher should never fail to make the symbolism mean what it says. Otherwise, it won't continue to work. Thorndike found experimentally that the two words "right" and "wrong" are strongly motivating in their effect. His studies indicated that a child is motivated far more positively when the teacher can say "right" than when the teacher has to say "wrong."

The principle of *interest* is related to the principles of symbolic drive and satisfaction. Briefly, the principle of interest says that the more natural interest there is in the subject matter to be learned, the easier it is to learn. This principle is almost axiomatic. Tommy, who runs a motorboat on the lake each summer and is vitally interested in motors and boats, is a ready subject for learning any new material dealing with the topic of either boats, motors, motor fuels, or safety regulations in or on the water. He is naturally interested. This principle is recognized by all teachers, whether psychologically trained or not. Of course, all children must learn, and learn well, certain things that may not appeal to them nor immediately interest them. These learnings, however, are usually at the drill level.

Each of the principles named above has to do with the teacher's personal relationships with pupils. Because children differ so much from each other, the same motivation will not work for all equally well. One child learns a certain thing rapidly because of the satisfactions he gets from the learning. Another learns by being inhibited from useless, wasteful, inefficient, and dangerous learning through punishment. This is negative only and does not teach the child to do the good or desirable act. A third child responds beautifully when the symbolic words "right" and "wrong" are used, although there is no tangible reward or satisfaction present. Still another child responds readily to praise (satisfaction), while a companion is inhibited by the least criticism (dissatisfaction).

## MANAGEMENT AND THE LEARNING SITUATION

From the management viewpoint, at least four factors appear which are basic as far as the teacher is concerned. The first deals with *how* children learn. This has been considered very briefly and will be considered more completely later in the text. The other three factors deal with *what* children learn, *when* it should be learned, and *who* can learn it. Since the four factors, when taken *in toto*, are the basis for all teacher education, no more than a superficial statement can be given here.

Good learning in a schoolroom is planned. To a certain extent, the planning procedure is a tactical campaign, with the teacher as the top officer. A good officer gets results from the effort of his men; he never willingly wastes this effort. The teacher's work is comparable. He plans the campaign, and the planning is a personal problem in school management.

The ability to learn is inherent, but this does not mean that every child will learn *what* he should learn or will learn what he should learn *when* he should learn it. This is where the planning part of the campaign comes in. It should be kept in mind that the teacher does not do the learning and that his effort is not a pouring-in process. His work is organizing, planning, preparing, setting the stage, and evaluating. Definitely, it is possible for a pupil to learn to learn. This is saying that pupils can be taught how to study. Study is frequently, but not always, concerned with reading. Reading is, in school, a part of learning.

**Improvement of Reading.** Since this book is not intended to be a text in methodology, but rather one in the broadly administrative phases of classroom procedures, these statements regarding reading, and in some cases the suggestions for improving reading, are intended to be managerial in nature only:

1. Reading is not a luxury; it is a necessity. It is well to remember also that a person can be well educated and be a poor reader. The correlation is sometimes low.
2. Children are poor readers largely because of bad reading habits. These habits are acquired early in a child's reading life.
3. Reading speed is improvable. For a child of normal intelligence, there is practically a mechanics of improving reading speed.
4. As a teacher your big problem is to prevent children from struggling with words rather than with ideas. Reading is no more than getting the thought or idea from a written or printed page.
5. As was stated above, a good reader's eyes pause to gather only groups of words which embody ideas; the oculophotometer (ophthalmograph), mentioned earlier, bears this out. He does not read single words.
6. The ability to scan rapidly and to get the thought without reading in detail is becoming more and more a demand made upon all business and professional men and women. Children should be taught to scan.
7. Studies show that many top executives read only 160 words a minute. This is reading at a walk. These are probably word-by-word readers.
8. Children should be taught to avoid rereading when they are reading for content. Rereading should be only to pick up a needed detail, or when the beauty of the expression can be enjoyed thoroughly only by rereading.
9. Reading authorities suggest encouraging pupils to read consciously for speed. They should be taught constantly to pick out the main idea in the thing read. It is not a bad practice to have children read against a clock or even a stop watch.
10. A good practice is to estimate the number of words in an article and then encourage pupils to read it within a specified number of minutes. Their comprehension may be spot-checked with a little test.

11. Children should be encouraged to know the difference between light (say, fiction) reading, and reading where the content is more difficult. No one would encourage a child to read the directions for getting to his new school for the first time at the same speed he would use in reading *Tom Sawyer*.

12. Mechanically, all of these practices are undesirable:
    a. Reading one word at a time, making sure one understands it before going on. The child should be taught to read phrases; thoughts are rarely expressed in a word.
    b. Rereading. Going back to reread words or phrases which one thinks he may have missed.
    c. Reading everything at the same speed, regardless of the difficulty of the reading material. Readers who do this are sometimes called "one-gear" readers.
    d. Following the line with a finger or a pencil while reading.
    e. Stopping to look up in a dictionary every word about which there is doubt. The child should be taught to go on; the context usually will clarify the meaning, and the word can be looked up later, if necessary.
    f. Swinging the head back and forth to follow the movement of the eyes across the page. Some specialists encourage the child to look at a line of type and try to see how much of it he can encompass without allowing the eyes to move. This tends to increase peripheral vision.
    g. Daydreaming. The child should be encouraged to get into his reading fast and to engross himself as much as possible. Dawdling and dallying are bad habits which do not lend themselves readily to reading competence.

Although there is something of methodology in the suggestions above, the teacher who has been in the classroom any length of time will realize that the process of improving reading is more one of management than of methodology. At best, the two complement each other perfectly.

Another type of reading which the classroom teacher cannot neglect is the reading of maps, charts, graphs, and profiles used to express thought in a form that is readily accessible from the visual standpoint. This, too, is reading, but it differs from word reading in form and in what it is intended to convey to the reader. Much of this type of reading follows patterns of understanding which embody both a methodology of teaching and a management of the learning process. To sum up in a sentence or two: Teaching a beginner to read is basically a problem in methodology; getting him to read with avidity, to read much, and to read skillfully is partially, at least, a problem in school management. The child's personal relationships are decidedly involved. His reading habits are not coldly impersonal or personal to him only; he is much influenced by what his group is reading, by the children's librarian, and by his teacher.

**Obstacles to Good Reading.** Reading ability is not inherent. Frequently it can be improved when it is inferior. The improvement is largely the result of a managerial operation. There may be methodology in the improvement also, but to a great extent the improvement is mechanical. There are two factors which are of prime importance in the improvement. The first is the child's desire to improve. The second is the elimination of inefficient reading equipment and of inefficient reading habits. Some of the principal obstacles to good reading are discussed below.

*Faulty Vision.* All authorities agree that good eyesight is an essential to reading efficiency. Not all children have good vision. Teachers should learn early to look for indications of vision deficiency, such as headaches, redness of the eyes, squinting, and excessive fatigue. The important thing is not to neglect the slightest indication of defectiveness in a child's vision.

*Schoolroom Lighting.* Light in the modern schoolroom is to a great extent under the teacher's control. It is thus a managerial problem. There have been many good studies of the effects of the various types of illumination upon eye fatigue. All point to the desirability of indirect lighting as opposed to direct or semidirect. The intensity of the light is not so important as is its uniformity. A schoolroom is better lighted for reading purposes with uniform underillumination than it is with brighter illumination but with shadows. Green and blue lights have been found to be bad; natural daylight, when uniform in intensity, is best.

*Inefficient Eye Movements.* Many studies prove beyond doubt that some persons are poor readers because of one thing only: their eye movements are inefficient. It is about as easy to develop bad habits in eye movements as it is to develop bad habits in any other motor skill. Playing the piano, tennis, golf, or baseball—all are to some extent motor skills. All are based on habits. When the performer develops bad habits, he develops efficiency slowly or not at all. To some extent, the same is true of reading. Reading is, in part, a motor skill. A good reader has good eye movements, and no person with bad eye movements is ever a good reader.

A machine, the ophthalmograph, has been devised which records clearly the movements of the eye in reading. The eye, in reading, moves in jumps; it does not glide. The jumps are rapid, taking usually a fiftieth to a twenty-fifth of a second. Good readers spend about 90 per cent of their time in fixations, where the comprehension takes place, and 10 per cent in jumping. Poor readers make short jumps, sometimes taking in but one word at a jump, and when they make longer jumps, frequently do not get all the words and have to go back and reread. Poor readers also overrun the lines at both ends and thus waste effort.

A teacher will probably make four jumps to an average line such as in this book; his pupils will probably use from four to seven. Again, the good reader does not pause for a long period at the fixations. Experiments show that the number of stops per line can be decreased by practice and that the length of time at the stops can be lessened. The good reader is like an express train: he makes few stops and goes at a high rate of speed. The poor reader finally gets there also, but he stops at every station. Techniques of improving reading are definitely worthy of study and are included in specialized methods courses in teacher education.

*Vocalization.* Frequently poor readers form each word with their lips as they read it. This is called vocalization. Vocalization lowers the reading rate, as the movement of the lips tends to be a brake upon the reading speed. One cannot read faster than he can say the words. As comprehension tends to be greater with rapid readers than with slow, vocalization tends to have a negative effect upon comprehension also. Poor readers do not always vocalize, but when a teacher notices vocalization in a poor reader while he is reading silently, he has a clue which may lead to improvement in the child's reading. This work on the teacher's part will not teach the child to read better, but it may remove something which is impeding his progress.

## SOCIAL DYNAMICS IN THE CLASSROOM

This is a text in classroom administration techniques. The word "technique" applies particularly to an art. It does not apply as directly to a science. Teaching is both an art and a science, but is commonly more the former than the latter. An art is controlled by the factors of creativeness, of ingenuity, of judgment, and of skill. All are marks of good teaching. A science is usually considered to be an organized body of principles supported by factual evidence, and is marked by the methods used in the search for and organization of those facts and principles.

The title of this section carries with it, if correctly used, the implication of creativeness, ingenuity, judgment, and skill. The word "dynamics," however, is rather specifically a word from science, denoting power, force, energy (leashed or unleashed) and, in general, activity as opposed to inertia. The teacher deals with energy of a special type, the dynamic energy of the child. Guiding, controlling, maneuvering, and channeling this energy into useful activities definitely requires creativeness, ingenuity, and skillfulness on the teacher's part.

The foregoing paragraph deals with dynamics as a source of energy. For the purposes of this text the term used could well be "social dynamics." The word "social" naturally refers to society or a form of society—that is, a social organism. The word "dynamics," which is today a keyword in all forms of business management, *indicates the influence one person exerts upon another or the influences of the group upon an individual in that group.* This is the lifeblood of all group activity, and a classroom is nothing if not a group. Two illustrations follow which show the impact of social dynamics in the classroom. The second demonstrates how mishandling of a situation by a teacher may decrease the dynamic urge in pupils.

Porter was in the sixth grade of the training school at the State Teachers College at Emporia, Kansas. His uncle gave him two arrowheads which the uncle had found in digging a cistern on his farm just outside the city limits. Porter brought the arrowheads to school. All of the pupils were interested. Other pupils brought Indian artifacts from their homes. They asked Miss Bonn, their teacher, if she could get them a case for their trophies. With a little, but not much, prompting from Miss Bonn, the class launched itself on a campaign of collecting and borrowing Indian relics for a room exhibit. Basketry, pottery, silver jewelry, arrowheads, spear points, blankets, a war bonnet (probably factory made), soapstone pipes, and a much-prized Indian-made bow nearly a hundred years old formed a most interesting, although small, school exhibit. The story was written up by the local newspaper; pictures were made of the collection; and Sunday supplements carrying the story were eagerly sought by the students.

Here was the social activity of a group involved in a project, in this case pupil-initiated, in which every child in the group influenced the actions of every other child in the group. This was group dynamics, always an interaction, at work.

Porter's uncle found part of a human skeleton near where he had found the arrowheads. Barbara Jean's father told her he had heard his father say that the Kaw Indians once had a permanent camp and burying ground on the spot now occupied as a farm by Porter's uncle. The children checked the story and found it to be true. Bryan, reading about the Kaw tribe, learned their subsequent history, which he reported to the class. Burton found an article which pointed out that former Vice-President Charles Curtis had been made a chief of this tribe, that he was part Kaw Indian and had always been very proud of the fact. Eloise read a newspaper account of a celebration at Haskell Institute, the government's largest Indian school, (located at Lawrence some eighty miles away) marking an anniversary of that institution. Nona had attended the celebration pageant and told the class of the various war dances and other dances performed by the Indian students, descendants of American Indians from tribes all over the United States. Knowledge became vital, thrilling, actual.

This teacher used the social dynamics approach to teaching history. The energy was there; her job was to direct that energy into channels which were desirable for children rather than detrimental to their growth.

In the seventh-grade class in United States history the pupils were studying about the interesting expedition of the Spanish explorer Coronado into the interior of the North American continent. Each member of the class had a part in the development of the historical drama. Preston had found an article in the Sunday supplement of his father's paper dealing with Coronado's quest for the fabled Seven Cities of Cibola. Not only had he read the article but he had cut the page from the paper, pasted the page to a large piece of cardboard that the pictures might be more readily seen, and brought the paper to school. Several brief reports had been given before Preston's turn came. The lad had just gotten a good start sketching material available in the text and reference books with a view to leaving the specially prepared material to the last, when his teacher interrupted him by saying, "There was an interesting article on this in Sunday's paper." "I've got it here," said Preston. "That's fine," said Miss Ward, the teacher. Without thinking what she was doing to Preston—and to the class as a whole—the teacher took the card Preston had prepared and without expressing any appreciation of the lad's industry and initiative proceeded to explain the material to the class, using Preston's card as she talked. Preston waited a minute, then sat down, his report uncompleted—by him. One thing he knew for sure: he wouldn't prepare another report.

Without doubt Miss Ward's action produced a certain degree of resentment in the class as well as in Preston, who was particularly hurt. It need not be pointed out that other members of the class would hesitate to make any unrequired contribution to the class development from then on. No pupil would be inclined to produce anything for class purposes that was not specifically assigned. Miss Ward had thwarted the dynamic urge which is present in all children, smothered it emphatically in Preston, decreased it in all other class members. It is as easy to reduce the social dynamics force in a group as it is to encourage it.

## DISCUSSION PROBLEM

### "Hold Him Another Year"

John was inattentive. He simply would not listen in class. This was clear to everyone when Miss Merkle, his teacher, would ask him what the lesson assignment for the next day was, immediately after she had made it, and John wouldn't know. When he sat at the front of the room he gave better attention; at least, he frequently answered questions correctly. John did average work in arithmetic when he worked at his seat, but he didn't seem to give Miss Merkle the least attention when she explained a problem at the blackboard for the class. Occasionally, just to catch him, Miss Merkle would ask him to repeat something she had just said, or to explain some simple step in a solution which she had just made clear to the rest of the class. Since John wasn't paying attention, he never knew. His inattentiveness seemed to increase when Miss Merkle talked with her back to the class, as she was compelled to do when working at the blackboard, explaining her work as she went along. Naturally, John was punished frequently for causing mischief, which he probably wouldn't have done had he been paying attention to the classwork.

There couldn't be much doubt but that John was inattentive —and perhaps lazy. He often proved he could do good work in arithmetic when he wanted to, by bringing to the class period some of the most difficult problems which he had worked out correctly, by himself, at his seat.

Miss Merkle couldn't understand John. At times he was so "dumb" and at times he did such fine work, especially when he worked by himself. She told the principal about him. Together, they looked up John's score on his entrance intelligence examinations.

"One hundred ten," said Miss Merkle. "I can't believe it!"

"Normal," said the principal, "in fact, a high normal. Hold him another year if he doesn't get down to business. That'll likely wake him up so that he pays attention."

Miss Merkle hated to have John disturbing her room another year, but since she couldn't think of anything else to do, she decided to follow the principal's advice.

### QUESTIONS ON THE PROBLEM

1. Sum up all the arguments in the problem which would seem to indicate that John was inattentive.
2. What factors can you suggest as tending to make John inattentive that might be entirely beyond his control?
3. Sum up all the factors stated in the problem which might indicate that the diagnosis "inattentive" was a poor one.
4. Set down in numerical order (1, 2, 3, 4) the steps you would follow were you the principal in John's school. A decision has to be made; list the steps in making the decision.
5. What does the principal mean when he says, "Hold him another year if he doesn't get down to business?" Does he have evidence that John is not trying?
6. Suggest as many ways as you can in which poor eyesight in a child might manifest itself.
7. What are the most common indications of a hearing deficiency in a child? Does John show any of these?
8. Does an individual (even an adult) know when his vision is impaired? Do you know definitely (if you have never worn glasses) that you do not need glasses?
9. Read the problem again. Are there any clues that John's vision is poor? Are there clues that his hearing is deficient? Pick these out.
10. See if you can list ten management problems which might have their genesis in the physical well-being of the children in the room. To illustrate: (1) A child is always tired and listless, as a result of which he rarely has his assignments well-prepared. (2) A child is inattentive and is thus hindering the accomplishment of the group. It is noticeable that he has a bad head cold.

## STUDY QUESTIONS

1. This chapter deals with the personal element in classroom management. What are some of the impersonal elements?
2. In a short paragraph write your answer to this question: What is the general objective of all management?

3. From the standpoint of the personal factor, list the advantages of a small class over a large class. Now turn the question around: From the standpoint of the personal factors involved, what are the advantages to the child of a large class over a small one?

4. Evaluate this statement: "Everything you do . . . must be evaluated in terms of what it may do to the child, perhaps in a way you never thought of." Try to think of a situation in your life where one statement from some adult influenced your actions in later life. To illustrate: Mr. Behmer said before his senior class one day when he was somewhat irritated: "This teaching business is for the birds! I'd never recommend it to a son of mine."

5. Do you agree that no one learns without motivation? Would you be inclined to agree with the theory that learning is practically in direct proportion to the extent or depth of the motivation? Discuss.

6. Many of our foremost citizens are (by ordinary standards) unsocial. They dislike crowds, talk little, and rarely speak to acquaintances on the street. Do you believe this personality characteristic has anything (little or much) to do with their usefulness as citizens?

## SELECTED READINGS

ALCORN, MARVIN D., HOUSEMAN, RICHARD A., and SCHUNERT, JIM R. *Better Teaching in Secondary Schools*. New York: Holt, Rinehart & Winston, Inc., 1954. Chapter 13. Makes good suggestions for developing skill in directing the learning of your class.

BUTLER, FRANK A. *Improvement of Teaching in Secondary Schools*. Chicago: University of Chicago Press, 1954. Chapter 13, "Teaching Should Provide for Individual Differences," applies significantly and directly to the teacher as the dominant personal factor in the learning situation.

JENKINS, GLADYS G., SCHACTER, HELEN, and BAUER, WM. W. *These Are Your Children*. Chicago: Scott, Foresman & Co., 1953. Chapter 13. This entire book deals with the personal element in teaching in a delightfully refreshing manner.

LINDGREN, HENRY CLAY. *Educational Psychology in the Classroom*. New York: John Wiley & Sons, Inc., 1956. Chapter 10 and pp. 451–55. The general theme of the chapter "Child-Centered Approaches to the Learning Situation," is directly applicable to the personal element in the learning situation as discussed in this chapter of your text.

McDANIEL, HENRY B., with G. A. SHAFTEL. *Guidance in the Modern School.* New York: Holt, Rinehart & Winston, Inc., 1956. Pp. 94–103. All of the book, but in particular the pages to which reference is made, deals with guidance in our schools as a personal rather than as an impersonal function of teaching.

MORSE, WILLIAM C., and WINGO, G. MAX. *Psychology and Teaching.* Chicago: Scott, Foresman & Co., 1955. Chapter 6. The psychology of the elementary school child is presented to the reader in a clear and informative manner.

PATTY, WILLIAM L., and JOHNSON, LOUISE S. *Personality and Adjustment.* New York: McGraw-Hill Book Co., Inc., 1953. The process of learning is the basis for the discussion in a large section of this textbook.

# 4

# RELATIONSHIPS IN CLASSROOM MANAGEMENT

If the teacher is to see his classroom organization clearly, he must be aware of its relationship to the entire process of teaching. The problem is never the elimination of organization but the development of that form which best fits the conditions under which the tactical commander must operate. If the classroom is a tent, a Quonset hut, a church basement, or a small rural school, the teacher faces an organizational problem entirely different from the one he would have in an ordinary public-school classroom.

## ORGANIZATION OF THE CLASSROOM

Each classroom presents an organization problem. The organizational plan of each teacher's room is only a part of a larger plan which, in turn, governs the entire school situation. The room organization is a small cogwheel always geared to a larger: the organization in the other rooms and in the entire school unit.

To illustrate with a problem: A teacher is assigned a classroom 24 x 40 feet. How would the organization differ were the room a square, 40 x 40? The school's organization is such that all the reference books must come from the general library. How would the room's administration differ if all references the teacher needed were in his own classroom?

The assigned room is on the north side of the building. There is no direct sunlight; the heating of the room under severe winter weather is ineffective. How would these conditions affect organization? If the assigned room were on the south side of the building, how would the room organization differ?

What would be the difference in room organization in a school building located on a much-used thoroughfare from that in one located in a park? What changes would be necessary if the assigned room were a part of a large school with twenty-four rooms and 750 pupils, rather than a part of a small school of five rooms and 150 pupils? It is evident that both administration and organization are based on the situation as it exists and are modified in such a manner as to realize the objectives of the school.

The entire school organization can never be separated from the whole environmental picture. If pupils must cross busy intersections in going to and coming from their homes, the problem is commonly an all-school problem. If the teacher's pupils come by bus or other school-furnished transportation, this aspect of room organization becomes a part of the all-school organization. The factor of timing is always vital in over-all administrative plans. If pupils are to cross busy intersections, the teacher's plan must coincide with the institutional plan to the extent that pupils are to be at the intersection at the time specified, in order to have patrol protection. Buses may not wait for pupils if the organizational plan causes too-close connections.

Material and mechanical aspects of the classroom play a significant part in management. Good lighting reduces eyestrain; reduced eyestrain means less fatigue. Less fatigue goes over into improved attentiveness to routine school work. Comfortable seating means less twisting and turning, less fatigue, fewer disciplinary problems, and greater school satisfaction for the pupil. Good floors mean less noise, freedom from dust, easy housekeeping, and personal satisfaction for teacher and pupils. Chalkboards at the correct height for the users reduce the organizational problem and make for reduction of school machinery. Cheerful pleasant surround-ings make for happy, cheerful children. The room's environ-mental factors, that is, its cleanliness and its furnishings (flowers, draperies, pictures) are to a great extent under the teacher's control. If the lighting is adequate, no room need ever be drab if the teacher wishes to make it otherwise. He can see that it is clean; he can see that it has bright pictures; he can secure bright, inexpensive curtains, even if the build-ing itself is old, weatherbeaten, and dilapidated. Cheerful-ness, brightness, comfort, and happiness in a classroom are, to a very great extent, a reflection of a cheerful, bright, happy teacher.

## CLASSROOM ACTIVITIES IN MANAGEMENT

Three factors are outstanding in the man-sized job of making desirable changes in the boys and girls who come into the classrooms. The child himself is first; the teacher is second; and the process, getting the task done, is third. The last-named factor breaks up into activities of two different yet interwoven types. Both are a part of the teaching act from the broader viewpoint, yet both are distinctly mana-gerial in form. Both are a part of education as much as a well-developed textbook assignment is a part of the educa-tive process. The first group of activities concerns itself pri-marily with activities of the teacher. The second group con-cerns itself primarily with pupils' activities.

**Activities of the Teacher.** Without much doubt, the Commonwealth Teacher-Training Study is one of the most significant researches ever conducted dealing with the ac-tivities of the classroom teacher. The list below, consolidated from the Commonwealth Study, gives the twenty activities in school and classroom management that have the highest ranking on the bases of importance, difficulty of learning, and desirability of teaching. The list of twenty items is made up from lists totaling 196 activities ranked as being worthy of consideration by teachers in the intermediate grades, elementary school principals, and college teachers of education.

1. Adapting teacher's procedures to physical conditions of classroom and equipment
2. Adapting teacher's procedures to individual differences
3. Conducting study exercises
4. Developing personal traits and habits
5. Developing pupils' initiative in useful ways
6. Developing pupils' interest and attention in correcting physical defects
7. Determining traits to be taught
8. Determining activities to be performed
9. Enforcing instructions to pupils in the formation of proper health habits
10. Enforcing instructions to pupils in the development of personal traits and habits
11. Enforcing instructions to pupils to safeguard against contagious diseases
12. Enforcing instructions to pupils in correcting physical defects
13. Exhibiting effective teaching traits
14. Giving instruction to pupils in the development of personal traits and habits
15. Giving instructions to pupils to safeguard against contagious diseases
16. Giving instructions to pupils in correcting physical defects
17. Giving instruction to pupils in the formation of proper health habits
18. Inspecting and evaluating pupils' behavior in developing personal traits and habits
19. Investigating difficulties
20. Providing worthwhile occupations[1]

The key words introducing the various activities are very important. Each deals with the administration and management of a single classroom. There is in this list but one activity dealing indirectly with the teaching process itself: "*Exhibiting* effective teaching traits." The other activities

[1] Adapted from W. W. Charters and Douglass Waples, *The Commonwealth Teacher-Training Study* (Chicago: University of Chicago Press, 1929).

are management activities. Thus the teacher, in the course of his daily classroom management duties, adapts, conducts, determines, develops, enforces, exhibits, gives, investigates, inspects, and provides.

One of the very real problems faced by every instructor in teacher education is that of making general, theoretical statements significant to the learner. Such general descriptions of teachers' activities as those listed on page 69 must be supported by concrete illustrations drawn from actual classroom procedure. For example, it is not enough to say that the teacher must adapt teaching procedures to individual differences; it must be demonstrated how this may be done with a specific procedure in the case of a particular child.

**Activities of the Pupils.** Pupils themselves never describe their activities in the abstract or in generalities; they are always concrete and specific. However, for the purpose of study, pupil activities can be described in general terms and placed in certain general categories. To illustrate: The activities of pupils are listed under four headings by the Educational Policies Commission booklet: self-realization, human relationships, economic efficiency, and civic responsibility. The first, self-realization, is expressed in general terms, such as health knowledge, reading, health habits, and interest in recreation. Human relationships deal with the child's concern for the rights of others, with developing friendships, with working with others, and so on. Economic efficiency is interpreted in terms of understanding the significance of work, of making a living, of knowing the value of money, and of knowing a "good buy" when one sees it. Civic responsibility expresses itself in seeing inequalities in human existence, in social understandings, and in items of a like nature. Each of these items is general in nature and thus to a certain extent is an abstraction.

What follows deals with the idea of analyzing some of the more common abstractions into terms of their specific application. This suggests to the teacher that all abstract statements must have meaning in relation to classroom procedures if they are worthy of study. It is easy to say that the teacher must help the child achieve self-realization, and that this means, in part, that she must teach the child to be courteous. That is still rather vague. Courtesy is a general term, and habits of courtesy are specific.

Again, to say that the teacher should concern himself with the child's *health habits* and that the child must concern himself with *civic responsibility* leaves the meaning of both terms in doubt. However, to say that the teacher should instruct the child to avoid anyone who has whooping cough or measles, and that the child must learn to obey the quarantine laws if he should contract either of these diseases, is to give a concrete illustration of what health habits and civic responsibility really mean.

The chart offered here suggests how generalities may be made significant to the child in terms of the learning situation. An analysis of the tabulation indicates the extreme breadth of the learning area in any ordinary classroom situation, even with subject matter omitted. A desirable activity as suggested from the first column may be expressed in any one of the four general fields as suggested by the Educational Policies Commission (second column) and may go over into a dozen specific activities which a child performs in reaching the desired objective (third column).

## AIMS OF EDUCATION AND CLASSROOM GOALS

Obviously, the teacher, the environment, and everything that happens in the classroom all lend themselves directly to the broader aims of education. The objectives of teaching, which are almost synonymous with those of learning, must concern themselves with making desirable changes in individuals. From a purely functional viewpoint, the objectives of a single classroom differ little from the general objectives of education as set down by the Educational Policies Commission: self-realization, human relationships, economic efficiency, and civic responsibility.

| Desirable Activity (Generality) | Educational Objective | Pupil's Activity (Specific) |
|---|---|---|
| 1. Complying with social conventions | Human relationships<br>Self-realization | Meeting callers politely |
| 2. Acting courteously toward others | Human relationships | Taking turns at the fountain |
| 3. Observing school regulations | Civic responsibility<br>Human relationships | Bringing a statement from home when returning after an illness |
| 4. Developing personal traits and habits | Self-realization | Listening attentively in class |
| 5. Meeting personal obligations | Civic responsibility<br>Economic efficiency | Paying one's share in class purchases |
| 6. Respecting desires and welfare of others | Human relationships | Sharing playground equipment |
| 7. Making field trips | Economic efficiency<br>Human relationships<br>Civic responsibility<br>Self-realization | Going with class for a week end at the state capital |
| 8. Conforming to school customs and traditions | Self-realization<br>Human relationships<br>Civic responsibility | Acquiring knowledge of and conforming to school customs and regulations |
| 9. Selecting and caring for personal property | Economic efficiency | Keeping clothes clean and protected from unnecessary wear |
| 10. Attending to routine activities | Self-realization<br>Civic responsibility<br>Economic efficiency | Taking part in school programs<br>Turning in written work on time<br>Buying athletic tickets |

72

| | | |
|---|---|---|
| 11. Engaging in school out-of-class activities | Self-realization<br>Civic responsibility | Participation in special day programs |
| 12. Conference with teachers | Self-realization | Help in diagnosing difficulty |
| 13. Utilizing school services | Economic efficiency | Selecting the best meal for the money at the cafeteria |
| 14. Observing regulations | Civic responsibility | Orderliness in the hallways, toilet rooms, and study hall |
| 15. Social equality | Civic responsibility<br>Self-realization<br>Human relationships | Selecting a member of the opposite sex as a working partner |
| 16. Doing class work | Self-realization | Writing a composition |
| 17. Orderly conduct | Civic responsibility<br>Self-realization<br>Human relationships | Not pushing when in line<br>Safeguarding against contagion<br>Covering the cough or sneeze |
| 18. Home duties | Economic efficiency<br>Self-realization<br>Human relationships | Delivering papers for pay<br>Promptness in obedience to parents<br>Mowing the lawn |
| 19. Care of school property | Economic efficiency<br>Civic responsibility<br>Human relationships | Closing a window when it is raining |
| 20. Responsibility for one's own acts | Self-realization<br>Economic efficiency<br>Human relationships<br>Civic responsibility | Returning borrowed property in as good condition as when received |

To show the relationship between the objectives as set down by the Educational Policies Commission and the classroom as a functioning entity, the key words from formulations by the Commission are discussed here. When taken in the larger sense, they tie up closely with the managerial activities just presented.

**Self-realization.** The objective of self-realization includes and implies an inquiring mind, the development of speech, reading, writing, and appreciation for numbers. It means health knowledge, skill in listening and observing, good health habits, and an appreciation for and knowledge of public health measures and recreation. It implies intellectual interests, aesthetic interests, and character formation. The latter would include moral, spiritual, and ethical development.

One of the pressures which is invariably put on the classroom teacher is to "mold" the child in terms of his future. The teacher is encouraged to think of the child's future economic efficiency, his future citizenship role, his future as a citizen. There is real danger that in seeking to satisfy this preparatory function of education, the teacher may lose sight of the real purpose of education. He may become so preoccupied with "preparedness" that the object of education, the child himself, is in danger of not being educated, but of being only trained. There would seem to be a fine but distinctive line between training for a job and education in the finest sense of the word.

Every teacher must remember that a child is first and last a growing individual. To think of the child as anything else is to think of him as a bit of formative clay which can be molded to serve the state and a state-controlled society. A child is entitled to his child-life. If self-realization is to reach its finest fruition it must do so in terms of the child's social growth, his physical growth, his moral growth, and his spiritual growth. Each child as he matures tends to write his own declaration of independence, an independence which should be largely intellectual and which should be unfettered by planning for a future which is to a great extent materialistic and has little to do with child-life. This is not to say that there is no place in school for planning for the future; it is saying that the goal of self-realization is not to be confused with that of economic efficiency, which has as its main purpose planning for the future.

**Human Relationships.** Boys and girls are social beings; they like to be together. Satisfactions are greater when shared with others. This is a normal human trait. Almost without exception, an individual can hardly wait to tell others of his good fortune—or of the troubles he is having. This tendency is one of which teachers should take full advantage.

When children are brought together in a class they are at first only an aggregate of young people. Superficially they are a group; in activity, however, they are individuals and may be—partially, at least—unaware of each other.

It is only when the individuals become a group in fact—a team, as it were—that anything which requires for success a group action, a common purpose, can be achieved. Obviously it is not necessary that the class group have only one goal, for besides the major group goal each child may have one or more individual goals. The team, a dynamic group, may have as its goal winning the game. An individual boy may have this goal in common with eight others, but have in addition his individual goal of being an effective shortstop on that team.

The methods of a group at work in concerted action—and a classroom is a group at work in concerted action—are almost always distinctive. The members of the group (1) know what their goal is; (2) share common beliefs about the desirability of attaining this goal or these goals; (3) work out among themselves acceptable patterns of behavior in reaching the goal; (4) set up rules (frequently unnecessary) for individual conduct within the group; and (5) plan (with the teacher) a course of action which offers promise of reaching the goal or goals or of solving the problem.

The very essence of any dynamic effort in problems involving human relationships seems to be the unity-of-thinking factor. This is at the heart of all team spirit. It would be delightful if one could say that this team spirit abounds in the classroom. Such is rarely the case. Classroom groups are rarely teams; the individual goal of each child tends to be *his* goal and not the goal for the group. If the group goal is to be desired—and attained—the teacher has to be the catalyst which brings this about. Children, by themselves, will not develop a group goal nor, under ordinary classroom conditions, a group spirit, possibly because the classroom is to a great extent an artificial situation. The children have been put together; they did not bring themselves together into a group. Boys building a raft for fishing purposes will develop a group goal as will boys building a tree-house. They unite themselves into a group. Little girls will develop the group (dynamic) attitude in playing "house," or later, in setting up a girl-scout campsite. However, a class in American history needs strong leadership if it is to develop as a group rather than as individuals.

*Group Behavior.* The study of group behavior, and of problems related to group behavior, has become a special area of psychological and sociological interest. Many studies are recorded in the field of group dynamics in the large area of industrial relations and of industrial production. In all of these studies there seems to be a common ground for action, a ground fertile and ready for the educator to till: this common ground lies in the need that *the leader create work for the group to do.* A study of activities of Army Air Force crews in World War II brings out emphatically that although the crews were thrown together by chance, they rapidly became united to each other by the strongest bonds. The men tended to identify themselves with their plane, and the terms, "my pilot," "my navigator," "my tail-gunner," were the rule rather than the exception. This, it need not be said, manifested clearly the unity-of-thought principle, and a definite job to be done, which could be done by a group only.

Groups are at their best when they have a purpose which can be satisfied best by collective action.

From what has been said above regarding the need for unity of thinking and for the leader to create work for the group to do if there is to be coordinated group action, it follows that the teacher must actually organize the working groups in the classroom. Schoolwork that can be organized readily for group effort is the first essential. Bringing the team together is the next task. Factors the teacher should consider are: the best size group for easy, effective working conditions; the best promptings for individual gains for each student; groupings which will bring reticent children into groups where they will be forced to participate; and adequate leadership for the groups.

*Group Leadership.* To discover the group's potential leaders, a beginning should be made by working up a sociogram, a device for revealing the preferences, likes, and dislikes obtaining among members of the group. Commonly this will determine also with some accuracy where the leadership in the group lies, if the questions used are so worded as to gain this information. The sociogram indicates where the cliques are; which children are more or less rejected by the group socially; which children are thought of by the group as being the leaders; and which children tend to become "mutual pairs" (pair off).

The mechanics of making a sociogram are comparatively simple. To make one for friendships (likes and dislikes) each pupil is asked to write, at the top of a sheet of paper, his own name, and below this the names of his three best friends in the class. An order of preference is not asked for. From this information, the teacher makes a chart on which he lists every pupil and by arrows shows each pupil's choices of friends. The first result is a jumble, especially if the class is large. The names are then rearranged so as to put mutual preferences together and to shorten arrow lines as much as possible. This arrangement gives a definite choice pattern, as is shown in the diagram below.

The pattern often produces surprises for the teacher. A group of 30 pupils means 435 possible pairs. Obviously no teacher can see the detailed social organization in a class of 30 as it actually exists. He has been able to spot certain cliques and he knows to a certain extent which children are chums and pals; he rarely knows which children are on the outside as far as all the others are concerned.

To save space and to avoid a complicated diagram, the sociogram on page 79 shows only ten seventh-grade boys. The question was, "List your three closest friends." The ten boys were selected from a group which commonly played together.

In the sociogram shown, Norman is selected as one of the "three best friends" by six of the nine boys; Irving, Tony, and Art are selected by four boys as "best friends"; Tom and Jack come close to being a "mutual pair" as Tom (only) named Jack in his first three, although Kevin and Tony also named Tom. Norman did not name Art, Jack, and Kevin, who named him in the first three. Steve was not chosen as one of "the three best friends" by any boy in the group. Steve will need special attention, as he is probably on his way to being, if he is not now, an unhappy boy.

A more definitive picture, but one not so informative on preferences, can be secured through a sociogram by asking a question such as: "Whom would you most like to work with from our class on any problem? It may be a school problem but might be any other sort of problem." In this the child is told to choose only one person. This choice will usually indicate, in a class of thirty, from one to three pupils whom the others think are the best leaders. In a class or group of ten, usually but one leader evolves, if it is made clear that the pupil is to pick not necessarily his best friend but the person he would rather work with on a difficult problem. It should be observed that the teacher is asking for two quite different things when he asks for the pupil's "three best friends" and when he asks for the "best person to work with on a problem."

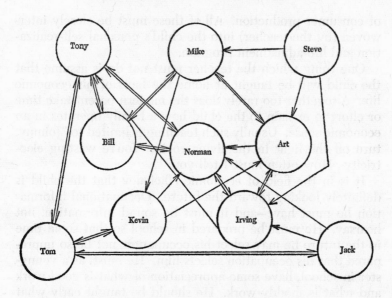

Obtaining judgment by peers through use of
the sociogram. In this group pupils were asked
to list "three best friends" in the group.

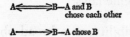

A⟺B—A and B
        chose each other

A——→B—A chose B

**Economic Efficiency.** In his effort to develop in his pupils
some understanding of the goal of economic efficiency, the
teacher, both directly and indirectly, seeks to develop appreciation for, and an understanding of, everyday functional
topics such as these: (1) the nature of work; (2) the occupations most commonly utilized by man in making a living; (3)
the information a person needs to have about these occupations; (4) the problems of adjusting to these occupations; (5)
the desirability of each occupation from various viewpoints;
and (6) what constitutes efficient work in each occupation.

The child needs to develop an understanding of personal
economics, of consumer judgment, of buying efficiency, and

of consumer production. All of these must be closely inter-woven (by the teacher) into the child's personal self-realiza-tion and life-adjustment program.

One thing which the teacher must not do is assume that the child will be taught at home the facts of his economic life. Altogether too rarely does the modern parent take time or effort to explain to the child how a family operates in an economic sense. Usually such teaching is limited to "Johnny, turn off the light in the living room. You're wasting elec-tricity. How often must I tell you?"

It is in the field of economic efficiency that the child is definitely looking toward the future. Occupational informa-tion he must have—and it must be sound information, not hearsay. He must be prepared in school so that some time in the future he may select his occupation, not be so unpre-pared that his occupation selects him. He must, as a young-ster in school, have some appreciation of what is good work and what is shoddy work. He should be taught early what money is, and how its value fluctuates—and why. Definitely he must realize that he lives in an economic world, and that his home and everything concerned with it (in a materialistic way) operate in accordance with economic laws.

**Civic Responsibility.** Civic responsibility, as a broad ob-jective of all education, becomes vital to every American boy and girl. If responsibility in the classroom is life at its best for the school child, then civic responsibility tends to be life at its best for the adult. Today, no one believes that a child goes from no civic responsibility to full civic responsi-bility simply by turning the calendar page and finding that he is twenty-one years old. Civic responsibility, with all that the term implies, is not something that comes suddenly. A child learns responsibility as he learns anything else, by experiencing it. This experience may be vicarious, but it is better if it is at least partially personal.

A child is naturally inclined to be self-centered. In prac-tice he may, if not influenced externally, be actually selfish. Because of this, it could be no accident if he were to prove to be sensitive to the disparities of human circumstances. If he not only knows and understands but feels that all boys and girls are not as fortunate as he, and if he acts to correct the disparities to the best of his ability, it is usually because a good teacher has made him conscious of his environment as a factor in his life and in the lives of others. If a school child recognizes social problems and exercises to the best of his ability some social understanding, it is rarely accidental. Some teacher has seen this recognition and understanding as being significant, and has attempted to develop this awareness in the child.

The teacher who helps his class to recognize propaganda and to judge it for what it is worth—whether a great deal, a little, or nothing at all—is making his classroom administration function to a greater extent than is one who carries on in a more mechanical manner. If he is able to develop tolerance for the opinions of others, especially of minority groups, aiding children to understand what minority groups are and that what is a minority group in one place may be a dominant group in another, then that teacher is much more than a hearer of recitations.

If the teacher, in a busy day of taking rolls, answering trivial questions, settling minor disputes, and carrying on the multitude of detailed work which constitutes school management, can take steps toward developing the idea of world citizenship, that is a greater achievement than correcting test papers. If the teacher is able to give a child a glimpse of the applications of science to our daily lives, his work borders on the superior in that it takes the child into a realm of thinking larger than his own limited one. The teacher who can help a child not only to know and understand but to feel that law observance is a duty is making classroom activities carry over into reality.

## A. THE TEACHER'S PERSONAL RELATIONSHIPS

The teacher's professional activities in the classroom concern the learning process directly. Pupils' activities in the classroom are always complementary to the teacher's. To this extent, and to this extent only, the teacher and the pupils have synonymous objectives.

The teacher is always a part of a complex situation. Although thought of as being academic, never is a teacher's work entirely so. Today, he is concerned with the life of the community in all its ramifications. Definitely, he is part of the community and, eventually, the community will be a part of him. He will work harmoniously with boards of education, with townspeople, with fellow teachers, and with school administrators.

A teacher's personal relationships are of the greatest significance. Never can he be a thoroughly good teacher in the classroom and be incompatible with fellow teachers, with the administration, and with the townspeople outside the classroom. The second becomes a part of the first. The qualities which make a teacher liked or disliked among his associates on the staff tend to go over into his classroom work.

**Nature of a Teacher's Work.** In a sense, a teacher is a member of a closed corporation. The other members of this corporation are the superintendent of schools, the principal, the supervisors, the co-workers on the teaching staff, and sometimes the school custodians. A teacher knows many things which he does not tell. To the teacher, as to the family doctor and the minister, come the confidences of children and, through them, of parents. Children tell of their home lives because they trust the teacher; he is very near and dear to them. Parents often tell a teacher of their most intimate desires and hopes and fears. Many confidences he has; no confidence does he betray.

The teacher in his professional career learns early never to talk "shop" publicly. What people too frequently want to know—and people who usually have no business knowing—are personal things about their neighbors and their neighbors' children. They are not particularly interested in generalities, and it is of generalities the teacher may speak, never of personalities. The answer to the commonly heard question, "How is school going?" is always the same one, "Just fine." If, in his opinion, it isn't going that way his opinion may be incorrect; and in any case, that opinion belongs, when it is asked for, to those who have a right to it, the administration of the school. Again, the teacher is not the person responsible for disseminating specific information concerning the school to the general public. This responsibility belongs, as far as the public is concerned, to the superintendent of schools and to the board of education.

From the teacher, parents are entitled to know about their children, but they are not entitled to know anything personal about a neighbor's child. Again, if he is really unhappy and finds it difficult to say anything good about the school which nourishes and shelters his professional growth, it is sound policy to keep still, and to keep still in such a manner that he implies no evil. Under these conditions, he is always planning to leave anyhow.

**Competencies in Human Relationships.** Educational authorities are in agreement on some of the competencies desired in teachers who are entering the profession. Among those commonly stressed from a human relationship viewpoint are respect for personality, and social understanding and behavior. Respect for personality implies treating all other human beings as persons whose purposes demand consideration and whose potentialities need encouragement. This implies respecting oneself and respecting others; understanding those with whom one is associated, learning from them, and in turn giving aid to thought and action. This reiterates what has been said earlier. A good teacher sees, hears, and speaks no evil. He reserves judgment until the evidence is all in; and since the evidence is rarely if ever all in, he reserves judgment.

It is in social understanding and behavior that a teacher will merge his own individuality with his environment, and in this ability he will grow while on the job. In-service training, which will be discussed later, is too frequently considered in terms of techniques, methodology, and the acquisition of academic and professional knowledge. These he cannot neglect if he is to mature professionally to the limit of his potentialities. However, in social understanding, the teacher takes his college course far from a college campus. Social understanding implies having more than an ordinary understanding of the society in which he works. It implies supporting a sound social philosophy with a grasp of the facts and relationships of contemporary social existence. It implies encouraging loyalty to the ideals to which our culture is dedicated. Oversimplified, this all means that a teacher understands society because he is not only part and parcel of it but also a most observant part of it, and that as a teacher he supports sound social ideas because he has a sound social philosophy.

The teacher with social understanding is first of all an intelligent participant in the society of his immediate environment. He participates in civic affairs, in church work, in clubs and forums, and in the recreation and fun of his community. Participation does not necessarily mean active leadership, for time for out-of-school activities is limited and the teacher's energies must not be dissipated. Active leadership might imply a group brand, and the teacher, serving all the people, must not be associated with cliques and factions. This, of course, does not mean that the teacher is not always allied with forces which exist for community betterment, but it does mean keeping out of unimportant community squabbles. Knowing the importance of democratic action, the teacher shares always in movements which tend to further such action.

**Administrative Relationships.** When a teacher fails to achieve cordial and pleasant relationships with the principal and the superintendent of schools, there may be one of two things fundamentally wrong. The first is that the teacher may be thoughtless or tactless in his relationships with these administrators. To illustrate: a woman teacher with a small sum in her room's treasury, a sum which had come from selling Christmas cards, asked a personal friend, at whose home she was having dinner, if she might use the money for some inexpensive drapes for her classroom windows. The friend said "Yes." The hitch was that the friend was a member of the board of education. The teacher purchased the material, the cost being negligible, and she and the children made it up. The superintendent of schools visited the room, admired the new drapes, and asked where the money had come from. She told him very frankly, and then added that the board member had given her permission to use the fund. She intended no wrong, but nevertheless she had violated a fundamental principle in teacher-administrator relationships. She had gone over the superintendent's head in a professional matter, small though it was.

The second cause for personal teacher-administrative unpleasantness is usually a dissatisfied teacher who deliberately makes trouble. This is, of course, unpardonable. Line-of-duty problems develop, but the teacher must learn to deal with these competently, without allowing them to become a cause of personal rancor against the administration.

In order to be more specific, some suggestions of a positive nature dealing with the teacher's personal relationships with the administration are offered below. There is no assumption that these include all such that exist:

1. Discuss with your principal and/or superintendent any problems which are worrying you. Don't consider these too trivial.
2. Go through proper channels for any aid you may need, whether that aid be a box of chalk, shades for the windows, or how to dispose of an attendance problem. Proper channels are the principal, the superintendent, or the supervisor if there is such. Don't go to the board of education or to some influential person in the city.
3. Support school activities of all sorts. These include projects such as Education Week, school plays, and school athletic events. Assure the administration of your active support and make good on your promise.
4. Be loyal to the administration at all times. You are inseparably a part of it. A teacher who is disloyal to the administration is a worthless teacher.

5. Make required reports promptly, completely, and with the greatest of care. You will be judged critically by these reports.
6. Be prompt in attendance at all required teachers' meetings and be cooperative in making such meetings effective to the best of your ability.
7. Know school regulations and obey them implicitly. Do not ask for favors from the central office.
8. Be human—and be forgiving even though you seem to be imposed upon.

On the negative side of the picture the teacher learns early that, as far as the administration is concerned, he should obey the following rules:

1. Never criticize a fellow teacher or an administrative officer. Inevitably, it will get back to the person criticized, and even though you intended no harm a rift in a friendship will follow.
2. Never speak disparagingly of the school to a member of the board of education under the impression that he is an administrative officer. His is a legislative function, not an executive one, and your criticism may do much harm.
3. Never belong to a faction or a clique. This means avoidance of being always with the same group for luncheon or for recreation.
4. Never take the credit to yourself when your pupils have done exceedingly well in anything. Give the credit to them; you lose nothing by so doing.
5. Never show your dissatisfaction to co-workers. Take the dissatisfaction to the person who is responsible for it or who can do something about it. Grumbling and complaining will not help any bad situation and may make it worse.
6. Never interpret administrative actions or decisions as being aimed at yourself specifically. To do so is like reading a medical text and diagnosing yourself into an illness that is non-existent.

**Community Relationships.** A teacher needs to know a good bit about a community's industries, its civic institutions and backgrounds, and its attitudes toward social practices and religion. Folkways and mores in smaller towns and cities sometimes place teachers in groups by themselves when items such as social dancing, an occasional cocktail, or cigarette smoking are under consideration. Parents all too frequently expect from teachers a conformity in social behavior which they are unwilling to enforce upon themselves. In general the teacher will do well to conform and not try to make the community over.

From the positive point of view, a teacher should in his community relationships conform to the following practices:

1. Always speak approvingly of the school and its administration. Avoid conversation in public which deals with personalities.
2. Patronize local stores as much as you can. The local community is paying a large part of your salary and feels entitled to your patronage. Distribute patronage as much as possible.
3. Speak approvingly of the community. Local residents may criticize it to you, but they will tend to resent your agreement with them and may even quote you as having originated the statement.
4. Be alert to the possibilities of interpreting the schools in a positive, forward-looking, and appealing manner to the public. You are always an ambassador for the schools.
5. Appear before community groups, such as service clubs, when asked to do so. Do your best, whether it be in singing, instrumental music, speaking, or directing a choral group.
6. Conform to local standards in dress and in social behavior in general. The teacher should always avoid extreme styles in dress.

Because the negative statement often clarifies thinking on abstractions, the following list of "don'ts" will illustrate positions for the teacher to assume in relationships with the community:

1. Don't try to make the community over. It was there a long time before you came and will resent your efforts. This does not mean you are not standing for advancement in any form which presents itself.

2. Don't fail to give credit to your principal, to your pupils, to your co-workers, and to your superintendent whenever you can. It is unlikely they will go up in popular estimation without your going with them.
3. Don't boast of your accomplishments even though they are considerable. Let your community find out about you from other sources. You will lose nothing by being silent.
4. Don't submit school news to local papers without first submitting it to your principal for approval. This relieves you of responsibility should there be criticism.

## THE TEACHER AND THE PARENT-TEACHER ASSOCIATION

The National Congress of Parents and Teachers came into being under this name in 1924. Previous to this time a National Congress of Mothers (1897) and the National Congress of Mothers and Parent-Teacher Associations (1908) had been in existence. Today, there are units of the National Congress of Parents and Teachers in thousands of towns, villages, and cities.

A teacher will make no mistake in affiliating himself with this organization. It exists for the good of the schools, and all in all it is doing a wonderful work in bringing parents and the schools into a closer relationship. He will hear the organization commonly spoken of as the "PTA."

One of the great advantages to the teacher in this organization is the development of a close acquaintance with the parents of the children in his room without too much time-consuming effort on his part. Again, he meets parents under informal conditions—a much better way of getting to know them than making an uninvited formal call. Later, after acquaintance, he will call upon parents, but it will be upon invitation.

Before joining the parent-teacher organization, the teacher should talk the matter over with his principal or superintendent. Usually they are in hearty accord. Occasionally, there is ill feeling between the school administration and the parent-teacher group, ill feeling caused by the latter's taking unto itself administrative functions which do not belong to it. This is rarely true; and where it is, the school, by encouraging consistent attendance of teachers at meetings, can discourage such mistakes.

The parent-teacher association can and usually does do much good. Through it the schools find valuable support and backing in projects exceedingly desirable for the school, which cannot succeed without community support. Usually, such effort is along lines of securing higher tax levies for school support, improvement in the school plant, increase of library facilities, and better salaries for teachers, raising money for school purposes for those items which may not come from the school's budget, and other functions of a similar nature. One is wise to take an active part, although a secondary one, as the organization must not be teacher-dominated.

Some teachers organize subunits of the parent-teacher association in their classrooms. Such groups make for a closer contact between the teacher and the parents than can be secured through the larger organization alone. The children gain in that problems suitable to children's interests are brought before them, and these problems tend to make children community-minded. These smaller groups are always working groups and get their inspiration from the larger group with which they are affiliated.

## DISCUSSION PROBLEM

### THE ENVIRONMENT CAN BE CHANGED

You have had an exciting morning. From among some thirty candidates for a position in the Tioga Rapids City Schools, Superintendent Barston has selected you. The work is in the fifth grade, and while you have not been assigned to a building, in rosy dreams you picture for yourself a well-equipped classroom.

Autumn comes and you attend your first teachers' meeting in Tioga Rapids. Although the meeting is not for all the teachers in the city, you are amazed at the number of teachers present. You estimate the number at five hundred, and you are conservative in that estimate. At this meeting, you find yourself assigned to the Lincoln School. You find it on the school map of the city, one of the smaller schools in the "across-the-tracks" region of the town. Your first impression of your classroom and of your building is dismaying. The building is old (you learn later that it has been tentatively condemned), and the classroom is disheartening. The floors, recently replaced, have been carelessly handled and are black with oil from a sweeping compound. The desks are old and dirty. The walls are drab; the pictures, relics of better days, are smoked and have always lacked brightness. All in all, the room is best described by the single word "cheerless."

School begins, and you find that the boys and girls in your room seem to reflect the atmosphere of cheerless homes and of the cheerless schoolroom in which half of their waking hours are spent. They are not happy-go-lucky, mischievous, wide-awake, industrious, or lovable. Instead, you find them to be undernourished, listless, somber, wistful.

A talk with your principal gives you little satisfaction. She has been in the school for years. Promotion has not come to her, although she has for years expectantly looked forward to it. Now, she is reconciled to her situation; discouragingly, she tells you that the situation is very bad, but that nothing can be done about it. You leave her to her resigned attitude, and go home to your own cheery room resolved to do what you can to improve conditions.

## QUESTIONS ON THE PROBLEM

1. Assuming that the janitor is unwilling to do any work for you which he is not required to do for other teachers, outline a program for improving the classroom situation or better, conditions, under which you are going to work. Can anything be done to improve the condition of the floors? What can be done about the desks? Would you be out of line if you should give them a good scrubbing yourself? Would two or three bright house plants improve the situation? Can you tie the PTA into this problem without stirring up a problem for the entire building?

2. Your principal does not promise to be of much help to you. What suggestions can you offer which might get her more interested? Would you be justified in asking the principal's

permission to talk to the city superintendent about the general condition of this building?

3. If the principal says, "Go ahead," to the suggestion in the question above, is there any probability that you will be considered a troublemaker by everyone? Would you do well to wait until you are more firmly established before trying to improve the situation in your room? Discuss.

4. Can you suggest a way in which the superintendent of schools might be made more cognizant of the bad conditions in the Lincoln School? If Superintendent Barston shrugs you off, would you be justified in talking to a member of the board of education?

5. Be specific in stating the things which you can do to make this room more livable for these underprivileged children, things which are entirely within your province.

6. Is there any reason for any American child today, one who is attending a public school, to be undernourished? This question implies that you should find out all that you can about the hot-lunch and the milk program for school children.

7. This is a poorer section of the city. Does this mean that the parent-teacher association cannot function as efficiently as it might in a wealthier section?

8. If there is no functioning PTA in this school, or if there has been one and it has died of neglect, is there anything you can do to organize one or to revive the non-functioning organization?

9. What one comparatively inexpensive item (which you can get from the janitor) will in itself make this room cheerier at once?

10. What can the children in your room contribute toward making their room more cheery? Would making the room brighter be a desirable group project? Would it (making the room brighter) be thoroughly in line with group dynamics as discussed in this chapter? Does the situation meet all of the requirements for good group action?

## STUDY QUESTIONS

1. What is implied in the word "environment" as applied to a school? What are the boundaries of school's environment?

Is the environment entirely a physical one? In a large city, is the school's environment the entire city? In a small city is the country around it the school's environment?

2. A child's environment is constantly increasing in size. This statement is made dogmatically. Can you show how this is true—or if you do not believe it is true in all cases, show how it is untrue?

3. Is a radio a part of the child's environment? Is a television set? A newspaper? A library? A professional baseball team? A slum area? A fine park system?

4. The key words in management as suggested on page 69 are all verbs. Would these words be equally effective as key words if they were nouns? Why? Why not?

5. Try to list as many things as you can which might properly come under the heading of self-realization for a child. Would being a good athlete be one? Could it be?

6. Is it presumptuous to assume that children, say in the fifth grade, can be taught anything about economic efficiency? List some things that might indicate a comparatively high degree of economic efficiency in a ten-year-old.

7. Can you illustrate what "civic responsibility" might mean for a seventh-grader? Try to suggest items which in a seventh-grader might indicate a lack of civic responsibility. To illustrate: a twelve-year-old boy deliberately broke on the sidewalk a Coca-Cola bottle which he had picked up. Do you believe it would have been possible to teach him, in school, general principles regarding civic responsibility which would have inhibited this action? Will talking about civic responsibility in class make children into good young citizens? If not, how will one get the job done?

8. Why is it so hard to talk about school to someone not in the profession and still avoid personalities in your discussion? Could you as a teacher talk to a doctor about his profession in an intelligent manner and avoid all personalities?

9. Is "talking shop" the same thing as explaining to the parent-teacher association the need for improving the lighting situation in the building? What is implied in the term "talking shop"?

10. What are some of the broader implications in the term "social understanding"? The term is hard to define with definiteness. Why?

11. In giving advice is it better to make the statements positively or in the negative? You are inclined to favor the positive. Why? Would the Ten Commandments be more effective if each was not a prohibition?
12. Pick out statements under the heading "Administrative Relationships" which in your opinion are questionable. Discuss each of these in class.

## SELECTED READINGS

ADAMS, HAROLD P., and DICKEY, FRANK G. *Basic Principles of Student Teaching.* New York: American Book Co., 1956. Pp. 200 ff., 310–21. Offers practical suggestions for maintaining an effective balance of freedom and security in the classroom. Chapter 8 stresses classroom management in the learning process.

BARUCH, DOROTHY. *New Ways in Discipline.* New York: McGraw-Hill Book Co., Inc., 1949. Discusses common everyday problems which all classroom teachers meet. Concrete examples make this book excellent material for the classroom teacher.

BURTON, WILLLIAM H. *The Guidance of Learning Activities.* 2d ed. New York: Appleton-Century-Crofts, Inc., 1952. Chapter 22. The last chapter in this book does a good job of correlating activities in terms of classroom organization and control.

BUTLER, FRANK A. *The Improvement of Teaching in Secondary Schools.* 3d ed. Chicago: University of Chicago Press, 1954. Chapters 15 and 17. The physical and social environment necessary for good learning, and the social dynamics phase of classroom management are clearly presented.

CHARTERS, W. W., and WAPLES, DOUGLASS. *The Commonwealth Teacher-Training Study.* Chicago: University of Chicago Press, 1929. An older publication which is still the outstanding study of the daily work of the classroom teacher.

GRIEDER, CALVIN, and ROMINE, STEPHEN. *American Public Education.* New York: The Ronald Press Co., 1955. Chapter 2 *et al.* Desirable reading for the student who desires a good over-all picture of the American public school system.

HANSEN, KENNETH H. *Public Education in American Society.* Englewood Cliffs, N. J.: Prentice-Hall, Inc., 1956. Chapter 7, "It Happens in the Classroom," is the title of a good chapter which emphasizes the position of the teacher as the director of the learning situation. Chapter 12, "The Teacher's Stake in Administration," also fits into the organization of the chapter in the text which you are studying.

KYTE, GEORGE C. *The Elementary School Teacher at Work.* New York: Holt, Rinehart & Winston, Inc., 1957. Chapters 3, 13, 14. Book in general is geared to the work of the classroom teacher.

MEHL, MARIE A., MILLS, HUBERT H., and DOUGLASS, HARL R. *Teaching in Elementary School.* 2d ed. New York: The Ronald Press Co., 1958. Chapter 18. This chapter puts emphasis upon the importance of group activity as a basis for creative learning.

SMITH, HENRY CLAY. *Psychology of Industrial Behavior.* New York: McGraw-Hill Book Co., Inc., 1955. Chapter 9 shows how the group dynamics factor operates in business situations. Examples presented are applicable to school group dynamics.

PART II

# CLASSROOM MANAGEMENT
# FOR PUPIL GROWTH

# 5

# ATTENDANCE AND
# NON-ATTENDANCE PROBLEMS

A basic principle of American educational policy says that whatever schools are provided for children by the government, those schools shall not only offer free educational opportunity for all children, regardless of race, color, or creed, but also shall offer equal opportunity for all.

The principle of free and equal educational advantages for all children has as a corollary the right of the state to compel children to attend school, either one which the state provides or one approved by the state under private auspices. Penalties for non-attendance are assessable against the parents in order to compel the child's attendance for a minimum school term and for a minimum number of school years. The length of the term and the number of years required vary much among the states, but the obligation for attendance is universal.

It is not enough that the well-trained teacher know the attendance laws of his state and the best methods of keeping school attendance at the highest point of efficiency; he must also know the underlying principles which have made the United States of America outstanding among the nations of the world as an exponent of universal education for youth.

Some seventy years ago, George H. Martin in *Evolution of the Massachusetts School System* pointed out that the Massachusetts Laws of 1642 and 1647, the first school laws in America, embodied all of the basic principles which under-lie the American school system today. These principles, which Martin derived from the Massachusetts laws, state:

1. Universal education of youth is essential to the well-being of the State.
2. The obligation to furnish this education rests primarily upon the parents.
3. The State has a right to enforce this obligation.
4. The State may fix a standard which shall determine the kind of education, and the minimum amount.
5. Public money, raised by a general tax, may be used to provide such education as the State requires. The tax may be general although the school attendance is not.
6. Education higher than the rudiments may be supplied by the State. Opportunity must be provided at public expense for youths to be fitted for the university.

Although it is more than three hundred years since these laws were enacted, the principle which they established has held in all laws dealing with American education since. The teacher who fails to grasp the basic principles govern-ing enforcement of the regulations, which are obligatory upon him, is on a well-marked route to trouble.

## COMPULSORY ATTENDANCE CONSIDERATIONS

Parents, under American law, may educate children in schools of their choice, or even privately, provided the mini-mum essentials required by law are clearly and obviously met. Compulsory attendance laws do not require attendance at public school; they do compel parents to satisfy the law that the child is being educated.

**Authority of the State.** Many court cases are on record involving the authority of the state regarding compulsory attendance. In the "Oregon Case of 1925" a state law, based upon a constitutional amendment, required all children be-tween the ages of six and sixteen years to attend the public schools. The Supreme Court of the United States ruled the law unconstitutional, as it violated the section of the United States Constitution which guaranteed life and liberty under the law. In general the law interfered with the rights of parents to rear and educate children as they saw fit. Specifically, the law tended to deprive private and parochial schools of their property (by making it valueless for the purpose for which constructed) without due process of law. However, the authority of the state to regulate, inspect, supervise, and examine all schools was clearly set forth. As Mr. Justice McReynolds wrote in the decision in *Pierce* v. *Society of Sisters* (the Oregon case):

No question is raised concerning the power of the State reasonably to regulate all schools, to inspect, supervise and examine them, their teachers and pupils, to require that all children of proper age attend some school, that teachers be of good moral character and patriotic disposition, that certain studies plainly essential to good citizenship must be taught, and that nothing be taught which is plainly inimical to the public welfare.

**Factors Affecting Enrollment.** The basic principle upon which compulsory school attendance rests is that universal education is essential to the well-being of the nation. An educated citizenry is imperative to a country which gives that citizenry the right to make laws, either directly or indirectly. Making available educational opportunities for all children, however, is not the same thing as requiring all children to utilize those opportunities. Laws requiring the furnishing of educational opportunity in all the states did not come about until less than a half-century ago. The first compulsory attendance law had been passed some seventy years before the last one became effective in 1912.

Although education is mandatory, laws governing education vary much among the states—for example, those governing compulsory attendance age. The average minimum age for compulsory attendance has been slightly higher than seven years; the average maximum age, slightly more than sixteen years. Seven to sixteen years has been the compulsory attendance age in more than half the states. The tendency is strongly to increase the number of years of attendance required.

Differences other than the minimum compulsory attendance age exist among the several states: (1) the average number of days schools are in session; (2) the average number of days attended per pupil enrolled; (3) the percentage of the total population enrolled in public schools, and (4) the percentage of school-age pupils (5 to 17 years) enrolled in school. To illustrate (with data for public schools only being available):[1] In Illinois in 1955–56, schools were in session an average of 186.9 days. In that same year in Arizona, the average number of days schools were in session was 165.2 —a difference of more than twenty days. The median of all states for the same year was 178.0 days. Illinois children had school opportunities of about nine days more than the national norm; Arizona children, some twelve days less than the norm.

In the same year, in California, the average daily attendance as a percentage of the number of pupils enrolled was 95.9; in Nevada it was 83.1. Here, again, there is a wide disparity. The average daily attendance in terms of enrollment for the United States as a whole for that year was 89.0.

The drawing power of the schools of the nation also shows wide divergence. For example, in 1957–58 the percentage of the total population enrolled in public schools in Georgia, highest on the list at that time, was 26.1. More than one in four of the total population was enrolled in public schools. Rhode Island had the smallest proportion of its total population enrolled in public schools, 15.2 per cent. For the nation as a whole, the figure was 19.8 per cent.

For the percentage of school-age children enrolled in public school in 1957–58 Nevada led with 98.7 per cent. As some Nevada children attend private schools, it would appear that Nevada had almost all of its school-age children in school. For the same year, Rhode Island had 69.2 per cent of its school-age pupils enrolled in public schools.

[1] Rankings of the States, Washington, D. C.: Research Division of the National Education Association, April, 1959.

(Rhode Island may have had many children enrolled in private schools.) The mean for the United States as a whole for school-age children enrolled in public schools was 82.9 per cent. One would like to believe that all the others were enrolled in private schools, but informed attendance officials know this is not true. The fact is that many boys and girls between the ages of five and seventeen are not attending any school. This is, of course, influenced by the maximum age of compulsory attendance being sixteen years in many states.

**Inequalities in Financial Support.** Equality of educational opportunity is an ideal not yet fully realized in American education. Some states spend on the average four times as much money per child for schooling as do other states; some communities within a given state spend thirty times as much per pupil as do other communities.

Two outstanding factors make for the inequality. First, the schools are state schools, not national schools, hence an inequality in financial support, as one state may have far greater wealth per pupil in school than another. Second, school district units within a state vary in their ability to support an adequate educational program. The variation is in size and in wealth. The ideal of taxing where the wealth is and spending the money where the children are is far from being realized. Only through a general state-wide tax can the inequalities within the borders of a given state be diminished. Even under broad, general school-tax plans, state-wide in effect, the inequality still exists. This is because such a large portion of school support is local in nature. To illustrate this disparity, the following data have been adapted from Hutchins and Munse.[2]

In 1955, the public schools of the United States as a whole were 41.4 per cent supported by the state in which the school existed; they were 50.2 per cent supported by the local district; the county contributed 5.8 per cent; and the federal

[2] Clayton D. Hutchins and Albert R. Munse, *Public School Finance Programs of the United States*, U.S. Office of Education, Miscellaneous 22, 1955.

government, 2.6 per cent. To show the wide disparity in methods of supporting schools, states with wide variation in the ways their schools are supported have been selected: Michigan and Nevada.

In Michigan for the same year (1955), the state support was 53.9 per cent; local support made up 45.2 per cent; county support was but 0.1 per cent and federal support was 0.8 per cent.

In Nevada, a state with many federal holdings within its borders, the following prevailed: the state support totaled 39.4 per cent; the local district support was 18.9 per cent; the county support for schools was 23.6 per cent and the federal government contributed 18.1 per cent.

## NON-ATTENDANCE PROBLEMS

When children are absent from school there are significant effects upon the school as a functioning unit of society.

1. State aid (school moneys distributed to the schools from the general school funds) is commonly based on average daily attendance (ADA). When a child misses school, the ADA for that school is consequently lowered, and the support for the school received from the state is lessened in exactly that amount. Only through perfect attendance for all enrolled children can a school secure maximum state payments.

2. It costs approximately as much per day to operate a school for half its enrolled pupils as it would were there 100 per cent attendance. Absences are wasteful for the school from a purely financial standpoint.

3. A classroom is a unit of society. It is to some extent like an athletic team. When part of the team members are absent, those present do not function as efficiently as when all are present. In some classwork activities, especially when pupils are functioning as groups, the absence of a few pupils severely impairs the over-all good for those who are present.

4. Regardless of what he may be doing when absent or how valuable such activity, the absent pupil is getting noth-

ing from the school itself when he is not there. To some extent, it is begging the question to say he is getting something of equal or greater value; the fact remains he is getting nothing of what the school offers.

**Causes of Absences.** The most common causes for absence from school are illness of the child or death of some member of the child's family, out-of-town family trips, work at home, illegal employment of the child, parental neglect, lack of suitable school clothing, dislike of school, distance from school, poor transportation facilities, and bad weather and roads. The last three causes are minimized when adequate transportation is supplied. The home is involved in absence in about one-third of the causes; the school is directly involved in approximately another third; and extraneous circumstances operate in the remainder.

In the elementary grades, Mondays and Fridays are the days when most absences occur. This is to be expected. Week-end trips with parents often start on Friday. Sunday is frequently a day of overeating for children and of greater exposure to weather conditions in playing outside. Consequently, children may be absent because of illness on Monday. There are more absences in March than in any other school month, because in many localities this is a month of very changeable weather, causing children to develop colds. Again, contagious childhood diseases frequently are epidemic in March. Approximately 80 per cent of the absences from elementary school come from less than 5 per cent of the pupils. Thus, a comparatively small number of pupils are responsible for the marred records.

Absence in rural schools is greater than in city schools. Distance from school, with roads frequently made impassable by storms, is a prime cause of absence. Also, health conditions are not as carefully supervised, generally speaking, in rural areas as they are in urban, and rural children are often absent because of illness. Another factor which operates to a lesser extent now than it did formerly is the scarcity of farm labor; with the advent of power machinery, fewer hands are needed to work a farm. However, a boy of fourteen can, with a tractor, come close to taking a man's place on a farm and may remain away from school to do so. The farm boy is less likely to be truant than is the city boy, as he does not have the parks, the movies, and other means of entertainment to tempt him away from school.

**Reporting and Checking Absences.** The method of reporting absences varies to some extent in different schools, and the teacher must conform with exactness to the regulations in his school. In general, the steps are as follows: The teacher reports the absence to the principal's office during the half-day in which it occurs, making certain that the exact date of the absence is noted. This is necessary, as legal action can follow unexcused absences. When the report is made to the principal, he consolidates it with the reports for the same period of the other teachers in the building. In larger cities, the principal usually reports each day to the attendance officer. However, because many absences are unavoidable and are of short duration, many principals make a checkup on the cause of the absence before reporting it to the attendance officer. This check is usually made by telephone. Thus the first report to the principal's office or his report to the attendance officer does not put this latter official into immediate action.

The attendance officer always waits until an absence has gone on for some time without explanation. At this point, his office steps in to determine why the child has not returned to school. The attendance officer may find that the pupil has moved from the district. This means a follow-up to be sure that he re-enters school at once upon arrival in his new location. A transfer of his school record is also indicated. The attendance officer may find that the child is truant and that the parents are definitely negligent; this is ground for legal action. In every instance the principal's office furnishes the attendance officer the data it has on the child. The amount varies in different schools, but it is always considerable. This case history is of vital importance to the attendance official, as through it he has a background of information exceedingly valuable and exceedingly difficult to collect, item by item, after the child has left the school's control. The attendance officer thus approaches the problem of absences more as a social worker than as a law-enforcement officer. Usually there is a definite maladjustment, either in the parents, the child, the child's health, the home situation, or the general environmental situation. Not infrequently, the school is at fault. Because the curriculum is not adjusted to the child, he has not responded properly to it and is taking the only escape method he knows.

The attendance service for large cities is broad in its scope, in that every child in the city is within its range of vision; it is also vital in its significance, as a child's future may depend on how well it functions. Because the work of this department covers a broad, general phase of school administration, rather than a single classroom, the general functions of such a department are not discussed in full here. The teacher is, however, related to its work directly.

Not an attendance officer, the visiting teacher is a mixture of social worker, teacher, juvenile worker, and all-round helper on attendance problems. Naturally this official's work begins with recognition of problem cases. These pupils may become juvenile delinquents if not reached; hence it is important that this work be most carefully carried out. Usually cases are referred to the visiting teacher by the principal, he in turn having been informed of them by the classrom instructor. Problem cases are commonly spotted by the fact that the child has absences and that he is deficient in scholarship. The latter is the most commonly found single index of problem cases.

A teacher will have neither an attendance officer nor a visiting teacher as an associate unless he is in a comparatively large city. However, the fact that such officers are not employed in the school situation does not imply that they are not needed. Commonly, one or both are valuable adjuncts to the school staff, even in smaller school systems. In rural schools the duties of these two officials will fall upon the teacher's already burdened shoulders. The county superintendent of schools is the legally appointed official in all situations where the attendance laws are being violated, and such violations should be referred to this official. Comparatively few cases, however, go to this office, as the teacher is held responsible for determining the why and wherefore of absences. Because of the overload which the county office carries in most instances and the shortage of help in these offices, the burden of attendance work usually falls upon the teacher.

**Responsibility for Makeup Work.** The teacher, whether or not responsible for the attendance checkup, is the one confronted with the problem of trying to repair the damage that has been done by non-attendance. When one considers that in large cities the absences on any given day amount to approximately 10 per cent of the pupils enrolled, the magnitude of the teacher's problem assumes even greater significance.

Making up work lost by absence is seldom entirely satisfactory. The good student, usually well above the class average in both ability and industry, misses little by an occasional absence as far as the classwork itself goes, although he may fail to benefit fully from the social life of the school. Makeup work for the poorer student—and too frequently it is the poorer student who misses school—is tremendously costly in both time and effort, as makeup work always involves individual instruction, and the poorer student needs more of it. Failure to make up the missed work at all or making it up in a superficial manner leads readily to maladjustment and unhappiness. The pupil may fall so far behind in his classwork that he fails to be promoted. Even if this does not happen, he may become emotionally disturbed and eventually lose all interest in his classwork. A teacher's responsibility is great. He alone must make the decision as to whether missed work has to be made up, whether the makeup need is immediate or not, and finally what means shall be used to bridge the gap for the pupil if the work is not made up.

**Absence Excuses.** The requirement of a written explanation from a parent or guardian following an absence is still in general use. A form supplied by the school is commonly used. The child gets this form from his teacher or from the principal's office, usually upon his return from an absence. Occasionally, planned absences (for instance, where parents take a child with them on a trip) are excused before the absence occurs. The excuse in no way constitutes an approval of the absence. It is simply a recognition of the legality of it. The form used for excuses usually carries a minimum of information: the pupil's name, the day or days absent, the cause of the absence, and the signature of the parent. These excuses are filed by the teacher or the principal, as they will serve as a justification for not setting the law in motion if the absence is a protracted one. The cause of the absence and the signature should be observed carefully if there is any reason to suspect forgery. The signature can be checked with the one upon the formal report card, which has been signed by the parent or guardian.

**Improving the Attendance Record.** A child's attendance in school usually depends as much upon the school as upon the child. It is not difficult to keep a child in school when he sincerely wants to be with his classmates. This is but saying that there is no better means of keeping attendance high than by keeping the school a pleasant, enjoyable place for all the children in the room. If one were to analyze the motives children have for going to school, he would probably find at the same time the motives they have for being absent. This applies, of course, only to the absences caused by the child's willingness to be absent.

*Using Attendance Incentives.* In improving the attendance record, the teacher will find that artificial incentives to attendance, such as gold and silver stars, publishing in the paper the names of those with perfect records, prizes, attendance certificates, and honor rolls, are only good to the extent that they achieve the result desired. They are a means to an end and must never be made an end in themselves. Items of this sort fail in their purpose if they become the main incentive to school attendance.

Probably the best device for improving attendance is one that enables the child to compete with his own best record. He needs to see the results of his effort in terms of his last month's record, as well as in terms of other children's records. Attendance graphs for each child are easily made, and when compared with a consolidated graph for the room they are readily understood even by young children.

*Using Extracurricular Activities.* The so-called "activity" program of the school is probably the best means of encouraging every child to be in school each day. The boy who plays shortstop on the seventh-grade team, although he may be the weakest student in the class, is reluctant to miss school if missing school means missing baseball practice and missing practice means not playing in the intramural game on Friday afternoon. The boy who is a poor student and who runs with a bad crowd in the evenings is frequently held in school and encouraged to enjoy better associates by the fact that his hot trumpet is at the heart of the school band. The history of the great entertainers of today's American night-club, radio, and television circuits is a history of boys (and girls) who did not care too much for school, but did like the place each held in the school orchestra or band, in school dramatics, in solo entertaining, or in talented, though often impromptu, singing and instrumental organizations at school. When the slogan "Every child in some activity which he thoroughly enjoys" is put into practice, attendance in school is usually good so far as the child's desire to be in school is involved.

## DISCUSSION PROBLEM

### May You Use Your Judgment?

What would you do in a situation like this? You teach in the fifth grade in the little town of Anandale. You have twenty-eight pupils. There is a total of 178 in the elementary school. Your nearest big town is Kansas City, Missouri, about 200 miles away. The community is rural and is given to stockraising. The big event of the year is the county fair held once a year. Many of the pupils in your community have never been away from home farther than a one-day drive in the family car.

A Friday morning comes and you find yourself at the building before eight o'clock. School begins at 8:40. Early as it is, someone is there ahead of you. "Good morning, Henry," you greet him. "My, you're early this morning, how did that happen?" The lad to whom you are speaking is a square-built, stocky chap, whose usually stolid countenance is this morning glowing with enthusiasm, interest, and importance. He is an average student, the son of a prominent livestock grower, Henry Vorak. Mr. Vorak has many farms, but Mrs. Vorak and their only child, Henry, are held to a rigid economy. Were you asked to name Henry's greatest school weakness, you'd likely say lack of interest. The things mentioned in books are, in general, unrealities to him. He has never, in fact, been outside his home county.

"Miss Bruce, please may I go to Kansas City with my father and mother? He's shipping two loads of cattle tomorrow, and we got four free railroad passes. Mother says if I can be excused from school for two weeks I can go with them to Kansas City and then we'll go to Davenport, Iowa, to see my Aunt Tillie. Please can I go, Miss Bruce?"

"But, Henry, two weeks is a long time for you to be out of school. Can't you go for just a few days?" you answer. "You're not very good in any of your school work, and I'm afraid you might fail because of being gone so long. I don't know that Mr. Grant would excuse you, even if I did recommend it."

"Mother says we can't afford to go to Kansas City unless she can see her folks in Davenport when we're that close. She can't go unless I do. We're going to spend four days in Kansas City, Miss Bruce, and—I've never been in Kansas City, Miss Bruce. I'd like to go awful well—and mother would like to go too. Father never said she could go before."

### QUESTIONS ON THE PROBLEM

1. What is your first inclination as you face this eager, enthusiastic lad, who never before has shown so much interest in anything?

2. List, in order of importance, the difficulties you face as you consider this problem. Assume that you cannot shunt this problem off on the principal or that he passes the responsibility back to you.

3. In your state, can school authorities legally excuse a pupil from school attendance for this purpose for a two-week period?

4. You have been reading about the life-adjustment education movement. Would the situation described above be considered as desirable—that is, if Henry is permitted to go?

5. If education has to do with life, rather than simply with preparation for life, will Miss Bruce be justified in telling Henry he may go?

6. Is a school lad getting value received from the life adjustment viewpoint, and from every other educational viewpoint, who broadens his interests and improves his understandings but does so at the sacrifice of his position in a class with the possibility of failing a grade?

7. From the class membership standpoint, how can you arrange for Henry to make the trip and strengthen his position socially rather than weaken it?

8. Were Henry the best student in your class, would you say "Yes" more readily than you are inclined to do with Henry?

9. Does a very good student need this trip as much as does Henry?

10. Can you suggest a solution which will allow Henry to go (granting the legal aspects are satisfactory) and which will not necessarily weaken his position in the class academically?

## STUDY QUESTIONS

NOTE. *Attendance is always concerned directly with the school laws of your state. Secure a copy of the school code, the most recent edition, and know the law.*

1. Having read the six statements from Martin, would you say that the idea underlying the Massachusetts Laws of 1642 and 1647 were socialistic? Were they democratic?

2. Does the state provide schools because it believes it can educate better than can the parents? If not for this reason, for what reason?

3. Many causes for absence from school are listed in the chapter. Which ones are subject to an improvement program in which you, the teacher, can take an active part? Suggest the means you would use in each case.

4. Would you expect a high positive correlation between poverty and poor school attendance? Which of the causes listed are most likely to have their inception in impoverished home conditions?

5. Is attendance usually better with children of native-born parents or with those of foreign-born parents? If you do not know, what would you surmise? Why?

6. In your state may a child who is leading his grade in school-work be kept at home to help his mother who is ill? How much time may he miss legitimately?

7. To what extent is the argument that the group suffers when any member is absent a legitimate reason for demanding regularity of attendance from all?

8. Do you agree that makeup work following an absence is rarely well done? If this is true, why is it so?

9. Suppose that a new family moves into your school district. How long might a child in this family be out of school before his absence is discovered? How are transfers into a city school district handled in order that the attendance law may be immediately effective? Does this same situation prevail in a rural neighborhood? Who is responsible for seeing that new children in a rural neighborhood are at once placed on the school attendance rolls?

## SELECTED READINGS

GRAMBS, JEAN D., IVERSON, WILLIAM J., and PATTERSON, FRANKLIN K. *Modern Methods in Secondary Education.* Rev. ed. New York: Holt, Rinehart & Winston, Inc., 1958. Record-keeping, classroom logistics, room organization, and general instructional routine are discussed in Chapter 12, "Managing the Classroom for Effective Learning." Discussion is clearly written.

HAGMAN, HARLAN L. *The Administration of American Public Schools.* New York: McGraw-Hill Book Co., Inc., 1951. Chapter 19, "The Administration of Special Facilitating Services," shows how good school transportation and an adequate school lunch program do much to reduce absences, as well as to improve school morale in general.

HANSEN, KENNETH H. *Public Education in American Society.* Englewood Cliffs, N. J.: Prentice-Hall, Inc., 1956. Chapter Three, "Money for Our Schools," indicates specifically the financial problems involved in supporting schools under widely varying economic situations.

KINDRED, LESLIE W. *School Public Relations.* Englewood Cliffs, N. J.: Prentice-Hall, Inc., 1957. Chapter 8, "Parent Relations," indicates the need for interesting parents more directly in the necessity of good school attendance for their children.

KINNEY, LUCIEN B., and DRESDEN, KATHERINE. *Better Learning Through Current Materials.* Stanford: Stanford University Press, 1952. Chapter 8 indicates how management problems may be lessened by varying materials of learning, thus avoiding the monotony which causes the desire on the pupil's part to miss school.

NATIONAL CITIZENS COMMITTEE FOR THE PUBLIC SCHOOLS. *Financing Public Education in the Decade Ahead.* New York: National Citizens Committee for the Public Schools, 1954. The report of a non-partisan committee, working with professional educators to formulate suggestions for dealing with school finance problems for the period ahead. Gives good national school finance data.

POWER, EDWARD J. *Education for American Democracy.* New York: McGraw-Hill Book Co., Inc., 1958. Chapter 2, "The Distinctive Features of Education in the United States," presents the historical background of American education in a condensed but still a reasonably comprehensive manner. Public-private school dualism is discussed.

REEDER, WARD G. *The Fundamentals of Public School Administration.* 4th ed. New York: The Macmillan Co., 1958. The problem of non-attendance from the administrator's point of view is presented with thoroughness in Chapter 19 (pp. 378–96). One of the best, if not the single best reference, on non-attendance as a management factor.

RISK, THOMAS M. *Principles and Practices of Teaching in Secondary Schools.* New York: American Book Co., 1953. The fourth unit emphasizes, while others include, the significance of good management and its everyday relationship to regularity of attendance.

# 6

# CLASSROOM CONTROL

"And, gentlemen, I say to you again, there is no true discipline other than self-discipline." The speaker is John Gorman, an elementary school principal. He is talking to a group of his friends, all businessmen. The quotation from the school principal presents the last words of Mr. Gorman's rejoinder, made when the businessmen had attacked the newer viewpoint implied in the word "discipline." All had insisted that the schools of today are lax in discipline, that they are permeated by a dangerous softness, that punishments are neither frequent enough nor severe enough. All tended to blame the school and its control for the social evils of the day.

## TYPES OF DISCIPLINE

The school today is not limited to giving preparation for life; for children of school age, it is life. Thus school control—it can be called discipline—is but an extension of the control exercised in the home, in the street, in the entire out-of-school life of the child. The word "discipline," although still in common use, does not express with any great exactness the idea of classroom control considered most desirable. If used in its best sense, discipline has to do mostly with control of the less mature actions of a child. In most cases, discipline concerns the child who has not yet the ability to do much reasoning. In some ways it is related to "conditioning" and is commonly one of the means by which conditioning is brought about. A very small child is governed to a great extent by external discipline or disciplines. However, in the modern classroom this is usually considered the least desirable form of control, as it is external and true control is internal. *True control is self-control.*

That the word "discipline" has many connotations is evident. Three different types of discipline are presented here.

**Military Discipline.** In the military organization discipline means a rigid observance of all regulations; it means unquestioning obedience; it means unthinking conformity. When given an order (he is seldom asked to do anything), the soldier does not ask "Why?" He obeys. The end desired is machine-like compliance with orders. Commonly, it has little relationship to self-control, which is always related to a truer form of discipline, self-discipline. Although not an end in itself, military discipline is almost synonymous with the end: implicit compliance with orders under all conditions.

**Baseball Discipline.** Commenting on one of the World Series teams, a prominent sport columnist wrote of them as a "well-disciplined ball club." This same club fought viciously for every advantage that might give it a victory in the all-important series. Base-runners went into bases with feet high and spikes flashing. When it seemed they might gain by it, they "rode" umpires to the point that another word would mean ejection from the game. If they felt there was a chance of gaining an edge by "jockeying" the other players, they expostulated, ejaculated, blasphemed, bullied, and denunciated. Yet the sport columnist was correct. They were a well-disciplined professional baseball club. A fighting ball team wins more games than does a meek, genteel one. Its entire objective is winning games. Bad discipline for professional ballplayers would be any behavior pattern which in itself led to failure in their objective, winning games. Discipline is a means to an end, never an end in itself.

**Classroom Discipline.** Self-control is the highest order of discipline. With it, authority is rarely called into play. Teachers try to guide children to exercise self-control. The following incident demonstrates the possibility of mistaking externals for the real thing and of not recognizing a desirable outcome when externals are superficially lacking.

Miss Bruce's room in the Horace Mann School was not a quiet one. The two most noisy boys were Bert Watson and Bill Morrill. The pupils, many of whom Miss Bruce had taught the previous year a grade lower, were doing schoolwork that, as indicated by the all-school testing program, was slightly better than the city norm for the grade. There was some bickering, quite a bit of whispering, some note-writing. Miss Bruce's room seemed noisy always, yet busy. The pupils liked Miss Bruce and she liked them, but the principal had implied frequently that Miss Bruce's discipline was poor.

During the first week of school, before a fire drill was held and before fire regulations for the year had been read, Miss Bruce thought she smelled burning wood. She left the room and opened a door at the end of the hallway. She was met by a billow of dense smoke which nearly choked her. Panicky for an instant, she rushed back to her room to be met by a wave of white, scared faces.

"Leave everything exactly as it is, your books, wraps, everything, and go at once to the fire escape." The pupils were badly scared, as was the teacher. Their actions, however, were even more deliberate than when they had entered the building from the playground an hour earlier. Miss Bruce followed Bill and Bert, the last pupils to leave the building. Although it had never been suggested to them, they were carrying Aline Beeson, an infantile paralysis victim who could walk only with crutches. Miss Bruce never admitted that she had forgotten her. The boys went down the outside fire escape carefully as Aline sat upon their "cat-cradled" hands, an arm around the neck of each.

Everyone commended Bill and Bert for their thoughtfulness and the room in general for responding to an emergency so beautifully. One other room had had serious panic trouble, although no one was injured in the fire.

Miss Bruce's noisy room had acted splendidly in a crisis.

## DEFINITIONS OF DISCIPLINE AND SOCIAL CONTROL

The three types of discipline mentioned here make clear various ways of interpreting the word "discipline." In the

*Dictionary of Education,* no less than six definitions of the word are offered. They are not, however, in any sense contradictory. One is archaic, and another applies to a specialized training that is spoken of as a "discipline." Four of the definitions have significance in relation to the classroom, although one of these is rarely if ever utilized. Because the various interpretations given by the *Dictionary* are all illustrated in the modern classroom, the pertinent definitions are quoted verbatim:

1. The process or result of directing or subordinating immediate wishes, impulses, desires or interests for the sake of an ideal or for the purpose of gaining more effective, dependable action.
2. Persistent, active, and self-directed pursuit of some selected course of action, even in the face of obstacles or distractions.
3. Direct authoritative control of pupil behavior through punishments and/or rewards.
4. Negatively, any restraint of impulses, frequently through distasteful or painful means.

The first two definitions taken from this authoritative source apply to the learner as the activity agent and the second two make the learner the recipient of the action. These latter two definitions imply or suggest inhibition and restraint. It would seem then, that discipline is both an active, purposeful, dynamic thing which impels one to take action and an inhibiting force which prevents action by making the results of the action painful. Evidently, the former conception of discipline is what is wanted in the classroom. The first two definitions carry connotations which fit the classroom situation. It would seem that only occasionally should a teacher be forced to use "the direct, authoritative control of behavior," as suggested in the third definition, or to apply the fourth, "Any restraint of impulses, frequently through painful means." Rarely do the impulses of a school child need to be restrained by punishment if the first steps in securing disciplinary control have been taken in the preschool life of the child at home.

The phrase "control of behavior" is used in the third definition instead of the word "discipline." In the classroom of today, control comes nearer to fitting the desired pattern of behavior of the pupils than does the older word.

The *Dictionary* defines "control of conduct" as "Those rules, accepted practices, social codes, authorities, or influences that act as restraints upon and provide direction for the activities of individuals or groups." Seems to fit to a dot, doesn't it? There is a heavy social implication in the words "rules," "accepted practices," "social codes," and "influences." The word "authorities" is used but is not placed in the significant first or last place in the definition.

Teachers will be told by those who do not know, that the modern school believes in allowing pupils to do as they please; that it believes in unrestricted, self-directed, individual activity; that it believes no child should be punished. The answer is, definitely, that the modern school believes nothing of the sort. The modern school goes along with all the definitions of discipline and social control quoted from the *Dictionary*. It believes that true discipline is "a persistent and self-directed pursuit of some selected course of action." It believes that true discipline, which is synonymous with self-control, deals with "directing or subordinating immediate wishes, impulses, desires, or interests for the sake of an ideal or for . . . more effective, dependable action." It uses punishment to inhibit an action detrimental to the individual or the group. It uses authority when necessary. But it is inclined to consider the use of authority and punishment as unnecessary in most instances.

## DEVELOPMENT OF SELF-CONTROL

Discipline in the best use of the word applies more correctly and more directly to the child who is very young than to the older child. It applies more directly to the immature person than to the mature. This is because the word even in its best usage carries with it the idea of restraint or inhibition. A small child needs to know the meaning of the word "no" long before he understands the reason back of the denial. If he does not know the meaning of restraining words and does not learn to heed them early in his life, he will always be in trouble, even in danger. To learn late in life that restraints must be observed is always very costly. It is with young children who have yet to develop self-control and with adults whose mentality is no greater than a normal young child's that "direct authoritative control of behavior through punishments and/or rewards" is indicated. *Discipline* then, in the older usage of the word, is the first step toward and a prerequisite to self-control.

The second step in the development of the child's behavior pattern for the classroom is commonly spoken of as *social control*. Here the kindergarten child who insists on going down the slide out of turn is made to realize that other children take turns, that he wants the other children to like him, that his teacher wants him to have the satisfaction and pleasure as often as do the other children but no more—in other words, he learns, without ever being conscious of it, the restraining influence of the social group. From a little individualist, who frequently has had to be restrained by the authority of another individual, he now becomes less individualistic, more group-minded, socially disciplined perhaps but socially controlled certainly.

Third in the order of development and the final step in development is *self-control*. This comes to the child who has learned early the discipline of authority. He has through authority been inhibited from detrimental, destructive, and dangerous actions. Later, through the influence of other children and of adults, both in his home and outside it, he has learned to subjugate his individual interests, impulses, and desires to those of the group. At this point he is not yet a "self-disciplined" child. He is still under external pressure. His actions are authoritatively, externally influenced. He does what he does to a great extent because of group pressure. He is, however, on his way to true discipline, self-discipline.

With the advent of self-control, the child rarely needs the restraining, inhibiting influence of punishment, and he less frequently needs a reward for satisfactory behavior. That many adults never reach the third stage of development goes without saying. In fact, a large number never get away from the first, the inhibiting, disciplinary state. These are unhappy individuals who are, as adults, always "in bad" with the law. Others are influenced by social pressure and have thus reached the second stage, but have never learned that they have freedom of choice between good and evil, and have yet to learn that they are, as Henley tells us in "Invictus," masters of their own fates.

## CAUSES OF PUPIL OFFENSES

An analysis of the causes of schoolroom offenses against the social group indicates that the basic causes are rather obvious ones. Causes must always be interpreted in terms of the child. It is to be remembered that he is a child, not a little adult. This approach tends to limit the number of causes of offense. Although a further breakdown of each item is possible, the list of causes is not large in itself, as is indicated in the following list:

Lack of general training and development
Unsatisfactory home conditions which are manifested in the child's behavior
Bad (physical) school conditions
Unsociability (commonly resultant of the first and second items)
Bad associates
Inherent tendencies in the child (probably far less significant as a cause than is commonly believed)
Physical defects
Too many school rules
Poor teaching
Poor school organization

Although the situations which can develop in the classroom, situations detrimental to both the individual and the group, are almost innumerable, the following are typical of classroom offenses: whispering while the teacher is explaining work, eating during the school period, gum-chewing, throwing anything, note-writing, irritating other children (or the teacher), showing off, talking back, impudence, forgetful violation of regulations, intentional violation of regulations, cheating, inattentiveness, crowding and pushing, tardiness due to dallying, slamming doors, deliberate destruction of school property, rudeness, and discourtesy.

It is evident that the list of offenses tends to dovetail with the pattern of causes previously set down. Some are definitely due to poor home training, others to bad home conditions, still others to bad school conditions. A school's poor organization is often a cause of school misdemeanors.

These schoolroom offenses are irritating but in the main are not serious in themselves. If uncontrolled, however, they may develop into behavior patterns which lead to more serious offenses. Experience shows that the minor offenses of school life originate in the classroom; the more serious offenses in the playground, toilet rooms, locker rooms, and going to and coming from school. Serious offenses which come from the schoolroom are those of cheating, lying, stealing, and deliberate disobedience. A teacher will be irritated most by the minor offenses; the more serious offenses frequently will never come under his observation at all.

## EFFECTS OF TEACHING SKILL AND OF ENVIRONMENT ON CONTROL

If the general steps in the development of control in a child are: first, the restrictive, *inhibiting* one; second, *the effect of the social group* in which the person lives; and third, the control of a well-integrated personality or *self-control;* then there are rather specific factors which are more or less under the teacher's direction which influence each of the first three. These factors for which the teacher is to a great extent responsible are: (1) his own teaching skill; (2) the impact of his own personality, or more generally, his social behavior, on the pupils; and (3) the physical environment under which the school operates. To put this more concretely: classroom discipline tends to be good or bad depending upon the teacher's skill in teaching, and his personal impact, and upon the physical environment under which the class and school operate.

**Impact of Teaching Skill and Personality.** With skillful teaching, problems of control are minimized. Through ineffectual teaching techniques a teacher tends to create his own classroom problems. On the other hand, by his actions and personality in the classroom a teacher can minimize problems. The parallel columns which follow illustrate the impact of teaching skill and personality upon pupils in the classroom. The operations of the poor teacher are shown in the left-hand column; those of the good teacher in the right.

### TEACHING SKILL

| *Many Problems* | *Few Problems* |
|---|---|
| Makes vague assignments or no assignments at all. Pupil doesn't know for certain what he is to do, so does nothing on his assignment. Undesirable activity often results. | Makes a clear and definite assignment. The pupil knows what is expected of him and does it. No time for undesirable activity. |
| Makes an assignment which is impossible for the child to accomplish. Pupil gives up as he sees no chance of succeeding, does something else —possibly undesirable. | Gears assignments to time allowed and to ability of students. Realizes that learning is tied to a successful completion of an act studiously attempted. |
| Speaks in a rasping, quarrelsome tone of voice indicating irritation. Talks too much, nags, scolds. | Controls and modulates voice. Remembers that nagging (symbolic drive) diminishes a teacher's effectiveness. |

## TEACHING SKILL (*Continued*)

| *Many Problems* | *Few Problems* |
|---|---|
| Fails to get attention of every person in his class before proceeding with oral work. Is sometimes competing with students for attention. Respect for teacher lost. Control weakened. | Gets attention pleasantly (if possible), but gets attention of every pupil before proceeding with oral work. There must never be any doubt in any pupil's mind as to who is in charge of the classroom. |
| Pays inadequate attention to classroom logistics (movement of students, handling supplies, student seating, etc.). Because pupils have not been instructed specifically, they fail to respond specifically. Confusion leads to disorder, which in turn leads to reprimands and illfeeling. | Is definite in setting up classroom routines. Allows no exception to occur until routines are established. Since the routine is definite and clear, the child has little reason for deviation. The child who deviates is definitely wrong and all the children know it. |
| Pays insufficient attention to the physical conditions of the room. Pupil discomfort causes restlessness, which in turn forces the teacher into some form of disciplinary action. | Notes physical conditions, (heat, light, ventilation) frequently, as these tend to vary with outside conditions during the day. The physically comfortable child gives less trouble. |
| Does not recognize, or if he does recognize, does not compliment an unusually fine effort on a student's part. Student feels effort was unappreciated, makes less effort on later assignments; may show resentment by unsocial activity. | Recognizes and shows appreciation for honest effort. Feels that failure to commend unusually fine work by a student is bad manners on the teacher's part. Student is inspired to further and better efforts; is not likely to make trouble in class. |

## PERSONALITY OR SOCIAL GRACE

| Many Problems | Few Problems |
|---|---|
| Is sarcastic in his criticisms. Hurts pupils' sensibilities. Pupils show resentment by being (in turn) ungracious. | Criticizes constructively; shows consideration of pupil's feelings. Always gives a child a chance to "save face." |
| Is inconsistent. Scolds a pupil for what has been condoned in another. Pupils will forgive anything in a teacher except what they consider to be injustice. | Is consistent although he may not always be right. Pupils recognize fairness in attitude of the teacher. Not inclined to feel resentfulness—one of principal causes of pupil behavior problems. |
| Sloughs off reasonable questions or gives a facetious answer. A reasonable (to the child) question is treated as a triviality. Pupil feels snubbed, shows resentment through undesirable behavior. | Listens seriously to a reasonable question, but if time is limited suggests the question be brought up again. Pupil pleased, feels important; therefore not inclined to resentfulness. |
| Plays favorites. Lets it be known when he dislikes a child. Child reacts much as would an adult. | Plays no favorites. Goes out of his way to alleviate a hurt which he may have unintentionally given. |
| Stops a student curtly when student is seriously discussing or reporting on an assignment. Gives impression that discussion is trivial. | Encourages discussion but controls a situation which is wandering or getting out of hand. Treats children as he would colleagues in same situation. |
| Disparagingly criticizes community social groups, forgetting pupils' parents may be members of groups. Pupils tell parents. Child may be advised by parents to "tell that teacher off." Result: discipline problem. | Avoids comments or discussions which tend to reflect in a derogatory way on any group or individuals. Teacher remembers that he is serving all of the community. |

To summarize, a teacher sets the stage for serious problems in his classroom control if he (1) makes vague assignments or makes no assignments at all; (2) makes an assignment which is impossible of accomplishment in the time allowed or in terms of the pupils' abilities; (3) speaks in a rasping tone of voice, or in a tone which indicates irritation; (4) fails to get attention from every person in the class before proceeding with any type of oral work; (5) pays inadequate attention to schoolroom routines which deal with handling supplies, taking rolls, seating pupils, routings for use of in-the-room facilities such as pencil sharpeners and reference books; (6) gives insufficient attention to the physical conditions under which the pupils are working (light, heat, ventilation); and, (7) does not recognize and give approval to unusually fine effort on the pupil's part.

Conversely, disciplinary problems are reduced in direct ratio to: (1) making good assignments, (2) gearing assignments to pupil's time, (3) controlling one's voice, (4) getting complete attention of everyone before speaking, (5) setting up definite classroom routines, (6) checking frequently on the room's physical conditions, and (7) recognizing the need for a sense of accomplishment for each child in something each day.

From the point of view of social graces, the teacher who indicates lack of ordinary courtesy (1) by being sarcastic in his comments or criticisms, (2) by being inconsistent, (3) by ignoring reasonable questions, (4) by playing favorites, (5) by interrupting a student who is seriously trying to be heard, and (6) by speaking disparagingly of social groups (sometimes minority groups), is definitely setting the stage for resentfulness, disobedience, fearfulness, impertinence, unhappiness, and sensitiveness. Each of these is a serious cause of unsocial behavior, and each is rated by the mental hygienists as having possibilities of creating more serious behavior problems later than is the ordinary vexing (but commonly inconsequential) classroom peccadillo.

**Importance of Physical Environment.** Usually there are factors in the physical environment of the classroom that operate directly on the behavior of pupils. Although the teacher may not be able to control the factors, understanding of them and recognizing that they exist may influence his attitude toward the behavior problem. Some of the physical conditions of classrooms which affect behavior problems directly or indirectly are:

1. Room humidity (desirable range is between 40 and 60 per cent)
2. Proportion of glass area to floor area (desirably glass area should be between 15 and 20 per cent of the floor area)
3. Direction from which light comes (desirably lighting should be unilateral and from the left)
4. Placement of windows (desirably no window should be nearer than six feet from the front of the room)
5. Quality of illumination (low illumination is not to be condoned, but in general, low illumination is not as bad as is uneven illumination—shadows and highlights)
6. Placement of chalkboards (in terms both of light and of correct height for pupils)
7. Condition of floors (good schoolroom floors are made for quietness, freedom from slipping, durability, ease of keeping in good condition, and suitability of both color and reflecting surface toward preventing eyestrain)

## METHODS OF ACHIEVING CONTROL

A teacher can achieve classroom control by two means: preventing trouble before it happens and correcting trouble after it happens. The wise teacher uses the first, and if preventive measures are wisely used, there is little occasion for correction. In general, misconduct is a result, not a cause. If misconduct is a result, then it is caused by something. The child's mental attitudes are frequently basic causes of misconduct. Probably children suffer from bad mental hygiene to an extent somewhat comparable to that of bad physical health. The poor mental hygiene is only more difficult to discern. Although one rarely thinks of the cause of school offenses in terms of poor organizational procedures, there is not much doubt that poor classroom organization more often causes than prevents misconduct. In general, the wise teacher sets the stage for good school conduct by keeping everyone profitably busy, building good school spirit, maintaining proper personal relationships with the pupils, and seeking permanent values.

**Increasing Pupil Activity.** For many years psychologists have been pointing out that there is a strong tendency for all thought to be translated into action. Put in the negative, this is saying that the child "with nothing to do" is on his way to doing whatever he happens to think of, which may mean that he is on his way to trouble. This is not primarily because his tendencies are more toward evil than toward good, as was held by earlier students of education, but because the schoolroom limits his physical activities drastically. Altogether too much of what the child can do in the schoolroom—that is, activity of a physical nature—is not approved as schoolroom activity. At home or on the playground, a child with no assigned work, or with his assigned work completed, has much opportunity for physical activity which is not distasteful to the society in which he happens to be. In classrooms, in spite of a desire to have it otherwise, there is still far too much sitting still, if one remembers that the child is a dynamo of activity.

It is unlikely that a teacher will have much trouble with pupil control in any school situation marked by abundant approved activity on the part of the child. This is true particularly if the activity is both mental and physical. The industrial arts, home economics, art, physical education, and music instructors rarely have any serious classroom control problems. The reason is obvious: their pupils have something to do, something which is both mental and physical. Hence, if a teacher has planned for plenty of desirable activity for pupils, both mental and physical, there will be far less inclination on their part to do something which is un-approved. Idle hands do something, but what they do is not necessarily bad. A schoolroom which limits its activity largely to sitting still and a normal school child have very little inherently in common.

**Improving School Morale.** Today the term "morale" is used in a multitude of ways and situations. There is the morale of workers in manufacturing plants, the morale of players on an athletic team, the morale of the men in the armed services. The word has significance in every life ac-tivity where people work in cooperation with others. It can, but less rarely does, apply to the person who works alone. In the classroom the word is synonymous with "good school spirit." It has something to do with building up an attitude of confidence in one's self and one's co-workers. It is closely allied to cooperation. It has to do with sublimating personal desires and personal ambitions to the desires and wishes of the group, that a greater good for the greater number may come about. Good morale has to do with being successful, which is again related to confidence. Morale is high in a classroom when there is the desire and the ability to over-come difficulties. When morale is poor or low, school unity is always lacking and behavior problems multiply. Below are a few suggestions for improving morale when it is low or for keeping it high when it is all that one can ask for:

1. Develop the parent-teacher organization for your room and use pupils in putting on room programs, demonstrating pupils' classwork, and making exhibits.
2. Routinize all the phases of your organization that you pos-sibly can, so that pupils carry on much of the room's daily routine work through force of habit.
3. Vary your classroom assignments from day to day. Same-ness is tiresome and monotonous. Morale goes down as monotony goes up.
4. Recognize good work from students by placing it on bul-letin boards or in other conspicuous places. Plan this dis-play work so that no child fails to be recognized in some way or another.

5. Work up a slogan for your room. Have the children develop the thought and the wording. This can become a creed for the room.

6. Make your opening exercises varied and interesting. Use pupils in these programs.

7. Recognize special days with programs, exercises, bulletin-board notices, and other room decorations. Don't let such notices and decorations stay up until they are dilapidated-looking.

8. Organize a student self-governing body for your room. This group leads in discussing school offenses, especially those which can lead to serious trouble, such as failure to observe traffic control regulations, "hooking" rides on trucks, and improper use of playground facilities.

9. Join in all-school movements such as Education Week, the Community Chest drive, crippled-children campaigns, support of athletic teams, and control of contagious diseases.

10. Develop intramural activities in conjunction with other rooms in the school: softball games, spelling bees, art competition, and anything else of a similar nature. This sort of thing keeps morale high and school offenses low.

11. Make your traffic control squad very proud of their assignment. Some sort of uniform helps much if you can arrange it. Enlist the help of city officials in impressing your pupils with the importance of these assignments.

12. Discuss morals and manners frankly in your group. Pupils do not grasp generalities. This does not mean sex instruction, as that is something which is a matter of all-school policy and lies outside your jurisdiction. If the lessons you wish to teach can be put into little plays or pantomimes, so much the better.

Always a sympathetic, kind, genial, and lovable teacher has a salutary effect upon the school spirit in his room. The teacher can eliminate resentment which has shown up, allay suspicions which a child is developing, encourage the fearful child, aid the sensitive child to see his trouble, and bring the child who tends to be unsocial into closer contact with his contemporaries. Offenses against authority always become less frequent when a teacher is an "honest-to-goodness" friend.

**Improving Personal Attitudes.** Not uncommonly a teacher encourages schoolroom misconduct by his personal attitude toward pupils and their offenses. The teacher should remember that an offense is almost never intended personally but is rather an offense against the teacher's position and the society the classroom represents.

The teacher who says, "You cannot do that in *my* room" is definitely taking a negative attitude toward an offense. It is not the teacher's room; it is the children's room. The offense was more against them than against the teacher. If one were to use a word of admonition to a young teacher on this subject it would probably be: "Never allow a pupil to create a situation which aligns the other pupils with the offender rather than with the teacher and the social group." Much better to say, "I'm sure that John did not think that he was hurting our room's reputation when he threw a snowball which hit a car that was passing. I know that you all agree with me," than to berate him for the offense, although it may have been deliberate. Other pupils, too, probably threw snowballs. John is now in a position where he can explain and admit the error of his ways. John, as would an adult, wishes to save face in the eyes of the group. It is usually wise to give him a chance to do it. An adult is resentful of the policeman who says to him snarlingly, "You can't double-park on my beat." The adult is guilty and he knows it, but the officer's attitude makes the offense personal. He is not wise nor is he an efficient officer. *One governs best when he does not seem to govern.*

## PRINCIPLES GOVERNING PUNISHMENT

If the members of the class have developed ability in governing themselves, the problem of what to do when an offense occurs is not so difficult. Personally, as far as the success of a teacher is concerned, what he does when dealing with an offense has far greater possibility of being disastrous than any other single item of a day's work. Ability to govern is always a first requisite of good teaching. Although pupil control and punishment are not the same thing, there is always a relationship between them. School authorities estimate that one-fourth of teacher failures can be traced directly to weakness in the teacher's ability to govern. If what the teacher does to correct the trouble is considered, the statement is probably more exact. Disorder, plus what the teacher does to correct it, is the hidden reef which has sunk many a teaching craft.

It is not the teacher's side of the question alone that tends to make the punishment factor so important. Improper punishments do irreparable harm to pupils. A schoolroom is a social organization. It is not a *training* for society in general, it *is* society in general for citizens of the school age. Improper punishments meted out by a teacher do to a school citizen exactly what an improper sentence meted out by a judge does to the more mature citizen. Punishment teaches little even when carefully chosen and well administered, and improper punishment always confirms rather than corrects the offender. The purposes of punishment in the modern classroom are commonly deterrence and reformation. Rarely indeed is punishment in school concerned with expiation or retribution. This is not saying that expiation is not necessary ever; rather it is to say that expiation must be accompanied by true penitence for the offense if any real good to the offender is to follow.

When it comes to the rules governing punishment in the elementary school and the junior high school, it would seem that the old adage is still a good one: Many rules for the teacher, few for the pupils. This only reflects the thought which should be dominant in a democratic form of government: that the fewer laws placed on the statute books, good government being taken for granted, the better. For the teacher, however, there are a few basic principles and corollaries which should not be forgotten:

1. The aim of punishment is never retribution. "Getting even" has no place in the classroom.

2. Suit the punishment to the offender, not to the offense. This may seem to be playing favorites, but what is light punishment for one child may be overly severe for another, even if the offense is identical. Again, the law always recognizes first offenders as deserving careful treatment.

3. No teacher should ever punish a pupil when either is angry.

4. To allow an offense to become personal indicates a lack of perspective on the part of the teacher.

5. The wise teacher defers punishment for a reasonable time. Offenders often realize the errors of their ways while waiting for the sentence.

6. The severity of the punishment does not necessarily prevent recurrence of the offense.

7. Certainty is a better deterrent than severity.

8. To punish the group for the offense of an individual in that group is not only foolish, it is also unjust. Incidentally, it is the surest way of losing support which would ordinarily go to the teacher, and securing it for the wrongdoer.

9. To avoid punishments which also punish the teacher is but to exercise ordinary common sense.

10. It is imperative that the teacher avoid the mistake of thinking that the student who knows of an offense and does not tell him is as guilty as the offender. Children, like adults, hate to tattle. Again, it is easy to assume that pupils know of an offense when they do not.

11. It is very unwise to have specific punishments (in school) attached to specific offenses. Circumstances alter cases. Again, the teacher represents the judiciary phase of school government as well as the legislative and executive, and must have leeway to exercise judgment.

12. It is much easier to correct the causes of control problems than it is to correct the problems themselves through punishment.

13. For a child old enough to reason, it is imperative that the punishment and the reason for it be understood if any real good is to result.

14. No matter what punishment a teacher metes out, if the child feels no sorrow for his offense and, if he has injured

another, has made no honest expression of his regret to the person, the punishment has done little or no good.

## DISCUSSION PROBLEM

Below are statements presenting varying viewpoints which are more or less pertinent to the question of school punishments. Only a few are directly concerned with the positive side of school control. Some of the statements are *sound* and may be taken as guiding principles; some are *unsound* and are certain to lead to trouble if followed; others *do not apply* directly to the general problem under discussion. Your assignment is to make three columns headed by the italicized words above, and to list by number and the first three or four words (for easy identification) each statement in the correct column. Your problem is to say that the statement is sound or unsound or does not apply. Be prepared to defend your arrangement of the statements.

1. Problems of punishment are merely problems of instruction.
2. The aim of punishment is never retribution.
3. It is easier to prevent discipline troubles than it is to correct them.
4. "Satan finds work for idle hands to do."
5. Teachers govern best when they do not seem to govern.
6. Noisy teachers are found in noisy rooms.
7. Punish similar offenses in the same manner. Justice demands this.
8. Suit the punishment to the crime.
9. Protect the interests of the other children.
10. If corporal punishment is used, it is wise to have an adult witness.
11. Never punish an angry pupil.
12. Punish personal affronts as such.
13. It is sometimes necessary to break the will of a spoiled child.
14. Immediate punishment for an offense is a certain deterrent to further offenses.
15. Good teaching consists mainly in good punishments.
16. Punishment makes an offender see his mistakes and repent of them.

17. Make no hasty decisions; it is often wise to postpone a decision for several days.
18. Avoid punishments that tend to punish you.
19. Corporal punishment is never justified.
20. Severity of punishment tends to prevent offenses.
21. Certainty is a better deterrent than severity.
22. A student knowing of an offense and not telling is as guilty as the offender.
23. Do not punish the group for the offense of an individual in that group.
24. Many states have capital punishment. This is recognition of the fact that severity of punishment is a deterrent.
25. The child makes the social group of which he is a part suffer; therefore it is but just that the child be made to suffer for an offense.
26. It is wise to have definite punishments attached to specific offenses. Thus: truancy—corporal punishment; tardiness —loss of recesses; insolence—a low grade in deportment; low grade in deportment—barred from scholastic honor roll, etc.
27. Make clear what you will do if a certain act is committed. Ignorance of the law is never an excuse.
28. No punishment is just unless it is fully understood.

## STUDY QUESTIONS

1. Be specific in stating the distinction the authors would make between discipline, social control, and self-control.
2. What is the significance of the statement, "The schoolroom is life, not only a preparation for life," in terms of school government?
3. If "true control is self-control," would you say that army discipline is not true control? If not, what is it?
4. Do you agree that self-control is of the highest importance in an individual's development?
5. Can a person display splendid self-control but not be a disciplined person? If you say "yes," illustrate.
6. Do you agree that the more serious offenses come from outside the schoolroom? If you say "yes," what would you call habits of indolence which have a schoolroom origin?

7. When is the statement that "Satan finds work for idle hands to do" not a true statement?

8. Is school morale a composite of the morale of the individual pupils or is it general in nature, so that the room morale can be low when the morale of most of the pupils is high? Discuss.

9. Can you show how a distrustful teacher makes for distrustful pupils? What has this to do with "proper teacher relationships"?

10. Name some permanent values a teacher should seek to develop in his pupils. Is it possible to be developing these when the morale in general is low? When pupils are intentionally disorderly? You are no doubt inclined to say "no." Does this mean "permanent values" are results of keeping everyone busy, good morale, and proper teacher relationships?

11. There are fourteen rules governing punishment listed in the chapter. Select the ten which you believe can be most readily omitted without weakening the whole.

## SELECTED READINGS

ADDICOTT, IRWIN O. *Constructive Classroom Control.* San Francisco: Howard Chandler, Publisher, 1958. This little forty-six page booklet, all devoted to the topic of classroom control, is the single best reference on this topic the authors of this text have found. Suggestions are practical; bibliography well selected.

ALCORN, MARVIN D., HOUSEMAN, RICHARD A., and SCHUNERT, JIM R. *Better Teaching in Secondary Schools.* New York: Holt, Rinehart & Winston, Inc., 1954. Chapter 3, "Improving Teacher-Student Relationships," indicates how good classroom organization, the teacher's attitudes, and physical and social factors influence behavior.

BUTLER, FRANK A. *Improvement of Teaching in Secondary Schools.* 3d ed. Chicago: University of Chicago Press, 1954. Chapters 7 and 15 are recommended reading. Latter deals specifically and clearly with the effect of the physical and social environment on pupil behavior.

CURRAN, CHARLES A. *Counseling in Catholic Life and Education.* New York: The Macmillan Co., 1952. Chapter 10, "Initiating Counseling Dynamics," proposes group techniques for counseling purposes. Much of this chapter has some relationship to the prevention of disciplinary problems.

CUTTS, NORMA E., and MOSELEY, NICHOLAS. *Teaching the Disorderly Pupil in Elementary and Secondary Schools*. New York: Longmans, Green & Co., Inc., 1958. A practical discussion of the general problem of schoolroom control in terms of the learning situation.

HAND, HAROLD C. *Principles of Public Secondary Education*. New York: Harcourt, Brace & Co., 1958. Chapter 7, "Establishing and Maintaining Good Discipline," develops idea that no class is under effective control unless the pupils in it have developed good work habits. Relates discipline to punishments in a clear way.

HARRISON, RAYMOND H., and GOWIN, LAWRENCE E. *The Elementary Teacher in Action*. San Francisco: Wadsworth Publishing Co., Inc., 1958. Chapter 8, which deals with classroom management and pupil control, emphasizes that "ideal control is the absence of control." Augments the theory set forth in Chapter 6 of your text, that true discipline is self-discipline.

LINDGREN, HENRY CLAY. *Educational Psychology in the Classroom*. New York: John Wiley & Sons, Inc., 1956. Chapter 12, "Discipline and the Learning Situation," treats the discipline problem from the slant of the educational psychologist. A discussion of group-imposed discipline indicates the tremendous force social control exercises on the behavior of the individual in the group.

OLIVA, PETER F. *High School Discipline in American Society*. Washington, D. C.: Bulletin of the National Association of Secondary School Principals, 40: No. 5–6, January, 1956. Among other directly pertinent items, presents many different definitions of education.

WILLIAMSON, E. G., and FOLEY, J. D. *Counseling and Discipline*. New York: McGraw-Hill Book Co., Inc., 1949. Part of this text is developed around the idea that school discipline is much affected by the environment and that discipline is very much a part of the modern student-personnel movement. Chapter 7, "Disciplinary Actions," is soundly written.

WRIGHTSTONE, J. WAYNE. *Class Organization for Instruction*. Washington, D. C.: Department of Classroom Teacher, American Educational Research Association of the National Education Association, 1957. This little booklet (33 pages), No. 13 in the series, "What Research Says to the Teacher," is worth reading for the student who is interested in classroom organization as a means of reducing in-class friction.

# 7

# THE TEACHER'S PART IN GUIDANCE

The establishment of guidance services has been a relatively recent development in the schools. Nevertheless, the good school has always made informal guidance services available to pupils, and the effective teacher has always provided both instruction and guidance to members of his classes. As a dynamic classroom teacher in a modern school, a teacher will wish to guide his pupils to the extent of his abilities and to direct them to further services of guidance specialists in the school and the community.

## RELATIONSHIP BETWEEN TEACHING AND GUIDANCE

Much confusion exists about the relationship between teaching and guidance. Some are of the opinion that the terms are identical. Certainly the teacher, directly or indirectly, is always giving guidance through word and deed. Teaching of the finest quality will have definite guidance values. Excellent guidance will make use of the learning situation, as does teaching. Others are of the opinion that guidance is a service offered by specialists and that teachers should not intrude in this area. This is an extremely narrow interpretation of guidance. Guidance is far more than a group of specialized services for people with problems.

In the American school pattern, teaching is a service intended for the benefit of members of a group, who are assumed to be alike in many respects. Although instruction is often individualized, the progress of the entire group is the teacher's main concern. Frequently it may be necessary for him to protect the welfare of the group to the detriment of an individual in the class. The more homogeneous the group, the less frequently will this circumstance arise. That this is a common problem is seen easily from a glance at the educational literature. Much has been written about what should be done for the gifted pupil, for the retarded pupil, for the slow learner, and for others who differ appreciably from the average individuals in the class. Teachers pitch their instruction at a certain level and are disturbed about those who vary too far from it. There is need for teachers to be concerned about this, because education in the last analysis takes place within an individual, but the teaching situation is a group situation.

On the other hand, guidance is addressed to the individual. At any moment the guidance counselor is occupied with a person who has a specific problem and needs help to cope with it successfully. Even when guidance services are offered on a group basis, for economy or some other valid reason, the intent is still to assist each individual as an individual.

Both teaching and guidance are intended for the development of the pupil. The emphasis in teaching is upon intellectual development, although physical, emotional, moral, and social aspects may not be disregarded. On the contrary, the dynamic classroom is one in which the teaching-learning process involves all phases of each pupil's development. The intellectual achievement in the dynamic classroom exceeds the result in a classroom where the teaching function is conceived as imparting information and the learning function as committing this information to memory. Nevertheless, the emphasis in the teaching of school subjects must be upon intellectual development of pupils. The emphasis in guidance is upon personal-social adjustment. Obviously the intellectual life of the individual being guided must always receive consideration, because a person whose intellectual talents are either unchallenged or overburdened cannot be considered well adjusted to himself or to society.

## PUPILS' NEED FOR GUIDANCE

An organized guidance program scarcely needs to be defended. The child is in school to be helped. He should be assisted in overcoming obstacles which interfere with the development of his potentialities. These obstacles can be traced to many sources. Urbanization and population shifts have created problems for young people. Mechanization and job diversity have puzzled pupils who have begun to think about their careers. Family instability, the result of divorce and war, has left its mark on many children. Increased dependence of youth, prolonged attendance at school, increased leisure time, expanded leisure activities—all these have had a profound effect on young people in the United States.

Although guidance is needed continuously for pupils, the need is more readily observed at particular stages in the educational process. When a child enters school for the first time he needs guidance. He finds himself in a strange place with strange people. He is confronted with a routine which he is required to follow, in sharp contrast to the free-and-easy existence he has enjoyed previously He does not receive the attention he has probably been accustomed to in an indulgent home. He needs more than instruction from the teacher who introduces him to his new life; he needs guidance. When he later enters junior high school and senior high school or when he transfers to a different school, his need for guidance will increase. When a shrub is dug up and replanted elsewhere, the gardener must take special care so that the plant will flourish. Likewise, the pupil transferred from one school environment to another must be given careful guidance so that his orderly process of education is not disturbed.

Occasionally the pupil must make key decisions that will seriously affect his life. When he chooses a high school curriculum, he commits himself to a program from which he can extricate himself only with difficulty and some loss. Hence the school must provide effective guidance so that the pupil makes a wise selection. Later he may narrow his program by choosing electives, thus restricting his educational and vocational objectives. Here again the school should provide guidance so that the pupil avoids mistakes.

## TEACHERS' BASIC GUIDANCE SERVICES

Knowledge of the learning process has increased; psychology and sociology have discovered much about changes in human behavior. The testing movement has yielded data which can be of tremendous assistance in guiding young people. Teachers have access to information about the intelligence, achievement, personality, attitudes, interests, and aptitudes of the young people they are teaching. This information can be invaluable for guidance purposes. The teacher should understand not only what guidance services are available to pupils now but also what guidance services have been available in previous years and what will be available in the future.

**Elementary School Guidance Services.** The classroom teacher bears the burden of guidance at the elementary level. Teaching and guidance are most closely allied at this end of the educational ladder. The teacher is in the best position to make the young child's adjustment to school a satisfying experience. The dynamic teacher will make use of the many chances to assist pupils through personal, social, health, and ethical guidance.

Many of the guidance services rendered to the elementary school pupil are often not thought of as guidance services. The teacher tends to think of them as part of the teaching experience. A teacher should be aware of the guidance implications in various teaching activities. Specifically, the elementary teacher gives guidance services such as the following:

1. Welcomes the new pupil to the school and tries to make him feel that he belongs to the class group. This is important whether the pupil is entering school for the first time or transferring from another institution.

2. Helps the pupil to accept the restrictions on his actions imposed by the nature of school organization. These may be quite distressing to the pupil when he first enters school. His movements are regimented by the school bell and the classroom desk. He is subject to adult authority which may be quite different from parental supervision. As he progresses through school the pupil faces additional restrictions. The school day may become longer, homework becomes a requirement, and longer continuous attention to a topic is demanded.

3. Organizes the classwork so that pupils are motivated to work hard but are not overstimulated.

4. Studies each child so that he can treat each as an individual developing along some distinctive pattern of growth.

5. Helps each pupil to find success in achievement. Every person, child as well as adult, needs to feel the satisfaction which stems from accomplishment of some task.

6. Provides the affection and security that are necessary if the pupil is to devote his attention to the business of learning. This can be done successfully only if pupils are encouraged to like, respect, and help each other.

7. Accepts the pupil as an individual entitled to a measure of respect and understanding. It is often a difficult thing for the teacher to accept a pupil whose cultural background is far different from the teacher's. If the teacher attempts sincerely to understand the pupil, he is likely to develop respect for the child as a person, though perhaps still rejecting the deficiencies in his background.

8. Provides assistance to the pupil in understanding himself. Increasingly, the child should learn to know his capabilities, his limitations, his values, and his attitudes. It is important that the teacher encourage self-acceptance as the pupil's knowledge of himself develops.

9. Inspires pupils to accept responsibility for classroom ac-

tivities. Each pupil must learn that his participation contributes to the welfare of the class. He must learn to take his share of responsibility willingly.

10. Assists the pupil to develop independence. The development of independence is a very gradual procedure. The pupil learns to make decisions, to act without direction from others, and to assume responsibility for his actions. The teacher should operate his classroom so that the development of independence is stimulated.

The elementary school teacher spends several hours a day with a group of pupils. He is very important to these children, who cannot help but be influenced by his words and actions. These children will learn from him far more than is outlined in any curriculum bulletin. Hence the teacher should give thought to the guidance responsibilities inherent in his task. He is in a position to observe and recognize symptoms of maladjustment before the problem reaches serious proportions. As he sees pupils in the classroom, in the halls, in the cafeteria, on the playground, in the library, he can come to know them far better than any other adult, with the exception of parents. Certainly no principal or guidance specialist can reasonably be expected to observe pupil behavior so completely as the teacher. It follows that the teacher should report any significant behavior *in writing,* so that all important data will be included in the pupil's record.

Usually the principal coordinates guidance activities in the elementary school, although this responsibility is sometimes delegated. In most school systems it is possible to obtain the services of specialists for children who have some particular need. The school nurse, doctor, visiting teacher, and attendance officer may serve the guidance program. A psychologist may advise teachers on tests, make case studies, and suggest programs for talented pupils. A psychiatrist may be available for pupils handicapped by serious emotional problems with which the ordinary school personnel cannot cope. The teacher can be of great help to guidance specialists as they assist children with problems.

**Secondary School Guidance Services.** Much of what has been written about the elementary school teacher's role in guidance services applies also to the secondary school teacher. However, there are significant differences in the guidance programs of the elementary and secondary schools. While the pupil is in elementary school he spends most of his school day with a single teacher, who comes to know him very well and is excellently situated to guide him. The secondary school pupil normally meets several teachers during the day. He must adjust to several teachers. Similarly, each secondary school teacher must deal with a greater number of pupils each day, which places a considerable burden upon him if he is to know each pupil well.

Departmentalism at the secondary school level has been considered necessary, since the fields of knowledge must be explored at a depth which requires specialized knowledge. Yet this departmentalism has given rise to problems which have troubled educators for many years. It is relatively easy for a secondary school teacher to center his class activities around his subject rather than around his students. It is rather natural for a teacher to do so if he does not know his students well and cannot estimate accurately their potentialities, their needs, and their aspirations. Adequate, accessible records can help teachers to learn about their students more quickly.

Today almost every secondary school has an organized guidance program. Various patterns may be found. Frequently one individual who has had special preparation is designated as the guidance counselor. He devotes all his time to guidance. If the school is large, there may be several full-time counselors. Another pattern assigns responsibility for the coordination of the program to one specially prepared individual, who is assisted by teachers released from classroom duties for one or two periods a day to counsel students. In some secondary schools the principal may coordinate the guidance program, and teachers are expected to accomplish guidance duties as part of the school routine.

In some schools the homeroom is strictly an administrative period to facilitate the taking of attendance, the reading of notices, and the handling of similar details of school life. In other schools the homeroom serves guidance purposes. A classroom teacher may find himself assigned a homeroom and expected to guide and counsel a group of students. The effectiveness of the homeroom for guidance purposes will depend on several factors, notably the time allotted for preparation of the guidance activities, the acceptance of the program by both teachers and pupils, and the coordination of the program.

Recently some secondary schools have organized their activities into a core program. The teachers of core are responsible for those activities that are considered necessary and desirable for all pupils in the school, no matter what their educational and vocational goals. Guidance under this arrangement becomes a responsibility primarily of the teacher of core.

Other forms of group guidance are found in secondary schools. Various courses have been initiated in schools to help students in such areas as study habits, self-understanding, educational and vocational planning, human relationships, mental and physical health, and adolescent problems. The variety of such courses and the frequency with which they appear testify to the fact that many needs of students are not being met adequately and that no school is certain that it knows how to deal satisfactorily with these needs.

A classroom teacher in a secondary school can contribute much to the guidance of young people. First and foremost, by effective teaching he can do a great deal to help young people adjust well to the school situation. No guidance program will be very effective in a school so long as the pupils resist classroom instruction because it is poorly planned, weakly motivated, or badly presented. Therefore, a secondary school teacher makes a real contribution to the guidance program when he teaches his subject—and his pupils—well.

Specifically a secondary school classroom teacher gives guidance services such as the following:

1. Helps the pupil to adjust to the departmentalized school program, which differs greatly from the elementary school program. This is particularly important in the junior high school.

2. Provides educational guidance by advising pupils on the selection of elective courses in accordance with their aptitudes and interests.

3. Supplies vocational guidance by calling attention to the vocational implications of whatever subject he is teaching. He may, under certain conditions, teach a unit on occupational information as part of his regular class schedule.

4. Helps the pupil to know himself. The teacher may do this by private discussion of behavior or interest, by interpretation of test scores, and by other means. The adolescent is in a stage of development when he is vastly uncertain about himself. An adult who is interested in him and yet can maintain an objective viewpoint can be most helpful to him.

5. Observes pupil interests, aptitudes, and attitudes which may be of great importance. Such data should be referred to the guidance counselor and placed in the cumulative record.

6. Encourages pupils to engage in a variety of extracurricular activities. Such activities not only help with the social adjustment of pupils but also afford opportunities for occupational exploration.

7. Cooperates in the development of the guidance program. He informs the guidance counselor of the non-instructional problems of pupils. He often assists in the devising of questionnaires and the selecting of standardized tests. He sometimes assumes certain counseling responsibilities for pupils.

The relationship of the classroom teacher to the guidance counselor is implicit in the discussion above. The classroom teacher and the guidance counselor are members of a team with one purpose—the welfare of the pupils. A secondary school teacher must recognize that his responsibility extends beyond the covers of the textbook. He must be interested in the rounded development of his pupils, not merely in their intellectual achievement. All areas of pupil growth—physical, emotional, social, intellectual, and moral—must be his concern.

**Training for Basic Guidance Services.** All teachers need formal training in guidance techniques. This does not mean specialized training of an advanced nature. It does mean some well-defined understandings of the everyday problems of school children. This is not to imply that such training will substitute for other general training or that there is any substitute for a thoughtful, considerate, understanding teacher. Guidance training is supplemental always.

The next to last sentence above only emphasizes the importance of the teacher's personality in all personal relationships with children, and guidance is always a personal relationship, never an impersonal one. However, sympathy is not enough. No doctor can cure his patients with sympathy only. Neither can a teacher do anything much toward correcting a physical, mental, or academic illness by the simple technique of being sorry for the child. First he must apply his technical training toward learning to understand the child. Then he must attempt to correct the difficulty through painstaking, consistent, daily effort.

Identifying problems of behavior requires training and understanding. Problems are to some extent geared to age groups. A type of behavior pattern may be quite common to one age group, rare in another. Failure to interpret behavior properly can be as injurious as the doctor's failure to diagnose illness accurately. Because of the importance of knowing each child's behavior pattern intimately, it is imperative that records be kept. These should contain not only information of the general type but also individual data concerning each child.

Under ordinary circumstances, the teacher proceeds always on a preventive line of approach. He tries to promote good school morale, keeps everyone busy, and looks for permanent values. He does not make the mistake of assuming that every deviation from the normal is something extraordinary. Temporary deviations are the rule, not the exception.

It is in the exceptional cases that the teacher should call in the expert. These are cases where the child's behavior pattern is decidedly abnormal and is of such a nature that the pattern remains unchanged in spite of a teacher's best efforts. The shy child who is becoming more and more a cry-baby; the resentful child who is showing his resentment in unsocial acts; the bullying, cruel boy who is daily becoming more feared and disliked—these are patterns of behavior which warrant consultation with the best mental hygienist or trained guidance expert available. Before asking for help, a teacher should be sure he has an extraordinary case. Then he should compile as many data as possible on the child's history and avoid coloring the data with personal reactions. A teacher must know specifically why he has asked for help. This is where adequate records are useful.

## FORMAL AND INFORMAL RECORDS AND PROCEDURES

The value of records is in proportion to their use. A classroom teacher should acquaint himself with the records maintained in his school, use them for the benefit of his pupils, and add to them all useful information that he gathers during the school year.

**Cumulative Record.** Most school systems have adopted a cumulative record which accompanies the pupil as he moves through elementary and secondary school. The content and form of the cumulative record vary considerably. Usually the following information is recorded: personal and family data, scholarship, scores on standardized tests, health, school attendance, school activities, and out-of-school experiences. These data may be entered upon a large card filed alphabetically in the school office. Frequently they are entered on a folder, within which may be deposited interview notes, correspondence, and other items of less permanent value than data entered on the folder.

The teacher adds to the cumulative record in many ways. He assists in the collection of information about the personal and family background of the student. He participates in the administration of standardized tests of intelligence and achievement. He contributes in a unique manner by reporting in writing on such things as classroom behavior, creative work of the pupil, conferences with parents, and results of sociograms. The teacher should remember that the more is known about a child the more possible it is to give him effective guidance. A notation made in a child's cumulative record during his early years in elementary school may prove useful ten years later when the child, now an adolescent, is being counseled just prior to leaving senior high school.

The cumulative record must always include all items that are indicators of special aptitudes, interests, or abilities a child may have. The teacher has the opportunity of observing him most intimately. For a teacher to fail to record the indicators of the child's potential interests and abilities is to neglect an important part of a teacher's work. These indicators in the elementary school child often point the way to a potential vocation for him later. There is no greater waste in the country today than the waste in manpower miscast into work which does not fit the individual's abilities, interests, and special aptitudes.

Does a child show mechanical aptitude? Is his work exceptionally neat? Does he like to draw, paint, construct things? Has he unusual musical interest—or no musical interest? The number of children spending futile hours at the piano to satisfy parental ambitions, not because the children have interest or aptitude for music, is appalling. Again, there is a probability that many a Toscanini goes unknown and unheralded because a teacher failed to record the child's exceptional artistic and musical interest. Does a child love to read? Does he express himself either orally or in writing unusually well for a child of his age? Is he a leader? Do other children tend to follow his leadership when he is put in charge? All of these and other indicators must be made a part of the cumulative record as well as of individual records of a more transitory nature.

**Anecdotal Record.** This record is probably more necessary for the child in the elementary and junior high school than are others which seem more specific in nature. This record deals with *incidents of behavior* particularly. It frequently offers a clue as to why a bright child does poor school work; why a child dislikes school; why a child is suspicious, fearful, resentful, or unsocial. The types of recordings found in an anecdotal record include: those dealing with what a child did or said in a situation which was troublesome; those that evaluate what or why a child's behavior is what it is; those that explain a child's behavior to some extent; and finally those that tell in a general way how or when or why a child reacted as he did. This record keeps those interesting, humorous, typical-of-the-child happenings, always with the view to interpreting and understanding the child better. Keeping the anecdotal record is time-consuming, but, once started, it is usually interesting and enjoyable work.

**Case Study.** The case study records a teacher's specific problem situations. The case study exists for the purpose of helping the child to understand himself better, that he may correct his scholarship, personality, or other deficiencies. It is especially good in that it takes an objective rather than a subjective approach; it is comprehensive rather than limited in scope; it offers a good background for counseling; and finally it brings together many facts about an individual, facts which in isolation mean little, but which assembled mean much.

In making such studies a multitude of little things are considered. Many of these in isolation have little significance, but when synthetized they can explain an abnormal behavior pattern as can no other single technique. Among items which should be included in a case study for an elementary or junior high school child are: his place (position) in the family; his childhood diseases; his likes and dislikes in foods, clothing, and the other everyday things; his out-of-school activities (undirected); moving pictures he attends; the radio and television programs he enjoys; the comics he reads; who his playmates are; and his attitudes toward God, toward church attendance, and toward wrong and right (in his own mind). Put together, these items explain a child's behavior more accurately and exactly than any other technique a teacher can use.

**Informal Procedures.** In the field of informal procedures a teacher gains many of his clearest understandings of his pupils. In this list such an important item as what a child does in his undirected moments both at play and in the classroom appears. The pictures he especially enjoys are noted. What he does in the so-called free-work or creative period of the day is never considered of little importance. In the school plays, the teacher notes his special interests, capabilities, likes, and dislikes. How does he finish a story which the teacher has left unfinished? What is his answer to questions such as "Who is the best man you ever knew?" "What is the best book you ever read?" "The best moving picture you ever saw?" "The most fun you ever had?" "The easiest subject in school?" "The hardest?" "The worst boy you have ever known?" "The nicest house you were ever in?" The response to *superlatives,* although an informal procedure, is more than an average indicator of a child's interest, feeling, and behavior pattern.

Informally the teacher can through discussions and conversations note a child's reactions. Especially valuable for those children whose behavior pattern varies greatly from the norm, the *free discussion* is often an excellent source of indicators of why a child is guileless or suspicious, resentful or forgiving, cruel or kindly, overbearing or humble, self-complacent or self-effacing, self-centered or unselfish. From the child who is no problem in any way the teacher secures a basis of comparison by which the extent of variation from the norm can be judged for the child who needs help. Another informal procedure which throws light on a child's interests, thinking patterns, and even general behavior is the writing of autobiographies. Children usually love to do this. That these can be factual up to the present and imaginary from the present on allows for a child's projection of his daydreams that may have vocational implications as well as indications of mental ill-health.

## TEACHERS' WORK WITH PARENTS

An elementary or secondary school teacher is constantly placed in a cooperative, coordinating position as far as pupils and their parents are concerned. Since teaching and guidance are inseparable in practice, a teacher works with parents with two purposes in mind: the improvement of the child's scholastic work and the formation of patterns of conduct which will make the child fit well into his group. Poor scholastic work and bad behavior patterns are frequently found in the same child, but this situation does not necessarily obtain. A child may be scholastically good and poorly adjusted or, occasionally, well adjusted and scholastically deficient.

To gain the greatest understanding with parents, five practices are common:

1. A conference or conferences with the parents
2. Parent-teacher meetings for small groups at the same time
3. Parents' visits to the school for observation of their child at work
4. Teachers' informal visits to the homes for observation of the child in his home
5. Reports to parents

**Parent Conference.** Any conference with parents is worthless or nearly so if it has no definite purpose. If parents are worried, they need to state their worry. If the teacher sees a difficulty, the teacher should present it to the parents. Every conference is specifically centered around the parent's child; never is it centered around children in general or around other children in the room.

In the conference the teacher learns things which he or she needs to know and does not know. To illustrate: How does Bob spend his time between school dismissal and dinnertime? What homework does he do? What books does Lucille read at home? What comics are Harriet's favorites? Does Frances do the dishes? Any other homework? At what time does Bob go to bed? Does he obey promptly? Who are his playmates? What does he do when left on his own? Questions of this sort are the basis for a better understanding of the child. A teacher, from such a conference, can determine (even if he does not make it known) a parent's part in a child's failure to do successful school work or to fit well into the general pattern of school life.

**Parent-Teacher Meeting.** The parent-teacher meeting should be a child-study meeting. Usually, it is a small meeting and, while no parent is unwelcome, not all parents are really needed. Usually, those who should come do not, and an extra effort will be needed to get them out.

A child hygienist who is not academic is a welcome adjunct to a parent-teacher meeting. He does not, however, give an address. He discusses with parents such problems as home discipline, punishments, reading readiness, home responsibilities, children's associates, and visual (television) and listening (radio) habits.

The parent-teacher meeting is almost worthless unless the leadership is excellent. Individual children are never discussed, of course, although the discussions are always kept relevant to the community life, the children in general, and common problems for all.

**Parent Visit.** Parents altogether too rarely visit the school in which their children live so much of their lives. The fault lies with both parents and the school. Commonly, parents feel they are neither needed nor wanted, and the school feels the parents are uninterested. Probably neither is true. The school errs in not specifically inviting parents to visit their children at work—and in not doing it frequently enough to get results. Haphazard visiting probably does some good but not nearly so much for the general good of the child as the planned visit. At the parent conference, the teacher can suggest what the parent should look for when visiting his child. Items worth suggesting include: what the child is doing, with whom he talks, what questions he asks, his responses to questions, his reaction to reading, his part in playground activities, and his interest in special subjects such as music and art.

The visitor will mark the teacher's techniques, the plans used for group work, discussion work, and the part the child takes in all activities. Following the visit it is always best to have a discussion or conference with the visitor so that erroneous impressions (if any) may be corrected and significant items re-emphasized. Again, no parent should be allowed to go home with an unanswered question in her or his mind.

**Teacher Visit.** It used to be a common occurrence for teachers to visit the homes of their pupils, often as a dinner guest. This custom is still frequently found in some smaller communities. There is considerable merit in home visitation. Both the parents and the teacher deepen their understanding of the child as they discuss his problems, his achievements, and his capabilities. The teacher has a chance to observe character traits and behavior patterns which may not be so apparent in the classroom situation. Finally, a bond between the teacher and the home is likely to grow from mutual interest in the pupil's progress.

**Report Card.** The traditional report card to parents has always been a liaison between teachers and parents—and, sad to say, it has never been a very good one. Too frequently it has been used as a motivating agency for improved classwork. In this it has commonly failed, as two teachers may grade entirely differently. One tries to note the child's individual growth, while another may compare him with the class. Again, the traditional card commonly carries a deport-ment, citizenship, or conduct grade. Parents are confused when a deportment grade is *F* for "fair" and scholastic marks are *E* for "excellent." The confusion is not lessened when the academic-conduct situation is reversed, and a child is marked *Excellent* in conduct and *Poor* in his scholarship. In either case something is obviously wrong.

The tendency today is to get the child's progress record to parents in some other way than through the traditional report card. Letter-form cards help much. Conferences are better. The latter is probably the only method of reporting that is both valid and reliable.

## DISCUSSION PROBLEM

### SCHOOL AND SOCIETY

"You go to hell!" The speaker is five-year-old Johnny Good-man. Johnny's teeth snap together and his little jaws clench in utter defiance as he lays down his ultimatum to you, his teacher. "I bought it, an' it's mine."

Johnny has been in school three days—two and a half to be exact. The first day he pulled the hair of blue-eyed, cherubic, golden-curled Anita Barber until she howled in sheer misery. He deliberately doused Harold Blue with the murky, dirty water into which he had been dipping his water-color brushes, and when you remonstrated with him, he stuck out his tongue at you. His second day found him arrogantly destroying the cooperative playhouse which was the joint effort of four happy youngsters. His latest outbreak, quoted in the opening words of the problem, had been occasioned by your telling him, upon seeing him mar-ring with a knife the little table at which he was seated, to bring the knife to you.

You had been warned prior to Johnny's starting school that he was a little terror. Spoiled, pampered, mishandled, improper home conditions, his father encourages him in his meanness, parents think it's cute—all these remarks and many others had come to your ears about the neighborhood's little bad boy before he was even of kindergarten age.

He is one of your pupils, and you won't admit that a five-year-old youngster is too big a problem for you. The lad is bright. He is attractive-looking. He is high-spirited, independent, and if properly guided may make a fine man. As he is now, he is a little outlaw who is doing much to disturb your happy social group. Basically, he is a guidance problem.

## Questions on the Problem

1. Select the tests you may find useful, if any, to begin your work with Johnny.

2. You are limited in your testing program because of Johnny's youth. What formal procedures can be used with a five-year-old?

3. What type of individual case history will you seek to build up on Johnny? Be specific in listing the items you will try to secure for this history.

4. Would an anecdotal record for Johnny throw any light on his conduct that you do not now have?

5. You are prone to jump to the conclusion that the boy's home training has caused the maladjustment which is evident. What evidence do you have of this? Is this evidence or hearsay?

6. You resisted the impulse to box Johnny's ears when he kicked over the playhouse during his second day in school. Is a good sound thrashing what he needs most?

7. Johnny, at this time, has no respect for law and order and no respect for authority. Will most of his social maladjustment be corrected when he gains this respect, or is this oversimplifying the case?

8. You are going to have a conference with Johnny's parents. Will you be satisfied if only Mrs. Goodman shows up? Why? Why not?

9. At this conference, what are the questions you are going to bring up with the Goodmans? List these in the order you will use.

10. If, after you have used every means at your command, Johnny is still a destructive element in your room, what will you do?

11. Do you believe it is possible to change this youngster's attitude without inflicting pain upon him, either physical or mental?

12. The case presented is a most unusual one and is offered because it makes an easy point of departure in clarifying the

theory expressed in the chapter. Can you fit every major item of the chapter to the situation?

## STUDY QUESTIONS

1. What are the essential differences between the guidance program of the elementary school and that of the secondary school?

2. "Good teachers are guidance-minded teachers." Is this statement always true? What distinction would you make between the good teacher who is not guidance-trained and for the equally good classroom worker who has had such training?

3. Why is the vocational aspect of guidance stressed so little for the elementary school child? How can a secondary school teacher increase his ability to help pupils with their problems of vocational choice?

4. How do you account for the fact that high school pupils are so poorly informed on questions dealing with future occupational opportunities?

5. What are some of the reasons why a school should have an organized plan for presenting occupational information to secondary school pupils?

6. Why are guidance workers disinclined to place children in type categories?

7. Would you agree that a school's guidance program should be broad enough to include the educational and recreational opportunities in the community? Would you include both? Defend your position.

8. What are some of the limitations and dangers in using tests for guidance purposes?

9. Do you think teachers' marks should be used in guidance? If marks are to be used, what recommendations would you make to the ones using them?

10. From the guidance point of view, work out a program which a school could use to improve the reliability of teachers' marks. Be prepared to explain your suggestions to the class.

11. "Any conference with parents is worthless or nearly so if it has no definite purpose." Can you suggest some purposes which a conference might serve when a pupil's academic standing is the immediate issue?

## SELECTED READINGS

BARR, JOHN A. *The Elementary Teacher and Guidance.* New York: Holt, Rinehart & Winston, Inc., 1958. Chapters 6 through 10 suggest ways in which the elementary school teacher can learn more about pupils for guidance purposes.

ERICKSON, CLIFFORD E. *A Practical Handbook for School Counselors.* New York: The Ronald Press, Co., 1949. The question-and-answer approach of this text should prove useful to the teacher seeking specific information about guidance.

JOHNSON, EDGAR G., PETERS, MILDRED, and EVRAIFF, WILLIAM. *The Role of the Teacher in Guidance.* Englewood Cliffs, N. J.: Prentice-Hall, Inc., 1959. This volume is intended specifically for the classroom teacher who wishes to perform his guidance functions more capably.

McDANIEL, HENRY B., and SHAFTEL, G. A. *Guidance in the Modern School.* New York: Holt, Rinehart & Winston, Inc., 1956. A broad overview of guidance is presented, useful for both the classroom teacher and the school guidance counselor.

MORTENSEN, DONALD G., and SCHMULLER, ALLEN M. *Guidance in Today's Schools.* New York: John Wiley & Sons, Inc., 1959. Chapters 6 and 7, dealing with techniques for understanding the individual, should be particularly helpful for the teacher inexperienced in guidance.

OHLSEN, MERLE M. *Guidance, An Introduction.* New York: Harcourt, Brace & Co., 1955. Chapters 2 and 3 should be particularly valuable to the classroom teacher who aims to relate guidance more closely to his teaching.

PETERS, HERMAN J., and FARWELL, GAIL F. *Guidance: A Developmental Approach.* Chicago: Rand McNally & Co., 1959. As the title suggests, the volume considers guidance from a developmental viewpoint; the role of the classroom teacher receives considerable emphasis.

SAALFELD, LAWRENCE J. *Guidance and Counseling for Catholic Schools.* Chicago: Loyola University Press, 1958. This book presents a thought-provoking and somewhat different attitude toward problems common to all boys and girls.

SMITH, GLENN E. *Principles and Practices of the Guidance Program.* New York: The Macmillan Co., 1951. This book is intended as an introduction to the over-all guidance program.

STOOPS, EMERY, and WAHLQUIST, GUNNAR L. *Principles and Practices in Guidance.* New York: McGraw-Hill Book Co., Inc., 1958. Chapters 2 and 3 contain many practical suggestions for acquiring information about the pupil.

# 8

# MOTIVATION OF CLASSROOM WORK

"It is foolish to take to hunt dogs that don't want to go," wrote Plautus many years ago. In good American idiom the statement might be translated, "You can lead a horse to water but you cannot make him drink." Both statements can be applied to the child's learning situation. If a teacher wishes a child to act effectively (and learning is always an activity) the child must always desire to act, to learn.

A teacher who has been teaching for any length of time has probably said more than once, "It is not what my pupils do which gives me the most trouble; it is what they don't do." This statement reveals one of the most significant problems which confront all who are in a teaching situation, whether in the home or in school. This is the problem of getting some children to care whether they close the door or not, whether they attend school or not, whether they prepare an assignment or not, whether they are successful or not. This is not to say that all or even many pupils are indifferent, but when a child is indifferent (and a child can be entirely a normal child and still be indifferent), the teacher finds teaching him a most difficult task.

No normal child is ever indifferent to everything. Such a child would be a sick child. A normal child may be entirely indifferent to the multiplication tables, to common fractions, or to the correct construction of a complex sentence, but intensely interested in learning to swim. If the teacher will remember that a child learns only when he has a reason for learning, or that he acts only when he has a reason for acting (illogical though the reason may be), the teacher is on the way to solving the problem. It becomes a question of finding what, to a child, seems to be a satisfactory reason. The teacher must consider the child's interests, motivation, and incentives.

Interest, as applied to the learning situation, is a word that everyone uses. "He has an interest in any kind of mechanical thing"; "Bob is right now much interested in collecting butterflies"; "Marie's only interest is boys"; "Steve shows much interest in his aquarium"; "Frank is interested in learning to box." But although interest is commonly used, to define it gets one into some of the complexities of educational psychology.

Technically, interest may be defined as a "subjective-objective attitude, concern, or condition involving an idea in attention, and a combination of intellectual-feeling consciousness." Breaking down the definition, it is seen that (a) interest is both a subjective and an objective attitude, concern, or condition; (b) interest involves attention to an idea or a percept; (c) interest tends to be partly intellectual in nature, partly emotional. From the definition it is obvious that interests may change from time to time or may endure for years. It would seem that an interest is something which comes from within, that is, it indicates some tendency within the individual, either inherited or acquired. If the interest is in the child, the thing which causes the interest must be closely allied to it. What causes the interest is spoken of as motivation.

To define motivation we must first define incentives, another word with much teaching significance. Simply put, an incentive is an influencing factor. Motivation is the utilization of incentives for the purpose of causing a pupil to act in a way which the teacher desires. In practice, the teacher selects and presents study materials which appeal to the child's interests so that the child will attack the work with enthusiasm and with readiness. In practice incentives tend to be external, although technically an incentive may be either intrinsic or extrinsic. In this chapter the word "incentive" is used to refer to external (extrinsic) motivation. The word "motivation" always implies behavior. Often we think of motives as long-range or persistent. To illustrate, "His motive in making the deal was to help his family; the result proved to be bad." "His motive was to make a quick fortune; the result was to lose his home." Both statements indicate an action or movement of some duration. Both indicate that the action is goal-seeking or goal-oriented. To be goal-oriented is a general characteristic of motives.

From the teaching viewpoint the problem is commonly not one of establishing new motives in the child. In general his motives have already been developed from his cultural background or possibly from his inherent development. The teaching problem is to influence his interests (his attitudes, concerns, conditions) to the extent that actions lead to desirable ends, to better things, and to more desirable meanings for his ideas. To illustrate, the motive to make a fortune may be more or less a development from a child's home life; the purposes, the ideas or ideals for which a fortune is desired are the result of education.

All formal learning is motivated. There may be unmotivated learning (incidental) but if there were much of this, schools would be unnecessary. Motivation tends to be the dynamic phase of all school processes.

The foregoing pages have dealt with motivation from the technical viewpoint. This discussion may seem to be unnecessary. It should, however, be remembered that no teacher is professionally well trained who neither knows nor cares about the psychological aspects of learning. Interests, motivation, and incentives are at the heart of all learning.

*Practical Aspects of Motivation.* Were one to put aside the psychological aspects of motivation and consider only the everyday, practical ways of inducing action into desirable patterns he would ask first, "What are the forces acting on the child which influence his motivation?" The list, of course, is large. Included in it would be:

1. Interest of the teacher in the child as an individual.
2. Interest of the teacher in his subject.
3. Vitality, enthusiasm, drive, energy of the teacher.
4. Desire of the child to be one of the group, to be accepted by his peers.
5. Desire of the child to identify. A child identifies himself with his favorite athlete, his father, a teacher.
6. Indirect influence of folkways, mores, and customs.
7. Influence of the values taught in the home. A child's values are largely home-determined and his values influence, in turn, his motivation.
8. Influence of the radio, television, professional athletics, urbanization, newspapers, magazines, record players, comic books, power machinery, the automobile, and other numerous factors which are a part of a child's environment.

Motivation implies positive attitudes, never negative ones. This is something teachers are prone to forget. "Because you haven't studied you'll get a test tomorrow." "Failure to turn in written work means a double assignment for the next day." "Bert hasn't studied, so we'll let him miss his recess and study." "No baseball game today because you flunked the last test." All such statements defeat good motivation. To some extent each of these statements puts a brake on any mental readiness the pupil may have had. Antipathy to learning cannot make a child want to learn, and negative approaches lead to antipathy. A pupil needs no motivation *not* to do something.

If student needs are clearly recognized by the teacher, if the needs are made clear to the class, if there is enthusiasm on the teacher's part, and if there is a clear goal in sight, motivation is positive and leads to desirable activity.

The problem of motivating students is difficult. What motivates Mary Louise has little effect upon Betty. A first-grader reacts quickly to an incentive which for a fourth-grader might be useless. What proves to be excellent motivation for an art class proves to be almost worthless for a history class. Any type of subject matter which involves physical activity has in it more interest-based motivation than does a subject which requires only mental activity. Because motivation is at the heart of teaching, and because one subject is harder to motivate than another, it follows that some subjects are harder to teach than others. A student who likes algebra is always a delight for the algebra teacher. The motivation is strong and the teaching is easy. His motivation is spoken of as intrinsic.

Previously some general aspects of motivation were discussed. To be more specific, the following suggestions are offered:

1. Use as wide a variety of learning activities and learning resources as you can. Audio-visual aids, library work, written work, lecture, free discussion, and short tests are a source of the activities teachers can use.
2. Keep students informed of their progress; and be sure there is progress, even though small, for everyone.
3. Show enthusiasm for good work and find something to praise if a pupil has tried, even though the work is perhaps not as good as this child can do.
4. Sell your subject. Pupils need to feel that there is a good reason for what they are studying.
5. Make success *in something* possible for every student. One must succeed if he is to desire to go on. Only extremely tenacious adults can and will continue to work over a long period of time if they do not achieve some success.
6. Set the stage for good work. Physical conditions make up a part of the environment in which the child operates. The teacher is a part of the environment. Make the room and yourself as attractive as you can.
7. Keep things moving. Children like an active situation. Procedures which drag have little appeal for anyone, child or adult.
8. Whenever possible, use suspense. A surprise always breaks monotony.

9. Inject fun and humor into the classroom. School is no longer a discipline in the unpleasant.

10. Give students as much responsibility as they can handle well. Children like responsibility. A child who has responsibility is usually well motivated.

## THE NATURE OF INCENTIVES

A thinking person works with an object in view; a child is a thinking person and must have an object in view. Perceiving the object clearly tends to make it more desirable. Perceiving the object dimly limits the desire to attain the object.

**Incentives in the Learning Situation.** In ordinary day-to-day classwork motivation commonly applies to selecting study materials that are attractive and presenting them in such a manner as to appeal to a student's interest. The idea, of course, is to cause the student to get into the work quickly and to sustain his interest until the work is finished. Because incentives are usually external, they tend to be artificial in nature. While they make the connection between the child and a task to be done, never should they remain the connection. A good incentive is one which makes a good, firm connection and then is forgotten by the child. As he develops a real interest, the artificial incentive (a prize, reward, commendation) becomes unnecessary.

A good incentive is always easy to manage. It is easy to set up and tends to eliminate itself as interest in the desired learning activity develops. Since all artificial motivation is a form of school machinery, it must give an educational account of itself. If the scheme means much work on the teacher's part, such as keeping a daily record for each pupil, the results probably do not justify the effort and time it consumes.

As a trained professional worker, the teacher will scrutinize carefully any plan he is considering for stimulating any activity. Such a plan is always marked by four characteristics:

(1) It is simple. (2) It is directly related to the activity the teacher wishes to stimulate. (3) It is practically self-administering, that is, there is little effort required to keep it rolling. (4) It is of such a nature that the probability of its elimination at an early date is easily foreseen.

**Incentives and Accomplishment.** Incentives are valuable only in terms of accomplishment. A good incentive gets the job done; a poor one does not. The monetary value of the incentive has little to do with its accomplishment. A boy may work harder, for longer hours, and with more concentration making a house for a puppy he was given at Christmas than he would if promised a ten-thousand-dollar building lot downtown. Again, he may work more diligently for a prize of a little turtle with a picture on its back than he would for a new suit of clothes. Children judge incentives by the value the group puts on the object. Prizes are worth little as incentives unless the children really want the prize.

**Incentives as a Means to an End.** It is imperative that the incentive be kept a means to an end and never be made an end in itself. For this reason, if for no other, no article of much value should be offered as an incentive. The greater monetary value does not increase the utility of an incentive, and there is danger that the incentive may become an end in itself rather than the means to an end. Such an incentive may distort a child's sense of values. A child who has never cheated in his schoolwork is sorely tempted to cheat when the external reward is very great, and when this reward seemingly is being lost after consistent and honest effort.

Prizes, in fact all incentives, are of greatest utility when they are closely related to the object or goal desired from the effort. Harry, who is practicing conscientiously on an old, battered trumpet, has before him a desirable incentive when a new trumpet is offered upon conclusion of his mastering fundamentals on the old instrument. The new instrument is closely related to the basic music fundamentals which he is mastering.

If, however, he has to be reminded constantly (the incentive dangled) of the new trumpet in order to keep him practicing, he will probably have little interest in either his music or the instrument when he secures it. If the artificial, external motivation is becoming an end in itself, it should be eliminated at once. Very good incentives have in them the quality of launching the child on the new endeavor enthusiastically and of disappearing almost entirely as interest builds up.

It is a common temptation for every teacher or parent upon finding that a child is uninterested in some desirable activity to try to stimulate interest in the activity. The first thought is usually to offer some sort of a reward. Mrs. G., upon finding that Junior was shortening his music practice, hit upon the idea of offering him a dime for every half-hour he put in practicing. Needless to say, Junior put in several hours in the vicinity of the piano. For teachers, a word of advice is sufficient: when tempted to offer a prize, to promise a half-holiday, to give some reward to pupils for anything *they are supposed to do in line of duty*, don't. There are two basic reasons for the negative injunction: first, a teacher is a poor teacher if he cannot make the desired activity reasonably interesting to his pupils without using artificial stimulation, and, second, a child needs to have a wholesome respect for his duty and for his work and there is no better way to develop this respect than by holding himself to a task, though it be unpleasant.

The use of prizes and awards is always open to question. Some of the reasons why prizes are in ill repute are these:

1. It is very difficult to relate a prize to the desired activity.
2. Prizes are rarely means to an end. They tend to become an end in themselves.
3. Prizes and awards of all kinds tend to be forgotten. This means that the teacher is forced to "dangle" the prize before the pupils.
4. A good incentive should have group appeal. It is difficult to secure any prize which has universal appeal to all students.

5. A good incentive makes a quick connection between the task to be done and the child—and then disappears from view.
6. Prizes tend to build for a wrong type of competition, a competition in which the prize is the object, not the desired learning which prompted offering the prize.
7. Prizes put little or no emphasis upon improvement, much emphasis upon final performance. Hence a child with high initial intelligence or skill may win a prize although he has improved little and has made little effort to improve.

**Incentives and Appeal.** As was stated earlier, the worth of an incentive depends very much upon the value the group puts upon it. An incentive forms a very poor generator of action when the group as a whole is uninterested. To illustrate, Miss Burke, a very good teacher, proposed to her class that she would, out of her own purse, buy a single-volume encyclopedia for the room if the class had the best attendance record for the building for the month. The result? Apathy. No one really wanted an encyclopedia. It had no group appeal.

Miss Burke and Miss Bruce in adjoining rooms purchased, with the principal's approval, a canary and its cage. The room with the better attendance average for the month (epidemic illnesses being excluded) was to have the warbler for its room for the next month. The result? Enthusiasm. The children really wanted the canary for their room.

A given incentive may have an entirely different effect on the pupil at different times. This is due to the fact that incentives (external and artificial motivation) are influenced much by other externals. An air rifle offered as a reward to Bob may be a good incentive toward his bringing up the wood from the basement for the fireplace each evening until Bill, next door, gets an air rifle and both boys use it. The novelty is gone. Ice skates appeal only while there is good skating. A book may have no appeal to the girl with a library at her command. A box of candy is worthless to a child who is not allowed to eat candy. Fishing tackle for the boy who is going to a lake for his vacation in two weeks is excellent because of immediate need, but it is worthless as an enthusiasm-builder immediately upon his return from his vacation. Relating the motivating agency to the learning situation directly is always the basic problem.

Incentives are often unnecessary. Some work has so much in common with a child's natural interests that there is no need for any artificial stimulus. Boys building model airplanes need no artificial stimulus when their older brothers are flight officers. When incentives are unnecessary in schoolwork, there is every indication that the subject matter and the child have much in common. This situation, sad to say, prevails altogether too rarely.

**Incentives and Competition.** Competition, an activity involving rivalry, either conscious or unconscious, in which one person or one group tries to outdo another person or group, has always been an effective motivating agency. The reason lies in the internal motivation aspect.

Group competition rates near the top as a motivating agency. Usually it brings out the best in children rather than the worst. Selfishness, complacency, and other undesirable attitudes tend to be eliminated in group competition. The goal and the means of attaining it are usually so closely allied in anything competitive that the danger of confusing means and ends is eliminated.

A phase of motivation which starts off as an incentive and soon goes over into interest is embodied in any plan whereby the child competes with his own best record. When this type of competition is encouraged, a teacher is on the way to inspiring enthusiasm and true interest in his pupils.

To keep children interested in their daily improvement in spelling, arithmetic, or any other subject in which objective scores can be obtained, many teachers use charts which they have run off on a duplicator. The charts carry the day of the week across the top and the subject down the side. Scores are recorded daily in the proper square. Each student records his own score and with his teacher's help makes a little graph of it for each week. He is thus competing against his own best record from day to day as much as against the record of his classmates. The charts, of course, tell the teacher quickly and accurately what progress is being made by each pupil. The charts are spoken of as "motivation charts."

Self-competition should definitely be encouraged, as should group competition. Individual competition—in which one child competes against another—is less valuable, as undesirable attitudes enter in more readily. Self-competition makes golf interesting for adults. Smith will buy the drinks for everyone in the clubhouse the day he pars the course for the first time, not because he beat Brown but because he has beaten his own best record and has shot theoretically perfect golf.

Work in factories is frequently stimulated by self-competition. Recognition of unusual production may bring a reward or honor, but usually the rivalry of record-breaking is sufficient to spur workers to high effort. The schoolroom can always use the same idea to advantage.

**Duty and Incentives.** The idea that all school work must be made interesting, appealing, and—if possible—pleasurable has grown with the modern school. In general, the idea is sound. However, there are some things in school and outside the classroom which a child should do, not because they are especially appealing or interesting, but because they are his work, his specific duty. Thus a negative precept can well be included with the best of the positive statements which form the basis of this chapter: Never use an incentive or any artificial stimulus to secure accomplishment of a service which a child owes his home, his parents, his teacher, his fellow students, or his school.

A child must learn early to do many things, not because he enjoys them or because he will get a reward. He must learn the meaning of duty and responsibility. Because of the softness which many believe is permeating American life today, parents and teachers must distinguish clearly in their thinking between the activities owed to parents, home, family, and school as obligations and activities of a learning nature which are not in themselves duties and obligations of a child. Discipline is one of the best routes to freedom in the nation as well as in our schools and homes. The satisfaction of a difficult task well performed is frequently self-motivation of the finest sort.

## PRINCIPLES GOVERNING INCENTIVES

Because one can rarely make the best usage possible of any instrument without understanding the principles under which it operates, the next few pages will discuss principles governing incentives and other forms of motivation. It is essential to keep in mind that an incentive is positive in nature; it is never negative. Hence, punishment is not an incentive.

1. *The need for incentives varies according to subject matter.* In general, external motivation is necessary in inverse ratio to the inherent interest in any phase of subject matter. When the subject carries with it much that is of natural or inherent interest to the child, artificial means of getting interest are not needed.

Drill subjects usually need more external stimulation than do other subjects because of the very nature of drill. Drill is necessary for habit formation and for the development of skills. Running the scales in music is imperative if skill on the piano is to result, but commonly this drill in itself is monotonous and tiresome for children and has little inherent interest. Hence an incentive to encourage drill may be needed, as the inherent interest is comparatively small after the novelty wears off. The very nature of some subject matter—for example, shop-work and physical education—makes for an inherent interest. It need hardly be said that good teachers seek to bring out the inherent interest in every subject and avoid artificial stimulations as much as possible.

2. *An incentive is as good as the motive behind it.* The efficiency of any incentive can only be measured by the motive

which prompted the child to seek the incentive. It must be remembered that the motive may be either good or bad. The motive back of a child's activity may be selfishness, greed, or some other undesirable urge or drive on the child's part, or it may be unselfishness, sympathy, or a thoroughly desirable reason for seeking the goal. Thus, the teacher always considers whether the prize, honor, or reward suggested as a motivating agency is going to call up in the child desirable or undesirable motives.

A good incentive calls into play desirable interests or motives; a bad incentive calls into play undesirable interests or motives. A given incentive may act in different ways for different children.

3. *Abstract incentives are better than material ones.* Incentives of an abstract nature are commonly more closely related to interests or inherent motivation than are material ones. Among abstract incentives which usually obtain satisfactory results are: commendation, publicity, honor rolls, group approval, special privileges, and leadership.

COMMENDATION. Usually a desirable form of external motivation, it is immediate in its appeal, makes for a closer relationship between teacher and learner, and is usually gained at the expense of no other child.

PUBLICITY. Frequently a desirable incentive, it stems from the desire to excel and from the pride inherent in all children. Displaying on bulletin boards a child's work or the work of many children encourages effort. Publishing the names of children who reach highest honors is good if names of those who have improved most in the same period are also made a matter of record. Contests for groups are good motivating agencies, and the accompanying publicity usually does no harm. The danger of making rewards, honors, and publicity ends in themselves rather than means to an end is always present, however.

HONOR ROLLS. These are usually considered desirable motivating agencies. The problem, however, is to confer honors for effort as well as for success. There is little honor due a brilliant child who ranks highest in his class and still is working at only 80 per cent of his ability. Honors, when conferred, should recognize effort, persistence, industry, and social worth to the group as well as scholastic excellence.

GROUP APPROVAL. Approval is always a sound motivating agency. The child who is voted by the class "the most conscientious student," "the best sport in the room," "the one who does the most for others," or "the pupil who does the most for the school" may well redouble his exertions because of the honor.

SPECIAL PRIVILEGES. Privileges are something which pupils understand. A child who works industriously and has completed an assignment is allowed to work on material of his own choosing. A boy who has finished in a satisfactory manner an assignment which was not especially interesting is allowed to read fiction taken from the school library. As incentives, special privileges are always good because of their relatedness to school work in general and because they are always open to all students.

LEADERSHIP. Being allowed to distribute materials, being chairman of a group, running special errands for the principal, and other items of a like nature have desirable incentive values generally. Circumstances always alter cases, and every good teacher utilizes judgment in all such assignments.

There is no assumption that the list above covers all of the possible abstract incentives in a schoolroom situation. The number is very great. What a child will particularly enjoy doing is always somewhat unpredictable. The wise teacher takes advantage of this and uses a child's particular likes to advantage in getting less interesting (to the child) schoolwork done well.

4. *Immediate need is always of great significance in the evaluation of incentives.* The degree of motivating power is in proportion to the nearness of the time when what is to be learned will be used. What is needed today is of importance. This is why fishing tackle is an excellent incentive for the boy who is going to the lake for his vacation immediately. The

tackle would have had little appeal after his return. Every teacher learns at an early date to gear learning to seasonal activities: for example, making valentines for St. Valentine's Day, writing letters to Santa Claus at Christmas, and studying birds in the spring when birds are plentiful.

5. *Audio-visual aids are devices for motivation.* Classroom work can be made more interesting through the use of the now quite common visual and auditory aids. These include the radio, television, record players, sound pictures, and sound recording. These in themselves are not incentives, nor are they motives. They are really devices. However, they can be made sources of good school motivation.

In establishing language usage standards, in developing and increasing interests, in bringing information to a child in a palatable form, and in creating desirable attitudes, the radio and television have possibilities still untapped. As motivating agencies for increasing children's interests, knowledge, and breadth of understanding, the potentialities of radio and television are tremendous. Some of the natural desires of children include desires to find out, to imitate, to express, to excel, to entertain, to share, to own, to master, to make things, and to develop. The radio and television carry with them satisfactions of many of these desires. Evidently the radio, television, sound recordings, and motion pictures are immediate sources of finding out, of imitation, of expression, of entertainment, and of development in general. As has been said, these are not motivations in themselves, but they can be used by the good teacher to stimulate interest.

## OTHER CHARACTERISTICS OF INCENTIVES

There are other characteristics of incentives which should be noted.

1. The same activity may spring from opposite motives in two pupils.

2. Motives come from stimuli, and stimuli vary much.
3. The sources of motives may come from outside the school.
4. Some motives are natural, since they are not acquired through learning.
5. Sustained attention is a goal of motivation. Children work for immediate goals. Mental maturity marks the person who can and will work in a sustained manner for a long-deferred goal.
6. Because spontaneous attention is desired by all teachers, anything that gets attention and holds it to the satisfactory attainment of the end desired is usable.

## THE TEACHER'S PERSONALITY AND MOTIVATION

The teacher's personality is an important factor in motivating pupils. The job is a salesman's task, and the teacher may well ask himself, "What personal qualities will play a part in the successful motivation of my pupils?" Among qualities which readily stimulate pupil interest and enthusiasm are interest in pupils, patience, persistence, sincerity, initiative and resourcefulness, enthusiasm, optimism, and the teacher's personal interests and inclinations.

A teacher who is a sports enthusiast, who loves games and reads the sport pages of the newspapers with avidity, will naturally be a source of motivation for almost any subject matter for pupils who are sports enthusiasts. The resourceful teacher has ability in originating new ideas or in adapting old ones to his purpose. His plans are never ready-made, nor need they be. Originality is always interest-getting, and a resourceful teacher is original.

The power of suggestion is always a strong motivating force. The teacher who can suggest what should be done without stating it always leaves the student with the feeling of discovery. Rarely does the student know where he has gotten the fruitful idea which has won him approval. Example is a strong form of suggestion. A teacher's personal habits tend to encourage desirable activity on the part of his pupils. A teacher who is always on time, who always makes good on a promise, who shows enthusiasm for school affairs, is usually one who has little trouble in keeping his pupils interested in school work. Neatness, accuracy, self-control, and cheerfulness are much greater motivating forces when exercised by a teacher than is generally recognized. In motivation as in all other forms of instruction, example is always better than precept.

## DISCUSSION PROBLEM

### "Dad's Crazy for Me to Make That Gold Roll . . ."

"Junior, your father will be very much disappointed if you fail to make the Gold Honor Roll again this month. It takes straight A's, and although you are making higher than a *B* average, that is not high enough for the Gold Roll. It will place you on the Blue Honor Roll, but your father tells me that he is most anxious for you to be the best pupil in your grade."

"I know, Miss Henry, Dad's crazy for me to make that Gold Roll—and I'd like to do it too, 'cause he gives me a dollar for every *A* I bring home—but boy! I've got a good chance to win first with my model airplane in the Scout contest for the District. That's a mighty big honor, Miss Henry, the biggest honor a boy can get, an' besides I'm going to be a pilot when I grow up. You know I won first in our contest here. Did you ever stop to think why a monoplane flies steadier than a biplane? Come over here an' I'll show you—I've got a model for each kind."

Junior, nine years old, places his beautifully made miniature plane on the arrow-marked landing field he has laid out on the floor, while you wish heartily that his father would not be so insistent on his making an *A* in every school subject. The Gold Honor Roll pupils, as well as the less coveted Blue winners, are listed each month in the town's daily paper, and you wonder to what extent the father's interest is personal pride rather than a serious interest in his son's scholarship.

There isn't the least doubt about it, Junior is seriously interested right now in airplanes. The worn and tattered *Popular Mechanics* as well as the more technical aviation magazines scattered about bear silent but effective testimony that he is reading everything he can find on the topic. You ponder. Should the Honor Roll be eliminated? Is it a good incentive?

## QUESTIONS ON THE PROBLEM

1. The Gold Honor Roll is available to all the boys and girls in Junior's class. Does this imply that every pupil in the class has an equal chance of making it? Upon what condition would this be true?

2. Which pupil deserves a place on an honor roll, a student whose ability is high but who rarely measures up to it, or a pupil whose natural ability is much lower, but whose efficiency, due to industry perhaps, comes much nearer to approaching his inherent ability? Which is most likely to be found on an honor roll? Is any honor roll open to every student on exactly the same competitive basis? Suggest one which could be.

3. There is a term "efficiency quotient" which is used to express the extent to which a student's accomplishment approaches his ability. His ability is sometimes expressed as his "intelligence quotient" (possibly erroneously). Why not base a student's position on an honor roll on his efficiency quotient?

4. If a procedure such as is suggested in 3 were followed out, would the honor roll become a better or poorer incentive than it now is? Why?

5. Supposing there were an honor roll in Junior's school for efficiency in any worthwhile, desirable activity for a boy. How would Junior be likely to rank? Why?

6. Junior is now much more interested in airplanes than he is in the Gold Honor Roll; judging by results only, the airplane contest plus his interest in flying must be greater than the honor roll contest plus his interest in it (to say nothing of the reward for A's). In your opinion which dominates him in the first instance, internal motivation or external in the form of a contest?

7. To what extent do you believe that honor rolls and other forms of publicity are incentives to parents rather than to pupils? Sum up all the good points you believe are inherent in honor rolls as far as parents are concerned. Do the same for pupils.

8. Junior's interest in airplanes is much greater right now than is his interest in a school subject, say spelling. What would you say to teaching him aerodynamics *now*, in a formal manner with much emphasis, and teaching spelling *now* with much less emphasis?

## STUDY QUESTIONS

1. Be clear in distinguishing between motives and incentives. When are they the same thing? Ever?
2. Write out and bring to class as large a list of school incentives as you can. List in order from the best to the poorest.
3. What are the good points of Miss Burke's and Miss Bruce's plan of using the canary for the room as an incentive for better attendance? Are there any bad points?
4. Is all-round improvement a good basis on which to award prizes? Why? Why not?
5. In your opinion, which student has the greater chance for all-round improvement, a good one or a poor one? Give reasons for your answer.
6. Will a bright child improve more under good teaching than a poor one? Why?
7. Can you show that self-competition is motivation rather than an incentive? Is it?
8. Does it make much difference whether any discrimination is made between *incentives* and *motivation*?
9. Is a chart or a globe an incentive? If not, what is it? Can a device be made an incentive? Show how, if you say "Yes."
10. What (if anything) is wrong with rivalry as an incentive? Is group competition rivalry? If "Yes," why is it better than individual competition?
11. Do you agree that the less consequential the subject matter is, the better the incentive needs to be? Does the question imply that rich subject matter is always inherently of interest to the child?
12. A child must learn to spell. This is commonly uninteresting. Does this mean that it is poor subject matter? Why? Why not?

## SELECTED READINGS

Alcorn, Marvin D., Houseman, Richard A., and Schunert, Jim R. *Better Teaching in Secondary Schools.* New York: Holt, Rinehart & Winston, Inc., 1954. Section 6, "Teaching Your Class," discusses how and why students are motivated. Suggestions are practical.

Briggs, Thomas H., and Justman, Joseph. *Improving Instruction Through Supervision.* New York: The Macmillan Co., 1952. The discussion of motivation as a factor in everyday learning is entirely usable for the classroom teacher. The general idea that learning is goal-seeking dominates the discussion of motivation and incentives.

Garrison, Karl C., and Gray, J. Stanley. *Educational Psychology.* New York: Appleton-Century-Crofts, Inc., 1955. Chapter 11, "The General Nature of Learning," considers the meaning of learning, some conditions affecting learning, the effects of practice on learning, the problems of motivation, and other related topics.

Grambs, Jean D., Iverson, William J., and Patterson, Franklin K. *Modern Methods in Secondary Education.* Rev. ed. New York: Holt, Rinehart & Winston, Inc., 1958. See pp. 106–8 for a discussion of motivation in the classroom; pp. 172–73, for a discussion of learning through use of devices of various types.

Herrick, Virgil E., Goodlad, John T., Estvan, Frank J., and Eberman, Paul W. *The Elementary School.* Englewood Cliffs, N. J.: Prentice-Hall, Inc., 1956. Chapter 5, pp. 95–124, deals with types, natures, and concepts of learning. Motivation, transfer, and the roles of teacher and pupil are among items discussed.

Mehl, Marie A., Mills, Hubert H., and Douglass, Harl R. *Teaching in Elementary School.* 2d ed. New York: The Ronald Press Co., 1958. Chapter 6, which discusses basic principles of learning and the place of motivation in the process, presents a good discussion of incentives.

Sawrey, James M., and Telford, Charles W. *Educational Psychology.* Boston: Allyn & Bacon, Inc., 1958. A technical but thoroughly readable discussion of the motivation for learning opens this text. This chapter is recommended reading for the student who is interested especially in the psychological implications involved in motivation.

Skinner, Charles E., *et al.* (ed.). *Elementary Educational Psychology.* Englewood Cliffs, N. J.: Prentice-Hall, Inc., 1950. Chapter 9 discusses the dynamics of learning with emphasis given to the place of motivation in the learning process. Excellently written, the chapter presents many different phases of the learning process.

# PART III

# WAYS AND MEANS
# OF SECURING RESULTS

# 9

# ORGANIZING ACTIVITIES FOR
# TEACHING EFFICIENCY

If a teacher is to do a good job of teaching he must observe at an early date that his work falls into two distinct but inseparable parts: the one is the child, the individual, the unit of his thinking; the other is the school machinery, the more or less mechanical organization by which the child is made to develop and grow most efficiently. It is obvious that the second exists only for the first, and that the first does not develop or grow without the second. In other words, school organization—in fact, anything and everything connected with schools—exists only for children; but children profit little from schooling unless the organizational work of the individual classroom teacher is complete, thorough, and efficient.

The teacher entering a new position, or even one who has been in the same position many years, cannot afford to wait until the first day of school is upon him before planning his work. He learns early in his professional life that the person who plans carefully is usually the master of a situation. Some work, even for the teacher experienced in a given teaching situation, must be done before the first day of school, and is not so well placed in his calendar of yearly planning if done later; still other portions of his work must be under complete organization by the end of the first week. From the efficiency point of view his work tends to break down into (1) preschool activities, (2) classroom activities of an organizational nature, and (3) organizational activities related to the other parts of the school, to his home, and to the community.

From the responsibility angle, the teacher's work is threefold in nature. He has specific responsibilities to the school administration (principal, superintendent, supervisors, boards of education) and to his fellow teachers in the school; responsibilities to the community which is his home and of which he is a highly respected citizen; and finally, responsibilities to the boys and girls who are directly and immediately his charges.

## ORGANIZING PRESCHOOL ACTIVITIES

The experienced teacher has learned to consider, almost without conscious thought, certain things before school starts. Some of these activities are listed below. Ordinarily, not all of the items fit every situation. The teacher, of course, will give attention only to those which fit his needs.

1. Obtain a good rooming place. Your room is your home (if you are unmarried) and is a poor place on which to economize.
2. Obtain a boarding place. If possible, it is desirable to eat where you room, especially if you are in a smaller town or city.
3. Learn all the facts you can about your teaching situation and the equipment with which you will work.
4. Check on school supplies for your room or classes.
5. Obtain, if possible, the probable list (or lists) of your students.
6. Plan your teaching assignments for at least the first week.
7. Find out what the plan is for homeroom (if the homeroom is used) and for opening exercises and general assemblies.
8. Look over the school library, giving special attention to your teaching field.
9. Study the school plan in use, if extra teachers are utilized in any specialized fields (music, physical education, remedial speech, etc.).

10. Learn what you can about school routines (lunch rooms, cafeteria, class changes, etc.). Get the handbook for teachers, if there is one.

11. Familiarize yourself with the plans of entrance and exit; regulation of heat and light; location of drinking fountains and toilet facilities; indoor and outdoor facilities for play; location of maps, projectors, charts, pictures, and other auditory and visual aids.

12. Consider your personal program for the year (your reading, recreation, etc.).

13. Get your clothes in good order.

14. Meet your minister and arrange for changing your church membership card if such is necessary.

15. Write down in detail items you must not forget; check each off as it is accomplished.

## MANAGING FIRST-DAY AND FIRST-WEEK DUTIES

Although no hard and fast rule can be applied to what the teacher should do the first day of school, the following list may have some useful suggestions:

1. Get your pupils seated properly. You probably will not be arbitrary about this the first day, but will reserve the right to make seating changes as you see fit. As a general rule, though, bad combinations should be broken up early. Alphabetical seating may be considered, but has disadvantages.

2. Make your seating chart and start in at once to learn the names of all your pupils. You will have trouble associating names and faces without the use of a seating chart for each class.

3. Study fire-drill instructions carefully and follow regulations set down implicitly.

4. Arrange for calling (or taking) the roll accurately. This requires exactness; the regulations regarding attendance will come to you from administration offices.

5. Note how your classroom register or class book is arranged. Do not list names in it the first day, however, as later changes will disarrange your alphabetized lists.

6. Make clear and definite assignments in all classes. Be specific. A poor assignment means poor preparation tomorrow.
7. Arrange your room, or at least consider how you will want it arranged when you get more time.
8. Exercise care in your "first-day" report. It commonly asks for numbers in classes and suitability of the room to class sizes. Many schools do not use a first-day report.
9. Start your routine machinery operating, but leave final arrangements for a time when you can get pupil participation. It is the pupils' room even more than yours.
10. Be pleasant, but firm in making decisions; first impressions tend to be lasting.

By the end of the first week a teacher's operations in management have included:

1. Getting your seat work and library work planned. This, of course, will vary with the organization of the school.
2. Using your recess periods to best advantage. In high school these include between-class periods and your "vacant" period (or two if you are fortunate).
3. Enlisting the cooperation of your pupils in every possible way. You are establishing yourself with them.
4. Attending (probably) an all-school faculty meeting.
5. Stimulating self-activity of a desirable sort for your pupils. Seek early to include everyone in this.
6. Discovering your leaders. (You may wish to make a sociogram in order to be more certain).
7. Perfecting your organization; eliminating the wasteful and what seems to be unnecessary procedure as evidenced by a week's work.
8. Getting acquainted with your co-workers, the custodian, and your pupils. Get a biography of each pupil.
9. Studying carefully the results of any formalized tests that may have been given for classification or other purposes.
10. Putting all of your routine machinery into its final form. Examples: library use, dictionary use, roll-taking, use of pencil sharpener, traffic routes for classes, care of waste paper, absence from room, passing of class materials.

## ORGANIZING CLASSROOM ACTIVITIES

Children differ in their ways of learning and in their rate of growth. This thought must dominate the thinking of the classroom teacher at all times. All school administration takes this into account. The child must develop (as an individual) continuously, and no arbitrary standard can be set up which fits all of the children in a class. Readiness is the key word in all development. The child can develop through formal education only when he is physically, emotionally, and intellectually ready for that development. The inference, which is well taken, is that no two children are exactly alike in terms of these three factors. As a group boys are commonly slower to mature physically and intellectually than girls. This means that more boys than girls are found in remedial classes. However, boys do equal girls when both attain mental and physical maturity. Again, boys who are late maturing physically (54 to 61 inches in height at eleven years of age) commonly are of the same height and weight as the early maturing boys (61 to 64 inches at eleven years) when both reach seventeen years. This is true, of course, for groups, not for individuals.

**Organizational Patterns and Principles.** Because the educational program is in a general way set up for a mythical "average" student, schools commonly adopt various grouping patterns to meet the differences in abilities and aptitudes of the pupils. These groupings (by abilities and aptitudes) also serve the teacher in meeting his instructional problems. Identical grouping patterns are rarely found, as each school uses the organization that best fits its needs. If the school is striving especially for social and emotional growth, one type of grouping is used; if it is working particularly for subject-matter mastery, another grouping is used. Such groupings are commonly spoken of as *homogeneous*. A teacher is always informed through the administrative or supervisory officials of the organizational plan in use.

The needs and educational goals of the individual school determine the general school objectives which in turn reflect the school's philosophy. The latter remains a constant; the goals and needs are to some extent variables. From the above it is evident that the setup is rigidly organized when the needs are considered as being mainly academic; less rigid when the objectives are considered to be principally social and emotional.

Certain principles have been derived from the studies of research workers and psychologists which a teacher must consider:

1. Children's learnings are not at an even rate. This is to say a child may learn rapidly in one area (mathematics) and learn slowly in another (English).

2. Children of the same age do not grow and learn at the same rate. In general, girls mature more rapidly than boys, but an individual boy may be more mature than an individual girl.

3. Learning is continuous; it is not discrete or saltatory.

4. Within a grade, children vary widely in abilities. A fourth-grade boy may read better than a seventh-grader. Because of this, the term "grade level" does not mean too much. Actually there is no grade level for all children within a given school grade. Grading is more or less a mechanical device for putting children together in groups for economy of teaching time and effort; there is no assurance the pupils are at the same level in any or all of the things which count.

5. The word "promotion" is to some extent a misnomer. Children mature naturally; they are not promoted physically, emotionally, educationally, or mentally. They may be "promoted," administratively speaking, but actually promote themselves as each matures.

6. No simple plan of grouping can be devised which takes into account all of the individual differences in children.

7. Achievement grouping (most commonly used) puts together those whose subject-matter abilities are of comparable strength; it may be bad grouping from the point of view

of the child's physical, social, and emotional growth. This is the main argument against grade-skipping.

When it comes to application of the principles set down above, a teacher will, of course, follow the procedures used in his school. However, if he is to be effective he must be thoroughly cognizant of the variability which actually exists among the children in any class he may teach, regardless of the grouping plan utilized.

**Heterogeneous and Homogeneous Grouping.** As was stated above a teacher must follow the grouping plan which has been adopted for his school. He will need to understand both its purposes and its organizational routine. Today, homogeneous (ability) grouping in the elementary school is probably less used than it was twenty-five years ago. Heterogeneous (age-grade) grouping is in quite general use. The argument against homogeneous grouping is that there are wide differences even in a so-called ability group class, and that labeling classes "bright," "average," or "slow" is hard to avoid. There is something repugnant to a teacher's thinking when pupils within a grade are so classified.

The arguments for heterogeneous grouping are: (1) that homogeneous grouping does not actually eliminate wide disparities; (2) that homogeneous grouping tends to be undemocratic; (3) that heterogeneous grouping provides a normal social situation; (4) that children in the heterogeneous atmosphere profit much from working with other children who may have more or less ability in a specific area; (5) that personal and social learnings are greater in the heterogeneous group; (6) that parents of children who have been placed in lower-level groups academically may with some reason complain that their children are being stigmatized by a label; (7) that the child who is pigeonholed as "low-achievement" loses much in social development; and (8) that homogeneous grouping tends to put all problem children together, which is a bad arrangement.

Those who favor ability grouping within an elementary school grade make claims for it that are not always sustained by research on the subject. The following statements are commonly heard: (1) Teachers like it; pupils are easier to teach when the ability disparity is not great. (2) Slightly greater gains are made under ability grouping. (3) Ability grouping is most effective for dull children (who need the best teaching effort), less effective for average children, least effective for bright children. (4) There are no verifiable data as to what ability grouping does to the child as a person. (5) Such studies as have been made concerning the social values and parents' opinions of ability grouping as opposed to heterogeneous grouping are inconclusive and indefinite. (6) Homogeneous grouping reduces to some extent the range of differences in achievement.

At the secondary school level there is more conclusive evidence that ability grouping gets good results. Everyone primarily concerned likes it: students, teachers, parents, and administrators. But the ability grouping plan is not completely effective; the groups as put together are commonly not of equal ability. The difficulty, of course, lies in trying to find a common denominator upon which to base the groupings. Mental capacity (intelligence tests), reading ability, mathematical ability—all are used. General achievement, which is influenced by mental ability, is most frequently used but is not necessarily best, as it often brings together wide physiological age differences within a group. As a whole, however, studies of ability grouping at the secondary school level indicate the desirability of the practice. As seems to be true in the elementary school, the greatest good accrues to the dull pupils. This factor may be the only significant one in weighing the balance for homogeneous over heterogeneous grouping.

**Planning for the Intellectually Gifted.** One of the more difficult problems a teacher faces is giving the bright pupil enough to do. Classes in elementary schools and in many high schools are geared to the average child. If all pupils in a room were of exactly equal ability, there would be little reason for time-wasting by any pupils. This, of course, is not true even under homogeneous grouping. As a result, the bright child usually completes an assignment in a fraction of the time utilized by his less gifted neighbor. If time is to give an educational account of itself, this bright child must be kept employed, and profitably employed. To do this, the teacher in planning his work must break it into three categories: the minimum assignment, which represents the least amount of work which can be accepted as fulfilling requirements; an average assignment which will be fitted to the larger portion of the class; and a maximum assignment, which will offer a challenge to the very bright youngster. Keeping a bright child employed to the extent of his capabilities is even more important than expending extra effort upon the least gifted child in the room.

Research available on the general characteristics of bright children warrants these statements:

1. Bright pupils are able to criticize themselves. They should be challenged to utilize all opportunities to criticize their own work.
2. Bright pupils reason well and if given the opportunity can analyze a difficult problem situation. This should be encouraged.
3. Bright pupils tend to be original. This quality of originality should not be discouraged, as it is from this group that America's leaders must come later on. Initiative, which they possess, should be encouraged, not discouraged.
4. Bright pupils express themselves better than do average pupils; every form of self-expression should be encouraged.
5. Bright pupils see relationships readily and must be encouraged to relate all school activities to out-of-school situations. They can engage in long-range assignments such as term papers, play production, larger projects in shop work, and composition of an original nature in English and music.

A teacher must encourage the bright child to do more and better work both inside and outside the classroom. This usually takes the form of more extensive reading, work on special projects, planning individual learning activities, and experiences for leadership in its various forms.

Bright pupils are taught to read a newspaper carefully and critically, are required to make scrapbooks on subjects allied to schoolwork, and in general, are encouraged to think critically. In mathematics, bright pupils are taught to see the relationships of their mathematics to daily life and to science, to apply the principles of mathematics to reasoning problems, and to work on individual projects which involve mathematics. They are taught to report accurately scientific experiments and to use information gained through these experiments.

In the social sciences, current events are utilized in classwork for these high-ability pupils, and the use of source materials, such as encyclopedias, almanacs, and reference works is encouraged. Use of the library is especially stressed for this group.

**Planning for the Slow Learner.** When it comes to setting up the organization for teaching the slow learners, the teacher faces a more difficult problem. A slow learner makes many errors and possesses limited powers of self-criticism. He does not know when his work is poor. Therefore it is easy for a teacher to smother him, so to speak. Since complex mental activity is above the slow learner, he moves forward slowly. Too many associations at one time only confuse him. The teacher must go straight in as far as his teaching approach goes. He must be direct and specific. He must always be concrete, definite, and detailed. The child must understand a thing thoroughly before a teacher can proceed. Therefore, a teacher of slow-moving groups must organize shorter teaching sessions, with specific, short-term assignments.

**Planning Daily Procedures.** A teacher's daily procedures are almost too numerous to list. A few of the more significant include directing of pupils to and from classrooms, bookcases, dictionaries, drinking fountains, and pencil sharpeners; caring for library books, art and music materials, classroom supplies (paper, pencils, pen and ink, chalk); mechanizing roll call; handling maps; written work; supervising lunch-room, cafeteria, locker, desk, and other facilities. The time element appears in all of these procedures, most of which eventually become habitual. Some of these items must be routinized very early; others at a later date. Still other procedures, fewer in number, are never habituated, although the action may become to some extent mechanical. Routinization of procedures justifies itself in that both time and effort are conserved when an action, of necessity performed daily, is habituated.

The activities mentioned above are significant in the formation of desirable habits of neatness, punctuality, industry, and courtesy. Directly, this work of the teacher serves to eliminate details leading to the actual teaching process as it involves the acquisition of knowledge, the control and appreciation of values, and the general academic program. Again, most of the organization work in a room facilitates learning but is marginal to the actual mastery of curricular content.

Few good teachers call the roll to determine absentees in the modern classroom. It takes but a few seconds to record absences from vacant seats. In situations where exact time records must be kept for absences in fractional parts of an hour, because state money is paid upon the basis of attendance, the teacher is commonly furnished forms from the central office for recording such absences. Where written excuses for absences are required from the home, these should always be carefully filed by the teacher, as they constitute his legal reason for not further investigating the absence.

A classroom procedure which must function efficiently, is *relating the work of each unit to the preceding work and to the unit which follows*. This is, of course, a phase of methodology. Failure, however, to tie all the various elements in a subject field together so that good understanding may result is a procedural weakness. It is a classroom procedure which must account for itself in the eventual learning situation.

Another classroom procedure is *leading pupils to acquire new skills and information, and to apply such skills and information to the end of obtaining clearer understandings.* More concretely, this statement says that drill practices from which skills develop and informational material which results largely in knowledges must be acquired with as little waste, both in effort and in time, as is possible. Knowing the best time allotments for the various drill subjects illustrates the significance of the statement as far as drill is concerned. What is the best length of time for a drill period in the multiplication tables? How long should a penmanship period be? How many words should be included in a spelling assignment for the sixth grade? Obviously, a waste results if the periods are not long enough. Again, a period which is exhaustingly long probably gives little educational account of itself after pupils begin to tire. Plateaus tend to develop, and learning ceases at least temporarily. The well-trained teacher knows these basic principles of educational psychology and applies this training to his daily work.

Developing efficiency in *teaching pupils how to study* is another procedure which must not be neglected. Selecting the useful from books and discussions and rejecting the parts which are unsuited to the learner's purposes is largely a matter of correct procedure. Many pupils go through high school and even enter college without having mastered any technique of discrimination. A child who knows how to study, as distinguished from memorizing, has acquired a most valuable ally in his educational advancement.

Another classroom procedure deals with *the formation of study habits and attention habits.* A child inattentive to his classwork is wasting time. An attentive child with poor habits of procedure in a given field is wasting both time and effort. Children do not acquire habits of attention or of study accidentally. If they listen attentively to speech which is not always of interest to them and if they study efficiently with very little wasted effort, someone has taught them either directly or indirectly. A teacher seeks to eliminate useless effort and to encourage, motivate, and instruct the child in techniques which bring desired results.

**Planning for Individual Differences.** The teacher whose classroom organization functions efficiently in all its details finds himself recognizing that his pupils differ much in their ability to learn, in their personal characteristics, in their physical abilities, in their home conditions, and in their social backgrounds. To reconcile some of these differences, a teacher must consider each child as a person. This expresses itself in various ways, among which are:

1. Tact in aiding the child who needs help but hesitates to ask for it
2. Concern for the very rapid learner as well as for the slow learner
3. Recognition of physical differences by adjusting seating, lights, and other physical appurtenances to aid the physically handicapped child
4. Organization of work to permit individual assistance
5. Discovery of differences by utilizing the best known available tests in the various fields
6. Especial aid for the maladjusted child so that his school days may be happy and profitable

Finally, a teacher consciously gears his explanations and his instruction to fit that larger group of pupils who are well adjusted academically, mentally, and physically for the grade.

**Planning for Social Growth.** The American school is fundamentally a social institution. By his association with children of comparable ages the child grows and develops in every way.

It is rather difficult for the teacher in a classroom filled with active youngsters to realize that the classroom organization either promotes, neutralizes, or actually hinders the development of correct social relationships. It is possible to set up any workshop, and a classroom is to a great extent a workshop, so that dissension, friction, and misunderstanding will result. It is equally possible to plan the organization in such a manner that practically all reason for personality clashes is eliminated.

From a social viewpoint organizational procedures are consciously planned to promote the development of certain habits which are significant in two ways: first, the child as an individual profits from possessing them; and second, his companions are happier and more contented because the child has these habits. Habits which develop from good room organization, and which are basically habits of social relationships, include:

*Punctuality:* keeping appointments; obeying promptly; performing tasks promptly; returning borrowed articles promptly; arriving at school on time; turning in written work on time; retiring and getting up at regular hours; promptness in acknowledging kindnesses

*Obedience:* obeying willingly and cheerfully; obeying intelligently, without thought of reward, without being watched, and without reservation; obeying constituted authority; obeying the rules laid down for a good citizen; obeying without asking "Why?"

*Social honesty:* returning borrowed property promptly; fairness (not cheating) in examinations; respecting the property of others; keeping promises; avoiding exaggeration; sticking to what the child believes is right in the face of opposition

*Courtesy:* awaiting his turn; refraining from loud talking and laughing which disturbs others; refraining from interrupting other; observing rules of "good manners" for a child; performing small services for others such as holding open the door, picking up dropped articles, and offering his chair

*Cooperation:* working and playing with others; working for the good of all; helping keep the room, building, and grounds clean; doing one's share in assembly programs; aiding cheerfully in all kinds of school undertakings; doing well a job that is disliked; accepting responsibility; working hard on all cooperative enterprises

*Industry:* systematizing work; doing more than is demanded; performing tasks thoroughly; using leisure time well; performing all of every task; accuracy in doing work he can do; keeping up daily assignments both in school and at home; giving his best effort to whatever he does

*Fair play:* not taking advantage of an opponent; being a cheerful loser and a modest winner; appreciating skill in others; consideration for sensibilities of other children; abiding by officials' decisions without questioning; loyalty to personal ideals of fair play; being able to win in games without boasting and to lose without alibiing; being willing to sacrifice personal interest to the interests of the group

*Health:* concern about his posture; obedience to health rules —such as drinking plenty of water, eating only at mealtime, eating little candy, brushing his teeth; rigid obedience to safety rules; making his personal appearance good; aiding in keeping up sanitary conditions at school—toilets, lavatories, etc.; getting plenty of exercise; observing such health rules as "covering the cough and sneeze"; keeping mind and body mentally and physically healthfully occupied; aiding anyone in the room who is temporarily injured or ill.

## ORGANIZING SCHOOL AND COMMUNITY ACTIVITIES

A teacher's room is a social organization within a larger school social organization. This is always true in any school situation except the one-teacher rural school. In the rural school, the relationship is more directly between the school and the community. In all city schools the organization of one room directly affects the organization of every other room. Naturally, the organizational procedure relates itself directly to cooperative action with other teachers, to professional ethics, to cooperation with parents, to relationships with school administrative officers, and to adapting oneself socially to the community. Loyalty to the community is a personal matter for each teacher.

**Working with Other Teachers.** A teacher in a school system belongs to the entire school, not simply to his room or his building. Because of the "one for all, all for one" situation, a teacher's work is always a shared-relationship job.

The sharing follows rather naturally if he has well-established patterns of courtesy and thoughtfulness for others. The ways in which a teacher cooperates with other teachers are far too numerous to name, but they include:

1. Giving assistance, willingly and graciously, to other teachers who are in need
2. Saving and selecting for other teachers magazine and newspaper articles and pictures which fit their work accurately
3. Showing true sincerity in recognizing a fellow worker's good fortune, excellent teaching results, or advancement, or in recognizing and sympathizing with any misfortune
4. Aiding a new teacher in every possible way
5. Being willing to grant each person a right to his viewpoint; never allowing an academic difference to become personal
6. Always giving full credit to a co-worker and never losing an opportunity to praise a fellow worker to patrons or administration

The very nature of teaching tends to make all personal relationships responsive to ethical standards. The code of the National Education Association indicates rather directly what is considered unethical for a teacher. However, many aspects of personal relationships do not come under a code of ethics, aspects which have much to do with general school efficiency.

A teacher's personal relationship with his co-workers is always friendly and gracious, but never is it allowed to become too familiar. That overfamiliarity leads to contempt is obvious. A teacher learns early to keep still when he is inclined to criticize a fellow teacher. The profession itself is what members of the profession make it—as strong as they are strong, as weak as they are weak. A teacher weakens himself indirectly every time he weakens a fellow worker either directly or indirectly.

**Cooperating with Parents.** A teacher's problem with parents is in developing a shared-relationship attitude. The criticism, so frequently heard from teachers, that the home is tending to turn more and more of the child's upbringing over to the school seems to be true. The fault is not entirely that of the home. The school is accepting, not too unwillingly, more and more responsibility and is attempting to do more and more the work once done by the home. Excessive urbanization of the population is basically the cause. There is no out-of-school situation which compares favorably with the school for the city child in terms of satisfactory employment of his leisure time. The rural child has much to do at home and is usually an asset financially. Again, employment of women in gainful occupations in cities has taken mothers away from home, and the school is actually *in loco parentis* in many instances.

One of the best means of vitalizing interest in the school is through the parent-teacher association. The organization can and does do much good. It will not, however, run itself. Attendance is the big problem. Parents too commonly expect to be entertained, and, when the show is not good on one occasion, they stay away on the next. Since the object of the organization is promotion of good relationships between the school, home, church, and community so that all may cooperate intelligently for the good of children, it follows that interest must come from learning about the child, his nature, and his needs.

The strength of the organization is in its leadership. A teacher should not shirk this responsibility. The extent to which the parents of the children participate depends much upon individual efforts on the part of teachers. If parents participate generously, a teacher will profit directly in his understanding of the children and indirectly by having the friendship and approval of many citizens of the town. The children are the liaison officers between parents and teachers. The wise teacher uses them to strengthen the parent-teacher organization.

**Adapting to the Community.** Many teachers succeed in the classroom but fail in their relationships to the community. The failure is not in generalities. It is in specifics. To illustrate: a teacher must consider carefully the organizations which he joins. One is known by the company he keeps. Certain places in every town, although frequented by the general public, are "out of bounds" to teachers. A few other "specifics" follow:

1. Failing to remember that the community is your home, that it pays your salary, and that it is loved much by others
2. Failing to patronize home merchants and to distribute your purchases among the various merchants
3. Failing to contribute to worthy causes and perhaps making a critical statement about the cause, a statement which is quoted, or worse, misquoted
4. Failing to "boost" the community; speaking of it as a "hick town" or in other disparaging terms
5. Becoming embroiled in controversy which divides the town when there is no moral issue at stake
6. Failing to be a good host or hostess either at your home or in your classroom
7. Neglecting to remember that the public has a right to expect more of you than of a non-public worker or of another public worker who is not influencing children

The community is both a teacher's playground and his workshop. Many phases of community life can be utilized to the improvement of classroom efficiency. A teacher may arrange for field trips to lumber mills, to packing plants, to factories, to large stores, to neighboring dairies, and to machine shops and garages. He may call upon professional and business men and women to contribute to assembly programs: a dentist with his charts could demonstrate good tooth care; a doctor could show slides of common ailments, with suggestions for care and prevention.

## DISCUSSION PROBLEM

To clarify your thinking as to the part your actual classroom situation plays in organizing your room, a sketch of a seventh-grade classroom in an older grade-school building (8–4 plan) with homogeneous grouping within the grade is presented. In size the room is not unusual, its inside dimensions (including the cloak-room) being 28 by 32 feet. The room is deficient architecturally, as are thousands of older classrooms in the United States. This, however, is not your problem, as you cannot rebuild the building. Your immediate problem is to take the room as it is and with this as a starting point build the most efficient school organization possible.

The room has new seats, individual, adjustable, for thirty-six persons. The class is divided into Seven-A (higher achievement group) and Seven-B. Your survey of the room on Friday before school starts on Monday discloses the following:

1. The teacher's desk is a large one of good quality, and is in the center of the room at the rear.
2. The bookcase at the left front is a large one, and contains an unusually fine collection of books for this academic level. The library is in good condition.
3. The pencil sharpener at the left front of the room is fastened to a little platform which is nailed to the wall.
4. The dictionary at the front of the room is held by a rack which is fixed to the wall. It can be moved without much effort.
5. The flag in the front of the room is held by a circular, iron-based standard which is fastened to the floor by wood screws.
6. The chair in the front of the room is a large one of the arm-chair type. It is movable.
7. There are blackboards across the front of the room and down the right side. The bulletin board at the front of the room occupies the same space as does one section of black-board which has been removed to make a space for the bulletin board.
8. The electric clock is near the center of the room on the right wall. Electrical connections make imperative that it remain where it now is.
9. The books in the front of the room are used by pupils in the sixth grade, which is in the room adjoining yours to the front. The sixth-grade library is inadequate and the use of supplementary books from your room is necessary.

## QUESTIONS ON THE PROBLEM

1. The teacher's desk is at the rear of the room. Is this a good place for it? State all the advantages you can think of for having the desk at the rear of the room. For having it at the front of the room.

2. As far as discipline is concerned, is the teacher at any disadvantage if he is behind the pupils rather than in front of them?

3. Should you decide to move the teacher's desk, where shall you put it? Justify your placement of the desk in the light of convenience. Of easy movement of pupils.

4. The bookcase, pencil sharpener, and dictionary being close together suggests a problem. What is it?

5. Is the pencil sharpener well placed? Why? Why not? If undesirably placed, where shall you ask the custodian to place it? Give your reasons.

6. The placement of school equipment constitutes one phase of school organization. If well placed it increases efficiency; if poorly placed, it causes commotion, disturbance, and disciplinary problems. Your assignment: Make a revised sketch of this room and place the equipment in a way that you believe will be more effective. Justify each change that you make. Give special thought to the bookcase.

7. The 7-A class is seated on the left side of the room, the 7-B on the right. Assuming that the bookcase cannot be conveniently moved, explain the machinery you will set up in order that books may be used conveniently by both groups.

8. The globe is suspended from the ceiling. Is it well placed?

9. Do you like the location of the flag? What is the official place of a flag in a classroom?

10. Two of the classroom doors open outward; one of the cloakroom doors opens into the classroom, the other into the cloakroom. Should classroom doors open in or out? What is the rule for corridor doors leading to the outside? Does the same rule apply to a classroom door opening into a corridor?

11. Show how the cloakroom can easily lead to a discipline problem. How are you going to keep this trouble from developing?

12. Is there a fire hazard in the arrangement of this room? If so, point out where and how it exists. Granting you have the

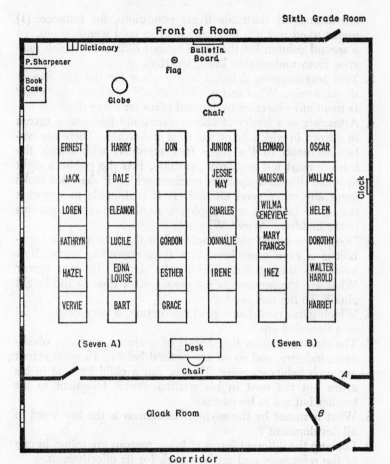

Front of Room

Sixth Grade Room

Dictionary

P.Sharpener

Bulletin Board

Flag

Book Case

Globe

Chair

Clock

| ERNEST | HARRY | DON | JUNIOR | LEONARD | OSCAR |
| JACK | DALE | | JESSIE MAY | MADISON | WALLACE |
| LOREN | ELEANOR | | CHARLES | WILMA GENEVIEVE | HELEN |
| KATHRYN | LUCILE | GORDON | DONNALIE | MARY FRANCES | DOROTHY |
| HAZEL | EDNA LOUISE | ESTHER | IRENE | INEZ | WALTER HAROLD |
| VERVIE | BART | GRACE | | | HARRIET |

(Seven A)

(Seven B)

Desk

Chair

A

Cloak Room

B

Corridor

authority, make any changes in the doors so as to minimize this hazard. Number the doors and state the changes you feel are desirable.

## STUDY QUESTIONS

1. Describe a situation in which you participated where the person who was best prepared was "master of the situation."
2. In one column list all the advantages you can think of which accrue from living in a home (when teaching) where there

are thoroughly desirable living conditions, for instance: (1) undisturbed rest, (2) sufficient heat in cold weather, etc. In a second column list the more serious difficulties which may arise from undesirable living quarters.

3. Your text suggests detailed lesson plans for the first five or six days only. What sort of plans should you have after that? Is there any objection to detailed plans for every day?

4. A teacher as a leader of children may not frequent a tavern in a town in which he or she lives and works. There are certain elements in the town (not criminal) with which the teacher must not regularly associate. Has the public a right to make demands upon its teachers which it does not make upon any other good citizen? It is reasonable to expect a teacher to be a better example for youth than are the parents of the children? Why? Why not?

5. "Keeping a bright child employed to the extent of his capabilities is even more important than expending extra effort upon the least gifted child in the room." Do you agree? What are the arguments for giving extra time to the bright child? To the dull one?

6. Which gains most from good instruction, a very bright child or a very dull one?

7. The chapter implies that habits of neatness, courtesy, obedience, industry, and so on are general habits. To what extent are such habits specific? That is, can a child be neat in his attire but not neat in his written work? Obedient to his teacher but not to his parents?

8. What is meant by the saying, "Readiness is the key word in all development"?

9. Look up the different forms of homogeneous groupings in one of the references and analyze each for its effectiveness.

10. Do good students use as many poor methods of study as do poor students? Substantiate your answer.

11. Is reading ability a sound basis for homogeneous grouping? Substantiate your answer.

12. What is meant by "being stigmatized by a label?"

## SELECTED READINGS

ALEXANDER, WILLIAM M., and HALVERSON, PAUL M. *Effective Teaching in Secondary Schools.* New York: Holt, Rinehart & Winston, Inc., 1956. Pp. 133–57. Gives a good breakdown of the teacher's classroom activities from the standpoint of when the activity should be emphasized.

BUTLER, FRANK A. *Improvement of Teaching in Secondary Schools.* 3d ed. Chicago: University of Chicago Press, 1954. Pp. 324–40. Places emphasis upon the physical and social environment as items in effective classroom organization and instruction.

CHAMBERLAIN, LEO M., and KINDRED, LESLIE W. *The Teacher and School Organization.* 3d ed. Englewood Cliffs, N. J.: Prentice-Hall, Inc., 1958. Chapter 17. The teacher's role in the use of buildings, equipment, and supplies.

KYTE, GEORGE C. *The Elementary School Teacher at Work.* New York: Holt, Rinehart & Winston, Inc., 1957. Chapter 13, "Planning Classroom Procedures," stresses the significance of good preplanning if instruction is to be effective.

MEHL, MARIE A., MILLS, HUBERT H., and DOUGLASS, HARL R. *Teaching in Elementary School.* 2d ed. New York: The Ronald Press Co., 1958. Chapter 21 discusses the various grouping plans in common use today.

NATIONAL SOCIETY FOR THE STUDY OF EDUCATION. *The Education of Exceptional Children. Forty-ninth Yearbook,* Part II. Chicago: University of Chicago Press, 1950. Services and procedures proved to be effective in teaching the exceptional child.

OLSEN, EDWARD G., *et al. School and Community.* 2d ed. Englewood Cliffs, N. J.: Prentice-Hall, Inc., 1954. Chapters 5 and 8. Using the community in the teaching process as a phase of classroom organization for instruction.

WRIGHTSTONE, J. WAYNE. *Class Organization for Instruction.* Subtitle: "What Research Says to the Teacher." Washington, D. C.: Department of Classroom Teachers, American Educational Research Association of the National Education Association, 1957. A 33-page booklet which summarizes research probings on topic indicated by the title.

---

Altogether too commonly the layman without professional educational background mistakenly conceives of teaching entirely as an instructional function. Not infrequently college instructors in academic departments make the same mistake. Both fail to see that the instructional function is interwoven with numerous details, details which have little or nothing to do with instruction directly. Among the problems of teaching are those concerned with marking, recording, reporting, and promoting. All are administrative in nature, and all require specialized training, as the problems involved are not problems that can be eliminated simply by having good academic background plus good intelligence.

## MARKING

The words "mark" and "grade," as applied to schoolwork, are commonly confused. Technically, a grade is a major division of the instructional program of a school; a mark is a measure of achievement in learning. The confusion exists when, as is commonly heard, a pupil reports a "grade of B," a "grade of 83," or a "grade of S." He is referring to an achievement *mark*. Strictly speaking, these are not grades unless the ratings are definitely secured by ranking the pupil in some methodical way, in terms of other pupils' achievements.

**Percentage and Other Marking Systems.**   When the pupil above reported a "grade of 83," he was stating what is known as a "centesimal grade." This is a percentage *mark* based on the traditional marking system. It implies that 0 equals no achievement at all and that 100 is equivalent to perfection. This plan of marking, now tending to obsolescence, states an arbitrarily selected point, usually between 60 and 75, as passing. Obviously the difficulty lies in determining an individual's achievement in terms of the small gradations. It is hard enough to be accurate when the passing range is broken into four large divisions, A, B, C, D, without breaking the range into thirty or more divisions. Divisions of Superior, Very Good, Average, Passing, and Inferior can usually be determined by comparison with other pupils, although the rankings would vary for any individual student were he compared to another group. A percentage mark, because in form it is absolute rather than relative, usually ends up either as a weighted guess or as a comparative (with the remainder of the class) mark expressed numerically. This makes it relative.

The trend is definitely toward evaluating a pupil's work in rather broad divisions and in terms of the remainder of the class. The A-B-C-D division is commonly used where the traditional report card to parents has not been supplanted by some other form of reporting. When the traditional card has been dropped, teachers can express accomplishment with much more detail and clarity in the form of a general statement of evaluation.

Numbers are sometimes used in place of letters. The significance is the same, 1, 2, 3, 4, 5 being equivalent to A, B, C, D, F. Somewhat descriptive terms are not uncommon and have the advantage of being comparative. Commonly used are Highest, High, Medium, Low, and Lowest. Even more descriptive terms, and as a result more comparative, are: Much Above Average, Above Average, Average, Below Average, and Much Below Average.

All marking systems are open to criticism. Because of the difficulty of assigning an absolute mark, there is the necessity of comparing pupils in a class relatively. This has the weakness that the mark does not indicate how well the objective has been achieved. A child may, on a comparative basis, be an A relative to the class he is in, when, were he in another class of much greater general ability, he might fall into the C group. All in all, however, the relative-marking system, based on a more or less homogeneous grouping of pupils as to ability, is probably as valid a basis of comparison as any.

**Distribution of Marks.** Schools using a five-letter marking plan commonly employ what is known as the normal distribution or probability curve. Graphically, this produces a symmetrical bell-shaped curve. This plan for distributing marks works well with large groups and is good if the sampling of pupils' achievement is large enough to make for reliability. Under the normal curve, different distributions are possible, depending upon the shape of the curve. Some schools give 7 per cent of the pupils A's; 18 per cent B's; 50 per cent C's; 18 per cent D's, and 7 per cent F's. Another distribution, also based on the normal probability curve, arbitrarily allocates marks 7-24-38-24-7, that is, 7 pupils in a hundred receive A's; 24 in a hundred, B's; 38 in a hundred, C's; 24 in a hundred, D's, and 7 in a hundred, F's. This is in actuality an estimate of the limit that would be approached if the number of observations were indefinitely increased and the class intervals were indefinitely decreased, while the total area under the curve remained constant. Obviously, the curve will not fit small groups with much accuracy, nor will it fit highly selected groups. In practice, a teacher's marks should approximate the theoretical distribution but never actually follow it without variation.

From the everyday, practical aspect, the teacher avoids trouble for himself and the administration if he remembers that the *average* tends to prevail in the academic sphere as well as in things physical. This means that he avoids extremes of high and low marks on the first reports he makes out for parents. Later, when he knows the abilities of his pupils better, he can move more accurately toward the extremes. On the first report to parents, the poorest pupil in achievement should probably be given the lowest mark, and the lowest possible *passing* mark. (This presumes, of course, that the group is unselected.) But the good students should not be given the extreme in high marks the first month. A teacher has no place to go the following month when they do better work if he has given the highest mark possible the first month. If marks are kept relative, pupils usually inform parents who fail to understand a lower mark than has been formerly received, "It's the best mark she gave, Mother," and the parent is usually satisfied.

There is always a question of whether a normal pupil who is making anything resembling a serious effort should ever be given a failing mark. If the child and the learning materials are appropriately adapted to the grade level, failure should at least be rare. The normal-curve idea may still be used even if all students are passed.

Although marks are incentives, to use them as such is a questionable procedure. The end desired from the learning point of view is not the mark but the control of the value represented by the mark. The child is inclined to make the mark an end in itself.

Every teacher recognizes the tremendous responsibility which is his when he sends a child home with a report card or with any other written statement which states with finality that a child is not being promoted to the next grade. A child must be promoted if he achieves up to his ability. His attitudes toward his school, toward his teacher, and toward his own ability to succeed are involved. He must feel some sense of accomplishment in what he is doing if his mental health is not to suffer. A failing child is an unhappy child, even when he covers his unhappiness with a front of indifference. On the other hand, to tell a child in black and white that he is an excellent student when he is only average is injuring his chance for academic success later, perhaps leading him astray in his vocational choice for later life. The wise teacher distributes marks with great care.

**Suggestions for Improving Standards.** Some suggestions for improving standards in testing and distributing marks follow:

1. Make your marks as objective as you can.
2. Make your tests *valid*. That is, try to make them measure what you have taught and what the pupil is supposed to know.
3. Make your tests *reliable*. That is, try to make your tests such that the same test would get the same results for a child were he to take it over again immediately. Again, if your test is reliable, another form of the same test, of equal difficulty, will get practically the same result for a given child. Keep in mind that a reliable test or a reliable evaluation of any kind is consistent; it will agree with itself and will not be influenced by subjective factors.
4. Avoid being influenced by outcomes of learning other than the one on which you are marking the pupil. That is, a child's poor handwriting or spelling should not influence his mark in history.
5. If you use a percentage distribution, recognize its limitations. Break the passing range by per cents into four parts and assign marks on a four-point basis within this range, keeping in mind that the large part of your class is average in ability in any given subject field and should receive an average mark for the range.

## DETERMINING GRADE LEVELS

Among the many difficult duties which the teacher and the principal share in the management of the classroom and the school, whether it be a small school or a building with many rooms and many teachers involved, is that of grading pupils for purposes of instruction. Basically, grading has but one purpose: that of bringing groups of subject matter and groups of children together for purposes of instructing the latter most efficiently in the former. Its prime motive is economy both of time and of effort.

**Class Plan of Grading.** As one studies the very precise and orderly arrangement of a school system by grades, he is struck by the mechanical precision of the entire plan. It is apparently simple, clear, and unconfused, but to the initiated the entire scheme of grading and promoting is one heavily cloaked by doubt and suspicion, by lack of clear purpose and of coordinated, logical thinking. The visible part of the machinery has tended to become the goal rather than the road to that goal.

Teachers at the close of the school year are commonly in doubt as to whether certain pupils should or should not be promoted. Parents and pupils press for favorable decisions. Thoughtless principals and superintendents cite "normal distribution curves" and imply that any scheme which treats all alike is certainly eminently fair and desirable. To the clear-thinking administrator and the well-trained teacher, however, the very fact that all are treated alike is evidence of unfairness. Treating all in exactly the same manner would be desirable only if all children were alike. Children differ much in their capacities, their likes, their temperaments, and particularly their adaptability to the content of the school's curriculum, commonly known as subject matter. To assume that all are alike and that all should be promoted on any single basis can lead only to a mechanical system of grading and promoting which crushes individuality without strengthening the group.

It goes almost without saying that, were the class plan of instruction to be abandoned, the problem of grading and promoting would take care of itself. The problem is at once one of economy and one of sound educational practice. There are many children to be cared for; there is a limited sum of money to be expended; qualified teachers are difficult to obtain, and there is a fairly well-defined body of knowledge to be taught. The problem resolves itself into the best and most economical method of making this common fund of knowledge directly and readily available for each child in a given community. When the Sieur de La Salle in or about 1684 instituted class instruction in place of the commonly used individual recitation, he not only made some education available for many children of the poor who otherwise would never have had it, but he also laid the foundation for two of the most vexing problems a teacher and administrator face: grading and promoting pupils accurately, fairly, and to the general good of the child.

**Promoting and Denying Promotion.** A teacher is to a great extent responsible for promotions from his grade, but under all conditions he should consult his principal or superintendent before denying the annual promotion to any child.

If scholastic marks are good, the child is promoted. Exceptions, rare indeed, would occur when the child is much too young chronologically for the grade he is in and when there is a possibility that a child's health, already poor, might be impaired by the strain an advanced grade would produce.

When scholastic marks are poor, two questions must be given consideration: Why are the marks poor, and shall promotion be made in spite of the poor marks? The two questions are interwoven and must be so treated. A teacher may be able to satisfactorily explain, even condone, poor marks—but still face the problem of denying promotion. Or a teacher may not be able to say why the marks are poor. As a basis of promotion, scholastic marks as the single criterion are definitely open to question. Usually such marks are based upon tests given once a month, upon the teacher's personal estimation of the pupil's academic ability, and upon the child's relationship to other pupils in achievement.

Factors which enter into the problem of denying promotion to a student are numerous. Among the most significant are those factors affecting the child's scholastic marks in terms of his:

Chronological age
Mental ability

Physiological maturity
Previous training
Environmental (home) situation
State of health
School industry, social development, adaptability, and general fitness for promotion as judged by his teacher

One of the first questions always asked when considering promotion deals with the child's *chronological age.* Is he old now for the grade he is in? If "yes," how much "out-of-grade" is he? Will keeping him in the present grade another year make a bad situation worse?

The child's *mental ability* is next on the list of questions for promotion. What is his mental ability? That is, what is the relationship between his mental age as indicated by good mental tests and his chronological age? More simply, has he the mental ability to do the work of the next grade in a satisfactory manner?

Next comes the question of *physiological maturity.* Is the child well matured or undermatured for his age? Socially, would he profit more by going to the grade above along with his classmates than he would by being held with children coming up from a grade now one year below him academically? Does he carry his load easily with advanced-grade pupils on the athletic field? Is he large for his age or small? All these are questions of maturity, but of a maturity that is not entirely chronological or intellectual.

Another question is one of *previous training.* Has the child a good or poor background? A child may be retarded, but his retardation may not be due to lack of mental acuity or maturity, either chronological or physiological. He may have had poor school advantages, have changed schools often, and have missed much formal schooling. Promotion under such conditions is probably warranted, unless it is to senior high school, on the ground that there is considerable repetition of work in the upper grades and that given the opportunity he can probably make up deficiencies. This is a case on record, for example:

Gerald C. in the sixth grade was doing work below the norm required for promotion. He was trying hard, and he frequently surprised his teacher by his reaction to questions requiring logical thinking. His attendance was good. He turned in his written work on time, although some of it was poor. He presented no discipline problem. These facts were determined in Gerald's case: He had come to the city from a neighboring town. He had been in the schools in that town for only three weeks, having moved to the town from a rural district in a neighboring state. This state required only eight months of school a year in its rural schools. Gerald's schooling consisted of forty months of work in a rural school under a teacher who taught on an average twenty-four classes a day and whose college training was limited to one year. Gerald's classmates in the sixth grade had been aided by forty-five months of schooling under a teacher who was a college graduate with good training for teaching and who specialized in a single grade. Gerald was doing work in language and geography for the first time.

There is every reason to believe that, in a situation like this, the child will catch up (approximately) with his classmates by the time he has finished the eighth grade.

The *environmental situation* under which the child lives poses questions to be considered. From what sort of a home does he come? Is it a home of culture and refinement, or is it a home where the children gain little or nothing academically from their parents? Is it a broken home? Are both parents living? Does the mother work to help support the family? Who are the child's playmates after school hours? How does he spend his leisure time?

All of these and many others of a similar nature are pertinent to the question as to why a child is failing a grade and as to whether he will be served better by being promoted or by being held in the same grade. These things a teacher must know before making his decision.

The child's state of health should always be considered when a child is not succeeding in his schoolwork. Although conclusive data are hard to assemble, there is evidence that approximately 75 per cent of school pupils are fairly normal as far as physical health is concerned. For the remaining 25 per cent, the abnormality runs all the way from slight or inconsequential deficiencies that the child will outgrow to such severe defects as bad vision and partially impaired hearing. A large number of America's children are undernourished. The disturbing thing about this condition is that a fat, roly-poly lad may be as undernourished as a painfully thin one. Dietitians estimate that some 10 to 15 per cent of children suffer from malnutrition. Possibly 2 per cent of the child population have a speech defect; a little less than 1 per cent have a measurable defect in hearing. Poor vision is the most common of child defects and frequently goes undetected even into adulthood. The number with diseased tonsils and enlarged adenoids is so great that every teacher looks at the failing student always with the question uppermost in his mind, "Is he physically well?"

Evidently, a child who has missed much school because of illness but who is well again can be promoted although the subject matter of the grade is not thoroughly mastered. The question is always what is best for the child, not what is most agreeable to the teacher.

Finally, in evaluation of the child's work in terms of promoting or not promoting, the child's *industry, social development, adaptability,* and *general fitness for promotion* are considered carefully. His parents are always consulted, and their cooperation is secured. To fail to promote, when parents feel the action is either unwise or unfair or both, is to lose the cooperation which the child's welfare demands. A child who remains in a grade for a second year should do so only with his parents' approval.

A child may fail because of lack of interest. Thus a promotion which is a change of scenery sometimes creates the necessary stimulation. Again, a child who is academically in a grade below the social group he plays with frequently lacks in motivation for doing good work.

A teacher's evaluation of all the factors suggested above, when summarized, clarifies his decision. Consciously or unconsciously, the teacher has considered each during his yearlong association with the child. He should not be in doubt, but if he is, generally the child is served best by keeping him with his social group. This is especially true if his mental and physical maturity fit him best for that group. Data from many studies indicate that in about 80 per cent of the cases studied, the pupil repeating a grade does no better work his second year than he did in his first year. Many pupils do poorer work. Probably not more than 20 per cent show any measurable improvement by taking work over.

**Acceleration.** Skipping a grade is commonly spoken of as *acceleration*. Studies made of the results of grade-skipping indicate strongly that:

1. Grade-skipping is practiced very widely.
2. Approximately one pupil in twenty in the elementary school is accelerated.
3. Semiannual promotion leads to more acceleration than does annual promotion.
4. There are no harmful results academically from grade-skipping for superior pupils as measured by teachers' marks.
5. Teachers generally are favorable to acceleration.
6. School administrators are, in general, opposed to grade-skipping by the child who is now in his correct age group. Reasons for the opposition involve the child's social adjustment and his mental hygiene. School administrators not infrequently argue that acceleration leads to hurrying through school, missing most of the fun of childhood, getting into high school at too early an age to profit most from the social influence, and getting into and out of college before maturity.
7. Educators and psychologists are not sure that grade-skipping is a bad thing. They argue that the child who is allowed to skip a grade is a gifted child and that gifted children have greater potential to think and work independently than is common for most pupils. They argue that gifted children should be graduated from high school a year or two earlier in order that they may get their professional training out of the way and start making their contributions to society. Again, there is accumulating a body of evidence that the gifted child who has been ac-

celerated is the one most likely to be accepted by his class-mates. This would indicate that the accelerated, gifted child is not socially maladjusted.

**Half-Year Promotion.** The half-year promotion started years ago, with the thought of breaking the rigid lock step of annual promotions. As far as age homogeneity goes, neither plan has an advantage over the other. There is more administrative work for both teachers and principals under the half-year promotion system, and some educators believe there is poorer articulation between the elementary school and the high school. The trend seems to be toward annual promotions. This may be influenced by the fact that with ever increasing enrollment, the administrative work load is great enough with annual promotions without adding to it through half-year promotions.

**Grouping Within the Grade.** Although regrading the pupil is an administrative problem, shared by the teacher and principal, the teacher being responsible for selection of the pupils for consideration, the job of grouping the pupils within the grade is largely a task which the classroom teacher must perform alone.

The question of whether the plan of grouping within the grade shall be used is in the hands of the administration. The policy being once determined upon, the classroom teacher faces the responsibility of making up his groups. The number of groups that can best be handled in a grade must be determined experimentally and depends, of course, on the size of the class, the range of ability of the students, the number of subjects in respect to which the grouping takes place, the physical room itself. Two or three groups to the room is most common, but the evidence is not conclusive that this number is best.

The grouping-within-the-grade plan has the big advantage of gearing subject matter more accurately to the child than is possible when but one group is used for the entire subject

**AGE-GRADE TABLE FOR ELEMENTARY SCHOOL ORGANIZED ON EIGHT-YEAR PLAN**

| Grade | 5-9/6-3 | 6-3/6-9 | 6-9/7-3 | 7-3/7-9 | 7-9/8-3 | 8-3/8-9 | 8-9/9-3 | 9-3/9-9 | 9-9/10-3 | 10-3/10-9 | 10-9/11-3 | 11-3/11-9 | 11-9/12-3 | 12-3/12-9 | 12-9/13-3 | 13-3/13-9 | 13-9/14-3 | 14-3/14-9 | 14-9/15-3 | 15-3/15-9 | 15-9/16-3 |
|---|---|---|---|---|---|---|---|---|---|---|---|---|---|---|---|---|---|---|---|---|---|
| 1 B | 10 | 130 | | | | | | | | | | | | | | | | | | | |
| 1 A | | 18 | 26 | 7 | 2 | | | | | | | | | | | | | | | | |
| 2 B | | 16 | 40 | 34 | 11 | 3 | 2 | | | | | | | | | | | | | | |
| 2 A | | | 8 | 10 | 30 | 7 | 5 | 2 | | | | | | | | | | | | | |
| 3 B | | | | 8 | 28 | 20 | 13 | 9 | 1 | | | | | | | | | | | | |
| 3 A | | | | | 6 | 7 | 13 | 6 | 5 | 1 | | | | | | | | | | | |
| 4 B | | | | | 5 | 13 | 10 | 15 | 4 | 2 | | | | | | | | | | | |
| 4 A | | | | | | | 3 | 15 | 5 | 5 | 3 | | | | | | | | | | |
| 5 B | | | | | | | | 10 | 10 | 15 | 2 | 1 | | | | | | | | | |
| 5 A | | | | | | | | 1 | 15 | 8 | 5 | 3 | 1 | | | | | | | | |
| 6 B | | | | | | | | | 10 | 15 | 9 | 1 | 1 | | 1 | | | | | | |
| 6 A | | | | | | | | | 1 | 2 | 8 | 4 | 1 | 2 | 1 | 3 | 1 | | | | |
| 7 B | | | | | | | | | | 5 | 9 | 6 | 1 | 3 | 1 | 3 | 3 | | | | |
| 7 A | | | | | | | | | | | 1 | 10 | 4 | 2 | 3 | 3 | 1 | | | | |
| 8 B | | | | | | | | | | | 1 | 12 | 5 | 6 | 5 | 9 | 6 | 15 | 8 | 9 | 1 |
| 8 A | | | | | | | | | | | | 3 | | 7 | 4 | 12 | 8 | 12 | 12 | 3 | 6 |

Legend (diagonal bands) with totals:

| | Category | Totals |
|---|---|---|
| Retarded | More than two years below grade | 31 |
| Retarded | Two years below grade | 13 |
| Retarded | One and one half years below grade | 26 |
| Retarded | One year below grade | 47 |
| Normal | One half year below grade | 79 |
| Normal | Up to grade | 683 |
| Accelerated | One half year above grade | 136 |
| Accelerated | Year or more above grade | 62 |

matter of the grade in question. Within-the-grade grouping also is good in that it keeps the child with his social group yet allows for some recognition of individual differences. The teacher's work of course tends to increase with the number of groups.

**Age-Grade Level.** The more or less standardized age-grade chart is the common means used by administrators to determine easily and with some accuracy the extent of over-ageness or underageness in a grade or in a school. Although there is some variation in different localities, in general the age-grade level is as follows: a child is "within grade" under these conditions: Grade I, 6 years to 8 years 3 months; Grade II, 7 years 3 months to 9 years 3 months; Grade III, 8 years 3 months to 10 years 3 months; Grade IV, 9 years 3 months to 11 years 3 months; Grade V, 10 years 3 months to 12 years 3 months; Grade VI, 11 years 3 months to 13 years 3 months; Grade VII, 12 years 3 months to 14 years 3 months, and Grade VIII, 13 years 3 months to 15 years 3 months.

It is evident that the range for the eight grades covers a period from 6 years to 15 years 3 months. This is saying that a child who finishes the elementary school at 14 years is exactly "in grade." At an age over 14 he is not "out-of-grade" until he is past 15 years 3 months in age. By making up an age-grade table for the class, the teacher can at a glance determine which pupils are young for the grade, which are about right in age, and which are laggards although technically they are counted "in grade."

On page 214 is an age-grade table for an elementary school organized on the eight-year plan. The situation shown is not abnormal, although there is slightly more over-ageness indicated than is commonly found. Attention is called to Grade 7-A where there is one student of approximately 11 years of age and one of approximately 16 years. Although such wide disparities in age within a grade are not customarily found, they show up when promotions are made on an achievement basis rather than on an annual promotion basis regardless of scholastic excellence.

## USING RECORDS

A record is a bit of school machinery and as such must give an educational account of itself. Records are kept to be used. If never used, they are of no value; and if used but rarely, they are of little more than historical value.

In the modern school there is much need for complete and reliable information on many subjects. Information about pupils, about equipment, about teacher-pupil relationships, and about a multitude of other details becomes essential if the school is to serve the pupils. Good records are invaluable, but records poorly kept are worthless.

Records are of service to three distinct groups of persons. These groups when taken together are the school. The first group served by records is the big group which comprises the *pupils* of the school. In the second instance records serve the *teachers*. In the third instance records serve principals, supervisors, department heads, the superintendent, and the board of education. These are the *administrative body* of the school. To a somewhat lesser degree and more indirectly, records serve parents and the taxpaying public.

**Value to Pupils.** The pupil is served by records in many ways, varying in importance according to the situation. The development of the pupil morally, spiritually, intellectually, physically, and socially is the great responsibiity of education. Emphasis today on these objectives has taken the form of guidance. It is a comparatively new word academically, but it is by no means new in its implications. Records, then, serve the guidance function in order that the pupil may profit.

The pupil is served distinctly by good records when he transfers to another school. With good records he loses very little by transfer. Without records he suffers.

The child is served when reports to parents are accurate, clear, and comprehensive.

Without good records no child can be classified accurately. Thus classification is best served by good records. Finally, without records the child suffers when a teacher cannot know the extent to which he is working up to his ability.

**Significance to Teachers.** The teacher is served by good records in a multitude of ways. Of these, those named below are of the greatest significance. With records a teacher is able to:

1. Speak with accuracy concerning a pupil and his school progress.
2. Preview a pupil's work before undertaking for that pupil the instructional function.
3. Know with considerable accuracy what can rightfully be expected from the pupil in everyday accomplishment.
4. Guide the pupil in his daily work and in maintaining good health, both physical and mental, and aid him in his adjustment both to his school environment and to his surroundings in general.
5. Recognize readily and encourage upon a sound basis of information any special aptitudes or abilities the child may possess.
6. Know with more than hearsay knowledge the facts concerning the child's home life, his social background, and what he does in his leisure time.

These are only a few of the ways in which records serve teachers. In a general way, records are the teacher's balance sheet for the pupils as an item in daily business and, when taken in the large, a ledger (or inventory, as it were) of where the teacher has worked to a profit, where to no gain if not to a loss.

**Value to the Administrative Body.** Records are indispensable from the viewpoint of the school as an institution. The administrative body uses records to:

1. Determine the extent to which public funds are being spent wisely.
2. Determine accurately the amount of state public funds to be allocated to each school on the basis of attendance.
3. Aid in placement of each pupil in a large school system to avoid overloading of buildings, staffs, and transportation facilities, but also to best serve the pupil's convenience.
4. Keep, as a permanent record, the vital statistics on each child enrolled.
5. Evaluate teacher load in terms of pupil-hours and classes taught.
6. Make possible, because of the permanent record feature, long-term studies of costs, retardation, building needs, and other researches of similar nature which depend upon accurate data for significance.
7. Interpret from data the causes of undesirable conditions and move intelligently to correct such conditions.

**Kinds of Records.** Records are good only in terms of the service they render. This means that the records in use must be scrutinized closely from two viewpoints: Which portions of this record serve no useful purpose now and give little promise of ever being of service? What data, if any, should be added to this record in order that those data now recorded may be more usable?

A list of records commonly used is given below. Not every school uses all of these, but each is used under varying school situations:

*Cumulative Records.* These are individual, permanent records that are kept continually up to date by the teacher or the school. Each one is an educational history containing fairly complete information about the pupil's school achievements, courses studied, attendance, health, and similar pertinent data.

*Health and Physical Records.* These are systematic collections of data concerning illnesses, immunizations, physical activities, and general physical condition of the pupils.

*Mental Test Scores.* These are records of scores made on tests designed to measure the child's natural ability or personality. Forms commonly used are standardized.

*Achievement Test Scores.* These are tests of knowledges, skills, and understandings in a given field taught in school. Sometimes called educational tests, they may or may not be standardized.

*Attendance Records.* These are "musts." State School funds are commonly distributed on the basis of attendance. Accuracy is imperative.

*Unit of Work.* This record is used where the curriculum has been broken into units. Records are kept of each unit accomplished by the child.

*Personality Traits.* These records are usually based on personality inventories, attitude tests, social adjustment, and the teacher's estimate of emotional stability.

Always there are records required either by state law or by mandate of the state department of education. Whether useless or usable, these must be kept and kept accurately. In general, these records are comparatively few in number, easy to make out, and of significance in terms of vital statistics. Usually such records deal with attendance, with health and physical conditions in the classroom and in the school, and with graduation. The administrative office of the school summarizes teachers' statements and makes elaborate reports to official state school offices as well as to the city superintendent.

## PREPARING REPORTS

Teachers often object to keeping records and making reports. There is always the feeling, "My job is to teach these children, not to waste all my time in bookkeeping." The reaction is a rational one, but the conclusion is wrong. A teacher's job is a double-duty one; that of instructor, and that of recorder, interpreter, and reporter. A teacher cannot be truly successful in the former if he is not reasonably concerned with the latter. In the words of Henry Van Dyke, "This is my work; my blessing, not my doom. Of all who live, I am the one by whom this work can best be done in the right way."

Teachers' reports fall into two main divisions: reports to administrators and reports to the home.

**Reports to Administrators.** Reports to administrators are of five types:

1. Reports at the beginning of the year only, on first week enrollments, attendance in general, seating, and textbooks and other supplies. This report is to the principal or superintendent.
2. Reports to administrative officials at the end of either the first month or a six-week period on attendance, health conditions in your school, expendable supplies, and so on.
3. Annual reports to administrative officers dealing with a large variety of topics, among which are attendance, honor rolls, promotions, and special achievement from the classroom.
4. Special reports, upon demand, to the central office. These may deal with age-grade progress (commonly by names of pupils), attendance, illness, honor rolls, supplies on hand, and items which can be used for general publicity by the superintendent's office.
5. Duplicate forms of reports to homes.

**Reports to Parents.** As records change, and take into account the fact that "the whole child" goes to school, reports to parents should also stress the fact that the child is growing as a whole.

Needless to say, it is very difficult to tell parents accurately about the progress of their children in school. The child is (presumably) developing in many ways, no two of which may be of equal importance. One thing is certain, the traditional report card, with its marks of 78 or 82, or A, B, C, does not tell any part of the story well, even that part which deals with the child's success in his school subjects.

The case is strong against the report card in its traditional form. Basically, its greatest weakness is in its lack of validity. This is to say that the report card does not do what it purports to do. It purports to tell parents clearly, concisely, correctly, and comprehensively of the progress or lack of progress of their children in their school life. It fails even to do the one thing most necessary (although this is not easy): to tell parents clearly, concisely, correctly, and comprehensively of the progress of the child in his subject matter.

Because of the official nature of the report card, it is usually given more significance by parents than it deserves. A difference of two percentage points is frequently taken seriously by parents. The card tends to make parents misunderstand the real objectives of the school, and usually fails to evaluate well, if at all, the child's growth in the more intangible outcomes of initiative, enthusiasm, attitudes, social growth, health habits, and appreciations. The trend is toward securing not only more accuracy but greater comprehension in reporting, toward reporting more specifically on the child's strengths and weaknesses; toward clarity; and toward a report which in general gives parents more understandable information about their child. This kind of report deals with behavior patterns; with a child's attitudes; with special difficulties the child has; with special aptitudes he shows; and with indications as to whether the child is working hard or not. It tries to anticipate questions a parent might ask if visiting with the teacher.

Many schools are asking parents to come in person for the pupil's report card. This allows for expansion on ideas suggested on the card. Time is set aside for these calls during the first two weeks of each month. A few schools use a "Parent's Night" for this purpose.

In a comparatively few instances, this detailed information goes to parents in the form of a letter, although, because of the large amount of work this entails for the teacher, the practice is not general.

The type of report now commonly used is quite large in size. A folder which folds to a size of 5½ by 8½ inches is not uncommon. Items are arranged in such a manner that the teacher may evaluate a child's progress by using such listed terms as "Satisfactory," "Is Improving," or "Needs to Improve." Many items dealing with other desired outcomes of education than subject matter are found. "Social Growth," "Work Habits," "Health Habits," and "Social Adjustment" are listed quite commonly for the primary and intermediate grades.

School subjects are evaluated in the same manner as are achievement goals in behavior. By evaluating the child's growth in a very wide range of activities, the teacher can give the parents a much more comprehensive picture of the school progress of the child.

**Conferences with Parents.** The conference between the parent and the teacher is probably the best supplementary aid to the report card that can be found. It cannot be used as a substitute for the card because of its unofficial nature. Some teachers write informal notes to parents asking if they would like to drop in for a brief visit, suggesting the time. The visit is definitely professional and should be terminated at once if parents are using the visit as a grievance springboard.

The teacher makes up his conference date-book for all convenient times during the month. It is not necessary to meet each parent every month, but in some cases where the child is failing to adjust well, a monthly conference is indicated. At the conference the teacher should have at hand all possible data concerning the child. He should lead the conversation into topics dealing with the child's problems. Special difficulties the child is having, the extent to which he is working up to his ability, his special aptitudes, and his social adjustment to his group are among the topics to be considered.

Before the conference-with-parents idea can be used successfully, parents must be educated to accept the idea of the conference, to see its significance, and to come when asked. Also, classroom teachers must have some formal training in this guidance technique before assuming the responsibility. Otherwise, the parents will often fail to appear for the conference or else will try to take the conference out of the hands of the untrained teacher. The conference is definitely a guidance technique and should be considered as such.

Reporting to parents, no matter what form is used, is one of the more difficult administrative problems of the classroom teacher. Confusion for the parent and actual injury to the child can be avoided only by the teacher's sound training, tact, and diligence.

## DISCUSSION PROBLEM

### Another Danger in Failing to Promote the Student

John failed in the sixth grade. Too bad that he did, but after all no one was to blame but himself. He didn't try more than half the time, and he was ill and missed much school. His mother is of the type who is always willing to write him an excuse whenever he requests it.

The boy's average for the sixth grade is 68. The school's required passing average is 75. John did passable work in history, which he liked very much. In the little work offered in nature study he ranked high, and he won first prize for the city system in the annual grade-school kite-flying contest.

Well—he failed, so he'll have to take the sixth grade over again. Too bad, because the seventh grade has shopwork and John has shown ability in doing things of that sort. It has been said, too, that the curriculum for the seventh grade in history is the richest planned for any single year in the school's entire offering. He probably won't take any work in either of those fields, as after another year he will be much behind the others and may drop out of school, since he is overage now. Can't help but feel sorry he didn't pass—mighty nice kid. And he might have done much better in the seventh grade—the offering in the junior high school really is more interesting.

## QUESTIONS ON THE PROBLEM

1. Is it sound that the only pupil permitted to take advantage of an especially rich offering in a single grade shall be a student who has passed successfully the previous grade? Discuss.
2. Which would you say is more fundamental to the best interests of John: attainment of 75 per cent in the work of the sixth grade or a chance to find himself in fields which seem to be better fitted to his natural interests and abilities?
3. May not a child who has been in the sixth grade or any other grade for a year, even though his work fails to meet arbitrarily set standards, obtain more benefits from the richer curriculum of the next grade than he would by remaining another year in contact with the old subject matter?
4. John is below average for his grade now. To what extent should this be considered in withholding promotion?
5. There is another child in John's grade who is not being promoted. He is exactly "in grade" now. Is it unfair to promote John and hold this boy, when the other boy is actually slightly better in all his work?
6. Present the argument, numbering your points 1, 2, 3, and so on, for *promoting* John to the seventh grade. Now carefully list the arguments for *holding* him in the same grade.

## STUDY QUESTIONS

1. Criticize this statement: "Basically, grading has but one purpose, that of bringing groups of subject matter and groups of children together for purposes of instructing the latter most efficiently in the former."
2. Can you state other purposes of grading which, if not basic, may be very important?
3. Name some instructional aids now under development which should make group instruction become even more predominant.
4. Is an intelligence test a sound basis for grading? If "Yes," what else would you add?
5. Should a normal child ever fail? Does he fail, or does his teacher fail, if you say "Yes?"

6. Why is it imperative that the teacher be trained in conference techniques before holding formal conferences with parents on pupils' work? Consider the following:

> The parent criticizes the entire school. What will you do or say?
> The parent informs you that he is paying your salary.
> The parent goes into a tearful story.
> The parent loses his temper.
> The parent tells you that *you* have failed.

7. What are the official (required) reports in your home state that must be made by teachers at the end of the first week? at the end of the first month? at the end of the year?
8. What are the obstacles in the way of preventing a teacher from promoting a child in the subjects in which his work is satisfactory and holding him in grade in the subjects in which he failed to meet the course-of-study demands?
9. Is the "fail in one subject, fail all" theory sound? What are the arguments for it? The arguments against it?
10. Promotion in high school is by subject. Why is the practice not more common in the elementary school?
11. Is there any real danger that in sending the parent a so-called comprehensive report that enough emphasis may not be placed on what the parent particularly wants to know: the definite facts concerning the child's academic progress?
12. Is there any reason why the reports made to parents should have a definitely official appearance, as most reports do now, rather than a more attractive format?

## SELECTED READINGS

ADAMS, HAROLD P., and DICKEY, FRANK G. *Basic Principles of Student Teaching.* New York: American Book Co., 1956. Chapter 10. Discusses measurement, promotions, evaluation, and reports.

ASSOCIATION FOR CHILDHOOD EDUCATION. *Reporting on the Growth of Children.* Washington, D. C.: The Association, 1953. Entire publication deals with general topic indicated by the title.

GARRISON, NOBLE LEE. *The Improvement of Teaching.* New York: Holt, Rinehart & Winston, Inc., 1955. Chapters 7, 9, and 10. The three chapters suggested as reading cover in a broad way the topics of evaluation, promotion, and reporting.

GRAMBS, JEAN D., IVERSON, WILLIAM J., and PATTERSON, FRANKLIN K. *Modern Methods in Secondary Education.* Rev. ed. New York: Holt, Rinehart & Winston, Inc., 1958. "Reporting to Parents," p. 509 ff. Sound suggestions on reporting to parents.

GRIEDER, CALVIN, and ROSENSTENGEL, WILLIAM E. *Public School Administration.* New York: The Ronald Press Co., 1954. Pp. 358–62. Recording, reporting, and promoting from the viewpoint of the school administrator.

HARRIS, FRED E. *Three Persistent Educational Problems: Grading, Promoting, and Reporting.* Lexington: University of Kentucky, Bureau of School Service, September, 1953. An excellent monograph which covers the topic with thoroughness.

MEHL, MARIE A., MILLS, HUBERT H., and DOUGLASS, HARL R. *Teaching in Elementary School,* 2d ed. New York: The Ronald Press Co. 1958. Chapter 20, "Recording and Reporting Pupil Growth," discusses mark distribution, marking systems, records, and reports.

OTTO, HENRY J. *Elementary School Organization and Administration.* New York: Appleton-Century-Crofts, Inc., 1954. Chapter 6. A discussion, from the standpoint of good administrative practice, of the problems involved in reporting and promoting.

SPAIN, CHARLES R., DRUMMOND, HAROLD D., and GOODLAD, JOHN I. *Educational Leadership and the Elementary School Principal.* New York: Holt, Rinehart & Winston, Inc., 1956. Pp. 262–74. Shows modern forms for attendance accounting.

# 11

# NATURE AND ORGANIZATION OF
# THE CURRICULUM

In the modern classroom the alert teacher utilizes every peg upon which he can possibly hang learning. From this point of view the curriculum cannot be narrow or limited or predetermined or static. Although definition is always difficult for any term which is to a great extent generic, the modern school curriculum becomes the sum total of those experiences provided for children that are consciously organized and directed toward the attainment of recognized desirable goals.

"What, then, is a course of study?" The answer lies in the difference between the general and the specific, between breadth and narrowness, between education over a wide expanse and education over a narrower area. A course of study is, strictly speaking, a curriculum guide. It is usually prepared by administrators, supervisors, and teachers, or any combination of these, for a particular school, as an aid to teaching a given subject or area of study for a given grade or grades. Sometimes a course of study includes aims and expected outcomes, the material to be studied, the textbooks to be used, even methods of instruction. It is to a great extent a manual or handbook, a compass as it were to keep the teacher on the curriculum route. To repeat, the curriculum is general in its scope, broad in its implications, comprehensive in its approach. The course of study is a specific road-map which directs the curriculum journey.

## NATURE OF THE CURRICULUM

The curriculum depends for its utility upon the extent to which the child's activities can be integrated and correlated, and this may come about in various ways. A teacher may gear his method of presentation of a subject very closely to what he is teaching; this is *adaption of techniques and methods* to the curriculum. He may organize his materials so that they include what he wants to teach and exclude what he wants to omit; this is *selection of materials*. Finally, he may put two or more courses together, omitting and adding as his judgment dictates; this is *integration* and *correlation*.

**Units of Work.** Materials of the curriculum may be organized in innumerable ways. This organization gives direction to the learning of pupils. Organizing around units of work has become one of the more common techniques. It brings together all of the materials that are in a large measure related, and arranges those materials so that the presentation to the child is sequential and sensible. These units are commonly put together from a functional viewpoint; that is, they are pointed toward a desired outcome or objective. If the unit is truly functional, it must change the child's behavior. This is the single best test of whether a unit of work is serving its purpose or not.

**Program of Experiences.** By putting the definition of the curriculum and the concept of organization together, it is evident that the curriculum is really organized life experiences. Not all of a child's experiences are included, of course, nor is it even possible to include in the formal organization all of a child's valuable experiences; but those experiences which can be controlled and which lead to the outcomes desired are consciously included.

The life-adjustment program, which is more and more being included in the elementary school organization, is only a broader concept of what the curriculum is and can be made to include. It would say that, because democracy is a way of life and as such deals with behavior, it follows that instruction should have as a major objective the development in the child of attitudes and appreciations, of skills and interests and habits and ideals, which are consistent with and derived from the democratic way of life. The life-adjustment movement has as its goal the integration of these patterns of behavior with that portion of the life around the child which best expresses the attitudes, appreciations, skills, habits, and ideals of the democratic way of living. Adjustment is achieved when the child's behavior patterns are consciously related to the life around him.

The teacher who follows a course of study slavishly is bound to produce an artificiality which is deadly. To illustrate:

Wallace W. is a farm boy attending a rural school. His parents own many acres of land, and Wallace is entirely interested in farm life. He expects to become a farmer and is encouraged by his parents, whose older sons, Wallace's brothers, have gone to the city to live. Wallace is a bright lad. He is interested in everything which pertains to the farm. Last year Wallace failed in his sixth-grade language work. He did good work in arithmetic, did passable work in his social sciences, and ranked high in his "activity" work.

The course of study in language, based on a poorly integrated and poorly conceived curriculum for a farm area, was identical to the one used for the fifth grade in the largest city in the state. Wallace (quite naturally) found the content totally uninteresting, as it was planned for city children. He was unable to work on it simply to please his teacher, and as a result he failed.

His teacher, in talking to Wallace's mother, pointed out that Wallace had the ability to do the work but had not seriously tried. The teacher said, for example, that Wallace had not handed in his copy of his acceptance to a party invitation. Wallace had told his teacher that he didn't want to know how to write a letter accepting an invitation to a party. No one seemed to have realized that equally significant values could have been found in other forms of writing, for instance, making out the order for a certain type of steel trap, buying his money order, and writing his letter to Sears Roebuck—all necessary activities for pursuing his favorite sport of trapping muskrats from the creek on his father's farm.

The illustration emphasizes (*a*) that the curriculum must be part of a child's everyday experiences, (*b*) that it must be made up of both activities and knowledges, and (*c*) that it must be organized by the teacher to fit the life the child is living.

**Sequence of Content.** Since a curriculum is always an organized, long-term plan for learning, its various units must of necessity be in some sequential order. The units vary, of course, in size and scope. Lessons may be broken up into written and oral work; they are a part of larger units which when completed are courses. Sometimes the sequence of work is logical in its order; sometimes it is chronological; again, it may be psychological. Reading tends to be psychological; history, chronological; and mathematics, logical. Regardless of the organization, there is always a relationship existing between what has been learned and that which is to follow.

Were one to look at the curriculum in terms of the chronological growth of the child, it is evident that early phases of the curriculum would, of necessity, deal with receiving and communicating ideas. If the phrase, "receiving and communicating ideas" is analyzed, quite naturally it becomes talking, reading, listening, and getting along with other children. Thus the first years of formal schooling always deal with reading, language work, numbers, development of manual dexterity, and the process of fitting the child into his social environment. The nursery school and kindergarten put the latter item first, as readiness for this usually develops prior to a readiness for reading or arithmetic.

From the social development slant, the home and its environment offer the first opportunities for growth. If nursery school or kindergarten is available, these offer the first formal introduction to schooling. Regardless, however, of whether the child is given formal schooling early, he is living in a social situation, receiving social impressions, and making social responses. The community is his laboratory.

Early in his life the child learns to like certain nursery songs better than others, to want certain bedtime stories told over and over again, to sleep with a tattered teddy-bear. He likes to hear his dad whistle and squeals with delight when ·his older brother stands on his head. Mother becomes more ·o him than just a sure source of comfort. He is developing ppreciations, recognizing outcomes. His curriculum is unfolding. He is fitting into his environment.

It is to be remembered that a child communicates as well as receives. Expression is closely tied to impression. While it is doubtful if there could be expression without impression, there is probably little lasting impression without expression. When impression fails to go over into action, there is probably little to go over.

In the reception and communication process, the teacher adapts, adopts, organizes, integrates, correlates, and distributes. To some extent his work is comparable to the function of the distributor in an automobile which receives the impulse from the generator (source) and then sends it to each spark plug.

**Characteristics of a Curriculum.** Basically a good curriculum always interprets activities and common knowledges in terms of the child's needs. It expresses minimum essentials in an understandable way. It provides for meeting the needs common to all children at the time these needs appear. Because children differ so much in their individual tastes and abilities, a good curriculum is so organized as to offer much more material than any one child either needs or can absorb. Since the curriculum is an interrelation of ideas and material things, it is concerned with both physical activity and intellectual impression. Generalizations are avoided, as the child lives and develops in specifics rather than in generalities.

Remembering that the inherent interests of children and school subjects of a formalized type usually have little intrinsically in common, the teacher is always confronted with a psychological problem of making changes either in the nature of formalized subject matter or in the interests of children or in both. The modern classroom is today recognizing "readiness" on the child's part as something which normally appears in subjects such as reading, spelling, penmanship, even common fractions. When the readiness does appear, the child and the formalized subject are usually at the point of closest proximity and the gap remaining is most easily bridged. The good course of study, based on a soundly organized curricular offering, takes this readiness into account.

Either by law or by regulation, the course of study (the curriculum guide for a particular school) provides the minimum essentials that may not be omitted. The teacher must keep to the area prescribed but may usually, at discretion, change the applications of materials to suit not only the class as a group but individual pupils as well. This freedom of application is another characteristic of a good general plan. The curriculum guide, like the federal Constitution, indicates the pattern of thinking and sets up both rights and restrictions, but it does not write the specifics. When the curriculum guide does the latter, it fails in its function.

The child's needs are always the force or forces which make for the modification of the teacher's approach to the curriculum. These needs are never conceived narrowly. They are intellectual, social, spiritual, moral, mental, and physical. No need may be neglected if the whole child is to be served.

## CURRICULUM ORGANIZATION

The preceding pages have dealt to a great extent with the nature of the school curriculum. How it is organized to fit the life of the child is, however, the *sine qua non* of the problem. The curriculum is the sum total of those experiences provided for children, experiences which are consciously organized and directed toward the attainment of desirable learning goals. The definition, which has the common weakness of all definitions of technical terms, is loaded with significant words: "sum total," "experiences," "provided," "children," "consciously organized," "directed," "attainment," and "desirable learning goals."

The child from birth is in a process of adjustment to his surroundings. Since the adjustment is a continuous process, it follows that the curriculum based upon life situations cannot be inflexible or fixed. Any school which boasts that it has revised its curriculum, implying that, as in remodeling a building, the changed organization is to serve for some years, has missed the true meaning of revision. The problems facing children, problems which come from their interaction with society, are never constants. Because of this, a curriculum adjusted to the child demands *continuous* modification and revision.

A beginning teacher will meet many descriptive phrases applied to the curriculum. *Experience curriculum* is one. *Activity curriculum* is another. *Core curriculum* is a third. *Areas-of-living curriculum* is a fourth. Basically, each of these varies from the other only in the focusing of the emphasis on the curriculum organization.

**Experience Curriculum.** The experience curriculum organizes all learning about the total experience of the learner. It is related to the activity concept, which emphasizes that knowledges have their basis in activities and activities their basis in knowledges. The activity-based program is very flexible and gets back to a philosophy of activism. Subject-matter fields are, of course, fused and integrated.

As would be implied by the above, the "experience" curriculum is involved in all forward-looking plans presented in this chapter. The implication, of course, is that the school and the pupil cooperate in selecting those learning activities which offer the most promise of achieving the child's educational goal. Care must be taken that the activity program characteristic of this type of curriculum does not become a hit-or-miss affair. The word "planless" must not be applied to it. Wide in its implications it can and should be; planless it must never be. If not most carefully planned, this curriculum leaves wide learning gaps in the child's program; if well planned, it fuses and motivates learning into a coherent unit which is rarely achieved through older, more formalized patterns.

**Activity Curriculum.** The activity curriculum has as its basic philosophy the thought that learning takes place through activity. This activity is not necessarily all physical. There is always a flexible organization of all types of learning around activity units as the principal type of learning situation. Naturally it involves a fusion or integration of subject-matter fields. The so-called project method is based to a great extent on this concept. It is an organized attempt to make the activity program readily available for all levels on the educational ladder. Always the activity curriculum carries with it a careful collection and sequence of materials for the group that are also suitable to the maturity, interests, and experiential background of any individual child.

**Core Curriculum.** The core curriculum commonly is organized around a unitary group of activities. These are arranged in advance in accordance with general objectives intended to provide a common body of experiences. Sometimes the core curriculum is defined as those broad areas of experience and learning which are required of all students before they are allowed to select a field of specialization. When used in this sense, the word "core" applies to a center of interest and emphasis about which all the other subjects are grouped or oriented.

One line of thinking considers the core to be those subjects required for graduation which are taught in the older, formalized manner. Thus the core could well be English, art, and social studies. If these three fields are the only fields required of all students, they do constitute a core. However, as the term is generally used, this interpretation does not satisfy. Core generally means a topic of interest based on present and future needs common to all students, about which materials and activities drawn from many subjects are centered.

Special fields and subjects have to be retained outside the core curriculum for pupils who have specialized interests. The core curriculum will not make available the quantity nor the right kind of mathematics for the students who desire to make careers of engineering or the science fields. Certainly, the mathematics will not be of the essential quality needed for the student who is to go on to advanced mathematics. In the elementary school, the core program can be made to involve practically all of the learning situations commonly found. With the beginning of the junior high school work in the seventh grade, the work which can be tied into the core program without artificiality is more restricted. The heart of the core curriculum lies in its lack of artificiality.

If core activities are to be carried into the junior high and senior high schools, it is usual to allow a longer block of time, usually a double period, to core activities. Where the core curriculum program is used, it is common practice to offer specialized and intensified courses to satisfy needs of pupils with special interests. Too many persons, even those in the teaching profession, assume that a curriculum integrated on the core plan will encompass all of a child's formalized learning, be it specialized or not. This is not true. The core organization does much to increase the child's interests, makes schoolwork more vital, and increases the area of the learning field. It does not satisfy the detailed work required for college preparation in the physical and biological sciences, in mathematics, in some social sciences, and in Latin and the modern foreign languages.

**Areas-of-Living Curriculum.** The areas-of-living curriculum organizes the school's program around large life areas such as health, civic responsibilities, homemaking, being a better citizen, getting an education, spiritual values, the development of ethical character, the use of leisure time, recreation, selecting a vocation, and other topics of a similar nature. There is always an attempt to make subject matter vital. Frequently the areas-of-living curriculum is community-centered and is then based on and adjusted to the life, culture, resources, needs, activities, and interests of the community in which the child lives.

**Subjects versus Activities.** Traditionally, the subject-matter curriculum is still entrenched, although many good school systems are placing emphasis elsewhere, making subject matter a means to an end rather than an end in itself. Regardless of the organization, however, the curriculum must include both knowledges and activities, and these must be drawn from the life the child is living, not from an artificial or fictional situation. Learning, if it is worthy of the name, must, as John Dewey has pointed out, have in it a desire for further learning. The teacher should never forget that the curriculum is made up of experiences and knowledges which are for the greater part consciously organized and directed toward desirable goals.

In the final analysis the school's problem becomes one of determining what the curriculum does to develop skills, interpret symbols, and express meanings. It strives to make activity combine physical and mental elements. Reading, spelling, numbers, and writing are activities rather than mumbo-jumbo when they are satisfying a child's felt needs. Readiness tends to become the key word in all conflict between subjects and activities.

Since the curriculum expresses itself in all of a child's life, not just in his "in-school" hours, it is evident that all of a child's activities must be carefully evaluated and appraised. He has much leisure time, and the curriculum of the modern school is much concerned with the utilization of this time. Play is not only desirable but imperative. Finally, the curriculum does not fail to recognize two other factors: the development of individual responsibilities and the need for self-discipline on the child's part. Because the older curriculum was more formalized, parents are prone to believe the present-day offering is "soft." Nothing is farther from the truth. Over and over again, the modern curriculum states in no uncertain terms the old maxim, "The boy who accepts the paper route must deliver the papers."

## CURRICULUM CHANGE

The very nature of the curriculum—that is, its over-all inclusiveness—tends to make change slow and laborious. Fundamentally, this is as it should be. The curriculum is an expression of school policy; it is a recognition of the permanency of American education and the American way of living; it is to some extent based on fundamental principles which time has tried and found good. On the other side of the picture, outmoded curricular materials get entrenched and are formalized in textbooks and in courses of study. The curriculum should reflect social change, but frequently the social change is well advanced before the formal curriculum makes any recognition of the change.

**Factors Affecting Change.** The delay in making curricular changes, a delay which prevents the general over-all guide for schools from keeping pace with changes in American life as those changes develop, is due to many factors. Among these are:

1. The old is entrenched. As a member of a Board of Education said: "It was good enough for me and for my father, and it is good enough for my children."

2. A curricular offering is assumed to be good until it is proved bad. Hence the useless, although it may not be actually detrimental, frequently stays in. There are vestigial remains in every curriculum.

3. It is difficult to distinguish the worthless from the valuable, as the results of schooling may not show up conclusively until a generation later.

4. Educators, who are specialists, tend to see problems differently from other teachers, who are in a way general practitioners in the profession. This hinders presenting a united front. Again, the schools belong to the people, and the people, although vocal, are not trained in a professional way. Always conservative in school affairs, the public resists change.

5. *Real* values are difficult to distinguish from *seeming* values. Frequently only time will tell whether a curricular change or movement was significant or not. Because of this element, what the layman calls "fads and frills" may be just that, or they may be highly desirable changes which should have been included in our curricular offerings many years ago.

**Influence of Textbooks.** Because textbooks, being always business ventures, can express only the more or less fixed phases of the curricular offering, they tend under normal situations to express only the more static, formalized portions of the curriculum. Again, a text must be used over a wide geographical area if it is to pay for its cost of production, and only the formalized portion of school curricula is in wide usage geographically. However, as was pointed out years ago by E. P. Cubberley (formerly Dean of Education at Stanford University), the American textbook represents the finest craftsmanship of its kind in the world.

Not uncommonly a publisher, frequently an educator by training and inclination, produces a book which is far in advance of its time; he offers it as a contribution to educational advancement. In general, however, textbooks follow the curriculum and to some extent make those portions of the curriculum which depend upon textbooks more resistant to change. Again, a textbook reflects a way of thinking, expressed by someone with prestige in the field. Because of this there is too frequently a halo around the printed word as far as the uncritical reader is concerned.

**Influence of Utility of Information.** There is reason to believe that only thoughtfully acquired information is usable at the time it is acquired. In other words, knowledge must have meaning to the child or he will make no attempt to use it. If the knowledge is unrelated to his experience (unmeaningful), he may translate it inaccurately into his experience with disastrous results.

Because of the necessity for relatedness between a child's everyday experiences and the information about things which he is storing up, the elementary school curriculum in general is suspicious of learning that will remain unused by the child for a long time. This factor greatly influences the position in the course of study of the various formalized portions of a child's school learning. When shall common fractions be taught? Shall a child be required to know how to spell a word he does not use now but may use later? Shall "percentage" in arithmetic be taught? If so, when? These questions illustrate an age-old problem as far as formalized education is concerned. One reason for the hesitancy in teaching in the elementary and junior high schools any material which is not of possible immediate utility is that there is a superabundance of material, equally significant from the child's development standpoint, which is entirely significant to him at the age-grade level which he occupies.

The above must not be interpreted to mean that there are no basic knowledges or skills. This would be untrue. The question is only when the child shall be exposed to these in a formal way. Many outcomes of learning, especially those which are acquired somewhat indirectly, are basic. A child's attitudes, appreciations, and ideals are not *accidentally* acquired. They may be *indirectly* acquired, but the two words differ in meaning. For example, courtesy and cooperation are somehow related to knowledges and skills. Outcomes of this type would seem to belong in the child's acquisition program at every level in the academic ladder. Literature, to illustrate, is replete with examples of offerings which are good at all levels. *Alice in Wonderland* and *Rip Van Winkle* are suitable to children's learning. They are not unsuitable to learning for the adult. On the other hand, "Thanatopsis," which has been memorized as a whole or in part by thousands of children, cannot have meaning at the time it is memorized by a child. Later, if it was "overlearned" sufficiently, it may prove to be a source of enjoyment to the mature person. This does not say it was not misplaced in the seventh grade, however. The *Gettysburg Address* is partially understood by intermediate-grade children because of its simplicity of wording. Its classical nature warrants consideration of it for the junior high school child, but only after the child has some understanding of the situation which produced it. The danger, obviously, is in assuming that, because only learning valuable to the race has survived, all such learning is valuable to everyone now. The curriculum of the modern school recognizes values inherited from the past, but never is it uncognizant of some real values for the present. The problem is one of recognition and utilization. The well-planned curriculum usually recognizes that something not quite so good but entirely suitable to the child is better than a classic which the child, because of immaturity, cannot understand or appreciate.

**Influence of Tradition.** In all his work, especially in that portion which deals with what the child studies, the teacher always works closely with the administrative officers of the school. If a teacher makes changes entirely on his initiative, they may prove not only embarrassing to the principal or superintendent but also actually detrimental to the children under his care. The interpretation of the curriculum is commonly a matter of school policy. A teacher can be theoretically right but be wrong in practice if his action is not approved by the public which supports the school.

To illustrate: Miss Burton decided that her classes in penmanship and spelling were wasting time and that the children were not doing their best writing on the work they turned in, and that the words they were learning to spell were not in their vocabularies. She decided to drop penmanship and spelling as subjects by themselves and to mark every student for his penmanship record on all the written work he turned in. This meant much more work for her. she also made it a point to require that every word the child used in writing be spelled correctly. When he missed a word, that word would go into his individual spelling list. These words would constitute his spelling "cripples" and he would be required to "cure" them. The idea was sound and in line with good methodology. What happened? You guessed it! A call from a member of the Board of Education to the principal; and an order from the principal's office to put both subjects back into her program in formal classes.

Miss Burton had failed to remember that social forces move slowly and that changes must be introduced only after the community has been educated to the change. The Board member said—and the public agreed with him—that he had never heard of such a thing as teaching spelling or penmanship except in classes; that he had been taught that way, as had his father. Tradition in the curriculum is, as in other school functions, frequently a fettering thing. Two years later Miss Burton's spelling plan was put into general use in the school after it had been clarified through the parent-teacher organization.

The chief school officer usually interprets public opinion more accurately and closely than does the individual classroom teacher. This is possible because of the liaison nature of his work. The teacher must remember that what is now required in a course of study for his school is either firmly entrenched or was placed there only after considerable thought had been given to the subject. Never does this mean, however, that the classroom teacher is not at the source of desirable changes either in the working manual, the course of study, or the more general outline of study, the curriculum. It does mean that he is not an entity unto himself and that a school presents a unified front on curricular changes. Because of the generally approved idea that, as with an accused person, one is innocent until proved guilty, what is now in the curriculum is considered good until proved bad. Because of this, changes are commonly difficult to make. The modern school is leading the way rather than following in these changes and in general the public is becoming more willing to leave all phases of the education process to those best trained for the work, the academic staff of the school.

**Influence of the Teacher's Philosophy.** Every good teacher interprets the curriculum to a great extent in terms of his training and experience. Because of this potentiality, it is possible, even probable, that teachers at the same grade level, using the same course of study derived from the same general curriculum, may develop in their classes quite different knowledges, attitudes, appreciations, and skills.

To illustrate: Miss Jackson has been teaching in the Blythe schools for twenty-three years. She is known as an excellent teacher and is much loved by the people of the little town, not a few of whom have been her pupils. In language class, Miss Jackson insists that each composition be, above everything else, grammatically correct; every bit of written work is done for the purpose of demonstrating the use of commas, periods, and other requirements of good punctuation. A misspelled word is graded down. Not a little attention is given to the mechanics of paragraphing, and to making the child see clearly the difference between narration and description. Miss Jackson's pupils get no particular fun or pleasure out of writing, but when they do write, each letter is made correctly, each phrase is properly placed.

In history, Miss Jackson gives a prize as an incentive for memorizing facts and dates. She says not infrequently that it is all right to tell students to think, but she doesn't understand how a student can think when he has few facts with which to think. Miss Jackson assumes that if one does not teach facts as such, the child will not get facts.

In physiology, her pupils can name the bones of the body, and they know which part of the tooth is found directly under the enamel. They can also name the teeth in order by the half-jaw from the front to the rear. It is true that many of her pupils do not have habits of tooth cleanliness, but that is not emphasized in the course of study. Miss Jackson's pupils test well on what they have studied, but have difficulty when trying to answer a "thought" question based on the facts they have presumably "learned."

Miss Jackson has a very quiet room. She puts much emphasis upon "memory gems" which she uses to teach courtesy and manners. Memory is stressed in all her teaching, and parents say frequently that her pupils "know what they are expected to know."

Miss Beeson came to the Blythe school two years ago, following three years' teaching experience. She uses quite different techniques. She does not follow the course of study as closely as Miss Jackson; in fact, she sometimes fails to complete all the work suggested by that guide. Miss Beeson places some emphasis upon memorizing facts, but not so much as she does upon developing the abilities to observe and to express.

Miss Beeson's pupils enjoy writing stories for their language classes. Many of the stories tell how to do things. She counts the best story the one which is easiest to understand and the one which the class likes best. She frequently points out to the class that clearness depends upon certain formalities, and that if a person fails to punctuate correctly it is difficult to understand what is meant. Her room is sometimes noisy and, to tell the truth, is rarely quiet. Her pupils like their classwork about as well as they do recesses. Undoubtedly, her teaching is dynamic.

The variation in interpretation of the meaning of the curriculum by the two teachers is noticeable. It is evident also that in each case the teacher's interpretation of the curriculum has become her working philosophy. From the illustration it is evident that teachers modify the curriculum.

**Influence of Recent Developments.** The more recent developments which are influencing the curriculum to some extent are:

*Scholarship Contests.* A sort of educational track meet, the scholarship contest idea has developed into significant proportions. Originally planned to place as much emphasis upon excellence in academic achievement and scholastic attainment as is accorded to excellence in extracurricular activities, the contest idea has served this purpose well. The tests are used for motivation purposes by schools for evaluating the achievement of their pupils and classes in comparison with those of other schools. Many have expressed concern that the contests tend to determine the curriculum of schools using the tests. To others the expressed concern seems rather unnecessary; but to say that the tests have not influenced procedure at all in schools would be incorrect.

*Quiz Contests.* Quiz contests are usually conducted by radio stations and newspapers. They are interesting to students who participate and to parents and others who listen in. As with other contests, they determine to some extent what is studied in school in preparation for the contest. In general, the effect on a good curriculum is probably slight.

*Radio, Moving Pictures, and Television.* To the extent that a child's experiences make up a great part of his curriculum, this type of entertainment for children is influencing what children see, hear, and appreciate. Radio and moving pictures are past the experimental stage as factors in education. Television for entertainment, however, is still an unknown factor in what it does to the child. Its possibilities are limitless, but if anything much which is usable or desirable for children is to result, popular program planning must recognize that children are not little adults. Good programs for children are exceptions, not the rule.

It must not be assumed that education as such is not interested in television. It is much interested, and many colleges and universities, as well as public schools, are offering good programs. It is the evening "entertainment" program which, too frequently, is worthless from the educational standpoint.

## DISCUSSION PROBLEM

### "Fads and Frills"

"Fads and Frills!" The speaker is a well-to-do businessman. His voice is rasping in its earnestness as he attacks the curriculum of the schools which his money is helping to support. "Sewing and cooking in school, automobile mechanics, typesetting, basketmaking, art and drawing, farm carpentry, and piano playing, how to entertain company, as well as how to bathe a baby! Bosh!"

His tones, as well as the closely clipped words, express plainly his utter disgust with the educational situation. "Wasting their time and the taxpayers' money. Hardly any arithmetic taught. My granddaughter can't spell at all, and her writing is terrible. What won't they clutter up the schools with next? They really educated boys and girls in our day, Harry."

"I believe you're wrong, John," said his friend sitting with the aforementioned businessman on the porch of the country club. "You're thinking of those subjects you've named as a body of knowledge to be memorized, which isn't what they're intended for. What the subjects you have mentioned are for, so that speaker at the Kiwanis Club told us the other evening, is to furnish a child while he is still in school with some experiences, mostly social, which give him a fuller understanding of occupations which have helped and are helping to make this country what she is."

"Besides," he went on, "I'll bet you two new golf balls that granddaughter of yours can outspell you right now. And," he chuckled, "I don't suppose that her arithmetic is much worse than ours was, or is now for that matter."

The conversation quoted in the previous paragraphs is typical of the criticism which is very frequently voiced concerning the curricular offering of the up-to-date twentieth-century school. It lacks in reality, mainly, in that the school and its offering are rarely so ably defended as by the second speaker.

To what extent is the first speaker correct? Are we running to "fads and frills"?

## Questions on the Problem

1. Can you picture typewriting being taught in a monastic school of the fourteenth century? Why or why not?
2. Can you picture home economics and baby care being taught in a pioneer school of seventy-five years ago? Why or why not?
3. Was such teaching unnecessary then? If you state that it was unnecessary then, is it necessary now?
4. "The difference is a difference in civilization." Do you agree?
5. "The curriculum must keep pace, if not lead the way, for a changing civilization. Change is a fundamental characteristic for a curriculum that fulfills its proper function." If this state-

ment is true, upon what condition should the curriculum drop its "fads and frills," of which the businessman complains?

6. How do you account for the fact that the curriculum remained static for so many years, almost centuries?

7. Automobiles are now commonly used. They are a part of everyday social life. In numerical order, name everything you can think of dealing with an automobile that might be introduced into our curriculum to help orient the student to this important part of his environment. Start like this: (1) Batteries: their use, make-up, life, cost. (2) Tires: composition, manufacture, utility, cost, adaptation, etc.

## STUDY QUESTIONS

1. Analyze this statement and be prepared to comment: "The formalized school curriculum is scarcely more than an incident in the sum total of a child's education."

2. If "the world is a child's curriculum," what is a printed course of study?

3. Consider for class discussion: "When the school curriculum fails to make any real appeal to a boy or girl, the child tends to make a curriculum of his own."

4. Name all of the sources of the curriculum that you can. Try to be specific. To illustrate: (a) the formalized school offering, (b) the home life of the child.

5. If we grant that the school curriculum should include both knowledge and activities, is there any preference as to which should come first?

6. If the activity is real to the child, can it be separated from knowledge?

7. A child is memorizing the multiplication tables. How can this satisfy a statement from the text that "both (knowledge and activity) must be drawn from the everyday actual life the child is living?"

8. Conceding that the multiplication tables fail to satisfy the requirement in 7 above, should the tables be withdrawn from the curriculum? If withdrawn, should they be reinstated? If "Yes," when?

9. Is Miss Beeson in the illustration given in the chapter building "upon the shifting sands of soft pedagogy"? If you say "No," why not? If "Yes," why?

10. Which child is going to be most approved for high-school work, one who comes from Miss Jackson's teaching or one who comes from Miss Beeson's?

11. What is Miss Beeson getting from her pupils that Miss Jackson is not getting?

12. Do pupils from "activity" schools do as well in college as those from more traditional schools?

13. Scholarship contest tests are made up by teachers thoroughly trained in the various subject-matter fields. To what extent is this evidence that the tests are valid, that is, that they agree with known criteria of what a test should measure?

14. A good school today is a child's school in a child's environmental situation. Was Miss Jackson's school as described in this chapter a child's school, or was it Miss Jackson's school? Which should it be? Discuss.

15. Can you show how a school's curriculum is always an expression of that school's educational philosophy?

16. "Sequence" and "continuity" are words stressed in the chapter. Does this mean that geometry must follow algebra or that a child may never skip a grade? If not this, what might be meant?

## SELECTED READINGS

AMERICAN EDUCATIONAL RESEARCH ASSOCIATION. (J. Galen Saylor, Chairman) *Review of Educational Research*, "Curriculum Planning and Development," Washington, D. C.: National Education Association, June, 1957. Chapter 2. Summarizes research materials on the general theme of the curriculum. Valuable to the research worker.

ASSOCIATION FOR SUPERVISION AND CURRICULUM DEVELOPMENT. *Action for Curriculum Improvement, 1951 Yearbook*. Washington, D. C.: National Education Association, 1952. Book tells how changes in the curriculum result from cooperation of pupils, teachers, supervisors, parents, and administrators. Is comprehensive in its treatment.

DOUGLASS, HARL R. (Ed.) *The High School Curriculum*. New York: The Ronald Press Co., 1956. Chapters 3, 4, 10, 14, and 21. One of the most comprehensive textbooks now in print dealing with the high school curriculum in its many phases.

FITZGERALD, JAMES A., and FITZGERALD, PATRICIA G. *Methods and Curricula in Elementary Education*. Milwaukee: The Bruce Publishing Co., 1955. A comprehensive treatment, clearly written, which analyzes the place of the various curricula used in the elementary school. Is especially good on the activity curriculum.

MacLean, Malcolm S., and Lee, Edwin A. *Change and Process in Education.* New York: Holt, Rinehart & Winston, Inc., 1956. Chapter 11, "The Emotional Basis of Teaching and Learning," discusses the child's emotional behavior in terms of the classroom situation.

Mehl, Marie A., Mills, Hubert H., and Douglass, Harl R. *Teaching in Elementary School.* 2d ed. New York: The Ronald Press Co., 1958. Chapter 5, "Basic Curriculum Problems," points out clearly many of the problems involved in curriculum construction.

Sands, Lester B. *Audio-Visual Procedures in Teaching.* New York: The Ronald Press Co., 1956. Chapter 29 relates the field of curriculum development and audio-visual aids in making the curriculum realistic.

Saylor, J. Galen, and Alexander, William M. *Curriculum Planning for Better Teaching and Learning.* New York: Holt, Rinehart & Winston, Inc., 1954. An easy-to-read book; a comprehensive treatment of curriculum problems common in our public schools.

Sears, Jesse B. *The Nature of the Administrative Process.* New York: McGraw-Hill Book Co., Inc., 1950. Chapter 2 shows how the administrative function cannot be separated from any phase of curriculum revision.

Smith, B. Othaniel, Stanley, William O., and Shores, J. Harlan. *Fundamentals of Curriculum Development.* Yonkers, N. Y.: World Book Co., 1950. The validity of educational objectives are questioned in terms of established criteria. Chapter 11 should be read.

# 12

# PREPARATION OF THE
# DAILY PROGRAM

A classroom is, first of all, marked by the *orderly* manner in which everything is done. There are many children who are not naturally inclined to orderliness. There is a given amount of *time* to be utilized. There are specific *subjects* to be considered. The teacher commonly faces the job of fitting the child, the subject, and the time into a harmonious but still thoroughly useful unity.

In a way a school's working schedule has in it something of the railroad timetable element. What type of trains are to run? At what times will they run? What are the accommodations offered? At this point the analogy ends, however, for railroad timetables exist for the purpose of serving the public in order that the road may make money, while a school program exists to serve the child in order that he may develop his capabilities to the fullest.

If the teacher is to see the class schedule as other than a necessary mechanical item in the day's work, he must learn to see it as a bit of machinery, somewhat formal in nature, which must give an educational account of itself. Since the program or, as it is sometimes called, the schedule, is a general plan of action by which the different activities of the curriculum involving pupils, teachers, and other school personnel are accorded a sequence and location, it follows that the "general plan of action" must be soundly conceived from both the utilitarian and the theoretical viewpoints.

First of all, the program reflects the school's curriculum. It places emphasis where the curriculum calls for emphasis; it omits what the curriculum intends to omit. The curriculum reflects to a great extent the community in which the school exists. Because of this function of a program, a school schedule sent out from a central office which covers a wide area both geographically and in interests is unsound in principle.

As a timetable, the program must be suited to the child from an educational point of view and, although this is not so obvious, to his parents and to the entire community from the standpoint of utility. A school program of studies that is out of step with a community's industrial timetable makes for confusion in the home and waste in family effort.

The program in itself is not as significant as is sometimes supposed. It is the effect the program has on other aspects of education that makes it significant. In themselves, space and time allotments, although significant, are not basic determinants.

Finally, the teacher must understand, and be certain to carry the understanding over into action, that the space and time allotments with whatever significance they carry are always considered in terms of the needs of the children in the classroom. The principles of both utility and adequacy in administration apply to the class schedule as they do to all of the broader aspects of administration.

## TIME FACTOR IN PROGRAM-MAKING

In every program the time factor tends to dominate the situation. Every phase of the schedule is limited by this factor. The day itself is limited by time. Subjects, as such, all have some value to the child. Emphasis on such value tends to be expressed in terms of time. The teacher who gives twice as much time to arithmetic as to social science is interpreting in terms of time his conception of the relative value to his pupils of these two subjects.

In every schedule the teacher has the feeling of being cramped for time. When there is more than one grade in a room, the time element is, of course, more significant. Always, two factors are constant in making the class schedule: the length of the school day, and the length of the school year. Commonly neither of these is determined by the classroom teacher.

**Time Allotment for Subjects.** The time allotted to school subjects has not (in general) been determined experimentally. Some experimental work has been done on those subjects which are distinctly drill in nature, but for the most part, time allowances have been determined through experience. It is something like the jeweler who set his big clock by the mill foreman's noonday whistle, and was dismayed when the foreman told him he had been setting his watch (for the whistle-blowing time) from the jeweler's big clock. Surveys have determined time allotments from analyzing working programs, and working programs have tended to base their time allotments on the published surveys. As is suggested by various commentators, this is probably why so little change has taken place through the years in the time allotments for specific subjects.

Again, experimental studies of time allowance for anything but drill subjects are most difficult to control because of the numerous factors involved. Arithmetic involves reading, reading involves English, English involves spelling, spelling involves penmanship, and so on. Basically the time has been governed by psychology as far as learning, development, and children are concerned, and by philosophical considerations in determining the values to be placed on the various fields as desirable learning activities. The individual teacher's subject preference is also influential. The teacher tends to spend more time on the subject which he thinks is important. This is pointed out by the demand of college departments for larger unit requirements for their major fields at the expense of limiting other fields of study or even eliminating them entirely. Give the teacher complete control of the time allotment (which is rarely done) and an unbalanced program may well be expected. Teachers tend to see values in terms of their specialized subject fields. This is less true of elementary teachers, generally true of high school teachers.

**Time Placement and Sequence.** Another phase of the time factor in making the schedule is the sequence of the subjects and activities. First of all, there is a frequent misconception that one time of the day is superior to another because of a lesser degree of mental fatigue on the pupils' part. Teachers assume that efficiency is higher in the forenoon than it is later in the day.

Experiments indicate that a child can do about as good work at one time of the day as another. Motor skill is apparently at its peak late in the day, but the time of the day makes little difference in arithmetic skills. If the motivation is good enough, a child can learn at 4:00 P.M. anything he could learn at 9:00 A.M. and in about the same amount of time. Boredom probably increases as the day wears on, and for this reason children need physical activity late in the day.

Ordinary common sense has much to do with making a time schedule. To place penmanship or art or any other physical-coordination subject immediately following a play period is bound to give disastrous results. To place a gymnasium period immediately before an intermission period is to place similar activities too close together.

In judging the time allowance for any given subject, the teacher must utilize the principles of educational psychology. When do diminishing returns in drill tend to set in because of time used? Is a twenty-minute period better than two ten-minute periods in penmanship? What is the best time length for a spelling class? For a drawing class? For a history class? Will this time period vary at different grade levels?

From the standpoint of ease of teaching, 10:00 A.M. is probably the best point in the day and 3:00 P.M. the poorest. In general, the subjects hardest for the pupils should be given the best times in the day and the ones with the most physical activity should be given the poorest. To keep purely mental subjects from massing together is sound in practice. Young children should have more classes in a day and periods of shorter duration. Their work is always in terms of activity learning.

Once a program is set down in black and white, a teacher should try it out There should never be anything final about it. A teacher may desire to shift the program each month, adopting what is sometimes called a "spiral" program. In this, if the traditional subject program is used, a subject given during the first period in the day for the first month goes to the second period for the second month. A subject which was in the second place during the first month goes into third place during the second month. Thus, the entire program shifts each month. Each subject in turn gets the "best time of the day"—if there is a best time. The mechanical way in which the plan operates is its weakness. Probably some subjects should never come at the first period of the day, nor certain others at the last period. This weakness can be eliminated by holding some subjects constant and shifting the others as good practice dictates.

## TIME AND THE CHILD'S NEEDS

Always the teacher should make the time program meet the pupils' needs. Needs, today, are determined by testing, using local, state, or national norms as guides. If the pupils are sixth-graders and hit seventh-grade norms in arithmetic and fifth-grade norms in reading, he has no choice as to where the time (and effort) must go. The child's needs are always determining factors in all matters educational.

**The Child as a Factor.** In planning the daily program, a teacher must remember that he is planning it for the children, not for himself. He must think of the children in terms of their interests, needs, nature, and environment. Among the questions a teacher should ask himself about each of his pupils are these:

1. What are his interests? What does he enjoy doing most?
2. What are his needs? How do they differ from his interests? How can his interests be made identical with his needs?
3. What is he like, himself? What is the environment from which he comes? What is his home life?
4. What portion of his needs and interests are quite well satisfied by his home life, church life, and social life outside the school?

Having considered his pupils as individuals in terms of the questions above, the teacher then considers the factors, some of which are more or less mechanical in nature, which operate in bringing about the behavior changes he desires to develop. He asks himself:

1. How will my program be modified by the number of children in my class or classes?
2. Having decided upon the sequence, time, and place given to each activity in my daily program, what measure do I plan to take to determine the correctness of such sequence, time, and placement?
3. What would I like to do for these children were I not limited by physical items such as the classroom, the building, and the equipment? Are these insurmountable difficulties, or are they merely difficulties which by effort I can control?
4. What are the limitations placed upon me by the official course of study? Having satisfied these, what do I have left in the form of time which can be utilized in an unlimited way as I desire?

**Time Distribution by Grades.** No program should be lifted *in toto* from one classroom to another. No two rooms can be alike when the needs and interests of the individual children are considered. Home backgrounds, intellectual abilities, previous training, personality characteristics—all are factors which make lifting a time-schedule from one grade to a similar grade a most undesirable practice.

To present time values common to the first eight grades (the variations are innumerable) the program below is offered. Certainly, no one should take this time distribution by grades for more than it is intended to be—information on time allotments, a guide-line. The time schedule presented[1] provides for a first bell at 8:15 A.M., an assembly signal for opening exercises at 8:20, and a tardy signal at 8:30. General dismissal is at 3:00 P.M. Grades I and II are dismissed at 2:00 P.M.

TIME DISTRIBUTION BY GRADES

Number of Minutes Per Week

| Grades | I | II | III | IV | V | VI | VII | VIII |
|---|---|---|---|---|---|---|---|---|
| Arithmetic | 100 | 100 | 150 | 150 | 150 | 150 | 150 | 150 |
| History | 125 | 125 | 100 | 150 | 150 | 150 | 150 | 150 |
| Language | 150 | 150 | 150 | 150 | 150 | 150 | 150 | 150 |
| Reading & Literature | 445 | 445 | 280 | 180 | 180 | ... | ... | ... |
| Spelling | 60 | 60 | 75 | 75 | 75 | 75 | 75 | 75 |
| Study | ... | ... | 100 | 150 | 150 | 180 | 150 | 150 |
| Writing | 75 | 75 | 75 | 75 | 75 | 75 | 75 | 75 |
| Literature | ... | ... | ... | ... | ... | 150 | 150 | 150 |
| Auditorium* | 75 | 75 | 120 | 120 | 120 | 120 | 120 | 120 |
| Art and Crafts | 135 | 135 | 120 | 120 | 60 | 60 | 60 | 60 |
| Geography | ... | ... | 150 | 150 | 150 | 150 | 150 | 150 |
| Industrial Arts | ... | ... | ... | ... | 60 | 60 | 90 | 90 |
| Library and Study | ... | ... | 120 | 120 | 120 | 120 | 120 | 120 |
| Music | 60 | 60 | 60 | 60 | 60 | 60 | 60 | 60 |
| Play (Health & Phy. Tr.) | 150 | 150 | 150 | 150 | 150 | 150 | 150 | 150 |
| Science and Health | 125 | 125 | 150 | 150 | 150 | 150 | 150 | 150 |
| Recess | 150 | 150 | 150 | 150 | 150 | 150 | 150 | 150 |
| TOTAL | 1650 | 1650 | 1950 | 1950 | 1950 | 1950 | 1950 | 1950 |

* Opening exercises in non-platoon grades.

*Note:* Literature may be taught during either homeroom or platoon time according to which is better suited for a specific school schedule.

From the tabular material shown, it is evident that school programs are forced to make recognition of *the group as a unit*. This is, of course, unfortunate, as one child's academic needs necessarily differ from another's. One child may need more time than is allotted to arithmetic (150 minutes a week

[1] Synopsis of Course of Study for Elementary Schools, Birmingham, Alabama.

in the sixth grade), but may not profit much from the 75 minutes given to penmanship if his writing is now above average for the grade he is in. It is only in his individual study program that correction for this can be made. A child must be helped where he needs help, and the class program is but one instrument for supplying this need.

Individual differences may appear in one or all of four phases of the child's maturity: emotional, social, mental, and chronological. The program must recognize these differences to the extent that the official course of study allows for such recognition. The teacher with thirty or more children in a room has little time for more than his formal class program, but his obligation to give individual help is always there, nevertheless.

The schedule is more or less a mechanical means of keeping the child in balance in his schoolwork. To this extent it protects him from himself and from well-meaning but sometimes poorly informed parents who would have him neglect one field of study or overemphasize another as his interests or their desires might dictate.

**Time Schedule and the Community.** In a very definite manner, every good program of studies serves the community. For one thing, it must be geared to the traffic situation to protect the child from physical injury. It should keep children in school or at home while traffic is heaviest for automobiles, trains, buses, and streetcars and keep children off the streets through maximum use of school playgrounds, park facilities, and other publicly supported places for recreation and play.

The school is, for a school child, his business. He lives at home with other members of the family who arise at a given hour, have breakfast together, go to work at a given time, and have dinner together in the evening. If a child's school program seriously interferes with this routine, the program (as far as time goes) must be changed, for the working schedules of other members of the family are by necessity more fixed. Thus a school's working schedule will differ to some extent if a large proportion of the parents of children in school are working in factories or in stores, or if most of the fathers are in executive positions where the time of arriving and leaving work is more flexible. Because of this, a school's time schedule frequently reflects the work of the community (as a unit) but not necessarily the work of an individual family.

In an industrialized area, the city school begins work a half-hour later or earlier if such action will reduce traffic hazards. If railroad tracks must be crossed, even though watchmen are posted, the program definitely is planned to avoid the heaviest congestion of trains at those crossings.

In a strictly residential area these factors are influential to a lesser degree. Here, the program considers the best periods for using recreational facilities such as parks and other public playgrounds. The child's leisure time is commonly less fraught with danger (to the child) in the residential area. It is in industrial areas that taverns, pool halls, and other places of like nature are found. These are places where adults gather to while away leisure time and are always "out-of-bounds" for children. The school's recreational program is always scheduled with this thought in mind. The installation of floodlights on school playgrounds so that playgrounds may be utilized for evening play is becoming more and more an accepted practice. In general, the school program determines what a child is going to do for the six hours or so of the school day and less definitely what he will do for the greater part of his waking hours. With the growing emphasis on teacher participation in school administration, the forward-looking teacher does not hesitate to suggest to his principal that his program be made to carry over into the child's leisure time. Otherwise, all that he does from the character development standpoint during the school day may be lost during the child's after-school hours.

The program in the rural area is specifically geared to the farmer's work schedule. Frequently the program starts earlier in the morning and closes earlier in the afternoon than it does in a city school. With the advent of power machinery, farm children, especially boys, are again an asset from a production standpoint, as they were years ago. With a tractor, a farm boy can do a man's work.

In some sections of the country, recognition is made of the harvest season by closing school entirely for a month or more while the big rush of work is on. The time is made up later.

The rural teacher, of course, faces a schedule-making problem quite different from that of his city cousin. The teacher has several grades in one room, possibly eight. To get the job done, the teacher combines classes, frequently putting Grades I and II together and calling it the D class, with Grades III and IV as the C class, V and VI as B, and VII and VIII as A. This can be done without loss because commonly there is greater variability in the individual scholarship of the children than there is in the subject-matter content between grades. Many sixth-graders are more advanced than are the weaker seventh, and the strongest pupils in the fourth grade commonly score higher on standardized tests than do the weaker fifth-grade class members.

Another technique used by the rural teacher is alternating subjects by years: for example, physiology one year and, if not limited by legal requirements, another subject such as civics the next year. At best, classes are always small, and much is gained in pupil interest by having more than one child in a class. The course of study is usually prescribed for the teacher by the county superintendent's office and commonly makes provision for both combining and alternating subject fields. The prospective rural school teacher makes no mistake in consulting with the county superintendent of schools about the school program before school opens in September.

**Time Schedule and the Curriculum.** Although the time factor is always present in all schedule-making, the dominant factor, so far as what happens to the child is concerned, is the school's curriculum, which determines where the emphasis shall go. If the curriculum is built around areas of living, then those areas will be recognized in frequency and amount of time in the daily program. A rural school's daily program is built around fields which are, first of all, basic to all learning, and second, especially significant to rural boys and girls.

When a subject-matter type of daily program is in use, it likewise reflects the curriculum, as subject matter is only a more specific form or a more limited aspect of a generalized curriculum. If, as is commonly recommended, the curriculum is integrated, all subject-matter boundaries are ignored in the daily program and everything is taught in relation to broad areas of study, so that the daily program reflects the integration.

It is not uncommon to find subjects which must be included in the daily program because they are specifically required by statute or by regulation. Usually the idea behind such regulation is that citizenship and loyalty result from subjects taught in school. Finally, an entire program can be built around a curriculum for a given age level.

## CONSIDERATIONS IN PROGRAM-MAKING

The foregoing pages have presented some of the more basic considerations in making the daily working program for a classroom. It is evident that time is a basic factor; that the curriculum determines the general content; that the locally prescribed course of study limits the offering; that the child is the unit of thinking; that the community enters into thinking when working out the program; and that laws, regulations, and state department of education restrictions must be enforced. This part of the chapter will consider each of these factors in terms of the practical problem of schedule-making.

**Programming Studies.** The curriculum always is the main determinant in what subjects shall be listed. The school's official guide, the course of study, is more specific. A teacher must program studies listed in the course of study. Under a unit organization a teacher may, however, group together several individual items under one general head. To illustrate: Under the heading "language arts," a teacher may list all the verbal skills used in expressing and communicating ideas, including reading, language (both oral and written), grammar, speech, spelling, and penmanship.

This allows him to use judgment as to where emphasis should go. However, if the curriculum guide specifies "reading" as a special subject, he will probably have to list it that way. Again, if the state law requires that the United States Constitution be taught, he cannot list this as social science and offer the course as a part of his history work.

**Order of Subjects.** From the standpoint of *ability to learn,* one time of the day is little if any better than another. This does not mean, however, that other factors do not enter in to make one time in the day better for certain subjects than another. The length of the school day has something to do with placement. The number of free activity, playground, and gymnasium assignments makes a difference. The school day is usually between 300 and 360 minutes in length. The tendency is toward a longer day, rather than a shorter one, with more physical activity for the child in the form of directed play, arts and crafts work, and directed music and physical training. Intermissions of fifteen to thirty minutes in each forenoon and afternoon, when vigorous play is encouraged, are usually prescribed.

Because of the tendency to boredom or physical fatigue as the day goes on, the most difficult subjects for the child, usually the most abstract, should come early in the day. Two difficult subjects should not follow each other. Study periods should be programmed as carefully as class periods. Writing or drawing should not follow an intermission. A teacher must decide which are the fundamental subjects, and never slight those when crowded for time. Young children should recite often, especially in reading. Drill periods in all fields are determined by the extent of the gain in terms of time put in. The economic law of diminishing returns operates in drill subjects. Drill periods, in general, lengthen as the child increases in age and the subject in complexity.

Experts in education and psychology agree to a considerable extent as to the order in which subjects should appear in the daily program of the elementary school. Studies indicate that the first period of the day in a traditional type of school can well be given to reading, the second to arithmetic, and the third, fourth, and fifth to language, spelling, and science or geography. Most educators put health in the sixth period, history in the seventh, civics in the eighth, and special subjects last. When subjects are integrated, such a plan will not apply except that guiding principles still operate.

**Time for Subjects.** Can a hard-and-fast rule be set down for the time allowance for each subject? Obviously the answer is "No." How important is skill in reading? Is civic responsibility a first aim of the school? Shall health information and health habits be considered more significant than skill in arithmetic? Answers to these and questions of a like nature determine the time allowance given to each. To say, "I consider reading skill to be the most significant item for an elementary school child" and then to cut reading periods to a minimum is inconsistent. The country over, reading probably uses more time in the first six grades than does any other one subject; arithmetic uses the second largest amount of time; and language and grammar, the third. This is not too significant, however, as reading is emphasized in all fields of study and language, grammar, spelling, writing, and speaking are frequently united under the head of "language arts" or "communication." Generally speaking, how well the reading is taught is more to the point than the total amount of time allotted to "reading" in the program.

**Combining Subject Fields.** Grouping subjects is really another way of developing the unit idea in instruction. Sometimes the grouping is by an area of living, sometimes by putting reading subjects together. Sometimes subjects are grouped indirectly by concentrating study on some selected activity such as transportation, communication, or industry. Thus reading, writing, spelling, art, and language can all be encouraged under the activity being studied. In a third-grade unit of work on transportation, for example, the children might cut out pictures of all ways in which men travel, make scrapbooks, or models of boats, trains, and airplanes.

The field is almost unlimited. History, reading, arithmetic, speaking, writing, and even general science can be tied together in the same manner.

Two sections of a class (if you have two sections) can best be combined where the subject matter differs little in difficulty, where one part is not specifically a preparation for the other, or where the children in the two sections are practically comparable in their ability to achieve. Health, physical education, penmanship, spelling, reading, and language all lend themselves readily to combining by subject.

**Arranging Study Periods.** Some programs are so arranged that the child always has a study period in a subject immediately preceding the class period in that subject. Other teachers reverse this and place the study period for arithmetic, for example, immediately after the class in arithmetic. These teachers argue that the study period immediately preceding the class period is conducive to "cramming" at the last minute, that the memorization so developed is dependent upon recency only, and that the studied material is not understood as well as it would be had immediate study followed the class demonstration period. It is evident that the nature of the subject determines which time is best suited to the end desired. Type-problems in arithmetic which the teacher has just developed in class will certainly be better remembered and more fully understood by the pupil if further study immediately follows. However, an activity program which has lasted an hour hardly needs immediate follow-up in order to make it more comprehensible to the child.

Many teachers, either by formal supervised study or in an informal way, divide the class period into a recitation period and a study period. This is probably the best answer to the question, "When shall the child study?" The weakness, of course, lies in the fact that the brilliant child does not need help, in fact, frequently has studied far in advance of the class. The study period for him must become a free activity period where he studies anything which interests him and which can contribute to his growth. The extent of the teacher's load eventually becomes a determining factor. The teacher with forty pupils and four grades in his room has little time for supervised study of either a formal or an informal type. The teacher with twenty-five pupils and but a single grade can do much.

**Planning for Homework.** The question of homework is the most generally discussed topic in the entire educational program. Parent-teacher association officials state that many parents complain because not enough homework is required; other parents in the same situation argue that the homework required of their children (and of them) is unreasonable. Needless to say, the teacher is caught in the crossfire. Some homework is essential (how much depends upon the thinking regarding the subjects). But much of a child's necessary preparation for the next day should be done on school time, rather than on the child's recreation time. Also, if homework is to be well done it has to be carefully planned, which, for the teacher, is a thoroughly time-consuming job since it must be planned for the individual rather than for a class.

Children differ much in their ability to do schoolwork in the time commonly allotted. Some need much time to do mediocre work, others little time to do excellent work. Certainly, many children have no reason for taking work home at all. The following are suggestions for a teacher to consider when planning homework.

*Homework should not be the same for all children.* It should place a premium on creativity and independent study rather than upon busy work. Without doubt there is something wrong with assignments that cause Mother and Dad to stay home from a pleasant evening's recreation in order to help Junior do his algebra. There is neither independent study nor creativity in this. The problem is, of course, that no teacher can make independent homework study assignments for 150 pupils a day, not an uncommon load for the high school teacher.

*Assignments should grow in the amount and quality of work as pupils progress in school.* It is probably unsound if not actually silly for pupils in the first, second, third, and fourth grades to be taking work home for study five evenings a week; it is entirely sound for juniors or seniors in high school to be doing so. There are plenty of hours in the school day for the six-, seven-, eight-, and nine-year olds to do what they should do. There are not enough periods for the eleventh- or twelfth-grader to do what he should be doing. His may be a six-period day with classes actually taking five of the six periods. Homework this student must do.

*Assignments for homework should be as concise, clear, and definite as it is possible to make them.* Meanings should be clarified, terms should be defined, illustrative problems should be worked at the blackboard—all with the thought that a child working alone on his homework is not stopped cold by something which was indefinite in the assignment. Parents can be of no help here.

*Assignments must be made meaningful and, if possible, challenging to the student.* An assignment lacking in clarity or meaningfulness can be clarified by the teacher making it, in the study hall or the supervised-study period. It cannot be clarified or made more meaningful when the student is on his own and the teacher is not available. Every teacher has had the experience of being called at his home to be asked by a pupil about a homework assignment. Such a call should not have been necessary.

*Reading assignments make the best homework.* This is, of course, because such assignments are easy to make clear and there is little chance of a misunderstanding clouding all of the work the student has done. Because of this, English, his-

tory, civics, sociology, economics, languages, and such subjects should be assigned for homework. In general, mathematics, and science can best be done at school.

If the mathematics is to be done by the parents, it is
surely not much good for them and is practically worthless
for the child. If a mathematics homework assignment is
type-problems, there is little justification for asking a high
school student to do many of them after he understands the
principle involved and has mastered the technique. Mastery,
though, he must have. To give him twenty problems to work
at home if he already has mastery is at worst useless, and at
best busy work. Again, to have his parents solve all of the
difficult problems for him is to do him an actual disservice.

"Dad, you missed that hard algebra problem last night."

"I did?"

"Yep. But don't feel too bad about it. All of the other
kids' fathers missed it too."

There is some exaggeration in the story, but not too much.
The writer's sister-in-law commented that her algebra was
surely good. "With my four boys going through high school,
I've reviewed my high school algebra four times in eight
years."

Some of the ways in which good homework can help the
student include: acquiring significant facts; practicing skills
(spelling, typewriting, reading, penmanship); analyzing what
has been read; classifying data; applying general principles;
comparing ideas; and attaining personal growth. The list
encompasses, of course, most of the techniques of good study,
whether it be at home or in school. Evidently, under only
the most ideal situation would a significant portion of these
goals be realized.

Homework can be made good, that is, interesting and
satisfying. Frequently, even commonly, it is neither. The
real value to the pupil of the assignment is the mian factor to
be considered.

**Arranging for Efficiency.** Although at first glance it is not
obvious that the arrangement of the program affects the gen-

eral efficiency of a teacher's classroom, such is actually the situation. Some subjects litter up a room more than do others. Some activities such as physical education need time in preparation for the activity and time afterward in order that the child's health may not be impaired. A child who sits for an hour in sweaty clothes after vigorous exercise is probably going to lose more than he gains from the activity.

For some activities two fifteen-minute periods are frequently better than one of thirty minutes, but the double preparation may be wasteful of time, and general efficiency may be lowered.

Finally, the teacher makes his program with recognition of the varying types of class activities which constitute the modern school day. When each period was a recitation period in which the child recited to the teacher the lessons he had learned, no time was needed in preparation for the next class. One class could follow another in rapid succession. Today, with so much emphasis given to various forms of the socialized class period, a time period must of necessity be allowed for clearing the room after each activity. Recognition of individual differences in pupils requires much more time than does teaching pupils as a group. The teacher who lectures can impart much information in twenty minutes, but the teacher who is using committees of children in his socialized work gets little accomplished in so limited a time. Twenty minutes is too short a time for a socialized period, although from the child's learning viewpoint the activity is of significant value. Drill on rules, definitions, dates, or fundamental processes takes little time in preparation. Drill for a Christmas program to which guests are to be invited uses much time. The more complex skill subjects, especially those of the type spoken of as "mental method" subjects, must have a place in the program which allows for both preparation and clearing up afterward.

The good teacher considers the daily program always as a time-saving, orderly guide to his day's activity, changing the program whenever another arrangement will serve the children better.

## DISCUSSION PROBLEM

### WHEN SHALL A STUDENT STUDY AN ASSIGNMENT?

"I don't like your program," said Miss Kent, the sixth-grade teacher, in her disarmingly frank manner as she scanned the program which had been the working guide for your seventh-grade class for some three weeks. "You know, I believe you're all wrong in principles. You have all of your recitation periods directly following a study period for the same subject. In my opinion, it ought to be the other way round. A study period should follow the recitation period in the same subject. That tends to fix everything you have done in that recitation."

With anyone other than Miss Kent offering this blunt criticism of the program which you had so painstakingly developed, you would have felt offended, but with this charming little teacher from the room adjoining yours, a teacher who in three short weeks has convinced you that she is thoroughly professional, you feel not the least resentful.

"You think I'm wrong? Well, I don't agree with you. Aren't recitations, if there is any reason for their existence at all, primarily for the purpose of determining if the student has studied his work well?" You shoot your half-serious, half-jesting question at Miss Kent and the argument is on.

### QUESTIONS ON THE PROBLEM

1. In numerical order, sum up all the arguments you can think of for having the recitation period in your class program immediately after a study period for the subject.
2. Make a similar summary for having the recitation period immediately followed by a study period in the same subject.
3. Think the problem of program-making through carefully with the so-called "laws of learning" as a guide.
4. Do you agree that the daily program, like the curriculum, should be open to change at any time? What are the objections to changes? When is a change of your program indicated?
5. What subjects should come early in the day and why?
6. Initial freshness is present in the morning. Is this sufficient reason for placing the most uninteresting subject for the children at that time of the day?

## STUDY QUESTIONS

1. Plan a program for a room with two grades. Show not only the recitation time and place but also the study periods for each group. Use any grade above the third and base the program on the conventional subjects for the grade you use. Do your work neatly and turn it in for your instructor's inspection.
2. Can you name some advantages a rural school situation has over a town school situation? Consider profiting from hearing older pupils, etc.
3. Obtain copies of classroom programs for various local schools and analyze these to determine the extent to which they agree with this chapter.
4. Start at the beginning of this chapter and write down every statement that you feel is significant for program-making. (These lists can be compared in class by placing in an orderly arrangement on the blackboard those statements considered by the class to be most important.)

## SELECTED READINGS

ALEXANDER, WILLIAM M., and HALVERSON, PAUL M. *Effective Teaching in Secondary Schools*. New York: Holt, Rinehart & Winston, Inc., 1956. Chapter 12, "Providing for the Individual Learner," discusses homework on page 367 f. Chapter 15, "Planning from Day to Day," presents various aspects of the organizational problem.

BARD, HARRY. *Homework: A Guide for Secondary School Teachers*. New York: Holt, Rinehart & Winston, Inc., 1958. A paperbound booklet which presents excellent suggestions for making homework meaningful.

GRAMBS, JEAN D., IVERSON, WILLIAM J., and PATTERSON, FRANKLIN K. *Modern Methods in Secondary Education. Rev. ed.* New York: Holt, Rinehart & Winston, Inc., 1958. Chapter 13, "Slow and Fast Learners," deals with some influences affecting good programming.

HAND, HAROLD C. *Principles of Public Secondary Education*. New York: Harcourt, Brace & Co., 1958. Chapter 11, "The Teacher's Role in Improving the Curriculum," and Chapter 12, "The Teacher's Role in Administering the School," stress the importance of careful class scheduling.

HARRISON, RAYMOND H., and GOWIN, LAWRENCE E. *The Elementary Teacher in Action.* San Francisco: Wadsworth Publishing Co., Inc., 1958. Chapter 4, "Home-School-Community Relations," points out that homework keeps parents interested in and informed on what their children are doing.

KYTE, GEORGE C. *The Elementary School Teacher at Work.* New York: Holt, Rinehart & Winston, Inc., 1957. Chapter 14, "Organization and Management," presents several working programs in a clear, concise manner.

LEONARD, J. PAUL. *Developing the Secondary School Curriculum.* New York: Holt, Rinehart & Winston, Inc., 1953. Chapter 10, "Reorganizing the Subject Curriculum," presents the more recent viewpoints as to placement of emphasis in curriculum making.

MEHL, MARIE A., MILLS, HUBERT H., and DOUGLASS, HARL R. *Teaching in Elementary School.* 2d ed. New York: The Ronald Press Co., 1958. Chapter 11, "Adapting and Using Instructional Materials," deals with the problem of programming and indicates some of the more common time allotments. Pp. 266–67 discuss home study in a general way.

MENDENHALL, C. B., and ARISMAN, K. J. *Secondary Education.* New York: William Sloane Associates, Inc., 1951. Chapter 5, "The Adolescent Learner," discusses the learner's growth in terms of home, school, and community.

# 13

# STUDY TECHNIQUES AND PROCEDURES

The word "study" is for the average child synonymous with "memorize." Only recently has recognition been given to the fact that studying, like reciting, not only can but should involve many different forms of activity.

The beginning swimmer tossed into deep water may succeed in getting out, but today no physical education instructor advocates teaching swimming by this method. The child who is tossed into the midst of a school subject and is told to "study" or be held responsible for not learning an assignment also flounders miserably. Frequently he does make his way to safety, but occasionally he fails to do so.

The tragic side of this deplorable situation is that the school too frequently does nothing about it. Parents can offer even less help to their struggling offspring than does the school, as comparatively few parents are professionally trained in teaching techniques and those few are inclined to teach their children as they themselves were taught.

Probably no other vital institution in American life has changed more in the last century, both in objectives and in methods of securing objectives, than has the school. The change has been in values, in the subjects studied, in means of support, in organization, in administration, in teaching techniques, and in the conception of correct classroom procedure to place a child properly in his niche as a young citizen in a democracy.

It is with the latter change, a change in the child's role in society, that this chapter deals. A child studies. How he studies concerns every teacher.

## STUDY TECHNIQUES

There have been many changes in the ways in which a child is required to prepare or study the work assigned or, if not assigned individually, under consideration at the time by the class. Most of the changes have been in the form of more freedom, less restriction. In general the change from little freedom to much freedom has manifested itself in the following ways:

1. There is freedom in choice of the content to be studied. The pupil is allowed, even encouraged, to follow up the thing which interests him if the relationship between his interests and the general content is reasonably close.

2. The child has freedom in selecting his own method of preparation. Suggestions are made as to possible "things that can be done" with the assignment. Activity rather than passivity is encouraged. No one method is considered the *sine qua non* of learning.

3. The child has freedom in selecting his working associates. Much of the modern elementary school work is co-operative enterprise. Pupils work together. Groupings, although carefully observed by the teacher, tend to follow what would be an adult pattern in a similar situation.

4. Freedom is allowed to each pupil in determining when he shall do his work. The pupil is not limited to specific time blocks in the program. When offered, such blocks are merely suggestive. He may not neglect a field, but he may decide to study any subject at a time selected by himself. His teacher has ideas about when, but does not insist or dictate. He suggests.

Nothing in the above should be construed as meaning that the child has no responsibilities. He has many. Freedom in the modern classroom is always a disciplined freedom. A child's obligations are obligations, nothing else. But, as with an adult, he has freedom within the bounds of the obligation. The modern schoolroom never neglects an opportunity to make the child a responsible person. It does teach and practice that responsibility and freedom, like responsibility and authority, must be found together. A school may be child-centered, but it can never be child-directed.

If the child is to have freedom, he must be taught to accept the responsibility which goes with it. Freedom with no responsibility tends to be freedom without discipline. A child "studies" responsibility as he does everything else, by participating in it. He learns early to accept responsibility in small things, things suitable to his level of development. Watering the flowers, arranging the chairs, feeding the goldfish, turning out the lights when leaving the room, all are ready responsibilities for the kindergarten child. As he grows older, responsibilities are greater and he in turn is given more choice, always limited by curricular bounds, as to what and when and how he studies.

### Child-Centered and Teacher-Directed Education.

Evidently there are many laymen (but few teachers) today who believe that the modern schoolroom is a place where children are encouraged to do as they please. The teachers know that learning is going on in the child-centered classroom. Many years ago, a splendid schoolman, William Chandler Bagley, expressed the point of view in an address before the National Education Association which best fits the thinking of today.

Public education is between two fires. On the one side, it is tempted by the soft sentimentalism of the extreme freedom theory; on the other side, it is assailed by the hard materialism which stigmatizes the budgets for public education as "sanctified squander."
. . . From between these opposing forces of soft sentimentalism and hard materialism we can climb to a new plane—the plane of a

virile, practical, and dynamic idealism. The only kind of freedom that is thinkable today is disciplined freedom. We cannot build our democratic structure on the shifting sands of soft pedagogy. There must be iron in the blood of education and lime in the bone. In the individual, as in the race, true freedom is always a conquest, never a gift.

Today, knowledge for its own sake is rarely, if ever, an objective of classroom study. Knowledge is valued for the possibility it possesses of going over into understanding. Cowper's injunction might well be a guide:

> Knowledge and wisdom, far from being one,
>   have ofttimes no connection.
> Knowledge dwells in heads replete
>   with thoughts of other men;
> Wisdom in minds attentive to their own.

The above says, in the poet's words, "Knowledge is insignificant until it is meaningful." It is meaningful in terms of activity. Activity is not necessarily physical. A child may be mentally most active and yet not be rushing around in either meaningless or meaningful action. It would, however, seem to be almost axiomatic that only thoughtfully acquired information is usable.

Any normal child will, if left to his own initiative, do something. Whether that something is purposeful, whether it is suited to his mental and physical development, whether it is in accord with his moral, spiritual, and social needs, and whether what he does is a logical and sequential part of the formal school curriculum depends upon his teacher. Activity is pupil-initiated. The direction the activity takes is the teacher's responsibility.

Because initiative is such a desirable adjunct to a child's development, no good teacher discourages it, but only directs it. The child with an idea is encouraged to go ahead. Only wrong procedure and wasteful procedure are redirected into correct channels. How the child does his work is one of his freedoms. Inhibition is rarely utilized, redirection constantly.

The teacher has the responsibility of making materials that

are meaningless to the child, but valuable as indicated by the experience of maturity, meaningful to him. Failing, the teacher has taught nothing, or at most little, even though the child can reproduce with some exactness the material considered. The teacher selects to a great extent the material to be learned; initiates, when necessary, the first steps in its learning; encourages the child when interest wanes; and clarifies his thinking when he is confused. The child ultimately accepts or rejects what is brought before him according to his inherent or acquired interests. He accepts by learning or rejects by ignoring the offering. The acquired interest is commonly the result of the teacher's ability to select, direct, clarify, and encourage.

**Study from Many Sources.** From a school which was teacher-dominated and textbook-centered, the modern schoolroom has become child-centered, teacher-directed, and community-vitalized. Moving away from the textbook as the heart and soul of a child's schoolroom activity, there has come a need today for "seeing" the child as he is, a significant citizen of the world in which he lives. The textbook could well be the heart of the school a century ago, when every child lived outside the schoolroom in a vitalized world. The child shared in all of the experiences of the family. Through personal experience he learned what made a farm or a ranch or a grocery store function. He knew his father's business. The daughter helped her mother, baked bread, washed and ironed clothes, canned fruit and vegetables. Modernization has changed all this, and the textbook today is but one of many side streets opening into the wide avenue of learning.

Other side streets leading into this avenue today, side streets through which the child studies, take many forms. Visual and audio aids—the radio, television, motion pictures, and sound recorders—all are utilized. The people of his daily life—the policeman, the doctor, the fireman, the dentist, the street commissioner—tell him of their work and his part in it. Trips of all kinds introduce the child to the industries which support the community. He not only sees, hears, and observes but also writes about, tells of, portrays, and even dramatizes what he has seen and heard. Through elementary laboratory experiences and nature study trips, he may photograph or draw pictures of the birds, observe the insects at work, collect and identify ferns and flowers. He learns of the world about him at first hand. Now he studies from a textbook on whose pages many things have made their record. The school and city library serve him. From magazines, daily papers, and comic books the child of today is exposed to more reading material in a week than the child of a century ago ever saw in a year. Each of these aids to the textbook carries with it activity. The information he gets is understandable, as it is thoughtfully acquired. Study today for the modern child is concrete, real, vital.

**Study as a Group Effort.** In the school of a half-century ago, two children studying together would be observed by the teacher with suspicion, if not with actual distrust. Study was an individual enterprise. In the modern classroom the opposite is true. Committee work is constantly in use. Learning is in the form of problem-solving, project-planning, cooperative effort, correlated activity, and community enterprise. Each child carries his share of the load, mastering the details in his part of the work. From what the others do, he puts together the framework which makes the combined effort meaningful for him. In the schoolroom he no more lives in an intellectual vacuum than does his father live in an industrial vacuum in his business or in a professional vacuum in his profession. Like his father, the school youngster understands thoroughly the details of his own work. As does his father, the child purposes, plans, executes, and judges the work he acknowledges to be his responsibility. Learning is rarely in segments but is commonly in relation to other learning.

By comparison and contrast the child is taught to see relationships. Unassociated ideas are meaningless. Study today carries with it the recognition of similarities and dissimilarities; it carries with it the necessity of singling out common factors; it contrasts right action with wrong action, good deeds with bad, mistakes with correct procedures.

In practice, the child tends to modify and influence his own environment. His everyday life experiences are of his purposing and planning and doing. The assembly program is his assembly program. He helps plan it not only for one day but for several days. He decides who best fits which part, how long it should run, when and how it best works into the daily program. Later, with his classmates, he judges and evaluates. Participants explain their difficulties and make suggestions for future productions. For the participants, memory work is to a purpose. Written scripts are written to be spoken. Arithmetic is in terms of feet and inches needed for light cords and distances on the stage. Spoken words are heard by a real audience, the content used is open to criticism when the audience fails to enjoy or appreciate it. The child's study today is not less arduous or less thorough, but it is more meaningful.

Continuity is always a mark of good study in the modern classroom. What is studied today is significant in relation to what was devised yesterday and what is coming up for tomorrow. One assembly program means little; six mean much more than six times one. The effect is cumulative. Publishing the school paper is today a pupil project, even in the lower grades. The learning develops from the continuity. Study is in terms of mistakes made, of successes gained, of effort that sometimes proves to be wasteful, sometimes extremely valuable. Reading, writing, composition, grammar, arithmetic, history, art—all are studied with great absorption on the child's part as the paper is produced because it is his paper, because his room publishes it, because he is business manager or assistant editor or sports reporter—study is significant to him. He works, but his work is play.

**Study for Production.** In the school of yesterday, study was almost entirely for reproduction. A child studied that he might "re-cite." Perfect reproduction meant that study preceding the class had been thorough. Today, the child reproduces in a more limited number of fields, and he reproduces less in any one field. He studies that he may *produce*, not *reproduce*. His study consists in refashioning, restating the meaning, putting the studied material into his own words. Because he is studying for a purpose, such as finding the answer to questions, solving a problem which for him is very real, or producing something which he is going to use, he is conscious of memorizing very little. Three other psychological factors tend to operate, all factors which are part of the memory process: *wide association, recency* in using the studied material again, and the factor of *enjoyment in learning*. What the child studies is (today) closely related to what he already knows. Associative hooks are not lacking. Material in use today is again in use tomorrow and in days which follow. Thus the factors of both recency and frequency enter into his recall and recognition. Finally, because the child is truly interested, he enjoys what he is doing, and psychological studies strongly support the theory that memories based on pleasant experiences persist not only longer but with more exactness than do those memories based upon neutral or unpleasant experiences. The child today does not need to memorize a great deal consciously.

**Study for Meaningful Understanding.** The traditional school believed that the study period was preparation either for answering fact questions or for exact reproduction. Under the new point of view, the purpose of study is rarely either. A child studies today for meaningful understanding. He memorizes, but the memorization is to a definite purpose. The difference is to some extent comparable to the difference between memorizing nonsense syllables and memorizing your grocer's telephone number. Since study is always associated with or followed by activity in which the study is utilized, artificiality is reduced to a minimum. To illustrate:

The Little Rustlers, one of the best teams in the Twilight League, were all members of Mr. Herndon's mathematics class. They were laying out their new baseball field. The rulebook told the boys that that the "diamond" (strange to say) is a square, ninety feet on a side.

They proceeded blithely to measure off ninety feet from the right of home plate. At this point they drove a peg and labeled the point "First Base." They proceeded from this point to another point somewhat to the left and considerably farther from "Home Base," which they labeled "Second Base"; from this point they turned again to the left and marked the point ninety feet away as "Third Base." Everything seemed to have gone well until someone suggested that it was more than ninety feet from third base to home plate on their new diamond. Measurements disclosed this distance to be one hundred and ten feet. By some juggling with their steel tape-measure, they reduced this distance to ninety feet. Then to their dismay the boys found that the distance from second to third was materially off. One of the boys standing on first base noticed that it was much farther from first to third than from home to second. Since the diamond is a square, he reasoned that these distances should be the same. The boys agreed. They continued working until darkness came on, the problem still unsolved.

The boys had had arithmetic and a little algebra, and the next day in class the problem came up. Mr. Herndon helped the boys, using the diamond as a real problem to develop the theorem, "The square on the hypotenuse is equal. . . ." To accomplish his purpose, he did not hesitate to take the theorem out of its original setting in their textbook.

The boys worked out in class the distances from home base to second and from first to third. That afternoon they completed their diamond measurements in thirty minutes. Study had been meaningful. Information had been thoughtfully acquired. Memorization had taken place, and each boy could state exactly the length of the hypotenuse of a ninety-foot square—yet no boy consciously memorized.

The changed purpose of study is but an echo of the change in objectives in the entire school program. Narrow and restricted subject-matter objectives have given way to broadly social objectives and adaptations. Study today is no longer preparation for life; it is participation in life.

**Study with a Purpose.** Purposefulness is always essential to good study. "What's the good of learning this?" is a child's way of stating that the study for him lacks in purpose. All learning has a purpose. Purposeful activity, then, is exactly what the word implies: activity full of purpose. Purpose always implies mind-set. As some one has said, it is "mind-set-to-an-end." A child with a purpose knows what he wants, why he is studying, what he is looking for. Good teachers recognize that artificiality in the purpose—that is, artificial motivation—is usually little better than the motivation of responsibility and duty.

Because all children must be taught that not everything in life can be made either pleasurable or interesting, the duty or responsibility function is not out of line with sound purposing. It is probably better to tell a child frankly, "The multiplication tables can be learned indirectly, but since they are a form of drill which when well memorized saves both time and effort, I'd suggest we memorize them." This direct attack is probably better than teaching those same tables by an artificial approach which the child recognizes as such. Purposefulness does not necessarily imply pleasurableness. Purposefulness may be satisfied by end results which come only as a consequence of serious effort. *The child must be taught not to retreat from realities of life which call for serious effort, frequently not pleasurable nor even interesting.* Mental maturity is not achieved suddenly but is developed gradually over a period of years through a process of meeting difficulties head on and overcoming them.

Motivation is frequently in terms of clarity of purpose. Seeing clearly why a thing, even though distasteful, should be done tends to purposefulness and to activity. Realizations must be satisfying, however. A child may exercise with a resulting satisfaction although he did not practice (at the time) with pleasure.

**Study with a Problem.** Study is at its best when it is related to a real-life situation. This is almost synonymous with saying that study is at its best when it deals with a real problem. Dictionary synonyms for "study" are "muse," "ponder," and "meditate." One might question whether a child is studying if he is deeply absorbed in an interesting detective story. Is the situation changed if the story is assigned reading? Are all study situations necessarily problem situations? The "study" question has many ramifications.

To illustrate: A teacher has suggested that a certain motion picture is worth seeing. The show takes two hours. It is being presented for the last time. You as a college student have a term paper to write. It is due next week. The cost of the show eats up your spending money for the week. You enjoy motion pictures. Shall you go?

Is the above a problem situation? Is it a study situation? Is attending the show itself a problem situation? A study situation? Is writing the term paper a problem situation? Necessity is present in the situation above, but the necessity is not pressing. Does the study situation differ if the necessity is urgent? Consider: You are driving your car on an unfrequented side road. The car coughs, sputters, stops. You are twelve miles from town; two miles from the nearest farmhouse, where there may or may not be a telephone. You are not an auto mechanic. The problem here is greater than the one above. Should the study be more intense? more prolonged? Were it possible to make all schoolroom study as definitely a problem situation as these two, there would probably be little tendency on the part of children to believe that memorizing is synonymous with study and that any considerable part of study is conscious memory.

Every teacher must keep in mind that schoolroom situations are real-life situations for children. How real they are is too frequently forgotten by teachers who have forgotten their own childhood. Childhood problems, particularly those of the classroom, are not lacking in reality nor are they merely preparation for life; they are vitally significant for school children. To illustrate:

Bobby was nearly five years old and had been admitted to kindergarten. Each day he told his mother, upon his return home, what had happened. He seemed contented, although he rarely showed real enthusiasm. Thanksgiving came, and with it, vacation.

On Wednesday evening before Thanksgiving the next day, Mrs. Barton entered the dimly lighted living room. She heard the muffled sound of a child crying, coming from the davenport.

"Why, Bobby dear, what's wrong? Why are you crying?"

There was no answer.

"Tell mother what's wrong, dear. It isn't like you to cry."

Still the tears and no answer.

"Bobby, stop crying and tell me what's wrong."

Mrs. Barton was growing alarmed.

Then the reply, the reply of a child with his first real problem in life. "Mother, I've—I've been in school three months and I can't read yet."

The story is not fiction. Children have real problems, and many of them are concerned with school happenings. There is little reason for artificiality in the classroom when the subject and object, the child, is never anything but vital.

**Essentials of Good Study.** When attention is given to the essentials of good study, one is likely to be surprised to find that the essentials differ little, if any, for the child in the first grade and for the candidate for the doctor's degree. The "essentials" seem to be inclusive in their implications:

1. The activity is purposeful, and the results tend to be satisfying.
2. Mental activity, as opposed to passivity, is always present.
3. Artificiality is absent; a life situation is present.
4. "Good" study tends to lead to further study; the process tends to be continuous.

Activity is essential for good study. That this activity takes many forms is emphasized by the following summary:

1. The activity may be mental only, but desirably it should be both mental and physical.
2. Through activity the pupil learns and develops. The process is unfoldment, not infoldment.
3. The child's knowledges and his activities are interrelated.
4. Mental activity unassociated with physical activity is one indicator of mental maturity. Only mature persons can and will "sit and think."
5. The activity tends to be both a cause and a result of the study. The study motivates the activity; the activity, in turn, motivates more study. Dewey's statement, that "All activity worthy of the name has in it a desire for further activity," is pertinent.

6. A given stimulus secures its response in terms of the child's activity. This is to say that if the stimulus is changed, the activity changes.

## STUDY HABITS

In the preceding pages the theory underlying study in the classroom of today has been discussed. Activity, both physical and mental, has been stressed as being imperative. The necessity of making what the pupil studies understandable, satisfying, interesting, pleasurable, purposeful, and vital has been emphasized. Changes in concepts of study as interpreted by educational theorists and psychologists have been pointed out. For a teacher in training the question becomes, "How can these requirements for good study be made available? What can a teacher do to make the theory go over into practice?"

Much of the emphasis has been upon study as a group effort. That is as it should be, but the impression must not be gained that the child does no individual work. He does much of his study entirely alone and on his own initiative. True study always begins with the individual child. He is the unit of all collective effort. He studies alone before he studies with others.

**Developing Study Techniques.** Children do not know inherently how to study any more than they know inherently how to ride a bicycle. All teachers take courses in methods of teaching; every child needs a continuous course in methods of study.

Without some training in study techniques children will try to memorize everything. Highly intelligent children usually memorize readily. This probably accounts for the tendency of bright youngsters to enjoy most those subjects which are based on reading, for they can memorize the content. Without training, reasoning subjects such as mathematics baffle them as well as their less gifted brothers. Mathematics in general cannot be memorized to advantage. Hence, because mastery does not come as easily as it does in factual material, the gifted child sometimes fails in complete mastery. The content is not at all too difficult for him, nor is he indolent. Having but one technique, that of memorizing, he meets for the first time a type of content which cannot be memorized to advantage. Not recognizing his difficulty, he attributes his failure to learn readily to the content of the material and assumes he is not "mathematically inclined," whatever that may mean.

The first step in developing study techniques for children is to *plan the time for study.* Time requires close budgeting. Budgeting involves making out an exact daily schedule with a time allotment for each subject based on the amount of preparation required. In preparing the study budget, subjects difficult for the child should be given preferred spots, usually at the start of the study period.

The second step is to encourage the child to *set the stage for study.* This means clearing extraneous material from his desk, arranging for good light, sharpening pencils, and getting his paper ready if he is to write. A comfortable chair and a suitable table or desk are a great help.

The next step is to *check up on the assignment.* What is the child to do? What is the problem involved? He should be able to answer for himself questions similar to these:

1. What is the scope, the content, and the form of this assignment? What am I supposed to do?
2. Did the teacher make suggestions as to the best attack? What were they?
3. Does any part of the assignment call for written work? What form best suits what I shall develop?
4. What are the apparent difficulties in the assignment? What aid do I need in order to attack them?

In an assignment based largely on reading, for example, a pupil's study steps may be something like this:

1. Make a preliminary survey to see what is covered in the assignment or in the problem situation.
2. Decide definitely what to look for.

3. Read headlines and introductory portions first.
4. Read summaries (if any) next.
5. Skim through material the first time over.
6. Try to associate main ideas. Write down facts which seem to be pivotal.
7. Take notes on important ideas.
8. Use the dictionary for unfamiliar words.
9. Outline the lesson after completing it.

Upon completion of study the teacher should test how well the material studied has been assimilated. Having the child tell aloud what the assignment covers is a good check.

**Diagnosing Study Difficulties.** No small part of a teacher's success in aiding pupils to study effectively will be in the extent to which he can diagnose study difficulties accurately. The child who is having trouble in learning should first be checked for the possibility of physical ailment. His vision, hearing, basal metabolism, and general health are given a careful once-over. Standardized tests of achievement will indicate fields of academic weakness. Diagnostic tests will indicate more specifically the weaknesses in these fields. Mental tests are indicated when the physical condition is satisfactory and the child, although putting in his time, is not learning.

Study difficulties appear in two forms—or better, perhaps, two phases—of the same difficulty: *wrong procedure* and *wasteful procedure*. Needless to say, it is not easy to detect the child's study difficulties. His study procedures are not readily observable. Sitting down with him and going over his technique is probably the best method. Below are some common indicators of study difficulties. They are not always in themselves the difficulty; frequently they are symptoms.

1. Is very slow in getting started to work.
2. Talks much and asks questions that are not pertinent.
3. Studies a little, looks around some, turns, twists, studies again briefly.
4. Memorizes the words of the text. Cannot express the thought in his own words.

5. Does not know how to use the dictionary, encyclopedias, and other reference books.
6. Fails to bring to class or have available the books or materials he will need for the period.
7. Shows evidence of distraction. A new word, sentence, or idea keeps him from doing anything that day.
8. Acts sleepy; shields his eyes from ordinary classroom lights.
9. Cannot see any application of ordinary classroom work to his own life situation.
10. Puts much time on items he enjoys; gives little or no time to distasteful things.

Pupils who study to good advantage are easier to pick out. A few of the most common indicators are these:

1. Reads carefully and writes afterward, or intermittently while reading.
2. Wants to know definitely what he is to do before he starts.
3. In a reading assignment, reads it through from start to finish without stopping the first time.
4. Writes down questions he wants to ask and asks them all at once.
5. Plans what he is going to do next and does it; keeps busy.
6. Skims through reading assignments once, then apparently reads carefully, writing as he reads if the material is heavily factual.
7. Keeps a list of all the words he has looked up in the dictionary.
8. Works well with other students; visits little.
9. Seems to get satisfaction out of having studied.
10. Is pleased when he overcomes difficulties.

## HOME STUDY

The question asked most frequently at parent-teacher meetings deals with home study. Any answer seems to evade the issue. The reason is that the need for home study varies according to circumstances and the individual pupil's needs. The illustration below probably presents the case more succinctly than does any exposition which can be offered. The first speaker is Mr. Boshtel, a hard-working citizen of the town, whose eleven-year-old son is one of the best students in the seventh-grade class.

"It's like this, Miss Burton. I think every boy of his age ought to be studying at home every evening. I know I had to. It isn't that Bill isn't a good kid, but he puts in nearly all his evenings reading books he brings from the library, most of them just stories. Oughtn't he to study more at home?"

"Well, Mr. Boshtel, I don't know that Bill needs to study much at home. He's doing very good work at school, don't you think? You see, he has more than two and a half hours a day for study in school, and Bill puts in his time well. The modern school with so much activity in it doesn't require much home study, but it does like to have all the children do lots of outside reading, as we call it. What does Bill do after he gets home before supper is ready?"

"Helps me some, usually. When I don't need him he sometimes plays a little ball. He keeps pretty busy usually before supper. He isn't a lazy kid at all, Miss Burton."

"That's exactly what I'm glad to hear. He spends the time outside in working and playing. That's good for him. Doesn't need to study much at home, although he does sometimes, probably, when he has a little extra work to do. Just so he doesn't loaf in the evenings and run around town, Mr. Boshtel. I believe you needn't worry about Bill."

"Then he don't need to work in the evenings on his schoolwork? That's a new one on me! I supposed all kids ought to work on their lessons in the evenings. I couldn't understand how he got such good grades when he didn't study none. Just supposed the school was kind of easy. He works two and a half hours a day on his lessons in school, eh? No wonder he don't want to work in the evening at home. Thanks for setting me right. I kinda felt I wasn't doin' my duty when he said he didn't need to work and I let him get away with it."

The discussion just presented does not answer the query about home study for every child, but it does indicate that in most cases home study is unnecessary as a steady diet. Supervised study in school is making for effective study. Time is utilized well. Much of the study in the modern classroom is done during the class period, a period of interaction between pupils and teachers. A child's work day, similar to that of his father in his office or business, usually ends when he leaves the school premises.

## DISCUSSION PROBLEM

### The Satisfactions of Serious Effort

Bert, nine years old, had spent nearly all of his Saturday afternoon fixing a broken pedal on his bicycle. He had made many mistakes, had retraced his steps, and late in the afternoon, just before dinner time, was whistling merrily as he laboriously tried to screw a nut, which didn't seem to fit well, onto the pedal-shaft threading. His brother, George, fifteen years of age, came along at this instant.

"Let me see that nut you're putting on there, Bert. Huh! I'll bet it's a left-hand thread." And without more ado the older boy proceeded to screw the nut on the end of the pedal shaft. He had just reached for Bert's bicycle wrench to finish tightening the nut when he chanced to see Bert's face—black as a thundercloud, eyes blazing.

"You get out of here!" screamed Bert, white with anger and kicking furiously at his well-meaning but thoughtless older brother. "I've worked on this all afternoon—an' just as I'm about to get it done, you butt in and spoil it all."

"I didn't spoil a thing," replied George, as he threw down the wrench and walked away. "I thought you wanted to get that old bike fixed up some time today."

There could be no doubt that some of Bert's pleasure and satisfaction in a serious effort were lost because of George's thoughtlessness.

### Questions on the Problem

1. In your opinion, was anything in the learning process lost because of George's well-meant interference?
2. Is there an undefined something in learning which holds itself aloof and out of the picture, as it were, until a learning act is completed? Did Bert sense that this something was just around the corner, and that it would never appear after George completed the act for him?
3. Bert was not only interested in getting his bicycle fixed; he was even more interested in doing it himself. That is to say, the satisfaction of the completed act was apparently less important than the way in which this satisfaction was secured. Have you

ever seen a situation comparable to this in a child's work in a classroom? Why are disappointments like Bert's rarely seen in the classroom?

## STUDY QUESTIONS

1. Do you believe that a child can be taught to study with the same degree of definiteness that he can be taught to swim?
2. We usually think of "methods courses" as designed for advanced students in teacher education. Is it preposterous to suggest that every child should take a beginning course in "Methods of Study" at some time shortly after he enters school, with perhaps a more scientific course coming near the close of the elementary school? That is, should the child be given a "How to Study" course just as he now is given a course in arithmetic or language usage? Discuss in class.
3. Is a child studying when he looks at the toys in a Christmas window? What is necessary to make this study?
4. Very frequently a boy or girl of high mental ability does much better work in one school subject than in another. We have been prone to assign this difference to some special aptitude on the part of the child; would it not be well to consider carefully the method of study utilized by the child on his different subjects?
5. Do you agree that one is not studying unless the "activities are intensely purposeful"? Apply this to:
    a. Listening to a lecture at general assembly
    b. Observing a balloon ascension
    c. Reading the most recent novel
    d. Attending a motion picture
    e. Attending a class lecture
    f. Witnessing an automobile accident and stopping to look it over
    g. Calling an ambulance and a doctor
6. What shall one do with a failing student during his study period? Should he be given more attention than a student who is doing passable work? What conditions or circumstances should govern the teacher?
7. Does it make you nervous to watch a person spending much time doing something which you could do in a fraction of the

time? Do you feel impelled to take charge of the doing? How do you account for your feeling?

8. The tendency to be more interested in the end-results than in the learning process seems to be an adult characteristic. Can you explain it? To what extent is true study, in your opinion, defeated by the tendency to help the person immersed in a problem difficulty?

## SELECTED READINGS

BUTLER, FRANK A. *The Improvement of Teaching in Secondary Schools.* 3d ed. Chicago: University of Chicago Press, 1954. Pp. 236–60. A well-written chapter which gives good illustrations of desirable study procedures.

CARR, WILLIAM G., and WAAGE, JOHN. *The Lesson Assignment.* Stanford: Stanford University Press, 1931. An old book which is still one of the best on the lesson assignment.

GRIM, PAUL R., and MICHAELIS, JOHN U. *The Student Teacher in the Secondary School.* Englewood Cliffs, N. J.: Prentice-Hall, Inc., 1954. Chapters 5 and 6. Indicates how group processes are used to facilitate the learning process. Geared to student teaching.

HAIMAN, FRANKLYN S. *Group Leadership in Democratic Action.* Boston: Houghton Mifflin Co., 1951. Chapter 5. Shows how group leadership develops under democratic processes.

KYTE, GEORGE C. *The Elementary School Teacher at Work.* New York: Holt, Rinehart & Winston, Inc., 1957. Pp. 55–71. Stresses the psychology of the elementary school child and how it functions in his group activities.

LINDGREN, HENRY CLAY. *Educational Psychology in the Classroom.* New York: John Wiley & Sons, Inc., 1956. Pp. 179–92. Theories of learning put in the child studying situation.

SMITH, HENRY C. *Psychology of Industrial Behavior.* New York: McGraw-Hill Book Co., Inc., 1955. Chapter 5. Shows how industrial groups solve common problems through the dynamic approach.

WIGGINS, SAM P. *The Student Teacher in Action.* Boston: Allyn & Bacon, Inc., 1957. Chapter 4, "Good Teaching," shows the dynamic aspects of learning.

# 14

# CLASS PROCEDURES

The change which has taken place in recent years in the interaction between the teacher and his class, although significant, is probably nothing like as great as it should be. Many teachers are still holding "recitations" in the old way. Pupils are assigned "lessons" from their textbooks. Pupils "study" (frequently synonymous with "memorize") these assignments. They come to class. They are asked questions by the teacher to which they give memorized or at least preconceived answers. Only good teachers make the recitation period what it should be: a vitalized interaction between pupils and teacher.

## BACKGROUND OF THE RECITATION METHOD

In order to present more vividly a quick survey of the historical background of the recitation and its growth and development, an excerpt follows from a report made to a graduate-school seminar in the history of education.

"As nearly as I can determine from my research, which I'll admit is not exhaustive, there has been little change in the method of handling recitations from the time the idea was first put into use up to the present. What I mean to say is that in practice there has been little change. Theoretically, I am convinced that the change has been significant, but I'm afraid that the mass of teachers, take them as they come the country over, are still holding the old type of class recitations."

"Would you mind enlarging upon the idea you've just expressed? Sketch briefly something of the history of the procedure called 'the recitation.'"

"To start with, the early view of education held that it was primarily interested in the acquisition of information; that facts, even though unrelated, were essential; that knowledge, a broader conception of the fact idea, might come about only through knowing many facts. Today, education seems to be primarily interested in making needed changes in individuals—character-building, if you will. Values are being emphasized. The old idea, which John Locke helped to popularize, held that learning consisted largely of writing impressions upon a passive mind. This has given way to the thought that learning is an active process in itself. It would seem natural that the present idea would develop a changed method not only in conducting classes, but also in the content of the material to be used. Personally, I think the change has been slow in materializing."

"Are we to understand that you believe the recitation today is practically unchanged from what it was two or three hundred years ago?"

"I wouldn't go quite that far. In my opinion there is a very large number of schools, it may be a majority of all the schools, that are recognizing a different aim in education in general and are using changed methods in order to attain that goal. These schools are not holding recitations in the old sense of the word, but I'm afraid there is a large number of schools, especially those in rural districts and in the more poorly developed villages, where most of the class period now, as in days of old, is given to having pupils tell back to the teacher what she has just told them or what they have just read out of a textbook. Occasionally, we see signs of this in college classes."

"Class instruction instead of the individual recitation is a contribution of the Brethren of the Christian Schools. The date is sometime around 1685. However, there is little evidence of group instruction as a general practice before 1800. It is probably not much more than a century ago when group instruction superseded individual recitations here in the United States. Grimshaw, writing in Barnard's *Journal* as late as 1855, deplored the time wasted by the old-fashioned and false method of teaching individuals instead of classes. Obviously at that date pupils *recited* in the truest sense of the word.

"Blackboards, which appeared in the United States sometime in the decade between 1810 and 1820, were an aid to group teaching. Another important development which made group instruction popular was the so-called monitorial system. In this country the development is credited to an Englishman, Joseph Lancaster. It was used in Europe before his time, however. The plan resulted in mechanical teaching and, in the eyes of teachers today, almost worthless teaching. It did, however, make for group instruction and for some education at very low cost.

"The introduction of the Pestalozzian technique into this country through the Normal School at Oswego, New York, about 1860, changed the structure of the recitation period to some extent. Both the Lancastrian and the Pestalozzian techniques led to a deadly formalism, although the latter had in it the germ of proceeding from observation by carefully graded, oral instruction to knowledge which was fairly systematic and rather well organized. Naturally, that made the recitation rather a mechanical affair, as I see it.

"The Pestalozzian method was based upon a psychology which stressed the significance of perception in learning. In general, the pupil accepted the subject matter handed to him. The pupil was given little or no choice for initiative, and any teacher following the plan closely was limited almost as much as the pupil. The teacher dictated the steps in the process, but the process was specifically outlined for her. The work of Herbart also tended to strengthen the group method of instruction, which in turn has perpetuated the recitation system.

"If I have given the impression that the group method of instruction, especially the recitation, has made little contribution to education, I'm sorry. It has made many valuable contributions. By making education more economical, it has sold the public on the great American experiment in universal education. Many of the educational problems of the past, although they have not been solved by the recitation method, have been materially lessened in their difficulty. The emphasis today is definitely toward recognizing the individual, and since this must be done in group instruction, our need is to develop the individual child's initiative, originality, and independence at the same time that we encourage him to live and study and work in classes with his fellows. Independence and freedom through cooperative effort could well be the slogan today."

Between 1900 and 1930 a great change took place. In 1897 Charles A. and Frank M. McMurray published a book titled *The Method of the Recitation*. In 1928, some thirty years later, V. T. Thayer devoted an entire book to *The Passing of the Recitation*. The change in thinking had come about largely because of a change in dominant educational philosophy. Receptivity had given way to activity. The John Dewey philosophy of learning by doing had begun to be felt in practice as well as in theory.

The problem now becomes one of improving an existing method which in some form or another will continue to exist for some time. When consideration is given to the fact that three procedures, broad though they are by implication, cover most of the work of the class-in-action period, the problem is not so confusing. The procedures are: introducing and setting the stage for new learning, drill and its concomitant of skill, and testing to determine both needs and attainment.

## PREPARATIONS FOR RECITATION

Because no other single word can be found which fits the pupil-teacher interaction better than does the word "recitation," that word is used, although it is really a misnomer today. Essential phases of the so-called recitation take on varied aspects, among which are the following:

1. Maintaining and providing proper physical conditions
2. Maintaining good order
3. Developing a pleasing yet thorough technique of questioning
4. Organizing and directing the activity for each day's work
5. Helping the individual child, yet maintaining a group effort
6. Testing the effectiveness of what is being done
7. Developing background material so that what happens is meaningful to each child
8. Setting the stage for the next work

It would seem to be stating the obvious to say that proper physical conditions must be set up and maintained if the class period is to be profitable, yet such is not true. It is obvious that children, like adults, work better if they can be seated around tables or in semicircles or in informal groups. Neither is it obvious that freedom from distractions, adequate lighting, and comfortable seating make for attentive youngsters. A cheery, light, attractive room is reflected in good classwork. *Set the stage for good classwork.*

Boys and girls at all ages are active. If interested, they are not disorderly intentionally. However, the wise teacher realizes that maintaining good order is no small part of his work. A good chairman maintains good working conditions in a meeting; a good teacher, in the classroom. *Do not allow intentional disorder to develop.*

The teaching process is a cooperative undertaking. Pupils ask the teacher questions, and he in turn questions them. Good questioning is both an art and a skill. It is an art when it deals with activities which involve creative ability, ingenuity, and judgment. The activities of a class under direction always lend themselves to a given end, which is another indicator of an art. Questioning is a skill in that it is something which can and commonly does improve with practice. Questions mean something only in terms of the thinking they evoke. A teacher questions when he feels that a child does not see the issue which is involved; he questions to bring out facts which are not stated; he questions when larger conclusions involved in the statement are going unperceived; he questions to bring out new information which is closely allied to stated facts; he questions to aid the child in organizing and assembling his facts into an orderly conclusion; and finally, he questions to determine whether the child has conscientiously prepared for the day's work and to test his knowledge of facts.

As a general rule, questions should not be used for drill purposes. Much better it is to reserve questions for thought-provocation. For drill purposes, questions are usually uneconomical of time. Types of questions usually avoided are those which can be answered by "Yes" or "No"; those which can be answered with one word; questions which involve only memory of facts (one should work factual material into thought questions); and questions which suggest the answer. However, if it is necessary to pin an answer down to "Yes" or "No," the wise teacher does not hesitate to do so. Intelligibility, accuracy, and completeness are always essentials of good questioning. *Consciously strive to improve questioning techniques.*

Probably the most significant phase of the recitation deals with organizing and directing the activity for each day's work. This is the whole field of "lesson planning." The interaction between pupils and teacher is planned, it doesn't just happen. *Plan the work carefully each day.*

Because the recitation is a group process, one of the most difficult phases of its management deals with the problem of bringing into the activity each individual in the group. It is so easy to use constantly and continually the bright, effervescent pupil who is, in military slang, an "eager beaver." To draw into the activity of the day each pupil in the class without seeming to call the roll of the class is the mark of the professional, as opposed to the amateur who allows a few pupils to monopolize discussions, initiate all activity, and (incidentally) get more from the class than do the more hesitant members. *Teach not only the group but also every member of the group.*

The class meeting commonly takes some form of testing. Questions are asked and the answers evaluated; drill is observed and ineffectiveness and weaknesses are noted and corrected; new learning is not only introduced but is also constantly being placed in its proper category, weighed and evaluated in terms of its pertinence and applicability to what is being considered for the day.

Formal testing, using more objective measures, is in constant use. Some good teachers test the child's memory, comprehension, and interpretation of studied assignments each day in a one-or-two-question test. The practice is sound. Assuming the child understands, without finding out for sure in the form of testing, is at best soft pedagogy and at its worst poor instruction. *Make tests frequent, varied, and comprehensive.*

In general, the assignment sets the tempo of the class movement. What happens for tomorrow in all group effort depends much on what happened today and upon what plans are made for tomorrow. Children are inclined to do little as individuals on any group project outside the group meeting period unless specific assignments are made. In this connection the teacher who wishes to make his daily work carry over into the child's thinking always asks, "What happens after this class meeting as a result of it?" This is, after all, the proof of the instructional pudding. Individual assignments, as part of a broader, more general assignment in order that the activity may progress, are the rule, not the exception. *Exactness, clarity, and completeness in assignments pay dividends in exactness, clarity, and understanding later on.*

The development of background material or, as it is more accurately termed, apperceptive material, is always a dominant phase of the class activity. This is really the process by which new content is related to the child's background of experience and through which this material is evaluated in the light of that experience. For example, reading historical novels is not the same as studying history; the novels are fiction, and historical characters may be placed in a setting and a period not true to fact. But the background material may be decidedly valuable to a child. The factual misstatements must be understood clearly, of course, and with this understanding the growth in apperceptive mass is most desirable. Good illustrations by the teacher are only bridges between understandings a child already possesses and understandings it is desirable for him to have. Audio-visual aids are really background materials. The same is true of moving pictures, general reading, a child's travel experiences, and his everyday life activities. *Consciously build up background material in every class taught.*

## FORMS AND OBJECTIVES OF CLASS ACTIVITY

The classroom procedure obviously takes many forms. Among those in most general use are socialized recitations, unit teaching, assignment—study—report, drill, project and problem, appreciations, testing subject matter, dramatization, panel discussion, and demonstration-performance. These procedures cannot truly be designated "type forms," as no class meeting is ever exclusively in any one form. The type lesson as such is gone, although it has left an imprint on modern teaching, and its successors resemble the parent.

**Socialized Recitations.** In socialized recitations learning comes about through participation by all the pupils in group activities. Discussion is usually led by the students, and informality marks the learning situation.

**Unit Teaching.** Unit teaching involves organizing activities, experiences, and reading around a central theme, a problem, or a purpose developed cooperatively by the pupils under the teacher's leadership. Unit teaching has in it most of the marks of project and problem teaching, as it purposes first, then plans, executes, and finally evaluates what has been done.

**Assignment—Study—Report.** In this form of socialized or unit recitation each pupil works on an assigned portion of a general problem. He studies carefully his portion, gathers his data into usable form, and makes his report to the class. The unified reports make a comprehensive whole. A report is always made to an attentive audience, as each child is dependent upon reports from others on different phases of the same general problem for his own understanding and comprehension of the unit. The teacher, or a pupil or pupils assigned for the purpose, synthesize the various reports.

**Drill.** The tendency away from drill today is based on the fact (which at first thought seems fallacious) that a child does not learn only through drill. Most learning actually happens before the drill takes place. One cannot drill on something he has not at least partially learned. Because of this, drill tends to perfect something partially learned.

Any learning which involves skill must be carefully introduced by the teacher before any drilling is to take place. Teachers who believe in drill for drill's sake will be amazed to find how much of a drill subject, such as penmanship, can be taught without the pupil's having a pen in hand. To drill before a thorough understanding of the skill or association has been developed is wasteful of time and effort. The statement "drill to acquire perfection" is sound; the statement "drill is the route by which pupils learn" is unsound.

Drill is one type of learning which is always teacher-directed. Some basic considerations for a teacher to keep in mind about drill include insuring a definite understanding on the child's part of what he is to do and exactly how he is to do it; working for accuracy always at first, speed or rapidity of association coming later; introducing any new phase of a drill process only after the preliminary phase is mastered thoroughly; and discovering difficulties and errors so that a child will not be perfecting himself in a wrong or wasteful procedure.

**Project and Problem.** This is a type of class activity which has grown out of the philosophy of learning through activity. A project is a practical unit of activity having educational value and aimed at one or more definite goals of understanding. It may involve investigation, problem-solving, and the use of materials and equipment. It is marked by being *purposed, planned, executed* and finally *evaluated* by the pupils.

The term "project" is frequently applied inaccurately to any class enterprise which involves pupil activity. Only a unit of activity, a complete act which includes the steps mentioned above, may be correctly termed a "project." The inference must not be drawn that the project is always of the mechanical or physical type. A project must take place in its natural setting but may be entirely free from manipulation of materials. Thus an appreciation project could be developed in which the children engage in an experience largely aesthetic and built entirely around enjoyment and appreciation. In this case the complete act would not of necessity involve problem-solving, producing, or constructing. If it is a true project, however, the four basic steps italicized above would still apply.

**Appreciations.** It is in teaching appreciations that a teacher makes use of his educational psychology training. Basically, appreciations are first cousins to emotions and idealisms. Appreciations deal with an awareness of the worth, the value, or the significance of anything. Feeling always enters into appreciations, although the foundation of appreciation is usually, if not always, intellectual. It is hard for anyone to appreciate thoroughly something he knows little or nothing about. This is especially true in teaching art, music, or poetry. These subjects are generally considered to have two distinguishable but separate components, *emotional* appreciation and *intellectual* appreciation. The first is based upon pleasure and satisfaction which comes from tone, color, beauty of design, rhythm, melody, and so forth. The second results from understandings of principles of art, of music, and of poetry and from the satisfaction of being able to recognize things of worth in art, music, and literature.

Because of the psychological aspects involved in teaching literature (poetry or prose), art, and music, as well as other subjects where emotional states are influential, the teacher evaluates all materials carefully before offering them to the child. The fact that a poem is a literary masterpiece does not mean that it is good classroom material for children in all stages of development. In art forms (music, poetry, art), more than in any other phase of learning, *suitability* of the material to be learned to the learner is basic. There are too many things entirely suitable to an age level in art, literature, and music for a teacher to use something unsuitable simply because of its acknowledged worth.

In developing appreciations, a teacher must consider the development, or better perhaps, the utility of each type of imagery. This is but to say that poetry is not only an appeal to the ear, but also an appeal to visual and other types of imagery. For children there is little if any appreciation for a thing if there is no enjoyment of it. Again, if nothing happens to the child because of his study, probably no appreciation exists. The appreciation grows and is in evidence when it goes over into action. If there is appreciation, a lecture on poetry stimulates learning, reciting, and writing poetry. The football "chalktalk" becomes no part of the boy until he tries out the plays diagrammed. Running the scales on the piano gets little appreciation, but a simple melody involving this exercise does. To paraphrase William James, appreciation dies of inanition if it is not fed through opportunities for expression.

**Testing Subject Matter.** In earlier days testing was usually in the form of recall. Today, testing may involve recall but is more likely to involve thought and perhaps recognition. The new type of test expresses in a concrete form the recognition of understanding, rather than memorization, as being basic to learning. "Tell in full," "Describe," and "Discuss" are giving way to "Why," "How," "How Much," "Would you agree," and "In what way" in the teacher's questioning. A later chapter presents in more detail the various forms that testing takes in the modern classroom.

**Dramatization.** Dramatization as a teaching procedure is used in the modern schoolroom from kindergarten through the college level. Children are taught in the first grade, sometimes in the kindergarten, to dramatize the stories they are told or which appear in their readers. This is not a substitute for reading. In the upper grades the school drama, usually in the form of a play presented as a part of the class, is common. The play may be before an audience of classmates or, more rarely, before a general audience. Frequently a bit of poetry is dramatized, a social situation, or an event from history. Always dramatization is tied into the general learning situation as a part of the regular classwork.

**Panel Discussion.** The panel discussion, an informal procedure, is rapidly increasing in popularity. The word "panel" was derived from the jury term and, as is the case with the jury panel, denotes a group of persons called to serve in a judging capacity. In panel discussions the attempt is made to approximate as closely as possible the spontaneity characteristic of a conversation. Each panel member should sit comfortably at a table to insure an informal atmosphere. The members, including the chairman, talk from a sitting position. Any number from five to nine is a desirable number. Four are usually too few and twelve too many.

The procedure is simple. The chairman first introduces the members of the panel, then reads the question to be discussed. Controversial issues promote the most interesting discussions. Audience participation is always encouraged.

**Demonstration-Performance.** For want of a better name, this designation has been given to the type of teaching where the instructor demonstrates first and the pupils respond with practice. A class in swimming, tennis, or gymnastics is based on this type of instruction. It differs from drill in that the imitation factor is not so large nor is there as much repetition. This type of teaching is sometimes the first step in drill teaching.

**Objectives of the Class Period.** From the various forms which the learning procedures commonly take, there is indication of the objectives or goals of the class period. These objectives and goals are, of course, varied in nature, but they are only component parts of the same thing, learning. One of the goals of every class meeting is *enriching the child's experience*. This experience enrichment is both personal and vicarious. The child learns at first hand and he learns indirectly from the experiences of others transferred to him through many media.

A second objective, general in nature, is *supplementing knowledge* the child already has. He knows something of a subject; a good recitation period adds much to what he already knew.

A third objective is *clarifying the child's understandings*. As a little knowledge is apt to be a dangerous thing, the wise teacher enriches the child's experiences, supplements his knowledges, and clarifies his understandings. One can hardly be developed without influencing the others.

*Fixing basic factual knowledges* is another desirable objective of the class period. There are basic facts in every subject field. A child must not be partially right on these; he must be entirely right.

*Developing appreciations and ideals* is not something which happens accidentally. The teaching of values should permeate the entire educational process. All of a school's resources should be used to teach moral and spiritual values. Appreciations and ideals are always desirable objectives in every class, not merely in the few which are labeled art, music, or literature.

## MODERN CLASS PROCEDURES

The modern class procedure follows no particular pattern. It has no specific form. It teaches the child first and considers the subject to be taught second. The recitation of other days was patterned; it followed a specific order. Today anything from modern dance to building an airplane, from learning common fractions to reading about the atomic theory, may be sound procedure for a classroom. The world is the child's curriculum, and the classroom is one of the more important of his laboratories.

That a teacher may appreciate the wide variety of activities in the modern class, a selection of such activities is offered below. Each is an actual situation. Not all are ideal situations; some are undoubtedly of questionable worth.

In the following paragraphs, a schoolman reports on what he saw in one school system in a week of visiting. Which of these situations is desirable, undesirable, partly good, partly bad?

1. Visited a spelling class, fourth grade, Williams School. Teacher pronounced words to class as a group. Each student wrote the words. Pupils changed papers to mark errors. Teacher collected papers at close of period.

2. Visited first-grade class at Oliver Wendell Holmes School. Class dramatized *Little Red Riding Hood*. When question as to correct procedure arose, one tot read from her book just what was said there. Every child participated, and the teacher was the audience. Many original interpolations on the theme were observed.

3. Visited a fourth-grade class in arithmetic. Class drilled on multiplication tables. Each pupil took turns reciting the entire table, then pupils quizzed each other.

4. Found a penmanship class in action at the Marquette School. Pupils were making ovals from a copybook. The teacher moved about the room, occasionally offering suggestions. Period lasted exactly ten minutes.

5. Spent thirty minutes visiting a seventh-grade class in community civics. Discussion dealt with the topic of "hot-rod" drivers and whether they could be kept off the highways and made to dispose of their cars after being arrested once. A student quoted the Fourteenth Amendment to support his contention that they could not be compelled to sell their cars.

6. The industrial arts class at the Marquette School was making a slide for the primary grades. A student had made the working blueprint which was frazzled from use. Boys worked in pairs under the teacher's direction. Pupils had asked to make the slide, had distributed the work among themselves, and were driving hard in order to finish by the end of the week.

7. A class in drawing at the Horace Mann School was doing profiles of two class members who posed while the others worked. Everyone was busy and interested. The latter half of the period was given over to criticism by the pupils and teacher of all the work.

8. A class in United States history used nearly all the period answering questions which the teacher asked. All were memory questions. Many were tricky and designed to determine accuracy of the reading. Details were stressed.

9. At the Williams school a spirited game of basketball between two girls' teams occupied the class period in physical education. Students acted as referee, umpire, scorekeeper, timekeeper, and coaches. Substitutions were frequent.

Everyone took showers after the period whether she had played or not. Everyone seemed to be having fun.

10. A seventh-grade class in "classics" had just finished reading London's *Call of the Wild*. A discussion, evidently carried over from a previous day, as to whether a dog would revert to the wild occupied much of the class time. One student read from an agriculture textbook to prove his point.

11. The junior high school paper, the *Lowellian,* is published by the pupils under teacher direction. News stories were being rewritten as student editors edited copy before the teacher approved it. Pupils worked feverishly as the paper deadline approached. Everyone had a job. Evidently earlier classes in composition and writing had assigned "stories" to be developed. As it was nearing the end of the school year, the organization was effective.

12. A seventh-grade class studying *Evangeline* used the class period in reading parts of the poem and in answering questions asked by the teacher to determine how carefully the pupils had read. Apparently no one but the teacher was much interested.

13. The entire fifth-grade class at the Horace Mann School had visited a dairy at the city's boundary. Pupils had taken notes and talked freely of what they had seen. Sterilization of bottles, pasteurization of the milk, refrigeration, the milking process, feeding the cows, and other phases of the industry were discussed freely. A child who seemed to be rather timid volunteered other information, as he had lived on a dairy farm. His importance was evident as other pupils asked him for information. The next day's assignment dealt with the distribution and price of milk.

From these examples it is evident that the school of today is embodying much of the best of the most recent theory in its practice. It is also evident that there is still present in most schools a considerable amount of "hearing recitations." Many of the recitations were socialized, some informally. At least two projects were in progress. The unit type of teaching was used in three or four situations. Formalized drill appeared in two or three places, although applications of

drill in the form of skills were seen many times. Appreciations were being developed in several instances, but were not
being realized in at least one situation which was definitely
designed to secure such. Testing was in the form of using
the results of study.

Again and again the modern classroom demonstrates that
the learner is working for himself, not for his teacher. The
procedure does not consist of a show with the teacher as a
one-person audience. Each and all have a part in the cast.
Applying the psychological "law of exercise," the modern
classroom is in a constant period of review work, although so
little of it is formalized that children do not recognize it as
being review. Useful things are utilized, the non-useful discarded. Teachers today are not hearers of recitations. They
are fellow workers with pupils, exercising control and authority through respect, admiration, and affection.

## DISCUSSION PROBLEM

In order to clarify your thinking concerning the present-day
aspect of schooling which substitutes for the old recitation, some
statements are listed below concerning it. Each statement is
taken from a textbook dealing with the subject. While several of
the books are more than fifty years old and reflect a point of view
concerning the "recitation" which is infrequently held today,
many of the statements represent the best in modern theory regarding this part of the teaching process. Your problem is to
analyze each statement in the light of the preceding chapter and
to place the numbers preceding the statements under the proper
headings. The three headings to use are: "Sound in Principle,"
"Unsound in Principle," and "Partly Good, Partly Bad." Class discussion will enable you to evaluate your classifications.

1. *White:* An aim of recitation is to test knowledge.
2. *Ogden:* The first aim of the recitation is to test the pupil's
   preparation.
3. *White:* An aim of the recitation is to test skill.
4. *Fitch:* An aim of the recitation is to test the power of the
   teacher.

5. *Ogden:* An aim of the recitation is to aid in comprehending subject matter.

6. *Swett:* A major aim of the recitation is to instruct the child.

7. *Swift:* A minor aim of the recitation is to cultivate expression.

8. *Fitch:* An aim of the recitation is to discover errors and difficulties.

9. *Sabin:* To measure the pupil with others is an aim of the recitation.

10. *Swett:* An aim of the recitation is to awaken inquiry.

11. *Lowth:* Every worth-while recitation trains the child in the art of expression.

12. *Lowth:* Another aim of a good recitation is that of *silent reading.*

13. *Harris:* To test the pupil's view of the subject is an aim of the recitation.

14. *Sears:* The aim of the recitation as far as the child is concerned must be very concrete.

15. *Harris:* One of the aims of the recitation is to supplement what the pupil knows.

16. *Lowth:* A good recitation develops initiative.

17. *Betts:* There are three great purposes to be accomplished through the recitation: testing, teaching, drilling.

18. *Hamilton:* The lecture method in the recitation renders the pupil's mind passive rather than active.

19. *Lowth:* The recitation period is the time to teach children how to handle books.

20. *Sabin:* An aim of the recitation is to clarify difficult points.

21. *Sears:* In some recitations the teacher's chief function will be that of auditor and spectator.

22. *Sears:* The management of the recitation is after all the real test of teaching skill.

23. *Stormzand:* Questions must have the purpose of stimulating thought or compelling study.

24. *Almack and Lang:* In the recitation, the teacher directs practice, corrects errors, checks previous learning, stimulates further effort, and continues the pupil's learning process.

(NOTE.—Statements from Fitch, Harris, Ogden, Sabin, Swett, and White are paraphrased from *The Recitation,* by Samuel Hamilton, Philadelphia: J. B. Lippincott Co., 1906.)

## STUDY QUESTIONS

1. What is the greatest objection you can think of to the recitation as we have known it in the past? Does being traditional necessarily mean being weak?
2. Try to describe a recitation in American history which would exemplify the best possible recitation under our dominant philosophy of education.
3. Is there reason for saying that the so-called academic subjects lend themselves more naturally to the old type of recitation than do subjects such as home economics, manual arts, commercial subjects, drawing, and physical education? Discuss.
4. "Good questioning is good teaching." To what extent is this true? When is it untrue?
5. Is there any specific difference between the aims of education in general and the broader aims of the recitation? If "Yes," what is it?
6. In a good recitation, will the teacher's aim and the pupil's aim always be the same? Should they be?
7. Would you agree with this statement: "Pupil activity varies inversely with the number of questions asked by the teacher"?
8. Should the recitation be a place for displaying knowledge? Is "displaying knowledge" a desirable aim either of the recitation or of education in general? Discuss in class.
9. To what extent is good oral expression by the pupil an indication of good teaching?
10. What are the dangers in the type of class study illustrated by the visit to the dairy farm? Can you teach spelling, arithmetic, penmanship, or English through such visits? Would you attempt to do so?

## SELECTED READINGS

Association for Childhood Education. *Grouping.* Reprint Science Bulletin No., 26. Washington, D. C.: The Association, 1954. One of the most comprehensive studies of class grouping and the class in action.

Haskew, Laurence D. *This Is Teaching.* New York: Scott, Foresman & Co., 1956. Chapter 6, "What Teachers Do in School," gives a good picture of the leader's activities in terms of coordinating the pupil-teacher effort.

LINDGREN, HENRY CLAY. *Educational Psychology in the Classroom.* New York: John Wiley & Sons, Inc., 1956. Chapter 5, "The Learner in His Group," puts emphasis upon the cooperative nature of all formal school learning.

McKIM, MARGARET G., HANSEN, CARL W., and CARTER, WILLIAM L. *Learning To Teach in the Elementary School.* New York: The Macmillan Co., 1959. Chapter 10, "Making the Most of the Total School Setting," deals with developing skills in human relations and in producing effective work habits.

MILLARD, CECIL V., and ROTHNEY, JOHN W. M. *The Elementary School Child.* New York: Holt, Rinehart & Winston, Inc., 1957. A book of case histories which does much to create a good understanding of the child in his relationship to his school, his teacher, and his classmates.

MORSE, WILLIAM C., and WINGO, G. MAX. *Psychology and Teaching.* Chicago: Scott, Foresman & Co., 1955. Chapter 12, "Ways of Learning," emphasizes how attitudes and concepts are formed in terms of group associations.

NATIONAL SOCIETY FOR THE STUDY OF EDUCATION. *The Grouping of Pupils.* Thirty-fifth Yearbook, Part I, Bloomington, Ill.: Public School Publishing Company, 1936. An older publication which is still one of the most authoritative, in a general way, on the topic of pupil-teacher relationships.

NATIONAL SOCIETY FOR THE STUDY OF EDUCATION. *Learning and Instruction.* Forty-ninth Yearbook, Part I. Chicago: University of Chicago Press, 1950. Chapters 10 and 11. Many sections of this excellent yearbook deal with coordinating pupil-teacher effort.

# 15

# EVALUATING AND USING TESTS

The twentieth century has brought to teaching a new element, or better, a refinement of a phase of teaching as old as the activity itself: more accurate measurement of teaching results. Teachers have always tried to measure the results of their efforts. But in the past their efforts were generally subjective. This is what happened, for example, about 1915. Two teachers are talking.

"Say, Nell, did Superintendent Kemp ask you to grade a paper in English the other day, one written by one of our sixth-graders?"

"Ye-e-es, he did—but he asked me not to say anything about it. Why? Did he ask you to grade it too?"

"Sure he did. Told me confidentially that it was a paper from one of the sixth-grade pupils here in the city. Said he wondered what I'd think of it, as he wanted it graded by an experienced teacher. You know, I've been teaching for fifteen years, and if I do say it, I've become a pretty good judge of the worth of papers pupils turn in. Wonder why he asked so many teachers to grade it? Helen Perkins told me, in strictest confidence, you know, that he asked her to grade it too. Told her about the same story he'd told me—experience, you know. Kind of a check on a beginner, I suspect. He didn't tell you that too? He did? Why, the big fraud! Pretty poor paper, didn't you think?"

"Well—it wasn't too bad. I gave it 89, if I remember right."

"You did? Why, girl, it was terrible! I marked it down to 66. Of course, I always have been known as a stickler for exactness in all my work. Well, tra-la. See you later."

The paper which Superintendent Kemp had given to twenty-two of his teachers to mark was one which he had lifted verbatim from the then new Harvard-Newton scale. He felt sure his teachers had not seen the scale. He had enticed a sixth-grade lad to copy the well-standardized exercise. Every error in punctuation, spelling, capitalization, in composition, in form and content was put into this sixth-grade lad's handwriting. Copies had been made mechanically. Mr. Kemp had then given a copy of the standardized composition (in the boy's handwriting) to each of the teachers in this elementary school. He had requested each to mark the paper, after studying it carefully, somewhere between 60 and 100, both inclusive. Sixty was the failing mark in the school. Marks over 95 were considered highly superior.

The standardized established value for the scale composition approximated a percentage mark of 83. Two of Mr. Kemp's twenty-two teachers had marked the paper with a value of 60. One teacher had given the paper a mark of 66. Another had marked the paper 95. The distribution of the other marks was from 66 to 93. After Mr. Kemp had explained the "experiment" and the results to the teachers they agreed that marking papers, in fact all grading, was rather subjective.

Measuring practices today are somewhat different. Two terms applied to giving marks, *subjectivity* and *objectivity,* are candidly discussed. The former recognizes the fallibility of marks due to the teacher's temperament, biases, prejudices, partiality, or physical condition. A subjectively bestowed mark is not verifiable by another scorer, since if it is subjective it is not susceptible to observation, physical measurement, or record.

Objectivity in grading is based on the impersonal, factual evidence and established truths, rather than on judgment, opinion, bias, hearsay, or untenable hypotheses. Traditional grading carried with it an element of the subjective, although every good teacher strove to be objective. Teachers today are not less subjective than their predecessors, but their measuring instruments, the tests, are commonly more exact and refined. Again, the object of the measurement varies to some extent in the ease with which results or replies on it can be measured. For instance, it is much more difficult to tell how often a boy has failed to answer correctly than it is to tell how often he has missed class entirely. The latter lends itself much more to objective measurement than the former.

The fact that some of Mr. Kemp's teachers approximated the established mark, 83, is not conclusive evidence of greater objectivity on their part than on that of the others. They may or may not have used more objective measures.

Measurement, then, tries first of all to be objective, as without objectivity there is no accuracy.

## PURPOSES OF MEASUREMENT

The purposes of measurement are to determine first where the pupil is now and, from this, what is needed in his instructional program; to determine as accurately as possible the extent of the effectiveness of the teaching; and to determine the child's understandings or ability to apply what he has "learned." The last purpose involves a check on memory of the mechanical type as opposed to utility of memorized materials, as well as on skills only partially or wholly mastered.

A teacher tests to find out where his pupils are; to determine what he has succeeded in teaching and wherein he has failed; and, finally, to find out whether the child's learning is significant to him or not.

Many types of tests are used, for the modern classroom teacher is definitely test-conscious. Some, in fact the greater number of the tests he uses are teacher-constructed. At certain times of the year, to compare pupils with other pupils who have taken the same tests, highly developed, standardized tests which are purchased commercially are given. These standardized tests are the work of experts in the field of test-making. Commercial tests are usually good tests; that is to say, they are valid tests. Standardized tests should be used in every classroom with some regularity, as they have norms based on a wide usage of the test. A *norm* is an average (it may be some other typical behavior) of some function of learning for a specified population. To illustrate:

An average for reading based on tests given to many sixth-graders would indicate where a particular sixth grade is when they are given the same test, in terms of the norm. The average is thus the "typical behavior" used; the "function of learning" is reading and the "specified population" is the sixth grade.

Except under extraordinary conditions a teacher will test his pupils for not more than five objectives. Some of these objectives will possibly be measured more or less indirectly.

1. Testing for *achievement in subjects* such as arithmetic and history
2. Testing for *skills and special abilities* in subjects such as penmanship, singing by note, and playing basketball
3. Testing to find out rather specifically *just what is causing the trouble* in a child's inability to learn some particular subject or phase of a subject (diagnostic testing)
4. Testing to *determine* a *child's mental age* in terms of a standardized measure (intelligence testing)
5. Testing to determine whether a child's *mental health is good or not*, and whether his personality development is well rounded

Tests have two major functions: (1) to determine needs, abilities, achievement status, interests, and personality characteristics of students, and (2) to appraise or evaluate the outcomes of learning. The five general reasons for testing stated in the paragraph above boil down into these two general characteristics.

## PROBLEMS IN MEASUREMENT

This chapter was introduced by a problem in measurement. In the problem the twenty-two teachers who marked the papers were good teachers; however, they had quite different ideas of the worth of a paper written by a pupil. They failed to agree on its worth. Evidently some of the teachers would have held the pupil in the grade for another year (if the test were used as a measure), while others would have promoted him, almost with "honors." Thus the problem of correct measurement—or testing, if you will—is a serious one. Constantly, it is involved in the problem of promotions.

Almost everything that happens in school can be measured, but not everything can be measured equally well. John missed school. This is measurable—exactly. John was tardy: measurable—but not so exactly. What constitutes tardiness? Being on the school ground when the bell rings? Being in the building? Being in the classroom? Evidently the measurement is not as certain as in total absence. Unless there are set rules, judgment enters in; hence a subjective (more or less) mark on the tardiness.

Three degrees of objectivity are possible in most school measurements. The first includes items which are definitely and accurately measurable. They include such items as attendance, the number of books in the library (not their quality), the amount of chalk and other supplies used, the number of times the principal visited a classroom formally and informally, the number of pupils with physical defects, and other items of a similar nature. From the measurement viewpoint, this group can be dismissed from a teacher's mind, as it presents no problem.

The second degree of objectivity concerns itself with measurements in school subjects, in group membership, in social standards, and in interest in school work. Here the measuring is less objective and as a result less exact than in the first group. This is, at present, the big field of measurement. It is not as susceptible to accurate measurement as a whole, however, as is the field in the first group. Academic achievement, in terms of pupil progress, is always the most significant measurement problem from the standpoint of its immediacy, or in terms of pressure put on a teacher. At present most measurement, or testing, is in this field.

The third level of objectivity, where at present sound measures are only partially developed or are totally undeveloped, lies in measurement in appreciations, attitudes, character traits, morale, spiritual and moral values, and other more or less intangible outcomes of education. No one doubts that these items are as important as, or even more important than, excellence in school subjects, but to date suitable measurements have not been developed.

It is possible to tell with finality whether or not a child missed school for the day; with rather a high degree of certainty whether he is strong, average, or weak in reading. But it is difficult if not impossible to measure objectively whether he is increasing his ability to take responsibility, to control his temper, to be thoughtful of others, or to participate in group action cooperatively, and whether he is growing spiritually and morally.

## WAYS OF EVALUATING MEASURES

There are five marks of a good test. It is valid. It is reliable. It is easy to give and to score. It has some established norms. There are equivalent forms available.

**Determining Validity.** Of these, the first-named, validity, is by far the most important. Validity deals with the extent to which a test or other measuring device measures what it purports to measure. It would also deal with the extent to which the scores obtained from a test (or a scale) can be used for prediction. In a general way, validity in a test refers to its all-round goodness. If the purpose is to measure a child's knowledge of history, but the test is of such a nature that his spelling, penmanship, and language usage cloud the result or purpose of the test, there is a strong indication that the test is not measuring what it purports to measure: history knowledge. If this is true, the test is invalid. If the test is valid, the items in it have been selected carefully. The test is about material which the class has studied.

**Determining Reliability.** The second mark of a good test is its reliability. If tests are to contribute to teaching excellences in general, and to a well-ordered relationship with other teachers, administrative officers, parents, and pupils in particular, a teacher will always have the reliability of his tests in mind. Only validity is a more significant measure of the worth of a test or examination. As with validity, reliability is essential for a sound measure of achievement.

The essential test of reliability is agreement. A good test agrees with itself, that is, if a test is split in halves, scores on the two halves agree with each other. If it is split by putting the odd numbers, 1, 3, 5, etc., in one test and the even numbers in another, pupil scores on the two halves thus secured will agree with each other. The extent of agreement is indicated by a term spoken of as a *coefficient of reliability.*

The layman's use of the word "reliability" is probably more exact than is his use of the word "validity." He does not always analyze just what his measure of agreement is, but he uses his measure constantly to secure reliability. The clerk in a store adds the bill twice. He adds up and he adds down. If his totals disagree, he may take it to the adding machine. He is seeking for agreement, reliability. The man telling of an accident calls on another observer to substantiate his statements. He seeks agreement, for agreement makes his statement more reliable.

The teacher secures reliability in his measuring intruments by exactly the same methods that are used by the layman, whether he is measuring attendance, the values in offering prizes, the justness of his punishments, the height of the seats from the floor, the accuracy of his promotions, or the determination of pupil achievement in a school subject. He compares his measurement with another measurement. This, if possible, is a measure of known accuracy. Agreement strengthens the reliability; disagreement weakens it.

**Ease in Giving and Scoring.** A good test is easy to give and easy to score. It is easy to give because it is clear, definite, and readily understood. It is easy to score because it is objective. An answer does not have to be evaluated at the time it is scored. This has been done previously. The answer is either right or wrong. It is evident that ease of scoring is tied up with objectivity, and objectivity wth reliability.

A good test is not easy to construct. The time and effort go into the construction, not into the giving and scoring. For the traditional essay-type examination, the opposite is true. It is comparatively easy to make but is extremely difficult to score. It is hard to score largely because it is subjective. While the determination of the answers in any test may be arrived at subjectively, once the answers are determined in the new type of examination, they are held constant. Furthermore, the questions are so worded that answers other than the ones decided upon as being correct cannot be considered.

**Using Established Norms.** Established norms are useful; however, a test may have norms established and still not be a good test. On the other hand, a test may be good but have no established norms, due to the fact that it has not been taken by enough pupils (perhaps not any) to establish what may be expected when the test is taken by many pupils. Norms refer to the extent or degree to which the test is standardized. If a self-constructed test has been given to many pupils, the teacher should know what should be expected from any group taking it—what is a high score on it, what is a low score, and what is an average score. These are the norms, and the norms form a basis of comparison. Without such a basis for comparison, the test lacks something in all-round goodness.

Probably the value of norms has been overestimated. Even the best of norms, those most carefully arrived at, are open to criticism. Norms are affected by the chronological ages of the children who have been tested, the length of the school year, local conditions governing what is taught, racial and economic background, mental ability variations, and other factors. Only norms developed locally are entirely significant for a given class. If records are kept, in the long run the norms on home-made tests will usually be satisfactory. In general, local norms should be established on any teacher's tests. Lacking such, standardized tests should be used, tests with established national norms. Without such norms a teacher has no evidence that his sixth-grade class is not a fifth-grade class in achievement, or possibly a low seventh if it is unusually strong.

Standardized tests, made by test specialists, not only have norms but also have a high statistical reliability which the amateur test-maker has difficulty in attaining. A standardized test measures well what it does measure. The validity of the test rests upon a basis more dependable than a single opinion. Commonly each item in the test has been validated separately. A classroom teacher has difficulty in doing this. Most tests on the market have a reasonable degree of objectivity in scoring. Without this, the subjective factor will react upon the reliability and consequently affect the validity.

Standard tests must be selected critically. All are not equally good. The purpose for which the test is to be used must be considered. Expert opinion in selecting standardized tests is highly desirable, almost imperative.

**Using Equivalent Forms.** As with norms, equivalent forms are desirable. The term applies usually to standardized tests. However, even with a home-constructed test it is desirable to have a second form of the same test for these reasons:

1. A pupil misses a test and a makeup test is called for. The equivalent form meets the need. Making a new test not only means too much work for the teacher, but inequalities of difficulty can hardly be avoided.
2. Doubtful cases can be retested, using the other form. Since it is equally difficult, the second measure verifies or indicates the reliability of the first test. Administrators and parents are often more satisfied if this is done.
3. Duplicate forms can be used in the same class; alternating the forms thus eliminates the possibility of copying.

## TYPES OF TESTS

Day-by-day measurement and evaluation is, of course, most desirable. Frequent testing with shorter tests is usually considered a more desirable learning technique than long tests at greater intervals. All tests have limitations, and the best of tests must be supplemented by the teacher's appraisal of the pupil's progress. Because of the impossibility of measuring accurately all of the desirable outcomes of education, the whole is not always the sum of the parts. An intangible something is frequently present which defies measurement with existing instruments. This does not mean that the teacher does not use tests and all other available measurements; it does mean that there is human fallibility in all evaluation.

In the past, the great objective of teaching has been to develop the ability to reproduce factual material. This, of course, represents a typical result of learning by memorization. Today there is recognition of greater values in other abilities. Instruction is now flexible, as opposed to the rigid and formal instruction of the past. The flexibility has led to recognition of a wide variety of objectives which can be classified under these divisions: functioning information; aspects of thinking; attitudes; interests, aims, and purposes; study skills and work habits; social adjustment and social sensitivity; creativeness; and a functional social philosophy.

With such a variety of objectives, it is difficult to evaluate progress in the schools. It is difficult to test pupils' growth in all items which are significant. Below are suggestions for making tests. Many types are illustrated, and the objectives mentioned above will be measured more or less directly, difficult though some of them are to measure, if a teacher will utilize all of the types presented. Only one or two illustrations of each type of test question are used.

**Essay.** The essay-type test has many variations and is one of the oldest test forms in use. The list below indicates that it has many forms. It shows how an essay-type question may test for many types of learning.

1. *Selective recall:* Name four important English poets of the early nineteenth century and show that each made a definite contribution to English literature.
2. *Comparison:* Compare the trade lanes of the Atlantic Ocean with those of the Pacific Ocean.

3. *Decision:* Who made the greater contribution to the westward expansion of the United States, Meriwether Lewis or Daniel Boone? Give reasons for your answer.
4. *Causes or effects:* Why does a planet always move in the same orbit?
5. *Summary:* Summarize the plot of *A Tale of Two Cities.*
6. *Analysis:* What are the characteristics of a good citizen?
7. *Relationship:* How did the French and Indian War lead to the Revolutionary War?
8. *Applying rules or principles to new situations:* Considering the impact of industrialization on farm production, what do you expect will be the status of farming by 1980?
9. *Discussion:* Discuss briefly the development of the short story in America.
10. *Outline:* Outline the steps in making a motion according to parliamentary procedure.

**Simple-Recall.** The simple-recall test usually asks for a single fact, based on memory. Examples:

1. Who wrote the pamphlet, "Common Sense"?
2. What is the formula for the area of a circle?

**Short-Answer.** The short-answer test differs little from the recall type except that it commonly requires discrimination or judgment in that the pupil weighs a number of facts before answering in a few words. This type of test is very useful. Examples:

1. How do we know that air is a real substance and occupies space?
2. What historical significance is common to Roger Williams, Lord Baltimore, and William Penn?

**True-False.** The true-false test is based on recognition rather than recall. It is really a multiple-choice item with but two multiples. It appears in many forms, such as true-false, right-wrong, and yes-no. The element of guessing can influence results, although there are ways of reducing guessing to some extent. Its reliability can be made high by making the number of items large. True-false tests may measure only the recognition phase of memory, but it is possible to word the question so that reasoning also is required. The factual type is illustrated by the following:

*Indicate by T or F your judgment of the truth of these statements:*

___ 1. Most bacteria produce disease and are harmful to man.
___ 2. Lincoln delivered the Gettysburg Address in 1863.
___ 3. Little Red Riding Hood was the name of a fairy.

The true-false question with a reasoning basis is illustrated as follows:

___ 1. Christopher Columbus refueled his ships at San Salvador.
___ 2. All transportation will eventually be taken over by the airlines.

**Completion.** The completion type test consists of simple recall items but varies in that each answer is commonly limited to one word, a phrase, or a number. Sometimes a form is used which omits key words and instructs that they be filled in by the pupil. It is usually more objective, and as a result is somewhat easier to score, than the simple recall test. Illustrations:

1. Cicero delivered a series of orations against _____.
2. A person who steps on a rusty nail is likely to incur the disease _____.
3. The Declaration of Independence was signed in July _____.

The mutilated-sentence type of completion test is of this sort:

1. Air expands when _____ and contracts when _____.
2. The two cities mentioned in *A Tale of Two Cities,* written by _____, are _____ and _____.
3. George Washington crossed the _____ River and attacked _____ at _____.

**Multiple-Choice.** The multiple-choice test question has several forms. It is a very good measure of higher mental abilities, or can be made so. It may test reasoning or deductive thinking in that much discrimination is needed to select the correct answer from among several, all of which seem plausible. Here are some illustrations of the more common forms of the multiple-choice test:

1. An instrument which measures wind velocity is
   a. anemometer
   b. barometer
   c. hygrometer
   d. thermometer
   e. ammeter

2. A house is painted to
   a. make it fireproof
   b. make business for paint dealers
   c. protect the house from the weather
   d. make it the most attractive house in the block

**Matching.** The matching test is of use largely for fact-finding. It is time-consuming usually, as pupils tend to make it a recognition rather than a recall test. Thus a pupil not recalling the answer must run through the entire list looking for recognition. Theoretically, it is too mechanistic to be one of the best tests. It can be used, however, for a survey of many facts which a pupil may or may not have. Example:

> *In the left-hand column is a list of poems; in the right-hand column is a list of American poets. Before each poem place the letter which identifies the author.*

| | |
|---|---|
| ___ 1. "The Raven" | A. William Cullen Bryant |
| ___ 2. "Ode to the Confederate Dead" | B. Robert Frost |
| | C. Sidney Lanier |
| ___ 3. "Thanatopsis" | D. Vachel Lindsay |
| ___ 4. "Chicago" | E. Henry Wadsworth Long-fellow |
| ___ 5. "Patterns" | |
| ___ 6. "The Arsenal at Springfield" | F. Amy Lowell |
| | G. James Russell Lowell |
| ___ 7. "Miracles" | H. Edwin Markham |
| ___ 8. "Birches" | I. Joaquin Miller |
| ___ 9. "The Defense of the Alamo" | J. Edgar Allan Poe |
| | K. Carl Sandburg |
| ___10. "Lincoln, the Man of the People" | L. Henry Timrod |
| | M. Walt Whitman |

When a question of this type is prepared, the teacher should arrange that it be complete on a single page, so that the pupil need not constantly turn pages to select the proper responses.

**Pupil-made.** Most teachers find there is a fine learning opportunity in allowing and encouraging pupils to make their own tests. After careful explanation of the type to be used and with good illustrations for guides, each child contributes questions which are assembled by the teacher. Editing is, of course, necessary. Being able to make a good question is usually as good an indicator of understanding of subject matter as being able to answer correctly.

**Battery Tests.** In order to get a more exact measurement, especially of abilities which are related, tests of the standardized form are commonly grouped so that they may be administered in succession to the same pupil or groups of pupils. This is, in test parlance, a *battery* of tests. To illustrate, a battery for Grades II and III might include tests in reading, word-meaning, arithmetic fundamentals, arithmetic problems, and spelling. From such a battery an over-all picture of the child's achievement can be made graphically. This graphic picture is commonly called a *profile*. The profile, which is really a line diagram, shows the child's relative position in each trait measured. From the profile, a teacher can see at a glance how the child rates on the various measures.

## USE OF THE RESULTS OF MEASUREMENT

There are four general aspects of testing from the viewpoint of the classroom teacher. The first deals with *how to test*. More is known of this than of the other three. The second aspect deals with *what to test*. Here, there is a growing accumulation of knowledge, as is shown by the effort in the direction of evaluating pupil progress in terms of all teaching objectives. No longer do teachers test memory only. No longer do they test subject matter only. The conception of what should be tested is definitely broadening. Emphasis on mental growth and development is opening up new fields in the area of what can and should be measured.

However, in the other two aspects of testing, *when to test* and *the why of testing*, very little has been done. No one has established for certain how often testing should be done, and even less attention has been given to the purposes served by testing.

**Guidance of Instruction.** It would seem that one of the big reasons for testing is to offer aid to the teacher as a guide and leader of youth and to aid in making instruction serve the child better. If tests are to serve well, common sense would say that the pupils must be given the results of the tests. If this is not done, a great part of the instructional values is bound to be lost. Only when an ability is being measured in which no improvement is or can be expected from instruction is testing valuable in and for itself.

To illustrate: a big-league manager wished to know for sure who were the fastest men in his baseball club. He tested all with stop watches. He was not trying to improve their speed, but he did wish to know his fastest men for sub-stitute base-running purposes. It made little difference here whether the players were given the results of the time tests or not. It need hardly be said that such a situation rarely exists in the schoolroom, whose reason for being is improve-ment of desirable conduct, skills, abilities, and other behavior patterns in children.

A teacher should help his pupils in interpreting their test scores, especially when tests are divided for the purposes of measuring individual abilities which are basic objectives of the instruction. A pupil needs to know wherein he is weak and, if the reason is explainable, why he is not succeeding. Interpretaton may indicate that he fails on memory questions largely and succeeds on understandings of principles or, more likely, the opposite.

There is nothing wrong and much that is right in allowing pupils to score their own papers. This, of course, utilizes two of the factors in memory: recency and frequency. Discussion during the correction adds much to instructional gains. Pupils cannot reasonably be expected to score any type of tests except those whose items are objective. Teachers usually rescore for accuracy.

**Measurement of Gains.** Not infrequently tests are used to show gains resulting from instruction. When used to show gains, two forms of the same test are needed. Form *A* is given before instruction and Form *B* following. The gains indicate whether the teaching was effective and to what degree. Loss is possible if the instruction is not fitted to the material tested. The principle of this type of testing is sound. Without such procedure the teacher does not know how much he has taught; he knows only what the pupil has at the end of the course. A pupil with the lowest terminal score may have made the greatest gains. It is probably sounder to evaluate a pupil on his net gain than upon an arbitrary standard to be met at the close of the instructional period.

## DISCUSSION PROBLEM

### LIMITATIONS OF THE OBJECTIVE EXAMINATION

"Do you know, this objective testing movement is making me terribly tired." The speaker is Miss Dorn, a thoroughly well-trained, conscientious, hard-working teacher, whose master's degree had been conferred by one of the country's leading universities. "First of all the so-called objective test, which in my opinion is far from being objective, limits the child's thinking entirely to the events which the teacher places in the objective question. As nearly as I can tell, and I believe my training is a fair cross section of the teaching population as a whole, the objection to objective tests, and I have yet to see one that isn't susceptible to it, is the guessing element. True-false, multiple-choice, the recall type, completion—I don't care what type you pick out —all are open to guessing on the part of the student. The best guessers get the high scores.

"While I'm at it I might just as well go on, then I'll have it out of my system. I don't believe there has ever been a test constructed which is as good a measure of a pupil's ability as the plain, unbiased judgment of a well-read, well-informed teacher. After all, a good teacher knows quite definitely how great has been the achievement of the pupils in her classes. If she doesn't know, I, for one, haven't much respect for her.

"Have you ever considered that the objective test completely neglects the language training of the child? Never a complete sentence does he write in an examination. A plus here, an underlined word there, a circle around this word, a check mark in front of that one—that is the extent of the oral and written expression bound up in the 'objective' examination. There isn't the least thing in a million of them to develop the creative ability which I believe is present to some extent in every normal boy and girl.

"Again, let us consider the limitations of the whole plan. There is never a problem present in one of these examinations. Life forces us to work problems, to meet situations, but the 'objective' tests teach us how to say 'true' or 'false' to them. Problems of life demand that they be faced fairly and squarely and that, entirely on our own, we think them through carefully and do something about them. We can't just remember facts about the problem and, through having developed a splendid objective-test ability, simply solve it by memory.

"Well, I feel better having gotten that load off my mind. It's your turn now, and I'm ready to be convinced. Right now, though, I'll have to say that I'm opposed to the objective testing idea in practically every phase of teaching and management."

## QUESTIONS ON THE PROBLEM

1. Do you agree with Miss Dorn in her attack on the objective test? If you agree, state definitely the points which you feel are well taken by her.
2. If you disagree with Miss Dorn, select the outstanding weakness in her argument, taking her attack as a whole.
3. In a well-thought-out sentence state the purpose of an examination.
4. Does the objective test limit "the child's thinking to the events which the teacher places in the objective question"? Were this statement true, would the objective test be either valid or reliable?
5. "I don't believe there has ever been a test constructed which is as good a measure of a pupil's ability as the plain, unbiased judgment of a well-read, well-informed teacher." What are the key words of the foregoing statement?

6. If "unbiased judgment" were possible, would Miss Dorn be correct?

7. If "unbiased judgment" were present, positively and completely, would the judgment of necessity be objective, or subjective? Does subjectivity preclude unbiased judgment?

8. Miss Dorn complains that the objective test limits the child's language training. Consider your answer to Question 3 above, then answer Miss Dorn's charge.

9. Are good tests primarily teaching instruments or measuring instruments or both?

10. What constitutes a "thought" question? If one knows all of the facts pertaining to a question to be settled, is the question for him more of a "thought" question or less so than it is for a person who does not know all of the facts?

11. Is there a criticism of the objective examination which could not be pertinently applied to the traditional examination? Which one or ones?

## STUDY QUESTIONS

1. If education is the process by which we make desirable changes in individuals, in what manner may the extent of these changes be best measured?

2. Define carefully the meaning of "subjectivity" as applied to marking a paper in a school subject.

3. Had Mr. Kemp, in the illustration used in the first pages of this chapter, used a problem in arithmetic, would the range in the marks have been as great as was true for the English composition? If you say "No," how would you score an arithmetic paper giving the wrong answer but using the correct principle? Would this be "subjective" scoring?

4. Is *validity* a term which is applicable to what a teacher presents to his class as well as applicable to his tests?

5. Name a field of endeavor (not necessarily school work) in which all of the tests are thoroughly *objective*. Can you name a field in which all the tests applied are apparently all *subjective*?

6. What makes a test that is very difficult to score (usually) a poor test?

7. Can you make a profile of all your marks received the past semester in college classes? Why is it not significant if you do it?

## SELECTED READINGS

ADAMS, GEORGIA SACHS, and TORGERSON, THEODORE L. *Measurement and Evaluation for the Secondary School Teacher*. New York: Holt, Rinehart & Winston, Inc., 1956. Part 3, "The Improvement of Instruction," emphasizes diagnosis as a necessary step in helping pupils to learn. Detailed suggestions are made for the construction of tests by the classroom teacher.

AHMANN, J. STANLEY, and GLOCK, MARVIN D. *Evaluating Pupil Growth*. Boston: Allyn & Bacon, Inc., 1959. Chapter 9 is an informative discussion of essay-test items. Suggestions are offered which should aid the teacher in constructing and scoring essay questions.

BARR, JOHN A. *The Elementary Teacher and Guidance*. New York: Holt, Rinehart & Winston, Inc., 1958. Chapters 6 and 7 deal with standardized tests and their particular application to the situation in the elementary school.

BRADFIELD, JAMES M., and MOREDOCK, H. STEWART. *Measurement and Evaluation in Education*. New York: The Macmillan Co., 1957. The reader's attention is called to the most primitive procedure for measurement in Chapter 4, "Observation." Suggestions are made which can help the teacher make more accurate use of observation for measurement, as well as for evaluation.

GERBERICH, J. RAYMOND. *Specimen Objective Test Items*. New York: Longmans, Green & Co., Inc., 1956. The teacher who wishes to improve his own achievement tests will find many illustrations in this volume. Detailed samples are shown for a wide range of subjects at different educational levels.

JORDAN, A. M. *Measurement in Education*. New York: McGraw-Hill Book Co., Inc., 1953. Validity and reliability are explained clearly in Chapter 2, "Characteristics of Measuring Instruments."

ROSS, C. C., and STANLEY, JULIAN C. *Measurement in Today's Schools*. 3d ed. Englewood Cliffs, N. J.: Prentice-Hall, Inc., 1954. Chapter 12 calls attention to the importance of diagnosis in the school situation. Preventable factors which lead to pupil failures can be discovered by suggested diagnostic procedures.

SCHWARTZ, ALFRED, and TIEDEMAN, STUART C. *Evaluating Student Progress in the Secondary School*. New York: Longmans, Green & Co., Inc., 1957. Chapters 6, 7, and 8 give some very practical suggestions for the teacher who wishes to construct better tests.

THORNDIKE, ROBERT L., and HAGEN, ELIZABETH. *Measurement and Evaluation in Psychology and Education.* New York: John Wiley & Sons, Inc., 1955. Chapters 12, 13, 14, and 15 should be useful to the teacher seeking information about measurement of personality traits.

WRIGHTSTONE, J. WAYNE, JUSTMAN, JOSEPH, and ROBBINS, IRVING. *Evaluation in Modern Education.* New York: American Book Co., 1956. The nine chapters in Part 2, "Major Evaluation Techniques," should be particularly helpful for the teacher in the construction of measurement instruments for his own pupils.

# PART IV

# PERSONAL AND PROFESSIONAL GROWTH

# 16

# THE TEACHER'S PERSONALITY

In no other field of endeavor engaged in by civilized man is the personality of the individual more significant as a factor in success than it is in teaching. One needs only to try to name another vocation which makes greater demands to find that teaching is first of all a "personality" job.

Personality is probably the greatest factor in success or failure in teaching. Two teachers may differ not at all in subject-matter training, insignificantly in mental ability, little or not at all in physical fitness and character; yet one is a marked success, the other fails. One makes friends; the other not only makes few friends, but may actually make enemies. The explanation? Differences in personal traits which go to make up that vague yet very real thing called personality.

There are many reasons why the teacher's personality plays so prominent a part in success or failure. The most significant is involved in the very nature of teaching. Intimacy marks teaching as it does no other profession except the ministry. Teaching is always a shared-relationship job. It always involves persons; it never involves only one person and a thing, as is common in most effort. One who teaches never teaches alone. Never can a teacher teach as effectively from an inner office, by radio, by television, by mail, or by telephone. No teacher today lives in an ivory tower.

Pupils want in their teachers what they want in their most intimate friends. At one and the same time the teacher is friend, counselor, confidant, confessor—and teacher. The impact of the teacher's personality on the child will show in the child's behavior.

## THE NATURE OF PERSONALITY

Probably no other word in the English language is more loosely and freely used than the word "personality." It has become a word which means all things to all people. In spite of its loose popular usage the word is entirely definable and understandable. The *Dictionary of Education* gives one definition: "The characteristic patterns of behavior through which the individual adjusts himself to his environment, especially his social environment." But personality is a little more than adjustment to one's environment through behavior patterns. It is the "behavior patterns" themselves. One's personality is the sum total of his habits—all habits—physical, mental, moral, spiritual, civic, and emotional.

It is not easy to distinguish between character and personality. In practice personality applies particularly to one's social surroundings. It goes over into social effectiveness, as behavior tends to be expressed in terms of others. When a personality is "integrated," it commonly is related closely to principles. When personality expresses itself in terms of a moral or spiritual code, it becomes synonymous with character. Thus, ethical character is really personality (habit or behavior patterns) expressed in attitudes, convictions, and ideals.

A teacher is not too interested in a philosophical analysis of personality and character. Suffice it to say that one's character may be excellent while his personality is a stumbling-block in the path of his success in his chosen profession. However, the converse could hardly be true—that is, that one could be of low character and possess a fine personality in the truest sense of the word. Since personality is in terms of behavior patterns, it follows that personality is modifiable. Probably no one has an entirely bad personality. He may have a few behavior patterns which are offensive to society, and these few may mar the total effect to the extent that his more desirable patterns of behavior go either unnoticed or unapproved.

**Personality and Human Relationships.** Getting along with others makes a teacher's work not only easier but more pleasant. Whether it is admitted or not the pupils are the customers, and to that extent they hire teachers. This could be called "public relations" or "pupil relations." Both terms fit, but the term "human relations" is better in that it is broader in its implications. Since human relationships are always the interaction of personalities, the best means of improving the former is through improving the latter. Good human relationships are results; good personality on the teacher's part is causal. Practicing good human relations is something of an art as well as a skill. It can be acquired if one does not have it.

Success, someone has said, is the result of saving little acts that make for success. This is especially true in human relations. One does little things all day long. Doing these little things correctly makes for good relationships with pupils, fellow teachers, the administration, and the community. It is not, it seems, only what teachers do but how they do it that makes the difference. This is but to say that a teacher may be technically and academically trained for his teaching work, but if he has not learned to say "Good Morning" and "Hello" pleasantly and heartily, as well as "Thank you" and "I'm sorry" when he should, his training is not entirely complete.

**Personality Characteristics.** The personality traits which appear to be the most significant in terms of the teacher's personality-influence upon others include intelligence, cheerfulness, friendliness, and congeniality of interests. It has been said that these are the traits men like most in other men. Men like in women the same traits, substituting beauty for friendliness. Women like in other women: intelligence, cheerfulness, helpfulness, and loyalty. And women (college students) like in men: intelligence, consideration, kindliness, cheerfulness and mannerliness.

Among personality characteristics which make for like-ableness are being a good listener, being a good conversationalist, being able to remember names, and having a ready smile. Two of these deal with the art of conversation. Conversation is a public relations item, as it always involves others. It involves:

1. Having something to say
2. Not being too positive about it
3. Not interrupting
4. Looking interested; avoiding antagonistic gestures and expressions
5. Watching your words

The traits just noted relate to adults and their reactions; but in general, in behavior reactions as reflected in "personality impact," children differ little from adults. They particularly dislike the person who talks down (patronizes them) and the person who withholds appreciation of good work they have done. As with adults, courtesy begets courtesy, kindliness reflects itself, and a friendly teacher has friendly pupils. This does not say, however, that children's patterns of conduct are identical. It does say that a teacher's attitude projected against a child's personality determines his behavior toward the teacher.

Strange as it may seem, people make their personalities what they are. The process is usually not a conscious one, of course. Children imitate their elders in almost everything. Saying that a child is the "image of his father" is interpreting the word "image" very broadly. What is meant is that he not only resembles his father in appearance but has made the father's characteristic habit patterns his own. Unconsciously, perhaps, the child has copied mannerisms of action, voice, and appearance.

Unpleasantness in personality can usually be described in terms of mannerisms. Mannerisms are personality characteristics, either pleasant or unpleasant to others, peculiar to an individual. They are atypical behavior patterns which are not displeasing to the extent of being obnoxious. In common usage, mannerisms are atypical when unpleasing to others; are considered typical when pleasing.

Even one or two unpleasant mannerisms, used continually, can make one's entire personality seem unattractive. By correcting the mannerism (substituting a desirable one for the poor one is the common method), one can usually improve the personality significantly. These non-typical elements in personality behavior are numerous. Among the more common ones are the following:

1. Not looking at people when talking to them
2. Looking "through" the person when talking—focusing the eyes behind him
3. Shaking hands with a limp hand
4. Fussing with hair or picking at face
5. Cracking finger joints while talking
6. Acting hurried; fidgeting
7. Raising voice when irritated or excited; shouting
8. Listening to another but not seeming to give attention; cleaning fingernails, sharpening a pencil, or performing some other purposeful act while listening
9. Speaking dogmatically; using a "this is the last word" tone of voice
10. Interrupting a conversation
11. Allowing emotions to "overflow" easily
12. Always telling troubles to someone
13. Arguing for the sake of disagreeing; developing a "negative" attitude
14. Saying "Thank you" without warmth in the voice and with the wrong inflection
15. Drumming on desk or table with fingers while talking

Some of these items are more than mannerisms, perhaps, as they may reflect bad mental hygiene as well as unpleasant personality characteristics.

**Personality Patterns.** Since personality is a unification of behavior patterns, resulting from combining many smaller patterns, it would appear that the sum total would be largely psychological. This would imply that the individual's personality will express itself in ideas and in emotional reactions to others.

Because of its combined intellectual and emotional nature, the individual's personality expresses itself in variations of four basic patterns:

1. Reactions to ideas
2. Reactions to people
3. Reactions to the individual's own self
4. Expressions of action and speech

The first, *dealing with ideas,* is manifested in innumerable ways. President Truman recalled General MacArthur from the Far East Command. This was an intellectual fact, an idea. Immediately, thousands of persons were angry and wrote indignant letters to the White House; other thousands sent telegrams of denunciation of the act; other thousands were sad and despondent; still others agreed thoroughly with the action and wired congratulations. The *idea* was the same in each case; the *reaction* expressed itself in terms of individual personalities. No two personalities can be exactly alike because behavior patterns are the resultant of many habits of thinking, doing, and feeling. A teacher expresses his personality then in the way he reacts to any idea.

An individual's *reaction to people* is another personality expression. Some persons love crowds; others like small groups of friends and deliberately stay out of large groups including strangers. They are not antisocial, but they react to groups differently than they do to individuals. Not infrequently, people who are usually talkative shut up like clams when thrown with strangers. Others are either the life of the party or have no fun at all. Both are expressions of personality in terms of the effect of people upon people and of their personalities upon others. An individual is attracted to some, repelled by others.

An individual's personality is both a cause and a result. Does he keep himself neat and clean? Does he use good English? Does he speak distinctly and clearly or does he mumble? Is he courteous to everyone or is he courteous only to his administrative superiors? When many patterns of these types are put together, the unification is expressed in personality. The personality is thus a result of many acts, both physical and mental. The personality may express itself in cleanliness, neatness, good English, clarity of speaking, and courtesy to all.

Finally, the fourth basic personality pattern is in terms of *saying things* and *doing things*. The man who says "yes" with a rising inflection irritates his hearer. The man who says "Yes, Yes," at regular intervals; the man who speaks dogmatically, uttering the last word (as it were) whenever he speaks; the man who interrupts a conversation; the man who raises his voice unpleasantly when he is irritated or excited—all express personality in terms of "saying things."

Fussing with one's hair, cracking the joints of one's fingers, shaking hands with a limp hand, picking at one's face, acting hurried or impatient—all these reflect unpleasant personality patterns in terms of doing things. Some men talk but do nothing; others write letters but do not talk; still others go into action both verbally and physically. The personality pattern expresses itself in saying and doing.

Each of the four basic patterns, of course, applies to the teacher more than it does to most other people. The reason lies in the fact that the teacher deals constantly and continually with ideas, with people, with his or her own habit patterns; and finally, he or she is constantly saying and doing. (Later in this chapter the four patterns appear again as specifically applied to the teacher's personality.)

**Personality and Appearance.** First impressions are largely in terms of appearance. If, as is said, first impressions are lasting, then the teacher's appearance when meeting the superintendent of schools, the principal, fellow teachers and pupils for the first time is all-important.

There are four significant aspects of appearance for the normal physique. The first is *good health*. From this comes a clear skin, an energetic and easy carriage, and the vitality which attracts others. The second aspect of appearance is *cleanliness*. This includes teeth, hair, hands, fingernails, clothing, and the body in general.

*Good grooming* is the third phase of good appearance. For women teachers this means conservative nail polish, adequate and appropriate use of cosmetics, hair attractively and modishly dressed (but not in the extreme of style), shoes shined and the heels well built up, clothes clean and well pressed, and stocking seams straight. The well-groomed man sees that his hair is neatly trimmed and combed; that his shoes are well shined; that his clothes are clean and pressed; that his neckties are attractive and in harmony with the shirt and suit he is wearing; that his linen is clean; and that he is clean-shaven.

Well groomed does not necessarily mean expensively attired. In fact, the converse might well be true. A teacher can be expensively attired and not be suitably dressed for teaching. In general, cleanliness, neatness, and variety in clothing are more significant requisites than are the highest quality and the latest styles. To think that children are not observant and that "any old thing" is good enough for the schoolroom is a mistake. Clothes become a part of the personality, and it is very difficult to see excellence in a carelessly dressed person. Athletic teams, musical organizations, and other entertainment groups learned this fact long ago. The New York Yankees, playing a World Series against the St. Louis Cardinals, both teams in blue overalls and red shirts, might give the impression that both were clowning, although they were actually playing championship baseball. Because of this tendency to see excellence in good appearance, a very strong superintendent of schools told his teachers: "You can afford to dress attractively, the board of education of the school will buy those clothes for you." He meant that excellence in teaching received better pay, and that distinguishing excellence from high average, if high average is more attractive in appearance, is most difficult to do.

## SELF-EVALUATION OF PERSONALITY

Improving one's personality is similar to reducing one's weight: no one can do it for you. Again, no amount of criticism from others or suggestions for improvement are meaningful if the "sufferer" does not sincerely wish to improve. In the words of Burns:

> Oh wad some power the giftie gie us
> To see oursels as others see us!

It would seem that every professionally progressive and aspiring teacher would be eager to help ascertain the qualities which make for better teaching. That these qualities are both personal and social, as well as qualities of training and technique, has been carefully demonstrated.

Self-improvement through self-evaluation is an old technique. Innumerable self-rating scales are available in the educational literature. Many deal with improvement of the personal and social qualities which make for success in the classroom. A teacher might use the scale offered here to check on the personal element in teaching. This scale is definite. Each answer is desirably affirmative. The extent to which a teacher's reply is equivocal indicates weakness on his part.

Personal and Social Qualities of the Teacher

To what extent does my success depend upon the personal and social factor that:

*I am neatly groomed:*
1. Do I care for my shoes, polishing or brushing them whenever necessary, and having runover heels repaired?
2. Do I wear fresh linen each morning?
3. Do I dress as carefully (and as appropriately) for my work as for a social function?
4. Do I vary my costume each day?
5. Are the lines of my clothes becoming to me—that is, they do not accentuate the fact that I am unusually tall or short, etc.?
6. If I wear jewelry, is it appropriate for the schoolroom?
7. Is my attire appropriate for the season?
8. If I wear glasses, are they becoming and always shining?

*I am clean in my personal habits:*

1. Do I have my hair shampooed regularly?
2. Are my hands and nails clean?
3. Am I free from disagreeable odors?
4. Do I brush my teeth each morning before school?

*I cultivate and develop desirable personal traits and characteristics:*

1. Do I look at people when talking to them?
2. Is my voice clear and well modulated rather than strident and harsh?
3. Do I convey an air of sincerity?
4. Is my smile friendly and convincing, or does it disappear too rapidly to seem sincere?
5. Can I appreciate but not take offense at harmless jokes?
6. Can I have fun with children and with adults?
7. Do I meet people easily?
8. Is my enunciation distinct?
9. Do I avoid curt replies, satire, and sarcasm in participating in my various activities?

*I am punctual in my daily living:*

1. Do I keep my appointments?
2. Do I return borrowed articles promptly?
3. Do I retire and arise at regular hours?
4. Am I prompt and gracious in acknowledging kindnesses?
5. Do I answer letters promptly; give requests my immediate attention?

*I have excellent health which permits me to participate in daily activities with enjoyment:*

1. Do I have a physical checkup each year?
2. Do I pay as much attention to my own nutritive habits as I do to the children's?
3. Is my attitude before children one of alertness which reflects my physical vitality?
4. Am I always on the job?
5. Do I work overtime willingly and uncomplainingly?
6. Do I feel like playing when time permits?
7. Am I free from remediable health defects?
8. Do I get some physical exercise each day?

*I have desirable personal habits:*

1. Do I remember that good posture adds to my appearance, and probably to my health?

2. Do I eat wisely in order to control my weight?
3. Do I have a variety of interests?
4. Am I habitually impartial in my handling of pupils as well as in my attitude toward others with whom I come in contact?
5. Am I habitually sincere?
6. Is there evidence of refinement in my manners and conversation?

*I have definite training in the development of good mental health:*

1. Do I keep calm under trying conditions?
2. Do I have the ability to endure criticism, slights, and abuse?
3. Do I put aside unhealthy images and ideas?
4. Can I smile in the presence of the annoying and irritating things of my daily life?
5. Do I sit, stand, and move in a natural way?
6. Have I learned to relax?
7. Do I try to accomplish today's work better than yesterday's?
8. Do I readily discard fears and apprehensions?

*My knowledge of mental hygiene contributes to my own moral, mental, and spiritual growth and to the growth of others:*

1. Am I a normal integrated personality?
2. Have I consciously given attention to personality development as a teacher's work?
3. Do I have coordinated purposive activity in the doing of worthwhile tasks?
4. Do I see the need and value of a significant task for every child in the integration of the child's personality?

*I am considerate of others:*

1. Do I ask for a favor, but rarely command?
2. Do I correct pupils in a quiet, friendly manner?
3. Do I, by my out-of-the-room attitudes, aid other teachers in developing self-discipline in pupils?
4. Am I sincere in my expression of welcome to school visitors?
5. Am I sensitive to a child's inferior ability or to physical defect and thus avoid embarrassment for him?
6. Do I exercise care in what I say about the town, school, or pupils?
7. Am I sensitive to social proprieties?

A teacher gains from a self-rating device of any sort if it is not used repeatedly. Outstanding personal weaknesses should be noted and a practical substitution made at the first opportunity. Good resolves mean little if not followed by corrective action.

## INTEGRATION OF PERSONALITY

Personality is the sum total of the individual's characteristic modes of behavior as expressed in habit patterns. Because personality traits are dynamic as opposed to fixed, there is always interaction among the traits. This interaction is the basis of integration. Integration is the unified and coherent functioning of the various larger elements in a personality. Mental hygiene consists in establishing environmental conditions, emotional attitudes, and habits of thinking conducive to the successful integration of personality. A "non-integrated" or maladjusted personality is often the result of poor mental hygiene.

The teacher's personality is extremely important when it is understood that the child's learning is rooted in the interrelationship between the teacher and the child. Each teacher sees in himself a reflection of the child. His personality, through the interaction, gives to and receives from each child something of support and strength. He gives support to the child in the face of conflicts, failures, and obstacles. He helps him to adjust to necessary restraints and in so doing helps himself to adjust to conflicts, failures, and obstacles which are around him. Because his own personality has warmth, is spontaneous and sensitive to children, the reaction from children is warm, spontaneous, and sensitive. Knowing, as he does, something of the psychology of emotions and of mental hygiene, he is free from excessive concern about the competitive, ambitious drives of children. He avoids rivalry with parents, overpossessiveness, and smothering the child with affection because he is emotionally stable, possesses good mental hygiene, and is an integrated personality.

The integrated personality is defined in the *Dictionary of Education* as: "An active, adapting personality, characterized by unity of action, in which the responses of the various parts have meaning only in terms of their relation to the functioning of the whole; that is, a personality in which all the tensions and forces that play a part in human life, physical, spiritual, social, emotional, moral, aesthetic, et cetera, work together in harmony with the purposes, desires, and needs of the individual concerned." The key words are "forces," "unity of action," "responses," "relation to the functioning of the whole," "work together," and "in harmony."

In more prosaic language, an integrated personality is one which "runs true to form." It reacts as would be expected. It is predictable. All of the forces work together in harmony with the purposes, desires, and ideals of the individual. In practice, the integrated personality is well adjusted and does not have many, if any, serious quirks and turns which tend to destroy or at least mar its functioning in everyday life. Thus integration is usually thought of in terms of desirable traits patterned into a harmonious whole.

Strictly speaking, of course, the personality can be integrated in terms of the desires, needs, and purposes of the individual and still be a most undesirable one. It is possible to have integration of personality in terms of undesirable desires, needs, and purposes.

**Non-integrated Personality.** Conflict, either conscious or unconscious, the mark of every rational human being, may lead to emotional disorders or to undesirable action. Conflicts usually grow out of inadequacy, either recognized or unrecognized. When a teacher's desires do not materialize because of inability to achieve, conflicts tend to develop. Conflicts are one, but not the only, phase of non-integration of personality. A conflict may be resolved. This in effect means that a personality may become more integrated by recognizing and admitting a difficulty. Once recognized and admitted, objective and realistic attack on the difficulty is possible.

For teachers, non-integration takes on many patterns. Among the forms it may take are the following; each is an indicator of poor mental hygiene.

*Indecision.* With indecision, desires conflict and are incompatible. Commonly one whose mental hygiene is good compromises and tries to reconcile the two conflicting desires. If this can be done, the conflict disappears. Procrastination helps not at all in reducing conflict, although it is the usual pattern if the choice is not pressing. Indecision is devastating to a teacher's emotional tone. A logical setting-down of pros and cons for each desire helps. Consulting disinterested persons is sound. Decision must be made. Pretended indifference to one or both desires and consequent withdrawal lead to the same unsatisfactory procedure when a similar situation develops again.

*Self-Satisfaction.* Self-satisfaction is poor hygiene in the form of complacency. It is reflected in such expressions as "I'm good at my work and I know it." "Why should I try to improve? I put in years of study getting here." The teacher with this maladjustment is in a rut and does not want to get out. Recognition of the trouble is the first step toward correction.

*Unnaturalness.* The teacher suffering from this phase of imbalance in personality has difficulty in reconciling what he is with what he thinks he is. The result of the indecision is unnaturalness. Children detect artificiality in a hurry. "Be yourself" is not a bad slogan for a teacher to adopt.

*Self-centeredness.* This form of non-integration is sometimes evidenced by self-satisfaction in a virulent form. Selfishness is commonly thought to be a synonymous term. Inability to interpret any action, either group developed or administratively offered, in terms of anything but self characterizes this personality. "What does this mean to me?" "How do I profit by this?" is this person's inner response to many in-service suggestions. This "sufferer" would deny being self-centered. "If I don't look out for myself, no one else will" is the rationalization commonly offered. Carried to an extreme, the personality is definitely maladjusted. Recognition—and more, agreement—that one is self-centered, is the first step toward correction. It is difficult to know with finality that one is self-centered and yet to persist in being so.

*Mental Dishonesty.* Mental dishonesty is not the same thing as social dishonesty. It is real unwillingness to face reality. The woman teacher who is unwilling to admit her own limitations but insists she sings as well as Miss A, dresses better than Miss B, is more efficient than Miss C, and is better liked than Miss D is probably the victim of this subtle but malignant form of mental ill health. Unwillingness to recognize or admit weaknesses in one's own daily life goes over into a personality non-integration which leads to disunity, manifest discontent, and unpredictability in the individual's behavior. Recognition of the weakness or the limitation is a first step. Avoiding going to an extreme of self-disparagement (the opposite imbalance) is a second. Hearty approval of the other person's accomplishments is a third.

*The Martyr Complex.* A martyr complex is one of the most common forms of personality maladjustment. Frequently, the person who takes himself too seriously exaggerates the common-sense attitude. If only for the sake of good mental hygiene, every teacher needs to do something occasionally which common sense would say could just as well be left undone. Honest-to-goodness fun is even more imperative for the teacher than for most professional workers because of the necessity for seriousness of attitude in the daily work. The teacher's recreation is the antidote or, better, the counteraction, for this imbalance.

*Inability to Take Criticism.* This is an imbalance which results in an emotional attitude which readily leads to personality maladjustment. Some indications, or symptoms: taking slights where none was intended; worrying, foreboding; introspection; frequently overrating ability; and exaggerated egotism. The correction? As usual, admitting the defect without reservations. Attacking boldly by stopping the negative attitude by doing something desirable, saying something nice about the offending person. Getting more exercise and improving the general physical condition usually helps, as mental ill health is commonly related to poor physical condition. Someone facetiously has said, "Life is worth living when everything is well with the liver." It is evident that in all phases of non-integration of personality as reflected in bad mental hygiene, the desired unity and coherence come about through elimination of the protuberances or bumps which prevent the personality circle from being perfect. Personalities tend toward integration rather than the opposite. Every individual has much capacity for adaptation and readjustment. The drive is toward positive health rather than the opposite. In general, personality is an emotional expression in terms of habit patterns. Feeling states are inclined to grow by expression, to become stultified by repression.

## DISCUSSION PROBLEM

### A Teacher Studies Herself

Miss Bann was "on the carpet." The school principal had actually called her to his office and had humiliated her to the extent that, try as she might, she felt sure she could never get over that crushed, shamed, humiliated feeling. True, he had said that there was nothing personal in the things he felt he must say to her and that he hoped every word was for her own good, but—the tears choked themselves forward again—he had really told her that she was proud, arrogant, unsympathetic, tactless, and yes, even thoughtless.

He was an old fogy, and she would resign at once. No man could talk to her in that manner, even though he did mask it all with a pretense of sorrow and distaste for the thing which he had done. She would not go to school in the morning, and she would officially resign before tomorrow night.

Elaine Bann was an only child of a wealthy family. As a child she had been waited upon by servants whom she had learned to order around before she had reached the age of four. Every scholastic advantage had been hers. Special teaching had developed the child's excellent natural ability; and intolerance for "dumbness," as she put it, had manifested itself while she was still in the elementary school. She had always been an attractive-looking girl, and her natural beauty had been enhanced by excellent clothes always in the best of the current style.

In college Elaine had rapidly made a name for herself. One of the best sororities had claimed her. Never popular, she had still been able to bring much recognition to her group because of her many accomplishments. She had been elected to Phi Beta Kappa. Her well-trained voice proved to be much in demand for solo parts in college musical presentations. She had represented her college in oratory and had won a regional tournament. Always she had ruled her set; always she had been first in everything. Brilliant, polished, reserved, cold, she was admired much, but her intimate friends were few.

Elaine had been graduated from college with honors. Her parents had taken her to Europe for a year, and she had spent nearly a year at her beautiful home before becoming dissatisfied with her surroundings. Although she did not need the position from a financial point of view and had never given a thought to teaching while she was in college, yet she had decided to teach for a year as an interesting experiment. She was legally certificated, as her liberal arts course had carried with it a smattering of fifteen hours of education courses which met the state requirements for certification. Only two months before, she had come to the Beehaven School for Girls as an instructor in art and dramatics. She had thought she was getting along splendidly, and then out of a clear sky this blow had fallen on her this afternoon.

Morning came, and pride made Elaine go to her work. Hollow-eyed and worn by a sleepless night of hurt and humiliation, she felt a wave of gratitude sweeping over her when a little girl in one of her classes said, "Miss Bann, you're not feeling well, I'm sure. Can't I do something for you?" She had never felt the need of sympathy before—and she did need it now.

The next day found Elaine Bann back on the job. She had decided, with the characteristic pride which had marked her since she was a child, to show the principal that he was mistaken. With the thoroughness which had aided in making her a brilliant student, she had set about analyzing her weaknesses. Perhaps the principal was not entirely wrong. Her analysis of the charges made by the principal—pride, arrogance, lack of sympathy, tactlessness, and thoughtlessness—produced the following questionnaire, her first method of attack upon her personality faults.

*To what extent have I failed as a teacher because:*

1. I measure my success only in terms of myself rather than in the success of my pupils?
2. I do not work as hard when I am an assistant as when I am in charge of an enterprise?
3. I have not succeeded in making my daily associates become my intimate friends as time goes on?
4. I have not always refused credit not due me?
5. I have evidently been untactful, as is evidenced by the fact that pupils rarely show me the results of their work unless required to do so?
6. I rarely encourage students to ask my opinion, and rarely show interest or sympathy in their troubles?
7. I have lacked in ordinary courtesy and thoughtfulness by failing to help those carrying heavy loads?
8. I have rarely helped anyone except in direct line of duty?
9. I have failed to be cheerful and hearty in my greeting?
10. I rarely if ever deliberately encourage anyone?
11. I have been guilty of telling my friends things which have come to me about them, things which could not possibly do anything but hurt them?
12. I have failed to commend those acts performed by my pupils and friends which were distinctly commendable?

## QUESTIONS ON THE PROBLEM

1. Is the assumption farfetched or well taken, in your opinion, that a teacher can be thoroughly well educated, attractive, and thoroughly conscientious in her work and still possess a personality so unpleasant as to render her success doubtful? Discuss.
2. Should the principal have been less direct in telling Miss Bann the facts about herself, granting that he was entirely right? Was this an indication of lack of tact on his part?
3. Do you believe that personality can be trained? Do you believe that it would be possible to improve personality by means of a college course entitled "Training and Developing Personality"?

4. Discuss this statement: No personality improvement is possible except as a recognized, felt weakness on the part of the personality needing improvement.
5. Did Miss Bann produce a consistent analysis of her faults, measured against the principal's assertions as a criterion?
6. Would you judge that Miss Bann will have any trouble in bringing about the desired changes in herself? If you state that you believe she will have difficulty, point out the particular obstacle or obstacles she must overcome.

## STUDY QUESTIONS

1. The statement that professional training in education is unnecessary and means simply time wasted is frequently made by teachers in academic fields who have had no strictly professional training. How do you account for the lack of excellence occasionally found in teachers who have had thorough professional training?
2. What specific habits have you consciously developed as a result of your desire to make a better appearance; to improve the effectiveness of your English; to improve your self-control; to develop your leadership ability?
3. Make a fifteen-item list of the personality traits required for successful teaching which would not be necessary for a secretary to the principal of the school.
4. Describe a personality trait which you have improved. How did you improve it?
5. A bright pupil in your eighth-grade class, in his enthusiasm, commonly interrupts others who are speaking. In other ways he is not a discourteous boy. Describe the technique you would use in securing from him a more desirable attitude. The habit is strongly intrenched.
6. Describe Robert B., a seventh-grade boy twelve years old who has fine mental hygiene and a well-integrated personality. Make this a personality sketch.

## SELECTED READINGS

BARTKY, JOHN A. *Supervision as Human Relations*. Boston: D. C. Heath & Co., 1953. Chapter 6, "Dynamics of Teacher Personality," puts the personality factor in clear perspective as a basic consideration where supervision is involved.

BRADFIELD, JAMES M., and MOREDOCK, H. STEWART. *Measurement and Evaluation in Education*. New York: The Macmillan Co., 1957. Chapter 15, "Personality and Character," deals with these items from the measurement standpoint. Illustrations are good.

BLAIR, GLENN M., JONES, R. STEWART, and SIMPSON, RAY H. *Educational Psychology*. New York: The Macmillan Co., 1954. Pp. 435 ff. Text discusses personality tests under the heading, "Measures of Character and Personality." This is a brief but interesting discussion of the tools used in personality testing.

COMMINS, W. D., and FAGIN, BARRY. *Principles of Educational Psychology*. New York: The Ronald Press Co., 1954. Chapter 10, "Personality and School Adjustment," gives characteristics of personality traits as seen by the authors.

ELLIS, ROBERT S. *Educational Psychology*. Toronto: D. Van Nostrand Co., Inc., 1951. Chapter 14, "Mental Hygiene in Education," deals with tensions as a factor in personality adjustment. Various theories of relieving tensions are stated.

LINDGREN, HENRY CLAY. *Educational Psychology in the Classroom*. New York: John Wiley & Sons, Inc., 1956. Chapter 18, "The Psychology of Being a Teacher," presents the various roles in which the teacher works.

MORSE, WILLIAM C., and WINGO, G. MAX. *Psychology and Teaching*. Chicago: Scott, Foresman & Co., 1955. Personality tests are discussed on pp. 195 f, and 402 ff.

PATTY, WILLIAM L., and JOHNSON, LOUISE SNYDER. *Personality and Adjustment*. New York: McGraw-Hill Book Co., Inc., 1953. Part Three, "Personality And Growth," is in itself one of the best treatments of the subject of personality growth and development available.

# THE TEACHER'S MENTAL HEALTH

Probably no phase of human life is more worthy of study than emotional attitudes. To one who has learned to interpret these attitudes, whether in himself or in others, they furnish a very good clue to personality.

The general term applied by the older psychologists to the long-enduring emotional attitude was *disposition*. Joy was expressed in a cheerful disposition; anger in a hostile disposition; love in an affectionate disposition; and grief in a despondent disposition. *Mood* was the term commonly used to describe a temporary state of mind; it also emphasized the constraining or pervading quality of the feeling (He's in a genial mood). Moods tend to be of short duration —sometimes lasting only for a day or two. A mood that becomes chronic may then be termed a *disposition* or, very freely, a *temperament*. Today, the terms mentioned here have given way to a general term which covers the field: *mental health*.

## MEANING OF MENTAL HEALTH

Mental health is difficult to define. The difficulty probably lies in the fact that the term is general rather than specific. However, as one who has good physical health is able to throw off quickly and easily the exposures to coughs, colds, sore throats, and other minor ailments, so does one who has good mental health adjust quickly and thoroughly to the minor vicissitudes of daily life. Mental health, then, involves the ability to adjust to the trials and troubles, the stresses and strains, the tuggings and the tensions of daily life which tend to make one unhappy. Good mental health implies effectiveness in dealing with personal problems both internal and external, and with problems arising from contacts with others. Perfect mental health for a teacher implies the presence of an emotional stability, a personality integration, a maturity in terms of the richest, fullest development. It involves physical, mental, and emotional balance. It implies the ability to withstand jolts and shocks to the nervous system, or better, the ability to rebound rapidly and completely from the more or less serious problems which every teacher meets in his everyday experiences.

Mental health is somewhat analogous to physical health in that it, too, is a variable. An individual may have good mental health one day and through one jolting incident lose it the next. Unlike a physical ailment, however, mental ill health is rarely recognized by the sufferer. An individual knows that he has a physical ailment—a headache, a sinus disturbance, a painful corn or bunion, a feverish condition; he seldom recognizes that he is supersensitive, overassertive, hypercritical, depressed, or unsympathetic. He tends to explain away his trouble, to rationalize, to compensate, and to substitute.

It is difficult to find a dividing line which separates the mentally healthy individual from the mentally unhealthy. There are so many types and degrees of mental health. Again, no one has all of the indications (symptoms) of mental ill-health or mental healthiness all of the time. As has been suggested by the National Association for Mental Health, one of the best ways of describing mental health would be to try to describe a mentally healthy person.

Mental health is indicated by characteristic behavior, not by temporary aberrations. In general, the over-all, day-by-day association with colleagues, pupils, families, and acquaintances is the index of mental health in a teacher. How

a teacher feels about himself and how he adjusts to unpleasantnesses indicates his balance or imbalance. If a teacher
controls his emotions well; gets satisfaction from simple
pleasures; is not ruined for the day when a fear, a bit of
anger, a little jealousy slips into his consciousness; if he is
tolerant of mistakes, can laugh at his own, and does not un-
derestimate or overestimate his abilities, he is indicating
good mental health. In terms of others, a teacher, if his mental health is good, feels a responsibility for his pupils and
makes their joys and pleasures as well as their unhappiness
his own. He does not run around with a chip on his shoulder;
neither is he willing to be pushed around by everyone. He
is not a lone wolf; neither is he a person who cannot be happy
except in a group.

Were one to describe the behavior of the person with
good mental health he would get a picture something like
this: (1) The person gives wholehearted effort to whatever
he does; (2) he recognizes his problems and does something
about them; (3) he does not shirk responsibilities; (4) he
plans ahead; (5) he has respect for the unknown but does not
fear it; (6) he makes use of his own capacities and abilities
to the utmost; (7) he is realistic about his problems; (8) he
makes decisions, and having made them, acts accordingly;
and finally (9) he has faith in a Power greater than his own.
Teachers with good mental health set attainable goals for
both their pupils and themselves; they not only build dream
castles but also take steps toward moving in.

## WAYS OF ADJUSTING

How teachers adjust to tensions is probably as good an
indicator of their mental health as can be secured. Adjustment tends to take many forms; the most obvious are presented here. Everyone makes use of the various adjustment
mechanisms, whether his mental health is good or poor. The
difference is in the manner in which the mechanisms are
used. If the mechanism is employed to obtain temporary

respite from tension in minor matters, it helps to preserve good mental health. If the mechanism is used frequently or for serious matters, it indicates poor mental health. Some mechanisms are potentially more dangerous to mental health than others.

**Rationalization.** Rationalization refers to the behavior pattern wherein a person tries to justify what he does, rather than acknowledge the actual reasons. Children rationalize; so do their parents. It is, naturally, a form of self-deception. One can rationalize himself into doing anything he wants to do, foolish though the action may be.

**Projection.** Projection applies to shifting the responsibility for something done (which is reprehensible) to another person. The individual remains guiltless in his own thinking because he has convinced himself he is not to blame. This is one of the first reactions of many children when they are guilty of wrongdoing. They blame someone else. "I'm not to blame. John pushed me," is the common reaction. Here is a small indication of mental ill-health.

**Substitution.** In substitution, tensions are eased by accepting lesser satisfactions than were hoped for. A person who cannot afford a new hat but wants something new for Easter buys new gloves and feels quite satisfied. Substitution as a tension alleviator can be good; it is bad when it makes an individual satisfied with imperfections.

**Compensation.** Compensation is a defense mechanism. A person builds up his self-esteem by compensating for a deficiency in one area through achieving recognition (which bolsters his self-esteem) in another area. For example, a boy who is a poor student becomes a good athlete; a boy who cannot make a team becomes the team manager; a teacher who lacks athletic ability learns to fly his own airplane. Tension is relieved often by compensating. Generally, compensation covers up a weakness or is used to achieve prestige. It may even do both.

Transferred compensation is really a form of substitution. The person diverts his energies from a desired goal (which he cannot reach) to a substitute goal which is within his reach. Mature, well-balanced persons use transferred compensation to gain goals which they convince themselves are equally good. Some substitution mechanisms are more adjustive than are others, a sort of making oneself the center of attention. In general, however, the substitution mechanisms tend to make for better mental health if the pattern chosen is a rational one. Of course, any mechanism for relieving tension is but potentially adjustive. If misused or overused, then the conflict is overcome only to have another pop up in its place.

**Identification.** Children frequently use the mechanism of identification to gain satisfactions through the accomplishments of someone else. In St. Louis a few years ago, a large segment of the junior high school-age boys in the city, when playing baseball, adopted the corkscrew batting stance of their idol, Stan Musial. When batting, they were Musial. Identification with parents is most common in small children. "My pop can do anything" is the proud statement of the small boy who lives in his father's real or imagined excellences. Usually, identification is abandoned after adolescence.

**Avoidance.** Mechanisms of avoidance provide teachers with means of reacting to frustrations and irritations. Being unable to solve the problem, the teacher simply walks out on it and quits worrying about it. The teacher learns that it is sound practice to avoid persons and situations which tend to throw him off balance. The mental health factor asks for but one thing: that the teacher recognize the avoidance mechanism for what it is, a way of releasing his tensions and, in embarrassing situations, saving face. It would seem, then, that the key to all corrective measures is for the teacher to see himself as he is, and to be able to laugh at his foibles. When a teacher knows he is grouchy, he ceases to be grouchy; and when he stops identifying himself with the great, he is usually a much more satisfying person to live with. When he catches himself being self-centered or selfish, he is well on the way to becoming more thoughtful of others and generous in his actions. It is unusual for a person's mental hygiene to continue to be bad when he is thoroughly conscious that it is bad. Getting himself into perspective is not always easy for the teacher to do, but once it is done, the teacher tends to see himself clearly as he is.

**Other Adjustment Mechanisms.** Many other mental mechanisms are adjustive in nature. In fantasy one substitutes imaginary satisfactions for real ones; by sublimation one redirects unacceptable emotional tension into socially acceptable modes of behavior. Repression forces distressing experiences, guilt-producing memories, and unpleasantnesses into the subliminal. Through regression one falls back upon satisfying experiences or behavior of earlier days, and tends to live in the highly successful moments of the past. Both children and adults use this mechanism.

## DEALING WITH TENSIONS AND ANXIETIES

Nervous tensions are not always an indication of poor mental health. In fact, tensions and some anxiety are a part of everyday life. It is only when the anxieties and tensions persist and become disproportionate that mental health becomes bad. Physical illnesses tend to follow emotional disturbance; psychiatrists are agreed that a great portion of our illnesses are emotionally induced. One who is functionally ill is as sick as is the person who is ill from an organic cause.

A certain amount of tension is stimulating. Tensions are the source of all excitement. When persons participate in or watch a competitive game they get pleasure out of the tension, the excitement. In viewing a drama on television; in enjoying a stage production, in seeing a ball game, in reading a vigorous story, they are, through the resultant tension, mildly participating.

Anxiety, too, has its place. It tends to prepare persons for difficulties ahead and aids in meeting them. Both tensions and anxiety tend to be self-protective reactions when people are confronted by any danger or threat to themselves. An overly vivid imagination is a developer of tensions. The imagined catastrophe may act as a preventive, but usually it merely causes needless tension.

Commonly a person does not recognize he is under strain or tension until that tension has been of some duration. He is apt to think of the strain as something new, although actually it is not. He has had normal tensions all of his life. It is also fallacious to believe that tension is a characteristic only of the fast-moving modern age. Individuals *are* under pressure today—they face the stress of great crowds, of severe competition, of the struggle for a living, of the threat of war, and of ever-mounting expenditures. But in the past, people faced the tensions brought about by fear of famine, of pestilence, of illness without recourse to medical aid, of danger from savages, and of the unrelenting attacks of the forces of nature (storm, drought, flood), which man had not learned to resist. Man has always faced tensions and stresses and strains. The difference possibly lies in the fact that everything today moves so fast that people are forced to much more rapid adjustments, and rapid adjustments are not easy.

**Tension Indicators.** The teacher must remember that everyone is confronted by threats; that he is not alone in having tensions. Anxiety and tensions mount when teachers are physically exhausted or have been under a constant sleep-losing effort. Emotions tend to take over and teachers think, say, and do things which would not occur to them were they not overtired. "Things will look better in the morning" is another way of saying that tensions will be lessened after rest.

The following indicators of overtension are suggested by Dr. George S. Stevenson (see Selected Readings). If a teacher's answers to most of these questions is "yes" he should seek assistance in making an adjustment.

1. Do minor problems throw you into a dither?
2. Do you find it difficult to get along with people, and are people having trouble getting along with you?
3. Do small pleasures of life fail to satisfy you?
4. Are you unable to stop thinking of your anxieties?
5. Do you fear people or situations that never used to trouble you?
6. Are you suspicious of people, mistrustful of your friends?
7. Do you have a feeling of being trapped?
8. Do you feel inadequate; feel the tortures of self-doubt?

**Suggestions for Alleviating Tensions.** Mental troubles tend to diminish when one recognizes the trouble as being what it is—trouble, and no more. Usually the teacher is capable of taking care of the situation himself, but the improvement will be so gradual that it will not be apparent at once. Again, determination and persistence are key words if a teacher is to rid himself of needless tensions and anxieties. It is suggested that the teacher try all of the following if he is conscious of needless tension and anxiety:

1. Do something for others. There is a satisfaction in this which improves one's outlook on life. Go out of the way to do a kindness. Compliment someone deliberately—and honestly. Give of yourself, not just money, to a community effort—the Red Cross drive, a church social, a school enterprise, in working with crippled children. Make an effort to be truly unselfish.
2. Talk the trouble over with someone. Confide in some down-to-earth friend. This can be a minister, a doctor, a respected colleague, a father or mother, a husband or wife. Talk it over. The stress will almost instantly be relieved. A trouble shared tends to be halved.

3. Never expect too much of anyone. Better to be pleasantly surprised than disappointed. Never expect too much of children. There's always a jolt when expectations are not realized. Do not consider yourself a failure as a teacher if your pupils do not measure up to your expectations. Better take the stand of the farmer with the load of hogs: "Well, they didn't weigh as much as I thought they would, but then, I didn't think they would."

4. Do one thing at a time. When a teacher faces a hard task there are so many angles to it that he is prone to feel the job is too big for him to handle. The task looks so large that it seems impossible to attack any part of it. The argument from the viewpoint of mental health is simple: plunge in. Tackle some segment of the problem. Take the most urgent portion of the task and do it. When the small portion is accomplished, what is left seems to be smaller proportionately.

5. Don't be left out. The teacher whose mental health is below par may feel that he is being left out of things. This happens to everyone. Someone else gets recognition; someone else is appointed; someone else gets the desired position—all are indications that you may not have made yourself available for the recognition, the appointment, the desired position. Make yourself available. Teachers who are in on things put themselves in. Be interested and show your interest. This advice, if followed, will usually do away with the being-left-out feeling—and your mental health will improve.

6. Give yourself a chance to relax. The necessity of driving yourself, of always getting there first, is an urge which should be repressed by all who come under the classification of being overly dynamic, too hard-working, overly conscientious, and perfectionist. If you are of the type who insists on edging out the other person, whether it be at a stop-light, on entering a store, on getting the services of a waiter, on getting marks into a central office first, or merely on getting in the last word, you are doing nothing to improve your tensions. Give the other fellow a break. Adopt the "what difference does it make?" attitude. By so doing you will make things easier for yourself—and if the other fellow feels you are no longer a threat to him, he will

stop being a threat to you. Physical tensions are subject
to conscious relaxation on your part. Deliberately "let
down" several times a day.

7. Cultivate your religious life. As Alcoholics Anonymous has
found, the man who has faith in a Supreme Being and
who expresses that faith in prayer tends to develop a mental attitude toward his problem which aids much in effect-
ing a cure. The person with tensions needs to have great
faith, too, if he is to meet difficulties confidently.

Mental ill health is the number one health problem.
Teachers still intepret pupil behavior in terms other than in
the frame of reference of modern mental hygiene. With no
understanding of mental hygiene, a teacher has trouble understanding himself, let alone understanding the youth he
is trying to instruct. Teachers are prone, as are others, to
think of mental disorders as something that other people
have. Each tries to convince himself that mental ill-health
happens only to the other fellow. This is unsound thinking.
One out of four persons will develop a physical ailment due
to an emotional cause; one out of twelve will be hospitalized
for mental disorder during his lifetime; one out of twenty-
two will develop a personality disorder which will interfere
with his work and happiness.

A teacher is under pressure, heavy pressure. It is easy for
analysts to talk of the pressures of the various businesses
and professions and to assume the stresses are greater than
those in teaching. This simply is not the truth. It is most
difficult to find anything more devastatingly destructive to
one's physical and mental well-being than attempting to
instil learning and good manners in twenty-five to thirty-five
squirming, twisting, noisy, and often deliberately irritating
children. Too commonly a teacher is expected to do the job
parents have failed to do.

It is only through sound emotional balance, through keeping things in their proper perspective, that a teacher can
keep what he had at the time he entered the profession:
emotional stability, integration of personality, and maturity
in good mental health and hygiene.

# DISCUSSION PROBLEM

## CLASSIFICATION OF ADJUSTMENT HABITS

Adjustment habits are the devices by which the ego is protected from jolts and discomforts; they are usually called mechanisms of adjustment. Each person uses or has used one or more of these. Classification of these adjustment mechanisms is not clear or definite, as they naturally overlap in the way they operate. In general, the child (or the adult) uses the mechanism (unconsciously of course) in one of three ways: *to avoid*—which enables him to get temporary satisfaction by taking himself out of the threatening situation; *to substitute*—which enables him to substitute the attainable goal for the unattainable (*compensation, substitution,* and *sublimation*); *to deceive*—which enables the child to change the situation so that he feels no threat to himself (*rationalization, projection, repression,* and sometimes *suppression*).

Below are listed four imagined cases, anecdotal in type, which present certain typical adjustment responses. Your problem is to classify each response under one or more of the headings discussed in this chapter, and then suggest a possible treatment.

1. Marie Becker is a girl who although in junior high school has never participated in any school activities which would put her into the foreground. Now, at age twelve, she plays enjoyably with children much younger than she is, seeming to like their company better than that of children her own age. She directs their play and seems to get honest pleasure out of being with them. She is a likable youngster and does good schoolwork.

2. George is a ten-year-old lad who is more than ordinarily interested in baseball. He likes to be called "Mick," as that is the nickname of his favorite baseball hero. He signs notes to his friends "Mick" and is trying hard to teach himself to be a switch hitter.

3. As an eighth-grader Hartley was wide-awake, clear-eyed, hustling, mischievous—the boy was a leader in everything. When eighth-grade work got too slow or monotonous, Hart was usually the person who spiced things up a bit. Although small for his age, he was good in all sports. He swam especially well. His work as a trap-drummer in the grade-school orchestra was always dynamic if not always exactly rhythmic. His teachers liked him.

Hartley entered high school. Too small for high school athletic teams and lacking in the skill needed to replace the high-school trap-drummer, he drifted into being a loafer, both in class and out. By the end of the first six-week session Hartley was "in bad" with all of his teachers. The boy was a troublemaker. He played less, studied little, was really good at nothing. Miss Burton, his eighth-grade teacher, when she was informed that Hartley was the ringleader of one of the worst boys' gangs in town, shook her head in disbelief. This was not the Hartley she knew and liked.

4. The Smiths had two children, Billy, aged twelve, and Mary Lou, who was eight. Mary Lou and her parents especially liked hamburgers and Coca Cola for a picnic lunch. Billy preferred wieners. At Alum Rock Park, a Smith picnic was ruined when Billy sulked and refused to eat anything when he found there were no wieners and only hamburgers for the bun sandwiches. When he continued to sulk, Mr. Smith threatened to spank him although Billy was twelve years old. This made matters worse, as Mrs. Smith intervened. The picnic was ruined.

## QUESTIONS ON THE PROBLEM

1. What is the common name applied to the mechanism Marie Becker is employing in Case 1? How would you handle the case? Is her case a difficult one? Why? Why not? Should she be prohibited from playing with younger children? Should she be given leadership responsibilities in her junior high work? Should she be told what she is (unconsciously) doing?
2. Is the mechanism of adjustment George in Case 2 is following in any way detrimental to him? What is this mechanism called? Can this adjustment be detrimental to a boy? Under what conditions? Give an illustration of a situation in which this type of adjustment is likely to prove dangerous.
3. What has happened to Hartley in Case 3? Is the situation far-fetched? "When the school curriculum doesn't fit a child, the child tends to make a curriculum of his own." Do you agree? Has this statement anything to do with this case? How would you handle Hartley's case now that so much damage has been done?
4. In Case 4, should Billy be held responsible for his actions, or are his parents mostly to blame? Should he be ignored when he refuses to eat, and without anything being said, allowed to sulk? Can his parents allow him to sulk and show temper over

his displeasure? What adjustment mechanisms is Billy employing? Should the parents have brought wieners for him?

## STUDY QUESTIONS

1. Describe some teacher you have known who uses some of the ways of adjustment described in the chapter.
2. Of the ways described, which are you most inclined to use? How do you do it? Do you tend to put off unpleasant duties? How do you justify (to yourself) this putting-off, if that is your weakness?
3. Do you use identification to any extent in your daily work? "Be yourself" is a commonly heard slogan—do you have any trouble doing this?
4. Have you encountered in your experience a badly maladjusted teacher? Try to describe this person.
5. Would you say that women teachers (unmarried) are more likely to be maladjusted than men teachers? Than married women teachers?
6. What are some typical classroom techniques that are questionable from the standpoint of the teacher's mental hygiene?
7. Should a teacher ever show anger in the presence of pupils? Infrequently? If he shows it frequently, is this evidence of poor mental hygiene? Poor physical health?
8. Some teachers have not outgrown their own childhood. Can you list indications of this in teachers you have known?
9. To what extent should paper work, lesson planning, detail work of all kinds be allowed to interfere with a teacher's golf or tennis or swimming?

## SELECTED READINGS

BEAUMONT, HENRY, and MACOMBER, FREEMAN G. *Psychological Factors in Education.* New York: McGraw-Hill Book Co., Inc., 1949. Chapter 5 shows relationship of frustration to behavior.

CARROLL, H. A. *Mental Hygiene.* 3d ed. Englewood Cliffs, N. J.: Prentice-Hall, Inc., 1956. Chapter 8. A good discussion of the effects of conflict and frustration on behavior.

*Fostering Mental Health in Our Schools.* Association for Supervision and Curriculum Development, 1950 Yearbook. Washington: The

Association, 1950. Chapter 11. Best single reference of a general nature available on the topic.

GRAMBS, JEAN D., IVERSON, WILLIAM J., and PATTERSON, FRANKLIN K. *Modern Methods in Secondary Education.* Rev. ed. New York: Holt, Rinehart & Winston, Inc., 1958. Chapter 16. Practical discussion geared closely to the general problem.

KAPLAN, LOUIS, and BARON, DENIS. *Mental Hygiene and Life.* New York: Harper & Bros., 1952. Chapters 12 and 14. Entire book is pertinent to the theme of this chapter.

SHEVIAKOV, GEORGE V., REDL, FRITZ, and RICHARDSON, SYBIL D. *Discipline for Today's Children and Youth.* Washington: Association for Supervision and Curriculum Development, 1956. A later slant of much of the material in the Association for Supervision Yearbook (1950) above. Applies well to chapter on discipline also.

PATTY, WILLIAM L., and JOHNSON, LOUISE SNYDER. *Personality and Adjustment.* New York: McGraw-Hill Book Co., Inc., 1953. Chapters 1, 2, 8, 9. A technical discussion presented in nontechnical language. Recommended for teachers especially.

STEVENSON, GEORGE S., *How to Deal with Your Tensions.* Bethesda (14) Maryland: Department of Health, Education, and Welfare. 15 pp. A little handbook which page for page is probably the most usable reference in this list.

SYMONDS, PERCIVAL. *The Dynamics of Human Adjustment.* New York: Appleton-Century-Crofts, Inc., 1946. Chapters 3 and 15. Although one of the older books in the field, it has a freshness in the way it attacks what was in 1946 not a common theme.

TURNER, C. E. *Personal and Community Health.* 11th ed. St. Louis: The C. V. Mosby Co., 1959. Chapter 13, "Mental Health," is recommended reading for all teachers.

# 18

# THE TEACHER'S PERSONAL RELATIONSHIPS

The teacher, being first of all a public employee and one who is known to everyone, faces problems peculiar to the teaching profession and different from those faced by another public employee such as a librarian or a city engineer. Occasionally restrictions are imposed upon the teacher's personal life which are both unnatural and unjust. However, because the teacher always lives a life which in its larger implications is exemplary in conduct, he needs but carry on out-of-class activities in a wholesome, normal manner to be praised rather than blamed. By saying little which can be misconstrued the teacher avoids criticism. Since in the main a teacher's relationships are positive rather than negative, a consistent policy of serving well the boys and girls in the classroom will gain for him far more love and respect than is given to, or merited by, any other person.

There is always the danger that the teacher will feel hedged about by restrictions. Part of this is due to the fact that educators are forced to stress the necessity of care on the teacher's part in personal relationships. The teacher's role is not a dual one, although at times it seems to be so. The teacher's existence is a very natural one. The teacher's personal problems tend but to be the relationship problems of any good citizen. Those problems appear to be emphasized more than are the problems of any other worker because of the public nature of the teacher's work, and justly so because of the nature of the materials. Whether the teacher wills it to be so or not, he is shaping the lives of children, and children do not imitate their teachers only when the teacher is in the classroom.

## LOCAL AND PERSONAL CONSIDERATIONS

**Living Quarters.** Probably no other single item contributes more to the beginning teacher's satisfactory personal relationships in the local area than does a wise choice of a place to live. The point can be best emphasized by illustration.

Miss Bailey comes to the county-seat city of Washington as the seventh-grade teacher in the Horace Mann school. She sees her superintendent of schools concerning a place to live. He has two recorded, both of which seem appropriate. One is with a young dentist and his wife, who have been in Washington for two years. He is building up a good practice. The home is new and attractive. There is one extra bedroom, and the desire to aid in paying installments on the new house prompts renting the unused room. Dr. Smith and Mrs. Smith have no children. They "travel" with the younger married set in Washington, which is the "sportiest" set in town; they are, however, entirely acceptable to the community. Miss Bailey is twenty-one years of age, is attractive, and, as is but natural, likes a good time.

The other place suggested by the city superintendent is with the Pattersons. They have a large eight-room house near the Horace Mann school. It is on a very large lot with trees and is set back from the street. The Pattersons are among Washington's most highly respected citizens. Mr. Patterson, commonly called "Uncle Jim" by the high school students, has been on the city council for many years and has served two terms as mayor of Washington on a coalition ticket. He is not now on the Board of Education but has served previously. His wife, "Aunt Dolly," as the younger generation affectionately designate her, is loved by everyone. The Patterson children, now grown, are all college graduates and do not live in Washington. Miss Bailey immediately likes the motherly Aunt Dolly. She had been captivated at once, also, by Mrs. Smith, the charming young wife of the dentist. The Pattersons do not need the money which her room rent would bring in, as they are in very comfortable financial circumstances. They had told the school superintendent they were lonesome and wanted a young person in the house.

The two situations pictured emphasize the need for careful selection of a place to live. Miss Bailey is inclined to go to the Smiths' home, as she feels sure she will have more fun. However, after talking to the city superintendent of schools again, and noting his preference for the Pattersons' home, she goes there. She has never regretted the decision. The city at once accepts her because she is the Pattersons' protégée. Aunt Dolly knows "who's who" among the Washington city matrons. She understands Miss Bailey very well also, having mothered a large family. Uncle Jim is able to offer a word of advice occasionally, which, because of his experience and maturity, is accepted by Miss Bailey in the spirit in which it is offered. At the Smiths, Miss Bailey might have been drawn into a fast-moving crowd. She might have had more fun, but inevitably she would have been criticized. Social activities partially condoned for married couples would have been attacked by the ubiquitous city gossips if engaged in by an unmarried teacher. At the Pattersons, she has been encouraged to invite the third-grade teacher to join her as a coresident of the four-bedroom home, and the girls find the owners not only cooperative but actually interested in seeing that they meet some unattached young men.

A teacher's living quarters can make the difference between success and failure in his work. Not only must they be comfortable and convenient; they must also lend something to, if possible, but certainly never detract from his work. It is always well to avoid the crowded rooming place as well as the hotel in the small city. It is only in the large city that the hotel is at all a suitable place to stay for a teacher—and there the expense is usually prohibitive.

**Purchases and Credit.** In the large city no one knows much about anyone else; in a small town or in a rural area, everyone knows much about the personal lives of others. Always, the merchants in the smaller city, usually good taxpayers, are interested in a teacher's patronage. They feel, and not unjustly, that they are helping to pay the salary and are entitled to a fair share, if not all, of the spending.

Whether the merchants are right or wrong in this assumption, a teacher makes no mistake by giving local merchants as much as possible of his buying. He will be getting much good will in return, and since he will be one of the highest-salaried persons in the small city or village, his patronage is significant. By distributing his buying carefully, especially of small items which, although they may not comprise a large part of the total spending, are frequent in occurrence, he will make merchants feel he is an asset to the town. The more important items may be secured in the city, where there is more choice, but the lesser items should be purchased locally.

Because a teacher has an established pay check, he will not only be invited, but in fact urged, to open charge accounts at all the local stores. Many teachers, newly out of college and earning money for the first time in any considerable amount, succumb to the lure and overbuy their earnings the first month they teach. Thus they start their professional careers with the handicap of being in debt. This is a dangerous development. Board and lodging obligations must be met on the dot. Definitely each new month must find every bill paid in full, or the teacher will suffer in numerous ways. To be known as "slow pay" is deadly. Shopkeepers carry what should be a teacher's private business to the superintendent of schools or to some member of the board of education.

A charge account met promptly and in full establishes a teacher's credit probably better than does paying cash, but the latter as a policy certainly is not to be criticized. Installment buying is in general not a desirable practice for teachers. For one reason, there is nothing more detrimental to one's piece of mind, which really means one's mental hygiene, than to find a garment or a car outmoded or badly worn and still unpaid for. In general, a teacher makes no serious error when he saves before he spends. The impression that one is living beyond one's means is always to be avoided by any citizen who desires to be sincerely respected, and installment buying too frequently gives this impression. Again, indebtedness is a fettering thing which teachers find restricts their freedom. To stop buying from the store to which a teacher is in debt in a small community is a most certain way to have his private affairs made public.

**Attire.** Clothes are a factor in the teacher's personal life which have much to do with success or failure. The rules governing a woman teacher's attire are almost obvious: (*a*) she dresses tastefully, (*b*) she dresses appropriately, (*c*) she avoids extremes in styles, (*d*) she varies her costume often, and (*e*) she avoids overdressing.

Tasteful dress for the teacher is exactly what it is for any other person. It means clothes that suit, harmonize or contrast becomingly. Appropriate dress is the correct attire for the occasion. For the classroom, prints in lively colors, suits, and semisports attire are usually appealing to children—and the teacher dresses for children primarily and for her own satisfaction and morale, secondarily. The teacher's street attire does not differ from that of any other well-dressed person.

Extremes in style call attention to the clothes, and good dressing never does that. Never is the woman teacher a "bobby soxer" or a pin-up girl. Always she is modishly dressed, in fact well dressed in every sense of the word. That is partly because such attire makes her better satisfied with herself and her work, and partly because she recognizes that it is easy for the public to see merit in the well-dressed person—and approval from the public should mean a salary increase for next year.

The well-dressed teacher varies his or her costume from day to day. Extremely high quality in clothes is not necessary, but variety, modishness, and utility for the purpose to be served are necessary. Children are very observant, and the well-dressed teacher loses nothing, as far as they are concerned, by the effort.

It is possible for the teacher to be too well dressed. Take the case of Miss Wood, for example. Miss Wood appeared at the Republic High School the day before school opened, driving an expensive new convertible. She was well trained, personable, talented, attractive—and beautifully attired. An only child of a wealthy family, she was teaching because she wanted to do something constructive. Always Miss Wood wore exactly the appropriate attire for the occasion. She spent much of her earnings on her appearance. Because she had means over and above her salary, she spent money freely, often buying cokes for a dozen high school girls at a time. Although she was an excellent teacher, she was not liked by the other women teachers. Only one explanation seemed plausible: she dressed too well, and her co-workers envied her. Unfair though it may be, to dress too well may mean to be ostracized.

**Social Activities and Friends.** Considering that more than two-thirds of the nation's teachers are outside the corporate limits of a large city, the reasons for a teacher's semipublic personal life is more evident. It is not that parents do not want teachers to be normal human beings. They do. The puritanical restrictions of a century ago are largely disappearing, but even now teachers are sometimes asked to refrain from social activities not barred to the average respectable citizen. This is not just, but it is just to ask that teachers absent themselves from amusement places commonly frequented by only the less desirable members of a community.

The unmarried woman teacher should give considerable attention to whom she dates. She should hesitate before dating twice the young man-about-town whose reputation is not good, even though he is always the gentleman in her presence. She should not attend roadhouses or other entertainment places which are "out of bounds" to the high school students. Constantly she should keep in mind that she is no longer a college girl; she is one of the community's most respected citizens. Whether she smokes a cigarette publicly or takes a cocktail at a private party is determined by the community's attitude toward such actions. In one community she will be severely criticized for such behavior; in another she will be subject to little or no criticism. Folkways and customs are changed slowly, and an unmarried woman teacher is foolish to martyr herself to the cause of "freedom at any price."

A teacher will do well to respect the mores of the community in which he works. This does not mean that he must agree with all of the restrictions, but that he never should criticize them publicly. Each community sets up its own standards, and, though many older residents may not live up to the standard, the community righteously demands that the teacher do so. If he fails, in spite of the fact that he is a good teacher he will be seeking another position at the year's end. A teacher will never make a mistake by asking frankly, before signing a contract, the community's reaction to his smoking, dancing, drinking an occasional cocktail, and dating.

A teacher's choice of intimate friends is extremely significant to his professional success. It is trite to say that one is always known by the company he keeps; but for a teacher this is especially true. This is partly due to the fact that in the smaller city or rural area everyone knows the teacher and his companions. Probably the same rule holds for the teacher as for everyone else: Make friends by the hundreds, but make intimates of comparatively few friends. This does not mean that a teacher will be aloof, but it does mean that he should entrust his distinctly personal affairs to very few. Nothing is so ruinous to a fine friendship as for one to suspect a friend has told something known presumably only to this person. Voluble friends are rarely reticent under any conditions. The teacher who gossips to you about colleagues is probably also talking about you to colleagues.

## ETHICAL PROBLEMS

Relationships more definitely geared to the position a teacher holds, yet not specifically or directly a part of his classroom work, have to do with co-workers, with the administrative officers, with supervisors, with community activity programs, with study clubs and other semieducational movements, with the parent-teacher association, and finally with the teacher's attitude toward his profession. These relationships are commonly spoken of as ethical problems and are worthy of consideration.

**Subscribing to Standards of Conduct.** Without doubt the development of a definite code of ethics is one of the marks of maturity in a profession. Ethics as such is synonymous with moral standards, and a code of ethics is simply a set of such standards of conduct, professional rather than personal in nature, to which members of the group voluntarily subscribe.

The development of such codes has become a major effort of the various state teachers' associations, and of many city organizations of teachers. Basically, such codes are statements of the "rightness" or "wrongness" of teachers' actions, either as groups or as individuals, in matters pertaining to the profession.

Because ethical guides must of necessity be stated in very general terms, each teacher faces the problem of interpreting personal behavior in terms of the ethical code. It is hardly necessary to say that one tends to rationalize oneself into thinking the code is not applicable when it conflicts with personal interests.

State codes of ethics for teachers differ to some extent to suit varying conditions, but in general they are influenced by the Code of Ethics of the National Education Association. Any teacher who conforms closely to the statement of the NEA Code (see Appendix) need not be concerned about the ethical soundness of any action.

A code of ethics is not a bill of rights for teachers. There is very much of the "thou shalt not" attitude expressed in all such codes. However, a teacher following rigorously a code of ethics such as the NEA statement is in a position to state in a positive manner what he has a right to expect from the profession in terms of permanency of tenure, suitable working conditions, adequate remuneration for effort, recognition in the profession, and "the same personal liberties which other respectable citizens assume for themselves as a matter of course."

**Working with Administrators.** Cicero in his *De Amicitia,* stated a principle basic to all relationships. He said:

> But I must at the beginning lay down this principle—*friendship can only exist between good men.*
> . . . We mean then by the "good" *those whose actions and lives leave no question as to their honor, purity, equity, and liberality; who are free from greed, lust, and vileness; and who have the courage of their convictions.* . . .
> Now friendship may be thus defined: *a complete accord on all subjects human and divine, joined with natural good will and affection.*

The success of every organization from an administrative viewpoint depends upon a mutual understanding of problems, upon a fine regard for the other person's interests, upon cooperation in all parts of the school machine, and upon a thorough and hearty accord on all matters pertaining to the school. Liberality in interpreting the actions of all co-workers, both administrative and instructional, is imperative in order that motives may not be questioned.

The quotation from Cicero offers an excellent vantage point for viewing the "valley of friendship" as the starting point from which all expeditions into the land of good relations must start. Good relationships cannot exist without mutual regard, trust, and friendship.

If a teacher is to work in harmony with administrative officers, the superintendent and the principal, he cannot but follow Cicero's injunction. There must be "complete accord on all subjects, human and divine, joined with natural good will and affection." That "accord" does not necessarily mean agreement on all professional matters is, of course, understood. It does mean that the lives of all concerned with the development and growth of children must be built on "honor, purity, equity, and liberality." That such lives must be free from "greed, lust, and vileness" is too obvious to require argument.

In a more prosaic, everyday way, the teacher in his relationships with administrative officers can interpret the Ciceronian injunction into definitely pertinent practices such as the following:

1. He is loyal to the administration in a sincere, consistent manner, keeping still in word and action when he cannot commend.
2. He speaks well, both in private conversation and in public, of the administration.
3. He is alert to aid officials in any way that offers itself.
4. He accepts responsibilities graciously and performs them with celerity and to the best of his ability.
5. He cooperates with all administratively appointed personnel, such as custodians and groundkeeper, that their work may be done without undue effort.
6. In school activities such as committee work and parent-teacher association work he cooperates heartily and without reservation.
7. He assists administrative officers by contributing in an active, dynamic way to faculty meetings.
8. When asked, he expresses himself forcefully and to the point on any issue, but he does not air his views promiscuously to the public.

## SEMIPROFESSIONAL RELATIONSHIPS

Another group of relationships which have a great deal to do with the classroom teacher's professional success are neither wholly professional nor entirely personal in nature. Frequently these relationships become duties, although there is no mention made of them either at the time the contract is written nor at the time the salary check for the month is handed out. These relationships, semiprofessional in nature, are concerned with community, co-workers, parents, and church.

**Community.** A wise teacher will from the beginning become a citizen of the community, not merely a resident, and will interest himself in civic affairs. He will visit homes and never refuse an invitation to be a dinner guest. Because he enjoys acquaintances and friends, he will take pleasure in associations with fellow teachers and other citizens of the community.

Always the teacher is a gracious host or hostess when opportunity offers. If his place of living offers no opportunity for entertaining friends at meals, the teacher should repay social debts at a local restaurant or hotel. Always a teacher meets his obligations as completely as he can.

**Co-workers.** Always a teacher should go out of his way to be agreeable to fellow workers. This cooperation takes such numerous forms that mention of only a few is possible. Suggestions would include: aiding fellow workers gladly when called upon or when he can see that the need exists; being sincere and gracious with compliments for work well done; offering his services to a new teacher sincerely and in such a manner that no "face" is lost by accepting; making his library available to other staff members; being friendly and gracious without being too personal or "snoopy"; keeping quiet about fellow teachers' actions when he cannot commend; refusing to gossip about anyone; and, finally, recognizing his obligations to co-workers as a step in his own professional growth.

**Parents.** A beginner in the profession will find it difficult at first to recognize and realize how much of his work is outside the classroom. When a teacher praises Bobby, scolds Marie, or promotes Lucille, he praises Bobby's parents, places Marie's in a position where they may question his motives, and leaves Lucille's father and mother beaming with pride. To better understand the children, a teacher should try to know their parents. A self-rating scale for the teacher in dealing with parent relationships would, of necessity, carry items of this nature:

1. Do I make it a point to get acquainted with the parents of the children in my room?
2. Am I sympathetic and sincere in talking to parents?

3. Do I visit the homes of my pupils?
4. Do I find out about home conditions without offending by being too inquisitive?
5. Do I encourage parents to visit their children so that they may compare school activity and behavior with home behavior?
6. Do I check with parents to evaluate success in the accomplishment of mutual purposes?
7. Do parents apparently cooperate willingly with me in analyzing the difficulties of their children?

To be friendly without being too intimate, to avoid "cliques," "crowds," and "factions," and to maintain a fine reserve with parents without being cold and impersonal, exemplifies what a teacher's public relations should be at their best.

**Church.** Upon arrival in the community, a teacher should contact the minister of the church in which he holds membership, or if unattached, affiliate with the church of his choice.

Because he teaches five full days a week, a teacher might graciously but firmly refuse to teach a Sunday-school class. Responsibility for teaching must not occur every day of the week. Neither should he direct a choir, even though he has the ability, for he cannot risk the comparison which may follow when a local celebrity in music, who may be a fine performer, outshines him. He may sing in the choir if it gives him pleasure, but he should avoid needless criticism by refusing a position of responsibility which can add little to his stature and may detract from it. Again, because he is a public employee, local jealousies will appear if he gives professional services to one church group more than to another.

Very frequently he will be in need of advice which can come from but one source, his spiritual adviser. He consults his pastor as he would his doctor were he physically below par. Always he should understand that his spiritual, physical, and mental hygiene are inextricably bound up with his community relationships and relationships with co-workers and with pupils. Especially will his pupils reflect his mental states. The teacher whose personality is well adjusted and whose mental hygiene is good has usually learned to put first things first and to "render to Caesar the things which are Caesar's." If the teacher follows the remainder of that beautiful injunction, personal problems will somehow solve themselves.

## DISCUSSION PROBLEM

### "What Shall I Join?"

What would be your attitude, were you a woman teacher in the elementary grades in a "good little city" of 4,000, toward questions of joining organizations which seek you as a member? You are one of the more desirable prospects among young women coming into the town for all types of organization membership.

At once you are "rushed" by many groups. Below is a list of organizations and movements of various types which ask you as a woman teacher to accept membership either for altruistic or other reasons. Your problem is to place the ones you believe should be given consideration in one list and those which you believe you should not consider, or better should let alone, in another. Give reasons for your placement in each case.

1. The YWCA. (This is supported by subscriptions.)
2. The Trend Club. (Members are younger women of some prominence in the city, nearly all married; this is a "study" club.)
3. The Country Club. (Older citizens hold memberships; the younger set runs it. Initiation fee is $200—dues $72 a year.)
4. PEO. (This organization has many fine members but seems to restrict membership.)
5. The League of Women Voters. (Prominent women are members. It works openly for various civic issues.)
6. The WCTU. (Members strongly oppose using liquor in any form.)
7. The Sphinx Club. (This is an older women's "study" club; has many of the most prominent women of the city as members.)

8. The BPW. (Members are business and professional women.)
9. The Parent-Teachers Association. (Many teachers belong, but there is no compulsion.)
10. The AAUW. (Members are college women.)
11. Soroptimist Club. (This is a service club for women.)

## QUESTIONS ON THE PROBLEM

1. "As much care is necessary for the teacher in selecting her associates when away from work as in selecting her associates at the school building." Discuss.
2. Make a general statement in which you set up a rule for the woman teacher to apply in joining organizations which seek her for membership. Try to make the statement all-inclusive, specific, and consistent.
3. State briefly the advantages of belonging to many clubs, lodges, and other organizations; the disadvantages.
4. Presuming eligibility, select (a) the professional groups, whether listed in the problem or not, to which you should belong; and (b) the professional groups which are desirable affiliations for you, but not imperative.

## STUDY QUESTIONS

1. Were you desiring to make a survey of community organizations and movements which you should consider for membership, how would you proceed?
2. In a paragraph or two, characterize the woman elementary-school teacher as you see her. Try to make this a personal character sketch depicting something of the most desirable type. Do the same for a man who is a high school teacher.
3. Has society tended to make teachers live lives different from those led by other people? If so, why? If not, give reasons for your answer.
4. Has society a right to expect more from its teachers than it does from other professional people? Why? Why not?
5. Are parents justified in asking that teachers live under a code different from their own? That is, are mothers who smoke justified in demanding that daughter's teacher does not smoke?
6. If an act is in good taste for another, is the teacher justified in insisting upon the right to engage in it herself? To illus-

trate: At a cocktail party, all guests partake; shall the teacher present do so? The party becomes quite hilarious; shall the teacher "go along" with the crowd? Discuss.

7. Is there reason to believe that the teacher militant in preserving personal liberties for teachers is more effective than the teacher pacifist in this regard?

8. Characterize the ideal rooming place for the elementary or junior high school teacher.

9. Is it actually anyone's business other than her own whom a young unmarried woman teacher dates? Discuss.

10. Presume you as a teacher need a car mostly for pleasure but to some extent for professional purposes. You have enough saved (only) for one-third down payment. You have fifteen months to pay the remainder, some $1800. You are not in debt. Present the argument for and against making the purchase.

11. Because of the nine-months pay situation and twelve-months living cost, the teacher under high prices and unfavorable salary conditions not infrequently needs to borrow money before drawing the first check in the autumn. Tell what you can of "credit unions" for teachers. How are they financed? Why is the short-term loan usually a dangerously high-rate loan? Discuss the various loan plans for teachers in class.

12. Teachers are sometimes the mark of unscrupulous representatives of "fly-by-night" publishing companies. These frequently offer (seemingly) something for nothing. Teachers who sign anything under such conditions usually find that later on they must pay the full price of the supposed gift. How can teachers and reputable publishers be protected from such impositions? Discuss.

13. Suppose you wish to buy a set of books which you have investigated. How do you go about making the purchase? Are you entitled to a professional discount? What use would you make of your school principal? The city librarian? The publisher of the books you want?

## SELECTED READINGS

AMERICAN ASSOCIATION OF SCHOOL ADMINISTRATORS. *American School Curriculum*. Washington, D. C.: National Education Association, 1953. Indirectly there is much discussion of the problems of the classroom teacher included in this excellent publication.

CAMPBELL, ROALD F., CORBALLY, JOHN E., JR., and RAMSEYER, JOHN A. *Introduction to Educational Administration*. Boston: Allyn & Bacon, Inc., 1958. Chapter 8, "What Is the Teacher's Role?" emphasizes teacher personnel concerns and the teacher's responsibility to the profession.

CANTOR, NATHANIEL. *The Teaching Learning Process*. New York: Holt, Rinehart & Winston, Inc., 1953. "Toward a New Teacher," pp. 226–62. "The Professional Self in Teaching," pp. 264–84. Presents characteristics of a good teacher with a section on the teacher's self-improvement.

CHAMBERLAIN, LEO M., and KINDRED, LESLIE W. *The Teacher and School Organization*. 3d ed. Englewood Cliffs, N. J.: Prentice-Hall, Inc., 1958. Chapter 21, "Engaging in Public Relations," and Chapter 23, "Maintaining a Code of Ethics," are both supplementary to the material presented in the preceding pages.

HAND, HAROLD C. *Principles of Public Secondary Education*. New York: Harcourt, Brace & Co., 1958. Chapter 6, "Maintaining Good School-Community Relations," emphasizes the teacher's personal life and his place in the community.

MEHL, MARIE A., MILLS, HUBERT H., and DOUGLASS, HARL R. *Teaching in Elementary School*. 2d ed. New York: The Ronald Press Co., 1958. Chapter 24, "The Teacher as a Person," lists qualities in the teacher which are appreciated by the student and the administrator.

OTTO, HENRY J., FLOYD, HAZEL, and ROUSE, MARGARET. *Principles of Elementary Education*. New York: Holt, Rinehart & Winston, Inc., 1955. A good description of what is required for an outstanding teacher is presented in Chapter 15, "The Teacher as Person, Citizen, and Professional Worker."

STINNETT, T. M. *The Teacher and Professional Organizations*. 3d ed. Washington: The National Education Association, 1956. The section, "A Teacher Looks at the Profession," makes many suggestions for good personal as well as ethical practices.

ZERAN, FRANKLIN R., ed. *The High School Teacher and His Job*. New York: Chartwell House, Inc., 1953. Chapter 7, "The Teacher and the Community," by Harold R. Bottrell, sets up the basic principles underlying good community relations as far as the teacher and the public are concerned.

# 19

# IN-SERVICE GROWTH

No one is ready to do a thoroughly good job in teaching at the time of finishing college and getting a teaching license. One only thinks he is ready. As with all highly skilled professions, the teacher at the time of graduation has a good supply of theory—an oversupply, possibly—and a decidedly limited amount of experience. As he works at the job, the converse becomes true: he gains much in experience and, comparatively speaking, gains little in theory. New theory is being developed constantly, is then tried out in the crucible of experience, and after time has elapsed either becomes common practice, is modified, or is dropped entirely.

Because of this constant development of both new theory and new techniques, the teacher, like the doctor of medicine, who does not keep up with new developments is actually retrogressing. No one may stand still in the teaching profession. Internship in the form of student teaching is at present of considerable importance, perhaps of great importance, but the initiated know that it is far from being anything but a sampling and a very small sampling at that.

Probably no other year in the teacher's professional life is more significant than the first. During this period the beginner puts into practice the theory acquired in teacher-education classes. For the first time he develops attitudes toward this chosen profession. Days become delights or dreads, which come and go either with anticipation and pleasure, or with apprehension and dismay. Fellow workers become friends in a joyous adventure or fellow sufferers in an ill-conceived enterprise. The beginner decides that he likes teaching or else is miscast, all according to his relationships with twenty-five or thirty boys and girls.

During the year a teacher's habits become somewhat fixed. The habits may be mental or physical, or they may be ways of doing things in the classroom. Only the most careful observance by the teacher himself can prevent the useless, the wasteful, and the detrimental habit from being developed. Fearing to ask for help or suggestions is a common mistake. Asking an older or more experienced teacher or an administrator for aid is sound practice from a common-sense viewpoint as well as from a psychological one. The common-sense viewpoint gets the teacher aid where and when he needs it; the psychological slant is served by gaining a friend, as a person is not only interested in but likes the person he has helped.

During the first year the beginning teacher's attitudes toward growth become crystallized. Watching the panorama of teaching unfold from day to day, the neophyte sees for the first time, perhaps, the significance of the college-class theory. Then the new teacher either goes back over college notebooks and revamps what he studied previously so that it may serve the more immediate pressing needs, or else adopts the attitude "that it was mostly hooey anyhow" and sets sail without compass on an uncharted sea, and with little or no hope of reaching any desirable destination.

Attitudes toward growth on the job are possibly as significant for later success as are daily practices in the classroom. A teacher must always keep in mind that, in baseball parlance, he is but a "rookie" on the way presumably to the major leagues, and that every item which makes for success must be saved; every mistake in procedure or in attitude must be discarded. It is during this first year that he learns or fails to learn to utilize the various sources of help available to every teacher, whether inexperienced or experienced, sources that are always available but which never intrude themselves, uninvited, into the situation.

## PLANNED IN-SERVICE GROWTH

The term "in-service growth" covers all of a teacher's activities after employment which contribute to professional growth. These activities tend to break themselves up into two groups: one rather formalized in nature, the other informal and mostly unplanned. To the new teacher, even the formal avenues of growth seem to be unplanned and informal. This is usually because of the lack of compulsion to enter any or all of these formal avenues. Only a few are "musts." The remainder are entirely a matter of choice, as no one will do more than suggest that one should utilize opportunities which are present. Usually the teacher is not entirely conscious of accepting or rejecting the opportunities for growing on the job. One thing, however, is sure: the teacher either takes advantage of the opportunities for growth or stagnates professionally—dies on the vine, as it were. The parade goes on, and either a teacher is part of it or else it goes on and leaves him standing on the sidewalk, an observer rather than a participant.

**Affiliation with Professional Organizations.** Among formal sources of growth, formal because they are organized and one must consciously accept or reject them, the first is affiliation with professional organizations. These are usually four in number: the city, county, state, and national associations of teachers.

The first, the city association, is imperative. Every school strives for 100 per cent membership. Here teachers meet fellow teachers, discuss common problems, work for a common purpose in a cooperative manner, and enjoy a social hour together. A teacher should attend city association meetings consistently.

The county organization can be passed up by the city school teacher, but in general membership reflects both money and time well spent. It is broader in its scope than the city association, and members develop much in their ability to think in larger units, always the mark of a liberally educated person. Selfishly, a teacher gains by becoming acquainted with leaders in the profession who are finally the selecting agency for new teachers in their schools. Acquaintanceship with leaders in the profession is always desirable for the young teacher working up the professional ladder.

The state organization is another "must" for the beginning public school teacher. Through this organization much desirable school legislation receives its impetus. Thousands of teachers in a state, tightly organized, can influence popular opinion in terms of desirable school legislation, desirable first for school children but also advantageous to the profession. Legislators listen when a strong organization speaks, and the state teachers' association is the best means of expression. Really professional teachers not only belong to the association, but are active in helping to solve the association's problems.

The National Education Association is the official representative of more than a half-million teachers and administrators. It is the agency which promotes growth in the largest body of professional workers in the world, the teachers of the United States. Membership fees in the NEA, as in other professional groups, bring value received in terms of publications, programs, and influence in school legislation desirable for the profession. Strong school men and women advise the beginner to affiliate with all four of the groups named above. A teacher's professional growth, as well as the quality of his teaching position, usually profits thereby.

**Participation in Workshops.** The workshop yields excellent dividend returns in the form of in-service growth for the forward-looking teacher. A workshop is a plan by which special facilities, including usually a wealth of source material and specialized personnel, are brought together for group and individual conferences. Usually the material resources are supplied by an institution of higher learning, although this is by no means necessarily so. A workshop may be set up in any area of special interest, such as administrative problems, curriculum development, guidance techniques, teaching of any subject, or improving the teacher in any felt need. Small groups work together on a common problem. Experience and training are pooled for the common good of all. No one lectures and no one "gives the workshop" as a course. Always it is a cooperative enterprise.

The workshop, which is both a place and an activity, is undoubtedly near the top in its in-service possibilities for growth for all teachers because:

1. It is a cooperative enterprise; a teacher learns both by doing and by receiving. Everyone shares.
2. The materials of study are fresh and vital.
3. Each participant is experienced; experience and theory are in balance.
4. It is concerned with immediate needs and problems, hence is immediately useful.
5. It offers an excellent opportunity for social growth in terms of friendships formed and in terms of democratic living.
6. The time utilized is short—a week end, a week, or a two- or three-week period—are most common lengths.

**Attendance at Summer School.** Teachers attend summer school for two reasons, one of which is included in the other. They attend always because of a felt need for more and better training. Those teaching on limited certificates attend to improve the quality of the certificate or to complete work on a degree, either baccalaureate or graduate. Naturally, this would be unnecessary if their training needed no reinforcement.

No matter how excellent the training, and this goes for the holder of the highest academic degree, an occasional summer-school attendance at a college or university is beneficial. Constant usage tends to dull academic tools even as it does those of the carpenter, and there is no other place which replaces the fine cutting edge more adequately and exactly than summer-school attendance.

Another outstanding value from the summer school is the more or less informal workshop which is going on constantly.

Teachers meet others engaged in similar work. They exchange and pool experiences. They make delightful friendships. They meet strong teachers in the college classrooms, leaders frequently in the profession. Good libraries, lecture programs, concerts, drama—all open their doors to the teacher.

The teacher who has satisfied all degree and certificate requirements can afford to combine a travel vacation with summer school. He can, in succeeding summers, browse among universities as one browses in a good library. This procedure is, of course, wasteful for the teacher working toward a degree, as the "year in residence" rule makes staying in the same school imperative until degree requirements are completed.

A teacher should attend summer school, whether required of him or not, about every third summer. If he is a workshop attendant frequently, the summer school is less vital and necessary. Many good schools pay part or all of the teacher's actual expense, and this practice is always the mark of the forward-looking board of education and chief administrative officer.

**Attendance at Meetings.** The chief value of the local teachers' meeting is to acquaint the teacher with the broader aspects of the school organization of which he is a part. This refers, of course, to the large group which is not workshop-organized. General objectives of the school are discussed, and clarification is given to items which a teacher knows something about but not enough to permit him to speak authoritatively. Attendance at these meetings, held usually once a month, is an obligation of teachers rather than a privilege. This does not imply, however, that such meetings are not sources of valuable in-service education; they are. Commonly topics of discussion deal with all-school problems such as pupil achievement, guidance responsibilities, athletic programs, out-of-class interests of pupils, and items similar in nature.

Though attendance at general meetings is practically required, taking the roll is not common. What a teacher gets from the meeting depends much upon himself. He can adopt the attitude of resistance or the attitude of anticipation. The teacher who participates grows. Meeting fellow teachers and the city school's administrative officers is among the rewards of attendance. A teacher makes friends and develops the feeling of belonging to a fine organization by attending regularly; he loses both in friendships and in standing in his profession when he rationalizes himself into non-attendance.

The academic meeting differs from the teachers' meeting largely in its purpose. The former is a meeting of the stockholders, better perhaps the board of directors or the department heads of an organization, to receive a report of progress. The academic meeting may be building-wide, city-wide, county-wide, or state-wide in its scope. Its prime purpose is stimulation, professional contacts, discussion of mutual problems, and explanations of the work being done in the various fields of instruction. As with professional organizations with which the teachers' meeting is usually an associated activity, a teacher cannot afford to be unenrolled or to be a non-supporter.

Attendance and participation through the years gain for the teacher recognition as a leader in his profession. He grows not only through the stimulation in content and techniques but even more significantly in professional standing. Teachers gain professional recognition, although few people stop to think about it, first by being good teachers; second, by writing for professional publications; third, by lecturing and taking an active part in teacher and pupil growth; and finally, by being recognized by the leaders in the profession as a wide-awake, hustling, enterprising teacher. The fourth is frequently a result; the other three, causes.

**Professional Reading.** Francis Bacon said, "Reading maketh a full man; conference a ready man; and writing an exact man." The quotation fits the teacher and his work exactly. A teacher must read if he is to grow and mature in the profession. Conference makes for readiness, and writing, another mark of the progressing as opposed to the receding teacher, makes for exactness. Thus the quotation fits the teacher well, because one will read, confer, and write in order to reach one's greatest possibilities. A teacher may be very successful, however, through reading consistently and constantly conferring with colleagues on professional subjects.

A teacher should read a great deal. He must be familiar with the new books in his field of teaching. Many of them he will buy because he can scarcely do without them. Publishers commonly are willing to send teachers their professional publications on a liberal week or ten-day examination privilege. These must be handled carefully if they are to be returned. Without much doubt, the single best external mark of the teacher who is growing is a professional library. It is difficult to conceive of a weak, uninterested teacher who has developed a good professional library. Strong teachers avail themselves of all the help they can get from books.

Many principals set up in their offices what is commonly called by the staff "The Bait Shelf." It is a small collection of books, books of all sorts—fiction, methodology, biography, history. These books are left on the shelf by the teachers. Mr. B., the principal, puts in a new book on audio-visual aids; Miss A., a new novel she was given at Christmas; Miss C., a book she purchased and found good on methodology; Mr. D., a new biography. Each teacher checks out any book available by signing a card and leaving it in a conveniently placed box. When the book is returned, he scratches his name off. Thus each teacher profits and the expense is kept to a minimum. Again, the reading is contagious, as discussion leads to more reading, and this in turn to more discussion. The teacher who takes pride in his professional library, selecting each book with care because it is to help in a felt need, is developing not only a source of encouragement and inspiration but also a very practical help whenever aid is needed.

Another phase of the in-service growth of the teacher is the consistent reading of the magazines for the profession. As with the book offering, the list is long and of fine quality.

Although public libraries subscribe to many of the better-known publications, the teacher wastes too much time by depending upon the library offering entirely. A teacher will find (if he is a beginning teacher) or has found (if he is mature in the profession) that he needs magazines of three general types for his professional advancement. First, he should subscribe for at least one, preferably two, magazines, specifically written for his field of work. Library browsing will enable him, before subscribing, to decide which ones best suit his needs. Second, he needs at least one publication of a scope national in nature (the *Journal of the National Education Association* is excellent) which fits itself to a pattern for the entire profession. Third, he needs at least one carefully selected news weekly. The latter is selected for its reliability and its faithfulness in recording vital news impartially. The three magazines, read faithfully, should keep a teacher fairly well abreast of developments both professional and general in nature. Consistent reading of the daily papers, with special emphasis upon editorial pages and the reviews of all sorts, is assumed for all educated persons.

**Scholarly Writing.** A number of years ago a large group of eminently successful teachers, ranging from the primary through the university level, were asked when, in their opinions, they ceased to be amateurs or semiprofessionals. All were agreed that the length of time in the teaching field was not the principal element. Answers varied. "When I appeared on my first professional program" was a common answer. "When I was elected an officer in our local association" was not infrequent. "When I represented our group at a state-wide meeting" was another. But the most frequently received reply was "When I saw my first professional article in print in a magazine."

If one believes that mental growth develops as insights do, it is easy to see that a single large mental-physical production such as writing an article might close the gap between being a teacher as a livelihood only and being a teacher also because of enthusiasm and zeal. In any case, scholarly productivity is one of the marks of the teacher who is growing professionally.

The teacher who is planning an article notes carefully the type of material the publication utilizes, notes the length of articles used, considers any new development or slant the writer may have to offer, and writes the article. Because the writing itself must conform to a plan, the teacher does well to own a writer's guide, a writer's handbook, which sets down the mechanical details to be considered. These books commonly list the types of articles each magazine accepts, the length of article desired, the frequency of publication, and the rate of pay, if any. But few professional magazines pay for articles.

Correspondence with editors of professional magazines is always desirable before writing an article. The publication may have already accepted many good manuscripts on the very theme the teacher is contemplating. Again, there may be a great need for another type which he can do equally well. The greatest mistake the beginner can make is to assume that he cannot produce for publication because an article is rejected. "Blue slips" are not unusual for any writer, even the professionals. The young teacher makes no mistake in consulting the more experienced author concerning an interest in writing. Experienced producers in the professional writing field take delight in encouraging the beginner.

## INFORMAL IN-SERVICE GROWTH

In-service growth for the classroom teacher depends more upon the teacher than it does upon the program. If there is to be growth, the teacher must desire to grow. The training is not something supplied by the principal, the supervisor, or the superintendent for members of the staff. It is largely supplied by the teachers for themselves. The growth must come where it is needed; it is not needed equally in every phase of a teacher's work. In some phases one may be very strong now; in others, only average, or even weak. Of necessity there must be some evaluation, and the evaluation must be to a great extent done by the teacher.

Many, if not most, of the more important things of life are caught rather than taught. Because of this, the informal, almost unconscious portions of the teacher's growth come about through sources and contacts scarcely recognized as existing. Recreation, day-by-day contacts with fellow teachers and administrative officers, informal visiting, vacations, travel, the social life of the community, and reading for enjoyment are all contributing agencies to in-service training and development.

If a teacher were to make a list of the informal items which have a possibility of leading to the improvement of the teacher in service, he would come up with sources which have been listed for many years in manuals, handbooks, and official and semiofficial bulletins. Among those which have been recorded, the following appear:

1. Visiting other teachers at work. A teacher has a chance to compare his work with that of others and to confer on the job with others who are doing the same type of work.
2. Reading along cultural lines. Teachers are forced to read professionally; they need to read the best in other reading material as it appears.
3. Attending conferences. These, if they are to be of the greatest good to the teacher, should be distinctly informal in nature. The conferences should be with administrative officers, supervisors, and other co-workers.
4. Traveling. The teacher is a communicating worker. He needs to have breadth of viewpoint as well as depth to his thinking. Travel is one means of adding breadth to the point of view of the classroom worker.
5. Self-rating. Good self-rating devices are available for almost every teaching level. Self-evaluation is much more acceptable than is evaluation by someone else and is usually more applicable to one's weaknesses.
6. Participating in community affairs. The teacher grows on the job who takes an active part in the community life.
7. Receiving some recognition for having made contributions to the well-being of the school. Recognition of good work

by administrative officials is a "must" for every teacher who is to grow on the job. To fail to recognize the commendable indicates lack of training on the official's part; to recognize and not to commend is unprofessional.

8. Participating in some form of recreation. A teacher should use leisure time in recreation in order to maintain his best physical and mental health.

## DISCUSSION PROBLEM

### Six Sources of Growth

"I've had four years of college, the last two of it given almost exclusively to teacher-training. My scholastic marks are respectable. I'm told that my rating cards rank me reasonably high in personality, health, adaptability, and in general professional promise. But I still feel that I'm woefully unprepared for the big job I'm undertaking." The speaker is one of the strongest candidates of a large class from one of the country's leading teacher-training institutions.

"I have the same feeling," her companion agrees. "I wonder if any person is ever graduated from a college or a university in any profession really thoroughly prepared to step in and do the job well from the first day on?"

"I doubt it very much. Well, since we've an assignment to work on dealing with this very subject, let's get busy. Let's see, according to my notes Professor Roper said that there were no less than six sources of growth always open to the teacher in the field if she would take advantage of them."

"That's right. Too bad he didn't name them himself instead of allowing everyone in the class to turn in his ideas of what they were. Now we have the job of selecting the six which we consider the most important out of the dozen or more which were left after the duplications were eliminated. Do you have the list that was made up from the different student contributions? Some of them seemed so crazy to me that I wondered why Professor Roper even listed them on the blackboard. Is that the list?"

"That's it. Heavens! Fifteen items altogether. Well, there's one thing sure. Some of them are out of the question because they are available only while one is in college classes, while others couldn't be worth much by any stretch of the imagination. What do you say about the first one?"

The list of possible sources of professional growth which the girls had copied from the blackboard compilation made by having each student in a class contribute his ideas of possible sources, the duplication of ideas having been eliminated, is given below. *Your problem: put yourself in the girls' places and select the six most important sources of professional growth for the teacher now on the job, from the fifteen items turned in by the class.*

1. Affiliation with lodges, dinner clubs, service clubs, social service clubs, bridge clubs, and other organizations which have for their purpose a good time socially, with community betterment in a general way as their commonly stated goal.

2. Affiliation with professional organizations.

3. Singing in the church choir, teaching a Sunday-school class, or conducting the church choir or orchestra.

4. Coaching community plays, directing community orchestra or band.

5. Frequent summer-school attendance.

6. Developing social prominence to the extent that one's name is found frequently in the society columns, along with those of the town's wealthiest and best-known citizens.

7. Securing the support of the younger set by aiding in the organization and direction of parties, dances, and other social affairs of a like nature.

8. Frequent attendance at teaching clinics in the form of demonstration teaching and an organized plan of visiting recognizedly strong teachers in their classrooms.

9. A constant and thoroughly planned reading program. This includes:

    a. Profiting from the teaching experience of others. This applies particularly to that field known as professional reading.

    b. Securing that wealth of information which reading and travel alone can give. This may be called informative reading.

    c. Receiving mental refreshment and stimulation, gaining at the same time physical relaxation. This may be called recreational reading.

    *d.* Being stimulated to wonderment and curiosity, ambition and desire. This is sometimes called inspirational reading.

10. Listening to well-organized lectures by experts in the field of teacher education.
11. A definitely planned and carefully organized travel program.
12. Personal contact with outstanding leaders in one's particular field.
13. A consistent utilization of the correspondence and extension offerings of colleges and universities.
14. Development of an active interest in the community civic affairs that only the strongest persons may be elected to offices, and that undesirable business activities from the school's viewpoint may be prevented from operating.
15. A consistent, regular attendance at all teachers' meetings with a demonstrated willingness to do one's part carefully and thoroughly when called upon.

## QUESTIONS ON THE PROBLEM

1. Be specific in naming the advantages which the young teacher just out of college has over the older teacher who has been teaching several years.
2. What are the advantages which the experienced teacher holds over the beginner?
3. How can the advantages held by the beginner be secured by the older teacher?
4. How can the advantages held by the older teacher be secured by the beginner?
5. Would you agree that a teacher's growth after leaving college should be as great as in the first four years in college? If you say "Yes," is this an argument that college training is unessential?
6. Name sources of growth for teachers in the field that are not included in the fifteen-item list.

## STUDY QUESTIONS

1. Cross-visitation or intervisitation is a source of in-service growth not discussed in the preceding chapter. Can you sug-

gest a plan by which teachers in an elementary school might be enabled to visit other teachers in the building or in the same system? Make your plan for an eight-grade school, with a teacher for each grade. Who will teach the room vacated by the visiting teacher?

2. Is the statement farfetched that the need for teaching clinics is as great in the teaching profession as is the need for clinics in the medical and dental professions? Discuss.

3. Can you learn anything from visiting a teacher at work whose skill is not as great as your own?

4. Demonstration teaching is sometimes used for in-service growth. What are its major weaknesses? Its strong points? Does the artificiality of the situation make the effort less valuable? Valueless? What is the difference between a "teaching clinic" and a "demonstration lesson"?

5. Presume you are given the task of making a recreational survey of the community in which you are to teach; how would you proceed?

6. Analyze your own inclinations toward recreation either as a teacher in training in college or as one on the job. Be specific in setting down the things you would like to do for recreation (while teaching) were these items available. From your list, are you the active or passive type in your enjoyments? With your recreational interests, should you teach in a large city, a small city, or in a rural situation?

7. "Miss Duncan works too much but not hard enough." What has such a statement to do with a teacher's recreation? Will Miss Duncan have time for recreation? If she has time, will her recreation be fun? Why? Why not?

8. "All work and no play makes Jack a dull boy." In the light of the previous chapter, analyze the old proverb.

## SELECTED READINGS

ALCORN, MARVIN D., HOUSEMAN, RICHARD A., and SCHUNERT, JIM R. *Better Teaching in Secondary Schools.* New York: Holt, Rinehart & Winston, Inc., 1954. Section 9, "Becoming a Better Teacher," puts much emphasis on growing professionally through conscious in-service effort.

ALEXANDER, WILLIAM M. and HALVERSON, PAUL M. *Effective Teaching in Secondary Schools.* New York: Holt, Rinehart & Winston, Inc., 1956. Chapter 16, "The Teacher's Role in Improving Instruction," lists professional qualifications needed by every classroom teacher.

BARTKY, JOHN. *Supervision as Human Relations.* Boston: D. C. Heath & Co., 1953. Chapter 16 emphasizes the need for in-service education and makes pertinent suggestions for attaining it.

CHAMBERLAIN, LEO M., and KINDRED, LESLIE W. *The Teacher and School Organization.* 3d ed. Englewood Cliffs, N. J.: Prentice-Hall, Inc., 1958. Chapter 22, "Belonging to Educational Associations," presents in detail the work of the various educational associations and suggests the place each teacher should take in these.

HAND, HAROLD C. *Principles of Public Secondary Education.* New York: Harcourt, Brace & Co., 1958. Chapter 12, "The Teacher's Role in Administering the School," emphasizes the growth of the teacher professionally through understanding the administration's position.

HICKS, HANNE J. *Educational Supervision in Principle and Practice.* New York: The Ronald Press Co., 1960. Emphasis of the book is on improvement of the processes of teaching. Shows how a supervisor can employ his personal resources to stimulate teacher growth.

LIEBERMAN, MYRON. *Education as a Profession.* Englewood Cliffs, N. J.: Prentice-Hall, Inc., 1956. Chapter 1 concerns itself with the nature of the profession. Chapter 13 deals with professional ethics.

NATIONAL COMMISSION ON TEACHER EDUCATION AND PROFESSIONAL STANDARDS. *The Teacher and Professional Organizations.* Washington, D. C.: National Education Association, 1952. Entire publication deals with the teacher's professional growth with emphasis on professional organizations as a means of attaining it.

UMSTATTD, J. G. *Secondary School Teaching.* 3d ed. Boston: Ginn and Co., 1953. Chapter 17 uses self-analysis as a possible means to professional growth.

WILES, KIMBALL. *Teaching for Better Schools.* Englewood Cliffs, N. J.: Prentice-Hall, Inc., 1952. Chapter 14, "How Do We Improve Our Teaching?" evaluates teaching and makes suggestions for improvements which are within the possible achievement range for every teacher.

ZERAN, FRANKLIN R., *The High School Teacher and His Job.* New York: Chartwell House, Inc., 1953. Section 9, "In-service Growth and Development" (John A. Dotson), and Section 6, "The Teacher and His Supervisor" (Edwin J. Brown), stress the growth of the teacher on the job as a requirement for professional excellence.

# 20

# REWARDS FOR EFFORT

The preceding chapters have endeavored to present the teacher's role in school administration, emphasizing the problems and situations in classroom management, in relationships with authorities as well as with students, and in entering and growing in service in the profession. No one pretends that the problems of the profession are not significant, nor does anyone assume that most of them have been solved. The most optimistic recognize that the profession is still something of an adolescent and, although a husky youth, has a long way to go before reaching full maturity.

Teachers are not demanding for themselves much, if anything, that is not necessary for all persons. They are justified in asking for salaries somewhat in line with their obligations and training, salaries which will enable them to have a decent standard of living; and for security in their chosen work based upon merit. Each teacher is asking reasonably that he be assured of a competence for old age or disability. Teachers are asking that their work be not so burdensome in its daily routine that it cannot well be done without undue risk of health impairment. They are asking that they be given time to assume a greater responsibility which now is denied them because of routine obligations, the making of the school the social force it can be. Finally, teachers are demanding that they be accorded all the rights and privileges of other citizens in the development of initiative and the honest expression of opinion.

## IMPROVEMENT IN THE EDUCATIONAL PROGRAM

The first step in improving the service which the schools can give is to keep the teachers themselves thoroughly informed of the social situation as it exists. Change is ever present, and it is only reasonable to say that those who teach boys and girls should be in the vanguard in recognizing that change. That schools should try to anticipate future demands to be made upon them and that teachers should seek to be ahead of the social procession would seem to be sound reasoning. In practice this is not actually the situation. The schools, which means the workers in the schools, have difficulty in keeping abreast of current developments. Too frequently teachers know less of the difficulties faced by businessmen, the reasons back of a strike by a labor group, or why parity regulations are imperative if farm production is to stay up than do other men and women of lesser intelligence and far less formal training. The reason seems to lie in the fact that teachers work for different results and with different materials than businessmen, organized labor, and farmers. The non-competitive nature of their work is inclined to make for complacency and less concern, rather than for greater awareness with its attendants of observation, reading, and study.

Economic workshops in many of our larger cities, costing up to $600 a teacher for a period of three weeks, are being completely underwritten by businessmen groups. The movement is not entirely altruistic. It is recognition of the fact by business that its very existence depends upon an informed citizenry, rather than upon a citizenry swayed by every wind carrying misinformation and blatant propaganda. That an informed citizenry depends upon an informed teacher group is not questioned. Teachers must have both time and training to teach young America the values in the heritage which is theirs.

Without doubt the school of tomorrow is going to be a better school than is the school of today, just as the school of today is a better school than was the one which served our parents. Greater recognition of the school as a social force and of the teacher as that force's agent will eventually go over into utilizing the teacher's potentialities to greater advantage. Less teaching load of the routine type, resulting in more time for other phases of instruction, would seem to be one means.

The changes which will take place—at least the need is greatest in these lines—should be first in a more effective educational program for citizenship. The next improvement will come in improving school working conditions. Obsolescent buildings and school sites are far too common today, and the overcrowded, worn-out building with ineffective equipment is still not an unusual sight in any city or hamlet in the land. A more efficient, better-balanced financial support for schools is imperative. Teachers must be better trained, more carefully selected, and paid for their services in terms of this training and competence. Educational inequality for American children must be entirely eliminated. Democracy is in danger of becoming a mere catchword when there is deliberate lessening of educational effort in one area over another because of race, color, or creed. Curricula will in time be geared to the community which the particular school serves. This is recognition of the school as a local, community-serving agency. Finally the over-all organization and administration of the schools can and will be improved.

Many needed changes are commonly recognized weaknesses and are dependent on only one thing for immediate improvement. This is, of course, better financial support and a better distribution of the tax burden as it now exists. Only by increasing the size of the unit of taxation can inequalities be even partially eliminated.

Although it is not commonly recognized, there is no other group in America so thoroughly capable of or so potentially competent in developing social leadership as are the teachers of the nation. Teachers are social-minded as a group. They are fairly well organized for anything they undertake. They are qualified by training for leadership. Teachers by the nature of their work with youth are in a position to make their leadership felt. If one adds to this the facts that teachers are willing workers, that they are publicly employed, that there are many of them, that no other group has a greater possibility of arranging for the time required, and that their opportunity for contacts is great, the first sentence of the paragraph takes on added significance. Teachers should be a leading force in America in every form of social betterment and development. That they are not to a significant extent such a force today must be charged primarily, it would seem, to inadequacy in leadership. Recognition of a failing is ever a first step in correction of the weakness. Social leadership, or what passes for it, cannot be allowed to go by default to social climbers, to selfish political aspirants, or to well-meaning but largely untrained lay workers. The future must see teachers exerting a new but no less powerful influence than they now have. A laissez-faire democracy was fairly adequate for an expanding, growing pioneer country where there was no deliberately opposing force. Maintaining democracy can no longer be left to chance. American children must know what their heritage is; must know what it means to them; and must idealize it in their innermost beings if that heritage is not to be lost. The teacher of tomorrow is to be one of many persons carrying the torch.

## VIEWS ON TEACHERS AND TEACHING

Believing that it might be interesting to teachers to get a glimpse of how writers in the past, writers who have left their names engraved in the pages of literature that are never to be erased, have regarded teaching and teachers, this section presents quotations from several. The picture thus presented, though not always flattering and possibly not always true to fact, is, to say the least, not bad reading. Pope starts us off well by telling us:

> Let such teach others who themselves excel,
> And censure freely who have written well.
>
> —*Essay on Criticism*, Pt. I, 1.15.

However, Browning is not so flattering:

> The hawk-nosed, high-cheek-boned Professor. . . .
> The sallow, virgin-minded, studious
> Martyr to mild enthusiasm.
>
> —"Christmas Eve," Pt. XIV.

Burns somewhat satirically admits, however, the ability of the teacher when he says:

> Here lies Willie Michie's banes:
>   O Satan, when ye tak him,
> Gie him the schulin' o' your weans
> For clever deils he'll mak them!
>
> —"For Mr. Willie Michie."

Carlyle speaks of "Respectable Professors of the Dismal Science" in his *Latter Day Pamphlets*, No. 1 (used with reference to political economy). And Cowper, paying allegiance to the sour-faced teacher, advises:

> A teacher should be sparing of his smile.
> —"Charity," I, 490.

Emerson, as always, gives credit where credit is due:

> He teaches who gives and he learns who receives.
> —*Essays, First Series: Spiritual Laws.*

and again, "The man who can make hard things easy, is the educator" in *Journals*, 1861.

Von Moltke paid tribute to teachers when he said: "The Prussian schoolmaster won the battle of Sadowa" in a speech to the Reichstag, February 16, 1874.

Oscar Wilde was trying to be funny when he wrote:

> Everybody who is incapable of learning has taken to teaching.
> —*The Decay of Lying.*

George Bernard Shaw, always more interested in being startling than in being accurate, backed up later on this: "He who can, does. He who cannot, teaches" in his *Maxims for Revolutionists.*

Elbert Hubbard is not so courteous as clever when in one of his epigrams he tells us:

> Now owls are not really wise—they only look that way.
> The owl is a sort of a college professor.
>
> —*Epigrams*.

Sinclair Lewis did not mean to be flattering to American English teachers when he said: "Our American professors like their literature clear, cold, pure, and very dead" in an address to the Swedish Academy, December 12, 1930.

Mencken, who possibly prided himself more on the pithiness of his remarks and his ability to shock rather than on the absolute veracity of the statement below, is unusually caustic:

> The average schoolmaster is and always must be essentially an ass, for how can one imagine an intelligent man engaging in so puerile an avocation.
>
> —*Prejudices*, Ser. iii, p. 224

But Shakespeare pays his homage to teachers when he says: "When I am forgotten . . . say I taught thee" in *Henry VIII* (Act III, Sc. 2, 1. 432).

Even the past has its negative contribution to make, as when a Greek proverb gives the teacher this dig: "The same persons telling to the same people the same things about the same things," a Greek proverb quoted by Isaac le Grange apropos of teachers.

However, Goldsmith in *The Deserted Village* (I, 193) gives a better picture of the schoolmaster of his day, although scarcely one to draw modern youth to the profession:

> Beside yon straggling fence that skirts the way,
> With blossom'd furze unprofitably gay,
> There in his noisy mansion, skill'd to rule,
> The village master taught his little school;
> A man severe he was, and stern to view;
> I knew him well and every truant knew;
> Well had the boding tremblers learn'd to trace
> The day's disasters in his morning face;
> Full well they'd laugh with counterfeited glee

At all his jokes, for many a joke had he;
Full well the busy whisper, circling round,
Convey'd the dismal tidings when he frown'd;
Yet he was kind; or if severe in aught,
The love he bore to learning was in fault.

And Whittier means every word he utters when he speaks of the young schoolmaster thus in *Snowbound:*

Large-brained, clear-eyed,—of such as he
Shall freedom's young apostles be—.

Dickinson it is, however, who presents the picture the true teacher likes best:

The twig is so easily bended
I have banished the rule and the rod:
I have taught them the goodness of knowledge,
They have taught me the goodness of God.
—Charles M. Dickinson, *The Children.*

## HIDDEN REWARDS IN TEACHING

If it is true that many of the most significant things in life are acquired without our knowing from whence they come, it is probably equally true that the greatest rewards of labor for the person who works toward human advancement in any form are rewards of the spirit. When a teacher discusses the "outcomes of education," he or she is always speaking of the intangible, of the hidden values in the work. The outcomes sought are rarely visible and may not appear until years later. Experienced school workers, retiring after many years of service to boys and girls, rarely express great satisfaction in the fine homes they possess, in the size of their estates, or the legacy in material things they are leaving their children. However, one needs only to talk to these men and women to appreciate their tremendous satisfaction in what they have done with the God-given equipment which was theirs. As Joubert said many years ago, "The evening of a well-spent life brings its lamps with it."

It would seem to be confusing to say that the reward for work well done can be in the attitudes toward life which one has acquired. This somehow is true, however, in teaching. Attitudes, a very good educator has said, tend to be the searchlight by which one discovers values in himself and in others. These values are not visible to all. This probably is but saying that happiness is in the person possessing it, not in the material thing which superficially would seem to be synonymous with happiness. The teacher by teaching efforts is never going to acquire wealth as the world knows wealth. By economy and care he or she can and does live respectably and with a fair share of comforts. Generally the teacher has peace of mind which in a way is synonymous with good mental hygiene in that there is far more security, permanence, and stability in the teacher's work than are usually found in more competitive fields of work.

In a physical way a teacher's work is commonly pleasant. His working associates are ladies and gentlemen. His working hours are not unreasonably long. He works under good conditions, as a rule. Vacations come when one wants them: at Thanksgiving, Christmas, Washington and Lincoln's birthdays, and Eastertime. Although summer vacation is too long when it is without pay, as expenses do not stop with the closing of school doors for the summer, this situation is being remedied rapidly. All in all, however, it is not the kind of work or its difficulties which prevent many of the strongest of college graduates from entering teaching for their life's work. It is the inadequate salary in terms of the excellences required both in personal qualities and in training. Those who say they would like to have a teacher's salary commonly fall far short in both expensive training and in the excellences of the personal qualifications demanded for the teacher.

Most professionals agree that teaching is only for idealists. The person with a materialistic slant toward life is always unhappy, always dissatisfied when found in the classroom. The hidden values in the form of the attitudes one develops within himself and those desirable attitudes toward life which develop in those with whom a good teacher works are not values for the materialist who sees success only in terms of substance and worldly accomplishment. As Browning puts it, " 'Tis not what man does which exalts him, but what man would do."

If education has something to do with making desirable changes in individuals, the teacher soon recognizes that those changes are identical for no two children. The longer the teacher teaches, the more he or she comprehends that the more important changes are other than those which can be measured readily by a battery of tests in subject-matter fields. Education, the teacher knows, is much more than teaching spelling and arithmetic.

The teacher's hidden rewards come in the form of changes in children's attitudes. He will see, under his guidance, the shy inhibited child grow in confidence and assertiveness; the suspicious, non-trusting child lose his fear of others; the cocky, ebullient youngster being toned down by his companions; the child from "across the tracks" finding his place among his peers because of his innate worth and ability. As a teacher sees in children cheerfulness appearing from gloom, clarity emerging from confusion, interest developing from apathy, hope arising from despair, joy in living and companionship taking over a child's life where there was only childish reserve and mistrust of others, he will see his greater rewards with a clarity possessed by no one who does not work with children. He will find that making the obvious significant to children gives him a joy and satisfaction no one can secure from owning a new television set or making the first down payment on a new car. Calmly and dispassionately he will see his work as a "thing of beauty," and always it "is a joy forever."

Several years ago the National Education Association presented the eulogy quoted below to each of its members. The message accompanying the card bearing the eulogy was worded, "Presented to one who loves the profession." There is no more suitable closing for a book dedicated to the profession, and therefore it is offered to the teacher, as both an inspiration and a reward for work with American youth.

### I Love to Teach

I do not know that I could make entirely clear to an outsider the pleasure I have in teaching. I had rather earn my living by teaching than in any other way. In my mind, teaching is not merely a life work, a profession, an occupation, a struggle; it is a passion. I love to teach.

I love to teach as a painter loves to paint, as a musician loves to play, as a singer loves to sing, as a strong man rejoices to run a race. Teaching is an art—an art so great and so difficult to master that a man or woman can spend a long life at it without realizing much more than his limitations and mistakes, and his distance from the ideal.

But the main aim of my happy days has been to become a good teacher, just as every architect wishes to be a good architect and every professional poet strives toward perfection.

—William Lyon Phelps.

As God illumined the morning
In pattern of perfect design;
Gave color to midday and dawning
Put in contour, perspective, and line;
He made for His world a new glory
To be judged by the God-head alone,
A pattern and guide for all artists
And PAINTING came into its own.

To man the gift to hold beauty
In music, in color, in verse;
The finest preserved as a duty
Life's glorious to live, not the worst;
This blessing God gave to His people
The gay ones—those saddened of heart,
The mind and the soul to know feeling
And this thing the world knows as ART.

When God projected the mountains
With their spires and minarets tall;
Formed streams with icy-deep fountains
Chiseled columns from precipice walls;
From His universe plant took His lighting
That we might have ev'ning and morn,
God gave to His world a profession
And ARCHITECTURE was born.

The doctor our suff'ring to lighten,
To the priest the uplift of soul
The lawyer some dark days to brighten
All serving—He gave them the goal;
All these He made to His purpose
That purpose, to save us, each one,
But when God wanted a TEACHER,
He gave to the world His own Son.

—EDWIN J. BROWN

# APPENDIX

## CODE OF ETHICS*

We, the members of the National Education Association of the United States, hold these truths to be self-evident—

- —that the primary purpose of education in the United States is to develop citizens who will safeguard, strengthen, and improve the democracy obtained thru a representative government;

- —that the achievement of effective democracy in all aspects of American life and the maintenance of our national ideals depend upon making acceptable educational opportunities available to all;

- —that the quality of education reflects the ideals, motives, preparation, and conduct of the members of the teaching profession;

- —that whoever chooses teaching as a career assumes the obligation to conduct himself in accordance with the ideals of the profession.

As a guide for the teaching profession, the members of the National Education Association have adopted this code of professional ethics. Since all teachers should be members

* Reproduced verbatim from the Code of Ethics of the National Education Association of the United States. This is the revised code prepared by the National Education Association's Committee on Professional Ethics and adopted in 1952.

of a united profession, the basic principles herein enumerated apply to all persons engaged in the professional aspects of education—elementary, secondary, and collegiate.

*First Principle:* The primary obligation of the teaching profession is to guide children, youth, and adults in the pursuit of knowledge and skills, to prepare them in the ways of democracy, and to help them to become happy, useful, self-supporting citizens. The ultimate strength of the nation lies in the social responsibility, economic competence, and moral strength of the individual American.

In fulfilling the obligations of this first principle the teacher will—

1. Deal justly and impartially with students regardless of their physical, mental, emotional, political, economic, social, racial, or religious characteristics.
2. Recognize the differences among students and seek to meet their individual needs.
3. Encourage students to formulate and work for high individual goals in the development of their physical, intellectual, creative, and spiritual endowments.
4. Aid students to develop an understanding and appreciation not only of the opportunities and benefits of American democracy but also of their obligations to it.
5. Respect the right of every student to have confidential information about himself withheld except when its release is to authorized agencies or is required by law.
6. Accept no remuneration for tutoring except in accordance with approved policies of the governing board.

*Second Principle:* The members of the teaching profession share with parents the task of shaping each student's purposes and acts toward socially acceptable ends. The effectiveness of many methods of teaching is dependent upon cooperative relationships with the home.

In fulfilling the obligations of this second principle the teacher will—

1. Respect the basic responsibility of parents for their children.

2. Seek to establish friendly and cooperative relationships with the home.
3. Help to increase the student's confidence in his own home and avoid disparaging remarks which might undermine that confidence.
4. Provide parents with information that will serve the best interests of their children, and be discreet with information received from parents.
5. Keep parents informed about the progress of their children as interpreted in terms of the purposes of the school.

*Third Principle:* The teaching profession occupies a position of public trust involving not only the individual teacher's personal conduct, but also the interaction of the school and the community. Education is most effective when these many relationships operate in a friendly, cooperative, and constructive manner.

In fulfilling the obligations of this third principle the teacher will—

1. Adhere to any reasonable pattern of behavior accepted by the community for professional persons.
2. Perform the duties of citizenship, and participate in community activities with due consideration for his obligations to his students, his family, and himself.
3. Discuss controversial issues from an objective point of view, thereby keeping his class free from partisan opinions.
4. Recognize that the public schools belong to the people of the community, encourage lay participation in shaping the purposes of the school, and strive to keep the public informed of the educational program which is being provided.
5. Respect the community in which he is employed and be loyal to the school system, community, state, and nation.
6. Work to improve education in the community and to strengthen the community's moral, spiritual, and intellectual life.

*Fourth Principle:* The members of the teaching profession have inescapable obligations with respect to employment. These obligations are nearly always shared employer-employee responsibilities based upon mutual respect and good faith.

In fulfilling the obligations of this fourth principle the teacher will—

1. Conduct professional business thru the proper channels.
2. Refrain from discussing confidential and official information with unauthorized persons.
3. Apply for employment on the basis of competence only, and avoid asking for a specific position known to be filled by another teacher.
4. Seek employment in a professional manner, avoiding such practices as the indiscriminate distribution of applications.
5. Refuse to accept a position when the vacancy has been created through unprofessional activity or pending controversy over professional policy or the application of unjust personnel practices and procedures.
6. Adhere to the conditions of a contract until service thereunder has been performed, the contract has been terminated by mutual consent, or the contract has otherwise been legally terminated.
7. Give and expect due notice before a change of position is to be made.
8. Be fair in all recommendations that are given concerning the work of other teachers.
9. Accept no compensation from producers of instructional supplies when one's recommendations affect the local purchase or use of such teaching aids.
10. Engage in no gainful employment, outside of his contract, where the employment affects adversely his professional status or impairs his standing with students, associates, and the community.
11. Cooperate in the development of school policies and assume one's professional obligations thereby incurred.
12. Accept one's obligation to the employing board for maintaining a professional level of service.

*Fifth Principle:* The teaching profession is distinguished from many other occupations by the uniqueness and quality of the professional relationships among all teachers. Community support and respect are influenced by the standards of teachers and their attitudes toward teaching and other teachers.

In fulfilling the obligations of this fifth principle the teacher will—

1. Deal with other members of the profession in the same manner as he himself wishes to be treated.
2. Stand by other teachers who have acted on his behalf and at his request.
3. Speak constructively of other teachers, but report honestly to responsible persons in matters involving the welfare of students, the school system, and the profession.
4. Maintain active membership in professional organizations and, thru participation, strive to attain the objectives that justify such organized groups.
5. Seek to make professional growth continuous by such procedures as study, research, travel, conferences, and attendance at professional meetings.
6. Make the teaching profession so attractive in ideals and practices that sincere and able young people will want to enter it.

# INDEX

415